There Is Simply
Too Much
to Think About

SAUL BELLOW

There Is Simply Too Much to Think About

COLLECTED NONFICTION

EDITED BY
BENJAMIN TAYLOR

VIKING

VIKING
Published by the Penguin Group
Penguin Group (USA) LLC
375 Hudson Street
New York, New York 10014

USA | Canada | UK | Ireland | Australia | New Zealand | India | South Africa | China
penguin.com
A Penguin Random House Company

First published by Viking Penguin, a member of Penguin Group (USA) LLC, 2015

Acknowledgments to the original publishers of the selections in this book appear on pages 513–16.

Some of the works were previously published in Saul Bellow's *It All Adds Up: From the Dim Past to the Uncertain Future* (Viking Penguin, 1994). They appeared first in issues of *Esquire, Forbes, Holiday, Life, The National Interest, The New York Times Book Review, The New York Times Magazine, Newsday, The Noble Savage, The Ontario Review, Partisan Review, The Reporter, The Times Literary Supplement*, and *Travel Holiday*.

"Israel: The Six-Day War" (as "Report on Israel") was published in *Newsday*, issues of June 12, 1967, June 13, 1967, and June 16, 1967. © Newsday Inc., 1967. Reprinted with permission.

"Nobel Lecture" is published by permission of The Nobel Foundation. © The Nobel Foundation 1976.

"Machines and Storybooks" was published in *Harper's*, August 1974. Copyright © 1974 Harper's Magazine. All rights reserved. Reprinted by permission.

"Before I Go Away: A Words and Images Interview with Norman Manea." © Words & Images, 19 Derech Eretz Street, Gedera 7047119, Israel. Words & Images is a nonprofit project dedicated to the documentation and dissemination of in-depth interviews with great Jewish writers of our time who are invited to explore the connections between their oeuvre and their Jewish identity. The project is conducted in conjunction with the National Library in Jerusalem.

LIBRARY OF CONGRESS CATALOGING-IN-PUBLICATION DATA
Bellow, Saul.
[Works. Selections]
There is simply too much to think about : collected nonfiction / Saul Bellow ; edited by Benjamin Taylor.
pages cm
ISBN 978-0-670-01669-3 (hardback)
I. Taylor, Benjamin, 1952– editor. II. Title.
PS3503.E4488A6 2015
818'.5209—dc23
2014038540

Printed in the United States of America
1 3 5 7 9 10 8 6 4 2

Once you begin talking, once the mind takes to this way of turning, it keeps turning, and it dips through all events. And perhaps it makes matters slightly more tolerable to let it turn. Though I can't see why they should be tolerable. It is really a frightful moment. But what can one do? The thoughts continue turning.

—*Mr. Sammler's Planet*

Contents

The Seventies

The Eighties

There Is Simply
Too Much
to Think About

Prologue: Starting Out in Chicago

What was it, in the Thirties, that drew an adolescent in Chicago to the writing of books? How did a young American of the Depression period decide that he was, of all things, a literary artist? I use the pretentious term *literary artist* simply to emphasize the contrast between such an ambition and the external facts. A colossal industrial and business center, knocked flat by unemployment, its factories and even its schools closing, decided to hold a World's Fair on the shore of Lake Michigan, with towers, high rides, exhibits, Chinese rickshaws, a midget village in which there was a midget wedding every day, and other lively attractions including whores and con men and fan dancers. There was a bit of gaiety, there was quite a lot of amoebic dysentery. Prosperity did not come back. Several millions of dollars were invested in vain by businessmen and politicians. If they could be quixotic, there was no reason why college students shouldn't be impractical too. And what was the most impractical of choices in somber, heavy, growling, lowbrow Chicago? Why, it was to be the representative of beauty, the interpreter of the human heart, the hero of ingenuity, playfulness, personal freedom, generosity and love. I cannot even now say that this was a bad sort of crackpot to be.

The difference between that time and this is that in the Thirties crackpots were not subsidized by their families. They had to go it alone for several years. Or at least until the New Deal (thanks largely to Harry Hopkins) recognized that a great government could *buy* the solution of any problem and opened WPA projects in many parts of the country. I think it possible that Hopkins and Roosevelt, seeing how much trouble unhappy intellectuals had made in Russia, Germany and Italy between 1905 and 1935, thought it a bargain to pay people twenty-three dollars a week for painting post office murals and editing guide-books. This plan succeeded admirably. If I am not mistaken, America continued to follow the Hopkins hint in postwar Europe and perhaps in Vietnam.

I know, for instance, that John Cheever has been conducting creative writing courses at Sing Sing. Writers and criminals have often found that they had much in common. And correctional officials seem to understand, thanks to the psychology courses they take in the universities, that it is excellent therapy to write books and that it may soften the hearts of criminals to record their experiences. Politicians, too, when they fall from power or retire, become writers or university professors. Thus Hubert Humphrey and Dean Rusk became lecturers, Eugene McCarthy became a poet and an altogether different sort of politician, Spiro Agnew, a novelist. Interviewed not long ago in *The New York Times*, Mr. Agnew said that, having suffered greatly, he felt the need to do something creative to recover his spirits and was setting to work writing a novel because he was not yet strong enough to do serious mental work.

But I started out to recall what it was like to set oneself up to be a writer in the Midwest during the Thirties. For I thought of myself as a Midwesterner and not as a Jew. I am often described as a Jewish writer; in much the same way, one might be called a Samoan astronomer or an Eskimo cellist or a Zulu Gainsborough expert. There is some oddity about it. I am a Jew, and I have written some books. I have tried to fit my soul into the Jewish-writer category, but it does not feel comfortably accommodated there. I wonder now and then whether Philip Roth and Bernard Malamud and I have not become the Hart Schaffner and Marx of our trade. We have made it in the field of culture as Bernard Baruch made it on a park bench, as Polly Adler made it in prostitution, as Two-Gun Cohen, the personal bodyguard of Sun Yat-Sen, made it in China. My joke is not broad enough to cover the contempt I feel for the opportunists, wise guys and career types who impose such labels and trade upon them. In a century so disastrous to Jews, one hesitates to criticize those who believe that they are making the world safer by publicizing Jewish achievements. I myself doubt that this publicity is effective.

I did not go to the public library to read the Talmud but the novels and poems of Sherwood Anderson, Theodore Dreiser, Edgar Lee Masters and Vachel Lindsay. These were people who had resisted the material weight of American society and who proved—what was not immediately obvious—that the life lived in great manufacturing, shipping and banking centers with their slaughter stink, their great slums, prisons, hospitals and schools, was also a human life. It appeared to me that this one thing, so intimately known that not only nerves, senses, mind but also my very bones wanted to put it into words, might contain elements that not even Dreiser, whom I admired most, had yet reached. I felt that I was born to be a performing and interpretive creature, that I was meant to take part in a peculiar, exalted game. For there are good grounds to consider this, together with other forms of civilized behavior and ceremony, a game. At its noblest this game is played, under discipline, before God himself—so Plato said and others as well. The game can be an offering, a celebration, an act of praise, an acknowledgment also of one's weaknesses and limitations. I couldn't have put it in this manner then. All that appeared was a blind obstinate impulse expressing itself in bursts of foolishness. I loved great things. I thought I had a right to think of that exalted game. I was also extremely proud, ornery and stupid.

I was, in 1937, a very young married man who had quickly lost his first job and who lived with his in-laws. His affectionate, loyal and pretty wife insisted that he must be given a chance to write something. Having anyone pay attention to my writing wasn't a real possibility. I am as often bemused as amused at the attention my books have received. Neglect would have been frightful, but attention has its disadvantages. The career of a critic, when I am feeling mean about it, I sometimes compare to that of a deaf man who tunes pianos. In a more benevolent mood I agree with my late father that people must be encouraged to make as honest a living as they can. For this reason I don't object to becoming a topic. When I visited Japan I saw that there were prayer-and-fortune-telling papers sold for a penny at each temple. The buyers rolled up these long strips of paper and tied them by threads to bushes and low trees. From the twigs there dangled hundreds of tightly furled papers. I sometimes compare myself to one of these temple trees.

So I sat at a bridge table in a back bedroom of the apartment while all rational, serious, dutiful people were at their jobs or trying to find jobs, writing something. My table faced three cement steps that rose from the cellar into the brick gloom of a passageway. Only my mother-in-law was at home. A widow then in her seventies, she wore a heavy white braid down her back. She had been a modern woman and a socialist and suffragette in the Old Country. She was attractive in a fragile, steely way. You felt Sophie's strength of will in all things. She kept a neat house. The very plants, the ashtrays, the pedestals, the doilies, the chairs revealed her mastery. Each object had its military place. Her apartment could easily have been transferred to West Point.

Lunch occurred at half past twelve. The cooking was good. We ate together in the kitchen. The meal was followed by an interval of stone. My mother-in-law took a nap. I went into the street. Ravenswood was utterly empty. I walked about with something like a large stone in my belly. I often turned into Lawrence Avenue and stood on the bridge looking into the drainage canal. If I had been a dog I would have howled. Even a soft howl would have helped. But I was not here to howl. I was here to interpret the world (its American version) as brilliantly as possible. Still I would have been far happier selling newspapers at Union Station or practicing my shots in a poolroom. But I had a discipline to learn at the bridge table in the bedroom.

No wonder a writer of great talent and fine intelligence like John Cheever volunteers to help the convicts with their stories. He knows how it feels to be locked in. Maybe he thinks the prisoners, being already locked in, may as well learn the discipline. It is the most intolerable of privations for people whose social instincts are so highly developed that they want to be confined in rooms in order to write novels. Nuns fret not, perhaps, but writers do. Bernanos, the French religious novelist, said that his soul could not bear to be cut off from its kind and that was why he did his work in cafés. Cafés indeed! I would have kissed the floor of a café. There were no cafés in Chicago. There were greasy-spoon cafeterias, one-arm joints, taverns. I never yet heard of a writer who brought his manuscripts into a tavern. I have always taken an interest in the fact that Schiller liked to smell apples when he was writing, that someone else kept his feet in a tub of water. The only person whose arrangements seemed to me worth imitating was the mys-

tic and guru Gurdjieff. Gurdjieff, when he had work to do, set forth
from headquarters in Fontainebleau with his disciples in several limou-
sines. They carried hampers with caviar, cold fowl, champagne, cheese
and fruit. At a signal from the master the cars would stop. They would
picnic in a meadow and then, with all his followers around him, Gurdjieff did his writing. This, if it can be arranged, seems to me worth
doing.

I am glad to say that I can't remember what I was writing in Ravenswood. It must have been terrible. The writing itself, however, was
of no importance. The important thing was that American society and
S. Bellow came face to face. I had to learn that by cutting myself off
from American life in order to perform an alien task, I risked cutting
myself off from everything that could nourish me. But this was the case
only if you granted the monopoly of nutrients to this business-indus-
trial, vital, brutal, proletarian and middle-class city that was itself involved in a tremendous struggle. It was not even aggressively hostile,
saying, "Lead my kind of life or die." Not at all. It simply had no interest in your sort of game.

Quite often, in the Hudson belonging to J.J., my brother-in-law, my
mother-in-law and I drove to the cemetery. There we tended her husband's grave. Her trembling but somehow powerful, spotty hand pulled
weeds. I made trips with a Mason jar to the faucet and made water
splotches about the nasturtiums and sweet williams. Death, I thought,
Chicago-style, might not be such a bad racket after all. At least you
didn't have to drive down Harlem Avenue in rush hour back to the
house with its West Point arrangements, with its pages of bad manuscript on the bridge table, and the silent dinner of soup and stew and
strudel. After which you and your wife, washing dishes, enjoyed the
first agreeable hours of the day.

J.J., my brother-in-law, born Jascha in the old country, practiced law
in the Loop. He was a Republican, member of the American Legion, a
golfer, a bowler; he drove his conservative car conservatively and took
The Saturday Evening Post; he wore a Herbert Hoover starched collar,
trousers short in the ankle, and a hard straw hat in the summer. He
spoke in pure Hoosier twang, not like a Booth Tarkington gentleman
but like a real Tippecanoe country dirt farmer. All this Americanism

was imposed on an exquisitely oriental face, dark, with curved nose and Turkish cheekbones. Naturally a warm-hearted man, he frowned upon me. He thought I was doing something foreign.

There was an observable parallel between us. As I was making a writer of myself, this exotic man was transforming his dark oriental traits and becoming an American from Indiana. He spoke of Aaron Slick from Punkin' Crick, of Elmer Dub: "Ah kin read writin', but ah can't read readin'." He had served in the Army—my wife wore his 1917 overcoat (too small for me) and J.J. told old, really old La Salle Street Republican sex jokes about Woodrow Wilson and Edith Bolling. It was common in that generation and the next to tailor one's appearance and style to what were, after all, journalistic publicity creations and products of caricature. The queer hunger of immigrants and their immediate descendants for true Americanism has yet to be described. It may be made to sound like fun but I find it hard to think of anyone who underwent the process with joy. Those incompetents who lacked mimetic talent and were pure buffoons were better off—I remember a cousin, Arkady, from the Old Country who declared that his new name was now and henceforth Lake Erie. A most poetic name, he thought. In my own generation there were those immigrants who copied even the unhappiness of the Protestant majority, embracing its miseries, battling against Mom; reluctant, after work, to board the suburban train, drinking downtown, drinking on the club car, being handed down drunk to the wife and her waiting station wagon like good Americans. These people martyred themselves in the enactment of roles that proved them genuine—just as madly wretched in marriage as Abe Lincoln and Mary Todd. Cousin Arkady, a clown who sold dehydrated applesauce on the road, giving dry applesauce demonstrations to housewives in small-town department stores, was spared the worst of it. He simply became "Archie" and made no further effort to prove himself a real American.

The point of this brief account, as I see it, is to evoke that mixture of imagination and stupidity with which people met the American Experience, that murky, heavy, burdensome, chaotic thing. I see that my own error, shared with many others, was to seek sanctuary in what corners of culture one could find in this country, there to enjoy my high thoughts and to perfect myself in the symbolic discipline of an art. I

There Is Simply Too Much to Think About

can't help feeling that I overdid it. One didn't need as much sanctuary as all that.

If I had to name the one force in America that opposes the symbolic discipline of poetry today as much as brutal philistinisms did before World War II, I would say the Great Noise. The enemy is noise. By noise I mean not simply the noise of technology, the noise of money or advertising and promotion, the noise of the media, the noise of miseducation, but the terrible excitement and distraction generated by the crises of modern life. Mind, I don't say that philistinism is gone. It is not. It has found many disguises, some highly artistic and peculiarly insidious. But the noise of life is the great threat. Contributing to it are real and unreal issues, ideologies, rationalizations, errors, delusions, nonsituations that look real, nonquestions demanding consideration, opinions, analyses in the press, on the air, expertise, inside dope, factional disagreement, official rhetoric, information—in short, the sounds of the public sphere, the din of politics, the turbulence and agitation that set in about 1914 and have now reached an intolerable volume.

Nadezhda Mandelstam, writing of poets in the Soviet Union, says of the Russian noise: "Nowhere else I believe were real people so much deafened as they were here by the din of life—One after another poets fell silent because they could no longer hear their own voices." She adds: "The noise drowned out thought and, in the case of millions, conscience as well." William Wordsworth, nearly two hundred years ago, had expressed his concern over the effects of modern turbulence on poetry. He was right too. But in the language of my youth—"He didn't know the half of it."

[1974–75]

The Fifties and Before

Spanish Letter

The police come first to your notice in Spain, taking precedence over the people, the streets and the landscape: the Guardia Civil in their wooden-looking, shiny, circular hats, brims flattened at the back, hats that are real enough, since they are worn and seen but, unlike the tommy gun that each *guardia* has in the crook of his arm, lacking in *real* reality. Next, gray-uniformed police with the red eagle on their sleeves and rifles hanging on their backs. Even the guard in the park, an old man in the costume of a Swiss chasseur, with a draggled feather, leather jerkin and shabby leggings, holds a rifle by the strap. Then there are the secret police; no one knows how many kinds there are, but you see a great deal of them. On the Irún-Madrid express our passports were examined by one who swung into the compartment and reversed his lapel, showing us the badge of blue, gold and red enamel. He was quiet, equable and unsystematic, sighing while he wrote some of the passport numbers into his notebook and ruffling the pages as if wondering what to do next with his authority. He murmured *adiós* and withdrew. The train labored on toward the flower-blazing villas of Santander, the wooden walls of the car quivering. The seats were long and seignorial, each headrest covered with lace, and in one of them sat a Spaniard who, as we were passing the harbor, engaged us in conversation, not casually, by design, preventing me from looking at the ships in the silver, coal-streaked evening water. He gave us a lecture on the modernity of Santander and invited us to ask questions on Spanish life, Spanish history, geography, industry or character, and without being asked, wrinkling his narrow forehead and shooting forward his palms like a photographer ordering you to hold still, he began to speak of hydroelectric power, very minute in his details about turbines, wiring, transmitters and whatnot. We were American and therefore interested in mechanical subjects. I was not an engineer, I told him. Nevertheless he finished his speech and sat as if waiting for me to propose a subject closer to my interests. He was a small, nervously mobile, brown man with measuring, aggressive, melancholy eyes. He wore a gloomy brown gabardine suit, shiny with dirt, and shoes that were laced through only half the eyelets. Already we were climbing into the thickening darkness; farms appeared below, remote in the steep green valleys. "You are on a holiday?" he said. "You will see many beautiful things." He enumerated them: the Escorial, the Prado, the Alhambra, Seville, Cádiz, *la taza de plata*. He had seen them all; he had been everywhere; he had fought everywhere. "In Spain?" I asked. In Spain, of course, and in Russia and Poland as a member of the Blue Division against the Reds. Essentially he was a soldier; he came of a military family; his father was a high-ranking officer, a colonel in the air force. He threw his hand open to me, displaying a white scar in the palm—his souvenir of Albacete. Just then a young *guardia*, lanky and sunburned, began to roll back the refractory door, and he sprang from his place, seized the handle and held it. He spoke a few rapid words in an undertone to the *guardia* and rattled the door shut. Someone, certainly not one of the Spaniards in the compartment, said, "*Hay sitio.*" There was room enough for two more passengers. But the colonel's son kept his counsel, and stepping over legs to his own seat, he resumed his conversation—with me alone this time, confidentially; and for a while something of the expression with which he had dismissed the *guardia* lingered on his face, the roused power of his office. Yes, he belonged to the police and made three trips a week between Irún and Madrid. He liked the job. Being an old campaigner, he did not mind the jolting or the noise—there was singing accompanied by rhythmical clapping and stamping in the next compartment; in his own good time, he put a stop to that. The pay was not enough for his style of life, but he was expecting a good *enchufe*, or sinecure, to which he felt himself entitled. Fortunately he could add to his income by writing. He wrote fiction, and at present he was busy with a long historical novel in verse. His eyes grew hot and visionary as he began to talk of the poets he admired and to quote, somber and reverent. I reflected that it was probably appropriate, since so many

There Is Simply Too Much to Think About

European writers were ambitious to become policemen, that the police should aspire to become writers.

Meanwhile the sky had grown dark and the train threaded its weak light among the trees and rocks or stopped briefly at stations as weakly lighted as itself. Crowds waited in the mist and the passage was filling. No one made a persistent effort to get into the compartment; everyone was turned away by the colonel's son. We, the Americans, were in his charge and he was determined that we should have a comfortable night, with space enough to stretch out and sleep. But somehow, by pressure of numbers, the vacant places were filled, and sensing our disapproval of such a thing, he did not try to evict the new occupants. He continued to be as solicitous as before. When I broke off a piece of the loaf I had bought in Hendaye, he was horrified to see me eat such inferior bread. I must have a slice of his tortilla. He dragged down his valise, touched the lock, and it sprang open. The tortilla was in a round tin box. Under it lay copies of *Green Hornet*, *Coyote* and other pulp magazines. He cut a thick gray slice of the cake. I ate what I could of it, excused myself from finishing and went into the corridor. Most of the people there were traveling between local stations, a crowd of *gente humilde*, sad, shabby and world-worn, resting between the walls, leaning on the brass rods along the windows, with gloom-deepened eyes and black nostrils; in muffling shawls or berets that fattened their heads and made a dis-proportion in their long, brown faces; melancholy, but with a kind of resistance to dreariness, as if ready to succumb so far but no farther to it—the Spanish *dignidad*.

The passengers in the neighboring compartment had become very boisterous, and now the colonel's son came out and subdued them. I returned to my seat and he to his. Immediately he opened a new topic. Tired of his conversation and of humoring him, I refused to respond, and at last he was silent. Then the shades were drawn, someone turned off the light, and we tried to sleep.

By morning the passage was bare, swept clean. The colonel's son said, "We will pass the Escorial soon, where the tombs of the kings are." I was stony to him. We were running downslope in a rush of smoke. The shallow fields, extending on either side to the mountains, looked drought-stricken, burned, desert, mere stubble and dust. We burst into the suburbs of Madrid and into the yards. On the platform the colonel's son was at my back, and in the sooty arcades and the hell's-antechamber turmoil of the station he hung on, rueful and anxious at my speed. Presumably he had to know where I was staying in Madrid to complete his report. From the hotel bus I saw his brown face in the spectator throng of porters, cabbies and touts for hotels and *pensiones*, watching the baggage being lifted to the roof, hot-eyed, avoiding my glance and looking on at the work. Successful!

First and last, the police. In every hotel there are police forms to fill, and passports have to be registered at the station. To obtain a railroad ticket you must make out a declaration stating the object of the journey, and you cannot travel without a *triptico*, a safe-conduct. No consulate or embassy is permitted to grant a visa without the police *salida*. The broad face of Seguridad, near the place where the first shots were fired on Napoleon's troops, dominates the Puerta del Sol with barred and darkened windows. The police license radios. The police go through your suitcase in a provincial rooming house. The woman living in the cave dug in the bluff near the Manzanares is quick to tell you, "We are here with the permission of the *policía*." Everywhere you hear that the jails are full. There is regular bus service for visitors from Cibeles, at the center of town, to the Carabanchel prison. On a trolley car near the Toledo Gate I saw two arrestees, an old man and a boy of about eighteen, being taken there. They were handcuffed and in the custody of a pair of *guardias* with the inevitable machine guns. The boy, with thick hair that grew sturdily down his neck and with prematurely deep creases beneath his eyes, had the precarious nonchalance of deep misery and deep hatred. There was a loaf of bread sticking out of his pocket. The old man was one-armed, filthy and scarred. His feet were coming through the rope-soled *alpargatas*. He was nearly bald and the lines of a healed wound spread under his thin gray hair. I looked at him and he gave me a gentle shrug of surrender, not daring to speak, but when I got down in Mataderos, among buildings demolished during the civil war, he ventured to lift his hand and wave it as far as the steel cuff permitted.

These were probably common criminals, not *Rojos*. Hundreds of the latter are arrested every month, and the trials at Alcalá de Henares continue endlessly. Political prisoners released from the overflowing jails

There Is Simply Too Much to Think About

are on conditional liberty and show you the cards on which they must have a current official stamp. Most of them are not granted work permits and live as they can in the streets, shining shoes, opening taxi doors, peddling lottery tickets and begging.

At the center of Madrid you occasionally notice shot-scarred buildings, but on the whole there are few reminders of the civil war in the better *barrios*. On Gran Via the shops are almost American in their luxury, and the early-evening café crowds that sit looking down the broad curve of the street at the mass of banks, churches and government buildings resemble those in New York and Washington bars. Hollywood pictures run in all the better theaters, and the craving for American good things—Buicks, nylons, Parker 51 pens and cigarettes—is as powerful here as in the other capitals of the world, and as in most of the capitals there are no dollars and the black market thrives. The police do not interfere with it. Peddlers go among the tables offering pens and cigarettes. Some of these, especially the pens, are obvious counterfeits; the Lucky Strike packages are beautifully done; the blue tax stamps are perfect; the cigarettes are filled with dung and crumbled straw. A boy comes with a huge gold ring to sell. He gives you glimpses of it in his cupped hands with exaggerated furtiveness, his face frantically thievish. It is a heavy, ugly, squarish ring, and you wonder who would ever buy it. He whispers, "It's stolen," and offers it for two hundred *pesetas*, one hundred, fifty, and then he gives you up with a sad, bored look and tries another table. Women flap their lottery tickets and beg tenaciously. Some of them carry blind or crippled infants and exhibit their maimed or withered legs. One, with a practiced movement, turns the child and shows me a face covered with sores and a pair of purulent eyes. Juanita, my Basque landlady at the pension, tells me that most of these children are hired out by the day to the professional beggars. It's all business, she contemptuously says.

In the dining room of the pension, the conversation is mainly about movie stars. The *comandante*'s wife is equally attracted to James Stewart and Clark Gable. The Sanchez sisters, who were born in Hong Kong and speak English well, are for Brian Aherne and Herbert Marshall,

British types. Even the *comandante* has his favorites and adds his dry, nervous, harsh voice to the rattle of the women. The *comandante* is lean, correct, compressed and rancorous and has a pockmarked face, a shallow pompadour, black eyes. He and the *señora* do not eat our ordinary bread. A black-market white loaf is delivered to them daily, and at noon he carries it under his arm like a swagger stick. There is a little military rush when they enter, she with small, pouncing steps, wagging her fan, he blind to us all but inclining his head. Even on the hottest day his tunic is buttoned to the throat. I offend him by coming to the dining room in a T-shirt and slippers. He sits down grimly to his meal, taking the *señora*'s fan to cool his soup. His is the *dignidad* of gnawing hauteur and dislike, the hateful kind.

There is an important person in the pension, an admiral stationed at the ministry, who never eats in the dining room and who often, in the afternoon, blunders through the dark, curtained rooms in his pajamas. Juanita enters his apartment without knocking and they are obviously on terms of intimacy. The Sanchez girls explain in an embarrassed way that the admiral is under a great obligation to Juanita, who during the civil war concealed and nursed his sick son, or perhaps his nephew, and he swore to reward her. The Republic was unjust to the admiral. He taught at a very low salary in the naval academy. The *comandante* served under Franco in Morocco and is now head of a military school. He has the reputation of being a great disciplinarian, the sisters inform me rather proudly. They themselves were educated in a convent.

The rest are middle class, people who must be well connected to be able to afford a pension as good as this one, beneficiaries of *enchufismo* or civil service patronage. (Literally, the *enchufe* is an electric socket.) An ordinary civil service job—and one must be, politically, as faultless as a sacrificial lamb to get it—carries a salary of five or six hundred *pesetas* a month or roughly twenty dollars, and since desirable things are approximately American in price (higher, in many cases; a pound of black-market coffee costs two and a half dollars), a man needs *enchufes* to live comfortably. If, through family influence or friends high in the church or the army, he has several jobs, he makes the rounds of the ministries to sign in and sign out. Occasionally he may be required to

There Is Simply Too Much to Think About

do a little work, and he does it *para cumplir*, to acknowledge the obligation, but as hastily as possible. This is in part traditional. All Spanish regimes have used the same means to keep the educated classes from disaffection. "Modern" government programs receive great publicity. Recently a social-security system modeled on the Beveridge plan was announced, and Sir William himself was invited for consultation. But the real purpose of these programs is to extend *enchufismo*, for the actual benefits to the sick or unemployed worker under this insurance scheme amount to about three *pesetas* a day, hardly enough for a loaf of bread. Franco has great-state ambitions, like Mussolini's, but Spain is too poor; the cost of staying in power is too high for him to realize them. The buildings called the New Ministries, which were to have gone up monumentally at the foot of the Castellana, stand in scaffolding, uncompleted and apparently abandoned.

For middle-class families without *enchufes*, the difficulties are terrible. One must wear a European suit, a shirt that costs two hundred *pesetas*, a tie. To appear in the rope *alpargatas* of the people is inconceivable. It is essential to have a maid. And then one's wife has to be properly dressed and the children clothed and educated. One must cling to one's class. The fall into the one below is measureless. Its wretchedness is an ancient fact, stable, immemorial and understood by everyone. The newer wretchedness, that of keeping one meager suit presentable, of making a place in the budget for movies in order to have something to contribute to polite conversation when *The Song of Bernadette* is discussed, of persisting to exhaustion among the stragglers in the chase after desirable things—the images of the earthly kingdom reflected in every casual American—is nevertheless not *the* wretchedness. That you see in the tenements and the inhabited ruins, old kilns and caves, the human swarms in the dry rot of Vallecas and Mataderos.

Summer is arid in Madrid, and cloudless. The sound of thunder is very rare. When it is heard, the maids cry out, "*¡Una tormenta!*" and dart through the pension, slamming the windows. Across the air shaft the blond Bibi calls "A storm!" to me in her tense, warlike voice, wavers behind the smoky glass and leaves the thick drapes trembling like the curtains of a stage on the last cry of a tragedy. Then the rain begins with a plunge, falling with the heaviness of drops of mercury.

In ten minutes it is over; ten minutes more and it has dried. On the hottest days the streets and the locust trees are watered morning and evening. The parks are divided by irrigation ditches and are grassless. The only grass I saw in Madrid, that before the Prado, was kept alive by continual sprinkling. As one goes out from the center of the city the green becomes thinner and thinner until, from the blank, sun-hardened flats of the outlying districts, overlooking the trenches that have sunk and are grown over with brown weeds and brown wires, there is only the scattered green of gardens on the immense plain, each garden with the diagonal pole of a well sweep rising above the Indian corn.

The Manzanares River is almost empty, yet on Sunday, in the section called the Bombilla, where in places the water has collected to a depth of several inches, there are hundreds of bathers and picnickers in throngs at the working-class cafés for miles along the shores, the *gente humilde*, choking the streets and bridges and lying on blankets on the dusty banks under the scanty acacias. It is like a vision of the first moments of resurrection, seeing those families lying in the smothering dust and milling in the roads. On the city side there are homes in the ruins, fenced round with the wreckage of bombardments and rolls of barbed wire. A few gypsies live in the Bombilla, in wagons. They are not like the Andalusian gypsies; they have a citified, depressed air; the women, filthy and gaunt, sit by their iron pots; the children lie naked on sacking. Goats are tethered to the wheels and axles, and under one wagon I saw two apes crouching spiritlessly. A factory that makes concrete tubes rises on the other side—a long, proudly lettered, modern industrial wall against which there are always a few men relieving themselves. Behind are the usual unfinished public works and miles away, far upland, is the intricate earthen blue of the Sierra that sends down the trickle of the Manzanares, more like the idea than the actuality of a river. It appears to be the idea, the *hope* of a river that attracts the gigantic crowd from the desert African dryness of the slums. The boys leap high into the air, as if the water were measured in feet, not inches, and the dust clings to their legs when they clamber up the bank. The river flows in a dirty green vein from shallow to shallow;

There Is Simply Too Much to Think About

gangs run yelling up and down the sand islands of its bed. A man leads his infant daughter, hardly old enough to walk, down to the water. She has soiled herself and he washes her with a certain embittered tenderness while she clings screaming to his lanky, hairy legs.

Among the trees surrounding the kiosks that sell wine and beer, the huge multitude is dancing, jogging up and down. Three young boys, self-contained, professional, indifferent to the dancers, play saxophone, guitar and drum, imitating the downtown version of American chic. Two drunken men are blowing the *gaita*, the hairy Galician bagpipes, for a group of drunken-looking friends. Madrid is said to be overrun with Gallegos; Franco himself is Galician, and in the old-fashioned Spanish belief in provincial loyalties they come to the city by the thousands for jobs.

The soldiers in the crowd look thickset and short in their coarse jackets, gaiters and big boots. They bump against the wheeling pairs of girls and try to force them apart. This is done seriously; there is little friskiness or gaiety and you see few smiles. The dancers tramp and shuffle but, though excited and sweating, keep a straight-browed, straight-lipped formality of expression and hold themselves apart with rigid heads and shoulders.

The kiosks and the cafés do not sell food. The people bring their own bread and chickpeas. You can buy a meal at middle-class prices in the bowery beer gardens set apart behind lattice walls and bushes growing in tubs. In one of these places, where I stop for a bottle of beer, there is a huge, time-eaten barrel organ that produces martial-sounding dances with missing notes, clanging bells and queer, mechanical birdcalls. The man who winds it has the pride-bitten look of someone who has come down in the world and gives me a glance of "too good for my destiny and every bit as good as you are." His wife sits beside him, evidently to give him support in his humiliation, for she does not spell him at the organ. The brass drum inside catches the late sun on its short spines as it revolves. He is bald and small and his cheeks are taut and hard as he faces me; his mouth is bitter. His wife is passive and sits with quietly folded hands.

People complain rather freely on very short acquaintance about the regime: the shortness of the rations, the inferior bread, the black market, the army, the police, the Falange and the church. Madrileños speak of the recent referendum on the law of succession as *el reverendum*, a priests' affair. It was conducted with the familiar, heavy-handed efficiency of fascist elections. Workers in the unreliable *barrios* of Mataderos, Vallecas and Cuatro Caminos received ballots beforehand with a printed *sí*. Ration books that were not stamped at the polling place to show that their holders had voted were invalid after election day. Nevertheless many people, monarchists as well as republicans, abstained, and even government figures acknowledged that a considerable number had voted *no*: 132,000 in Barcelona, 117,000 in Madrid, 36,000 in Seville. The socialists interpret the referendum as an attempt by the regime to convince the United States of its stability in order to obtain a loan. Franco has become very confident since the weeks after V-E Day, when it was thought that he had lost together with Hitler. The Germans did as they liked in Madrid during the war and everyone was therefore greatly surprised that Franco was allowed to remain in power after their defeat. But Britain and the United States did not stop selling him the gasoline without which his army, estimated at seven hundred thousand men, would have been paralyzed. And now, with the air of future allies, Spanish fascists tell you that no other country on the continent is so safe and convenient a base for the coming war with Russia. France and Italy are, or soon will be, communist. Spain is a strategic center owing to Gibraltar, and Franco's reliability as an old fighter against communism is appreciated by America. Besides, everybody knows what magnificent soldiers the Spanish are. It is curious how much national pride is mingled with the cynicism of the people who tell you this. Everyone, whether communist or socialist, has a touch of this pride, and fascists and socialists alike joke explosively about the Italian disaster at Guadalajara: "The order was *a la bayoneta* and they thought it was *a la camioneta*"—"To the trucks!" instead of "Bayonet charge!"

There is, judging from the number of political arrests and the frequency and violence of the attacks in the press on Prieto and other exiled leaders, a great deal of underground activity. Several republicans told me that between November 1946 and April 1947 ten thousand people were imprisoned. CNT, UGT and communist newspapers circulate in Madrid and other large cities, but there is little organized resistance except in isolated mountain districts in the north and in Andalusia. From abroad, both the socialists and the communists claimed leadership in the short Asturian coal strike that occurred in May 1947, but little is actually known about it. Many socialists and republicans admit that the communist underground is growing, mainly because the international situation favors it. Of the Western countries only France has boycotted Franco, and it is believed that the border was closed by the French government as a concession to the communists. The victory of the Labor Party did not change Britain's policy, notwithstanding the pledges of support made by Attlee to the Loyalists when he visited Spain during the civil war as his party's representative.

Alcalá de Henares, where I saw one of the political trials, is an ancient, decayed town, the birthplace of Cervantes and, in the fifteenth century, famous for its university. Ten men, tramway employees from Cuatro Caminos charged with distributing the communist paper *Mundo Obrero*, were the defendants. I was told by the son of one of them that they had been arrested sixteen months before. Such trials are theoretically public but they are never announced; embassies and the foreign press are notified by the underground or by relatives of the accused. I came with one of the embassy secretaries in a resplendent green embassy car before which soldiers and Guardia Civil gave way in the antique streets. *Diplomáticos*, we went unchallenged past the sentries and under rifles up the staircase into the long hall of the courtroom. It was lined with *guardia* and their machine guns. We sat down at the rear among the families of the accused.

The court was a tribunal of officers, for members of illegal political parties are in the category of criminals endangering public safety and come under the army's jurisdiction. Looking toward the narrow windows, we could see only dimly. The prisoners were on benches with their backs turned to us. The members of the tribunal had the light behind them and their faces, too, were obscure. In profile at either side of the room were the prosecutor and the officer appointed for the defense. Boots and scabbards shone under the tables.

A clerk hurriedly reads the depositions of the ten. On such and such a night Fulano de Thal met another conspirator in such and such a place and received or handed over money, instructions, papers. One by one the accused, called on by court or prosecutor, rise and acknowledge the confessions. Only one balks at a detail. He does not recall it. He is ordered to look at the signature of the deposition. Is it his? It is, but he cannot remember making the statement in point. Again, more impatiently, does he recognize the signature as his own? He does. Obviously, then, the statement is his. He is ordered to sit, and he stiffly obeys. All the prisoners with the exception of two elderly men rise and stand with a military bearing, infected by the manner of the tribunal. To see them play the soldierly game and stand like *hombres honrados* to verify confessions exacted, everyone knows, in the cellars of the Seguridad affects me painfully, like the injection of a depressant that thickens the heartbeat. No doubt it is very *castizo*, purely and essentially Spanish, that the prisoners should conduct themselves like captives in an honorable war, and probably it also sustains them to stand at attention, but I have a horror of this game as I do of the *comandante*'s bouncing and pivoting game in the pension, his peevish chivalry.

Each of the prisoners answers questions. The defense does not examine them, no evidence is introduced, and there are no witnesses. You become aware, when the prosecutor stands up, of his large hands and powerful body; they give an effect of incongruity to the meticulousness of his uniform. He makes a neat prosecutor's packet of the depositions: "It is admitted . . . it is admitted . . . according to the statements of Fulano de Thal . . ." Not until he concludes does he become bullish and exhortatory. He puts forth his strong voice suddenly. In cold blood, lifting up his chest, he begins to thunder that crimes "in a foreign spirit" against a whole people cannot be pardoned, and he asks that the leader of the ten be given a twelve-year sentence and the rest four years each. W. whispers that this is relatively lenient. Then the defense lawyer reads a short statement to the effect that in the Christian democracy of the Caudillo's government there is room for differences of opinion when the expression of those differences is temperate. These words cause a sighing stir in the gloomy end of the room where the families sit. The prosecutor speaks for another half hour in reply, his showmanship at times becoming perfunctory. This is a very minor trial. He towers be-

There Is Simply Too Much to Think About

fore the window in the clear morning light of Castile and makes his last summation, reads from notes, and repeats his demand for twelve years and four. The time served awaiting trial does not count. The president of the tribunal now asks each of the prisoners in turn whether he has anything to say before sentence is passed. Six do not. The seventh, however, the leader of the ten, starts to speak; the president says loudly, *"¡Cállese!"*—"Shut up!" The prisoner persisting, he rises and shouts, *"¡Cállese!"* startling everyone. *"¡Nada de la política!* Sit down!" He sits. "Stand up!" The prisoner rises. "You have been heard on the evidence. Nothing else is relevant. There will be no politics here. Be seated." There is no other disturbance. The trial is over and we file down under the guns with the silent relatives. I see the grieving face of a boy on the stairs and I talk to him. His father is one of those who received four years. Will he be allowed to see him? He does not know; since the arrest he had not seen him till this morning. He is now the eldest at home. There was an older brother but he disappeared in the last days of the war. He has another brother, eight years old, and two sisters. "How do you live?" I ask; he does not reply. Thin and tall, he stands pigeon-toed beside me on the street, drawing his long hands out of his pockets and thrusting them back. His face is narrow and his soft eyes seem almost without whites: all center. I make a low-voiced comment on the barbarousness of the trial. W. has meanwhile taken down the names of the condemned for his report and wants to leave so I say goodbye and we get into the car.

The uselessness of it afflicts me. Poverty and the harshness of the dictatorship make resistance inevitable and the relations of powers outside the country make it vain, perfectly useless. The Spanish problem will not be settled within Spain. Franco wants to bargain with America and the communist leaders, were they in power, would represent Russia. But people continue to struggle in the political spirit of past times, when they were still free within national boundaries to make revolutions and create governments. There is no such freedom now, as a growing number of Europeans are aware. "We liberated ourselves from Napoleon in 1812," a Spanish acquaintance said to me, "and we manifested the same spirit in 1937 when we fought Hitler. Against him, however, we were powerless. And perhaps we would have been swallowed by Stalin if in the civil war we had succeeded in defeating Hitler. I dread another civil war here for it would inevitably turn into the conflict of greater powers. The doctrines of 1789 are for us like the morals of Christianity: pieties. We are not strong enough to enjoy the Rights of Man. If Russia does not dominate us your country will. We must resign ourselves to remaining subjects and withdraw our hopes of independence from the realm of politics to another realm."

Nearly every conversation in Madrid eventually turns to the subject of national character, and more than once I was referred by other foreigners to Unamuno's essay on Spanish envy and was quoted Quevedo's line, used as an epigraph by Unamuno: "Envy is lean; it bites but cannot swallow." An Italian explained to me that the Spaniards were half Moorish and that I would not understand them if I forgot it for an instant, and according to a German lady who has lived in Madrid for many years, the great fault of the Spaniards was that they had no real feelings. After her brother's death several Madrileño friends came to visit her. "They did not console me," she said. "They sat and talked of their *marmotas* [maids] and their children. They knew I was in mourning. They really are heartless." On the other hand, Pio Baroja, with whom I had a conversation, found the German character inexplicable. "At first I could not believe that they were burning their captives in ovens. But then I met a young man who had lost his mother and a sister in that way. And to tell the truth, I found Germany a queer place when I visited it in the Twenties. In Hamburg a nudist family got on the streetcar: father, mother and little ones all as naked as my hand, a family of petit bourgeois carrying bundles and packages like any petit-bourgeois family that has been shopping. And the parents weren't even handsome. The father had a huge *tripa*, like a barrel."

All these discussions of national character were occasions of resentment, and the resentment was particularly strong when it was the American character that was discussed. A traveling salesman said to me, his eyes aswim with poetic heat behind thick lenses, "America is still looking for a soul; our soul is very old." Others spoke of "American emptiness," "unhistorical Americans who live only in the future," et cetera.

But people, of course, feel the sway of American strength and American goods and the loss of their own liberty and strength. Until 1898 Spain still considered itself an empire, and for a nation of traditionalists 1898 is by no means the distant past. The emphasis on national character is an emphasis on value. Take away the ignorant nonsense and there is still something left—namely, an assertion of worth in a world in which worth is synonymous with power, and power has passed to featureless mass societies for which the past has little meaning, and machinery, wealth and organization topple the old dignity to replace it with contempt and discontent.

Between Málaga and Granada, at the railroad junction of Bobadilla, shivering under the heat that darkened the stone hills and olive fields, I went into the station restaurant. It was a buffet doing a feverish business in bread, grapes, tortillas, ham, boiled eggs, jelly sausage and blood sausage, salami, cheese, chicken, a huge abundance without boundaries, spread on thick paper and shining with fat. There were two women and a man behind it. The man was middle-aged, gray-faced, and he coughed continually. Three or four strands of hair were arranged with elegant care over his bald head. He behaved toward me with iron *dignidad*. I was an American, therefore he refused to speak Spanish. He addressed me in a kind of French acquired, probably, in a restaurant in Madrid or Barcelona or in a luxury hotel on the Mediterranean and ripened during many isolated years in the desert wilderness of Bobadilla. *"Les oeufs son' a cinq cad'un, m'sieu."* He kept coughing softly and could not stop, obviously consumptive. *"¿Y qué precio tienen las uvas?"* *"Cuat' le demikilo, m'sieu."* Great politeness; fiery politeness. Meanwhile he stared at me secretly with his rather vindictive eyes, the cough blurting softly through his lips so that his cheeks shook. By my accent, by the cut of my clothes, the pattern of my shoes, and who knows what unconscious attributes, he recognized me as an American, one of the new lords of the earth, a new Roman, full of the pride of machines and dollars, passing casually through the junction where it was his fate to remain rotting to death. But he faced me at least with the proper *dignidad,* like the bitter organ grinder in the Bombilla.

The *comandante*'s dignity is something else again. The *comandante* is, after all, the tyrant's friend and the tyrant, too, believes in organization and is trying to trade his way into the new imperium. The *señora* wears nylon stockings and the *comandante* owns a marvelous cigarette lighter and I am sure he has a large supply of American flints.

[1948]

There Is Simply Too Much to Think About

Illinois Journey

The features of Illinois are not striking; they do not leap to the eye but lie flat and at first appear monotonous. The roads are wide, hard, perfect, sometimes of a shallow depth in the far distance but so nearly level as to make you feel that the earth really is flat. From east and west, travelers dart across these prairies into the huge horizons and through cornfields that go on forever: giant skies, giant clouds, an eternal, nearly featureless sameness. You find it hard to travel slowly. The endless miles pressed flat by the ancient glacier seduce you into speeding. As the car eats into the distances, you begin gradually to feel that you are riding upon the floor of the continent, the very bottom of it, low and flat, and an impatient spirit of movement, of overtaking and urgency, passes into your heart.

Miles and miles of prairie, slowly rising and falling, sometimes give you a sense that something is in the process of becoming or that the liberation of a great force is imminent, some power, like Michelangelo's slave only half released from the block of stone. Conceivably the mound-building Indians believed their resurrection would coincide with some such liberation and built their graves in imitation of the low moraines deposited by the departing glaciers. But they have not yet been released and remain drowned in their waves of earth. They have left their bones, their flints and pots, their place names and tribal names and little besides except a stain, seldom vivid, on the consciousness of their white successors.

The soil of the Illinois prairies is fat, rich and thick. After spring plowing it looks oil-blackened or colored by the soft coal that occurs in great veins throughout the state. In the fields you frequently see a small tipple or a crazy-looking device that pumps oil and nods like the neck of a horse at a quick walk. Isolated among the cornstalks or the soybeans, the iron machine clanks and nods, stationary. Along the roads, with intervals between them as neat and even as buttons on the cuff, sit steel storage bins, in form like the tents of Mongolia. They are filled with grain. And the elevators and tanks, trucks and machines, that crawl over the fields and blunder over the highways—whatever you see is productive. It creates wealth, it stores wealth, it is wealth.

As you pass the fields you see signs the farmers have posted telling, in code, what sort of seed they have planted. The farmhouses are seldom at the roadside but far within the fields. The solitude and silence are deep and wide. Then when you have gone ten or twenty miles through cornfields without having seen a living thing—no cow, no dog, scarcely even a bird under the hot sky—suddenly you come upon a noisy contraption at the roadside, a system of contraptions, rather, for husking the corn and stripping the grain. It burns and bangs away and the conveyor belts rattle. A double flame twists and roars within the generator. Three broad women in overalls stand at the hoppers and toss the ears of corn upward. A dusty red mountain of cobs is growing under the small dinosaur's head of the conveyor and the chaff dazzles and trembles upward. The hard kernels, red and yellow, race down the chutes into the trucks.

When you leave, this noise and activity are cut off at one stroke; you are once more in the deaf, hot solitude of trembling air, alone in the cornfields.

North, south, east and west, there is no end to them. They line roads and streams and hem in the woods and surround towns and they crowd into backyards and edge up to gas stations. An exotic stranger might assume he had come upon a race of corn worshippers who had created a corn ocean; or that he was among a people who had fallen in love with infinite repetition of the same details, like the builders of skyscrapers in New York and Chicago who have raised up bricks and windows by the thousands and all alike. From corn you can derive notions of equality or uniformity, massed democracy. You can, if you are given to that form of mental play, recall Joseph's brethren in the lean years and think how famine has been conquered here and superabundance itself become such a danger that the government has to take measures against it.

The power, the monotony, the oceanic extent of the cornfields, do indeed shrink and dwarf the past. How are you to think of the small bands of Illini, Ottawas, Cahokians, Shawnee, Miamis who camped in the turkey grass and the French Jesuits who descended the Mississippi and found them? When you force your mind to summon them, the Indians appear rather doll-like in the radiance of the present moment. They are covered in the corn, swamped in the oil, hidden in the coal of Franklin County, run over by the trains, turned phantom by the stockyards. There are monuments to them here and there but they are only historical ornaments to the pride of the present.

In the northwestern part of the state, the Black Hawk country near Galena, the land is hilly and the streams have a steeper gradient. This is the region in which Chief Black Hawk, in 1832, made his last resistance.

The principal city of that portion of the Mississippi is Galena, once a great center of trade but now a remote place beside a shrunken river. There is no historical mood about the flourishing towns. Prosperity wipes out the past or, in its pride, keeps the relics dusted, varnished, polished—sentimental measures like the Lincoln residence in Springfield. Entering such houses, you feel the past undeniably; only you feel the present much more. Ulysses S. Grant lived in Galena and his house is a museum, but it is a museum within a museum, for the town itself is one of the antiquities of Illinois and it has a forsaken, tottering look.

Galena is not deserted; it is inhabited and its houses are not in bad repair, yet they blink and lean on their tall hillside in the peace of abnormalcy. The streets are empty under the stout old trees. Of course even the streets of thriving towns are vacant five days a week. The emptiness of Galena, however, will never be filled. The long street of the lower town resembles that of a Welsh village when everyone is down in the pit. On the main street the store windows have no luster except the dull one given by rock samples. Lead enriched Galena in the first half of the nineteenth century. Its harbor was filled with steamboats. The boom started in the 1820s and continued about forty years.

Now if you lift up your eyes from the drab streets at the waterfront, you see on the hill something that confusedly resembles the antebellum South, old mansions of brick and stone, a few of them still handsome, ornamented with wrought iron in something like New Orleans style. Galena is an old, cracked, mossy place and looks a little crazy. An invisible giant tent caterpillar has built over it and the sun comes through the trees as through frayed netting. From an upper street you stare four narrow stories downward into a spinsterish backyard where a cat, in the easy way of all cats, is lying on a small plot of green. Within the long rooms are Franklin stoves, recamier couches, ornate wallpaper, and on the rooftops stand television antennae.

There are many towns in Illinois that have been thus bypassed, towns like Cairo and Shawneetown in the south. They flourished until the railroads made the steamboat obsolete and now they sit, the fortresses of faithful old daughters and age-broken sons who do not go away.

An old resident of Galena said, "The young folks leave. And they don't come back. Not alive, at least. Lots of them ask to be buried here, but whilst they live there's nothing for them in Galena."

Some twenty miles away, across the river, is Dubuque, Iowa, full of vigor and enterprise. The diesel trains run through there with deep, brazen cries, like the horns of the Philistine army, and the city rejoices. There is success, and here is its neighbor, failure. The inhabitant of the failure city bears a personal burden of shame. The old resident would leave too if he were younger; but what could he do now in Chicago or Los Angeles? Here he can live on his old-age money, his Social Security income. Elsewhere it wouldn't make ends meet.

The residents of the failure town are often apologetic. They talk of history and tradition, fusty glamour or the unrecorded sins and tragedies of the place, as though these were all they had to offer. By and by the old man points out a high hill in the distance and says, "There was a man lynched over there long ago. The whole town of Galena turned out and did it. Afterward they found out he was innocent."

"Is that so? Who was he?"

"They don't know. They killed him over there. Then they found out they were wrong. But it was too late to make it up to him then. It was before my time. I only been here fifty years. I came from Wisconsin when I was a young fellow. But they hanged that innocent man. Everybody knows about it here. They each and every one of them do."

When Illinois was a frontier state it attracted men of strange beliefs from everywhere, dissidents and sectarians, truth seekers and utopians. Those who did not depart were assimilated.

On the Mississippi a few hours south of Galena, the Mormons built a city at Nauvoo in 1819 and erected a temple. After the murder of the prophet Smith and his brother in neighboring Carthage, the Mormons emigrated under the leadership of Brigham Young, leaving many empty buildings. Into these came a band of French communists, the Icarians, led by Étienne Cabet. Their colony soon failed; discord and thefts broke it up. Cabet died in St. Louis, obscurely. And after the Icarians came German immigrants, who apparently sobered up the town. Now, unobtrusively but with steady purpose, the Mormons have been coming back to Nauvoo. They have reopened some of the old brick and stone houses in the lower town, near the Mississippi; they have trimmed the lawns and cleaned the windows and set out historical markers and opened views on the river, which here, as it approaches Keokuk Dam, broadens and thickens with mud. Sunday speedboats buzz unseen below the bend where the brown tide, slowly hovering, turns out of sight.

Nauvoo today is filled, it seemed to me, with Mormon missionaries who double as tourist guides. When I came for information, I was embraced, literally, by an elderly man; he was extremely brotherly, hearty and familiar. His gray eyes were sharp, though his skin was brown and wrinkled. His gestures were wide, ample, virile and western, and he clapped me on the back as we sat talking, and gripped me by the leg. As any man in his right mind naturally wants to be saved, I listened attentively, but less to his doctrines perhaps than to his western tones, wondering how different he could really be from other Americans of the same type. I went to lie afterward beside the river and look at Iowa on the other bank, which shone like smoke over the pungent muddy water that poured into the southern horizon. Here the Mormons had crossed, and after them the French Icarians. The Icarians held together for some years after leaving Nauvoo. But they were absorbed, as everything eventually was absorbed that could not be reconciled with the farm, the factory, the railroad, the mine, the mill, the bank and the market.

Some process of absorption is going on in Shawneetown, on the other side of the state from Nauvoo, where the Ohio and the Wabash rivers meet. This is the country called Egypt, the southernmost portion of Illinois. Its principal city is Cairo (pronounced Cayro), at the southern tip of the state. Cairo is not so thriving as it once was, but Shawneetown has changed even more profoundly in the course of a century. They will tell you there how representatives from a little northern community called Chicago once approached the bankers of opulent Shawneetown for a loan and how they were turned down because Chicago was too remote a village to bother with.

"Well, look at us now," my informant said to me.

We stood in the midst of wide dirt streets from which the paving had been washed out. About us were deserted mansions, dilapidated huge buildings with falling shutters, their Greek Revival pillars gone gray.

Such is old Shawneetown, in its time one of the great cities of the state. With the disappearance of the keelboat and the steamboat it would gradually have withered anyway, but its ruin has been made complete by the flooding of the Ohio.

A strange, Silurian smell emanates from the mud and the barren houses. The scene is Southern. Whittlers sit on boxes, and the dogs roll in the potholes; the stores sell fatback, collard greens, mustard greens and black-eyed peas. The flies wait hungrily in the air, sheets of flies that make a noise like the tearing of tissue paper. People in the river bottoms tell you that old Shawneetown is a rip-roaring place on a Saturday night; it swallows up husbands and their paychecks. The bars near the levee burst into music and the channel catfish fry in deep fat and the beer flows.

On higher ground to the west, a new Shawneetown sits under the hot sky of Egypt. It is like many another Illinois town, except newer. The state and the WPA created it beyond the river's reach. It is high and dry, spacious and rather vacant, for many of the diehards refuse to leave their old homes. Half ghost, half honky-tonk, old Shawneetown has a fair-sized population of traditionalists. Like old campaigners they name the years of disaster with a ring of military pride—"eighty-four, 'ninety-eight, nineteen and thirteen, nineteen and thirty-seven." The 1947 edition of the Illinois State Guide says that the flood of 1937, which rose six feet above the levee, "marked the end of Shawneetown's pertinacious adhesion to the riverbank." Reasonable people, the authors of the guide spoke prematurely. The pertinacious adhesion continues in spite of reason and floods.

Between the new and the old Shawneetowns there is a deep rivalry; the two factions express pity and contempt for each other. Old Shawneetowners tell of many who are held against their will up there, people whose children prevent their return. Some have moved back from the new town, bored by its newness and aridity. Nothing is happening up there. Sensible new Shawneetowners reply, as a fine portly woman with spreading short blond hair did, "If they want to degenerate down there and play hero"—a strange combination of terms—"that's their own fool business. I have cleaned house after floods too many times. And if you saw what it looked like after the water has been in it! Six inches of silt on the carpets, and just like a swamp. I sat down and cried."

In old Shawneetown a retired railroad man whom I met on the levee said that his wife was old enough to recall how the victims of '84 were laid in rows on the sitting room floor. "Right in here," he said, and showed me the red, ancient house. It had belonged to the first president of Shawneetown's bank, the very bank that had refused Chicago's request for a loan.

"We live here in the summer now," the railroad man explained. "This here is our little grandboy. We raised him up ourselves." And raised him all too well, I should have said, for at the age of eight he must have weighed about a hundred and fifty pounds. He looked at me with precocious significance, as if the manitou of this place had entered his fat little body.

The trodden earth of the levee makes you feel safe. Below, the river is fire blue. The summery Kentucky shore is green. The banks look supple and full as they decline toward the water. A new bridge of orange steel hangs in the air. The child says, "Three guys fell off it and got kilt."

"Oh, mercy." His grandfather laughs. "Only one was, because he hit a barge. The others went into the water and was saved. Three falling is not bad for as big a bridge as this one is."

From this old man I heard the first sensible explanation of the stubbornness of the old Shawneetowners. He said, "When you have grown up here and see the river every day of your life, it isn't so easy to move away and do without. And especially only a few miles away."

Between the Ohio and the Mississippi, Egypt lies low and hollow. Its streams are sluggish, old, swampy and varicose. Spring floods bring fresh topsoil to many areas and the corn is thick. Toward Cairo the farmers make good cotton crops. We are here farther to the south than Richmond, Virginia. To a Northern nose the air is slightly malarial. People's faces and their postures are Southern and you begin to see things for which no preparation is possible. A young Negro woman, her head tied up in a handkerchief, drives by in a maroon convertible; on her shoulder sits a bull terrier. That is a pleasant thing to see and all the better because of the slight start it gives you. In a river town, a place whitened by the local lime-burning, is a small bar and restaurant. You enter on a calm Sunday afternoon and see what appears to be a clan of working people eating and drinking. Anyone who wants beer may work the pulls for himself. Sliced bread and ham are on the bar and a woman is drinking beer while her baby nurses. North of Vandalia you are not likely to see a child at breast. And yet this is a sight that has no business to be remarkable.

On a road in Egypt a warm wind was booming across the flashing sky and turning the white clouds round, the corn leaves were streaming, and I saw a roadside marker that read Old Slave House. An arrow pointed, as roadside arrows sometimes will, skyward. It said Equality. Two spring-breaking and stone-embedded ruts under low willow branches led finally up to a bald hill on which a corn crop sadly petered out in gullies, ashes, old flivver bodies and various cast-iron relics. On the summit of the hill stood the old mansion or slave house, once the property of John Crenshaw: a brown structure, formerly white.

Because you know it is a slave house, it looks evil, dangerous; it also looks trashy; its brown color is disheartening. The evil is remote because slavery is dead. A sort of safe thrill passes through the liberal heart. But then, the evil is not altogether remote, because nothing has been done to make the house historic. There are no exhibits in glass cases. In a great vacant room the slaves' shackles lie on the linoleum-covered floor. The white form of a washing machine stands in the background. Its

There Is Simply Too Much to Think About

present owners live in the old mansion and it is both domicile and museum.

Slaves were imprisoned at the top of the house in narrow cells no larger than closets. Runaways or freed slaves were kidnapped by Crenshaw, so the story goes, and resold in the markets of the South. Lone sheets of foolscap framed on the walls give the history of the place. The writing is old-fashioned, the ink faded; the details are sinister. Crenshaw tortured his captives on crude devices made of heavy beams. These still lean against the walls. This is a dismal, chalky, low-pitched, aching garret. Many hands have left signatures on the plaster. The wind drives against the walls; the corn stoops in the bald, runneled clay.

The lady of the house has a great deal to tell about it. She is a Southerner and evidently a lover of legend. Mr. Crenshaw, she says, was a fearsome man. It is possible that he had to leave England for his sins and he became a great power in Illinois. His abuses of the black people were so horrible he was attacked by one of his own slaves and wounded in the thigh. The slave was cast alive into a furnace, said the lady, but Crenshaw lost his leg. Her catalog of horrors is very long; possibly endless. Crenshaw bred his captives. Made pregnant by studs, the slave girls brought higher prices. And yet, she said, Abe Lincoln was a guest in this house. She told me this with an air of triumph. When he campaigned against Douglas he came to visit Crenshaw, who was a Democrat. "Politics!" she said.

"And did he know what sort of a man Crenshaw was?" I said.

"Everybody knew. And he was waited on by slaves. But he was here to get the votes. Now looka here at the family pictures." Brown and yellowed people seemed to return my gaze from the framed portraits. Their hair and garments were heavy, their faces long, severe. In our day we have learned something about charm, the art of self-presentation, and are told to look sunny when we are photographed; but there is nothing to mitigate the austerity of these slave owners. They were masters and looked like masters; they scorned to enliven the expression of their eyes, the sullenness of their mouths. But why should they, the overlords, have looked so dull and sullen? "Now, here," said my guide, "is Crenshaw's daughter. She was waited on hand and foot and never even had to brush her own hair until after the Civil War was over." I must say that she sounded a little envious. Was she not the present lady of the house?

Egypt belongs not merely to the South but to the Deep South. Cairo is as Southern a city as Paducah, in Kentucky across the river. But even in Lincoln's own county of Sangamon I heard things said against him. In Sangamon the pioneer village of New Salem has been restored. New Salem was Lincoln's home before it was abandoned circa 1840. He had already moved to Springfield, eighteen miles away. In 1837 he helped to establish Springfield as the state capital.

There is a residue of old grievances still in Sangamon County, for North and South meet here. Northern Illinois was settled by New Englanders, the southern part by Kentuckians and Virginians. Slavery and its enemies, Union and Secession, struggled here. Sangamon County may be said to have been at the very center of this conflict, and despite the public worship of Lincoln's memory you meet people who say, the feuding blood still running strong in them, "We knew him here. Yes, they called my granddad Copperhead hereabouts, but what of it? Lincoln was for the big cities and the banks." But it is nothing but a residue. Most of the old differences have long since been composed; it is mainly the historical (feuding) sense that preserves them.

[1957]

The University as Villain

A re writers greatly harmed by teaching in universities? The first reply that comes to me is that a man may make a damn fool of
himself anywhere.

But the question probably deserves more serious consideration. Any
number of serious people have given it their best thought. Some believe
it is harmful beyond measure, others that nothing can be nicer for both
the writers and the universities. I was once told by Nelson Algren,
"Some teach school; some would rather run a poker game." Poker is
probably better but not everyone can be so lucky. I am too stupid a
poker player to make a living at cards.

Exactly twenty years ago I graduated from Northwestern University.
Of those twenty years five or six have been given to teaching, the rest
to writing, and I think I am able to weigh the arguments of either side
with an equal hand.

In 1952, when I was teaching at Princeton, I met in New York a
man I had known in Chicago in less happy times (for me) when he
was connected with the University of Chicago and I was connected
with nothing. He had been one of Chancellor Robert Maynard
Hutchins's assistants; now he was near the summit of a huge advertising corporation in New York. We had always been fond of each other
and we met with pleasure. He was dressed in such high style that I
could hardly keep from touching his tweed. He had a fine red, conservative straight face and was smoking the biggest and shiningest
pipe that Madison Avenue had to sell, so there was no need for me to
ask how *he* was doing.

"But what are *you* up to these days?" he said.

"Well," I told him, "you'll find it hard to believe, but this year I am teaching at Princeton."

It had never occurred to him that I might be connected with anything so classy and because of his respect for higher learning, probably absorbed from the chancellor, he was upset. So I was very sorry and I said, "It's only temporary."

"What do your academic colleagues think about this?" he said.

"Oh, it's probably a joke to them, but they still have most of the joint to themselves. What's the matter, Mack? Why does this bother you?"

"Well," he said, "writers have always come out of the gutter. The gutter is their proper place."

I can't think just now which of the one hundred Great Books of the Western World contains this historic idea. But perhaps the books were not to blame at all. And in justice to my friend I must make it clear that he was not upset because of the academic colleagues alone; he viewed the matter also from my side—a little. He seemed to feel that society was right to build universities to shelter men of learning and to pay them and protect them and keep them. It could not, however, do this for writers. It could not be friendly to them without softening and taming them and making them fat, checking their necessary vices, damaging their freedom and harmfully curbing their madness.

But I have seen full-blown lunatics in universities, too, and as for the vices, they may be found on the campus not less than on the Bowery. It seemed crazy to explain to the executive of a large corporation how powerfully pervasive life could be; and I didn't think it would be suitable to tell the chancellor's former assistant that his implied view of professors was not flattering. Were they fat, tame and lazy, or did they take no harm from the special protection of society? Were they too good for the gutter, or not good enough for it? How was it that a philosopher might live in the *tour d'ivoire* whereas a writer belonged out in the *marais de merde* by which Flaubert thought the tower to be surrounded?

Sharp questions. Too bad they didn't come to me then. But I like to continue old debates in my mind and today I can tell Mack that the old tower ain't what it used to be. From its remoteness there now come things like rocket-launched satellites that loop over us, the writers, as we sit in our gutters playing poker.

I will certainly hear it argued that professors of physics and professors of literature are altogether different, and it must be conceded right away that the differences are great. For the professor of physics is reinforced, as animal psychologists might put it, by a sense of being needed (by the Air Force and the Navy and Oak Ridge), whereas the professor of literature is likely to feel that the dull canal, all that remains of the once sweet Thames, is his only portion, and that he is foolishly watching the rats in the vegetation while he ponders the problem of Hamlet's uncle, unrelated to the gas tanks behind him and Sputnik overhead. Professors of humanities often have a keen sense of their inferiority to the great mass of Americans. Is the real realer where the mass is thicker? So they seem to believe. Perhaps, too, it is their feeling that there is something shameful for grown men in sitting with a parcel of kids in a corner. Callicles in the *Gorgias* accuses Socrates of doing just that. To which Socrates replies that if you follow Philosophy you must give it what it calls for. It is true that in the English departments to which writers find their way, there are sometimes to be found discouraged people who stand dully upon a brilliant plane, in charge of masterpieces but not themselves inspired, people who are to literature what Samuel Butler's clergymen were to religion. But belief does not end with the Reverend Pontifex nor literature with Professor This-or-That. If the professor will not give it what it calls for, somebody else will. And the writer, if he is a lively soul, does not need to feel so depressed. If he knows his own mind and if the university thinks it can get along with him—well, why not?

He will very often find good conversation in university communities, and he may find a Whitehead or an Einstein as well worth writing about as saloonkeepers or big-game hunters. Everything depends on the amount of energy he has the boldness to release, regardless of the restraints of his environment. Is he more likely to achieve this boldness in Greenwich Village; in the air; on the water; in the "literary life"; in the mines; on an assembly line?

If you, the writer, love rough company and need to knock around, why then, do as Walt Whitman did, go into the streets, ride up and down Broadway or go and dig clams. But under no circumstances should you select any of these things deliberately and do them for the sake of writing. *What* an idea! You must give the thing what it calls for. But there is no prescription to follow.

A man's life from the standpoint of Experience—and it is a notion about Experience which is at the heart of the gutter position—is made up from varied and balanced experiences of a specified sort. There are people who are intensely proud of having met the specifications and who have made very special efforts in the fields of sex, drunkenness, violence and even poverty. Not to have met these specifications can be, for them, a source of shame. The shame of never having been down and out! I have heard young fellows boast that they had been on the bum and that they have been run in for panhandling (not that there were no checks from home). I have even been envied my good luck in having grown up during the Depression.

Now I don't want to make jokes on serious matters, and it is serious when people feel that they must be able to demonstrate that reality has happened to them, certified and approved reality in the form of Experience. Have they met life, not fled it? That's fine. Very good. But Experience in this aspect is something resembling a merit badge; something like a commodity. Let us admit it, Experience with the capital E *is* something of a writer's commodity and the reason for this, I think, is that modern fiction has taken it upon itself to show experience as ever new and ever valuable. The very form of fiction is that of experience itself. Everything is to be viewed as though for the first time. The representation of things is imperative, for the things of a modern man's life are important. They are important because man's career on this earth is held to be important. Literature has been committed to the assertion of this importance for a long time. Unquestioned value. But what is the source of the value?

For some time now the whole fictional enterprise has been running backward. It is not importance that illuminates the facts. The facts as facts are assumed to be important. We bring forward characters, enumerate the facts and try to put it over on everyone that such numbering or naming is all that is necessary.

"He opened the door." Did he, now?

"She lit his cigarette." So what?

It is assumed that these declarations are important or will seem so. But why? Documentation, observation, details of action cannot by themselves give life, no matter how authentic or faithful to experience they may be. You can't construct a tree with twigs. You cannot give importance to events by the authority of Experience, merely.

The life of a civilized man is, increasingly, an internalized one, and toward this internalized life writers have been encouraged to take a gross and foolish attitude. They are the playboys of Experience. More Lord Byron? More Kipling? More *Noa Noa*? More Zola? These are very old-fashioned postures. It is ridiculous for writers to continue them.

Well now, does it harm writers to teach in universities? I am not sure the question is a real one. It is to some extent a *postural* question. It assumes that by doing the right things we get the desired results. Those right things are conventional. Leave your hometown; don't leave your hometown; don't write for the movies; travel; don't be a sissy; don't tie yourself down—and you will turn out fine. But the wind of the spirit is capricious. I have known men of foresight who avoided every trap of bourgeois life, some after the manner of Rimbaud, and some after the manner of Baudelaire; I have known faithful followers of Fitzgerald and Hemingway, and D. H. Lawrence-men, *semper fidelis*, grown old and wrinkled and red-nosed and cat-whiskered and bad-tempered. But that wind! It bloweth where it listeth. And in the end a correct posture can give you nothing more than the satisfaction that comes of fidelity to good form.

It is not easy to find the right way. You must learn to govern yourself, you must learn autonomy, you must manage your freedom or drown in it. You may strain the will after Experience because you need it for your books. Or you may perish under the heavy weight of Culture. You may make a fool of yourself anywhere. You may find illumination anywhere—in the gutter, in the college, in the corporation, in a submarine, in the library. No one man holds a patent on it. No man knows what it is likely to tell him to do. For this reason universities and corporations may find the illuminable type unreliable from a *personnel* point of view. A writer may do better in the anxiety of the gutter; he may do better in the heavy security of the college. Despite the purity of your posture he may do well. It's up to the spirit, altogether, and the spirit prints no timetable.

[1956]

There Is Simply Too Much to Think About

The Sharp Edge of Life

The great issue in fiction is the stature of characters. It starts with something like the Psalmist's question, "What is man that thou art mindful of him?" Responses range from "a little lower than the angels" to "a poor bare, forked animal." The struggle of the novelist has been to establish a measure, a view of human nature, and usually, though not always, as large a view as belief and imagination can wring from observable facts. The artist tries, Nietzsche once wrote, to exaggerate the value of human personality. This is a secular notion, for on the assumption that God exists a religious writer would deny that such exaggeration was possible. But novelists have been largely secular men in secular, doubting times. If we consider the humanistic art of the Renaissance that Nietzsche probably had in mind, and its near-divine creatures, we can agree with him. It made the human image very great. But even then there were doubts about the unaccommodated poor bare, forked animal, and since then the value of man has depreciated. We see the doubt in *Don Quixote*. Are nobility and great virtue delusions? Can there ever be a time when ecstasy will be the daily spirit and men and things be set in diamonds? Cervantes investigates what it means to will the highest and to insist on a superior reality. This contrast of a superior reality with daily fact is the peculiar field of the novel.

In the nineteenth century heroes appear as revolutionaries, great natures, born aristocrats, but the original humanistic doubt has made terrible progress. The great Russian novelists insisted on the Christian measure; even so, Dostoyevsky created the antihero of *Notes from Underground* as well as Prince Myshkin and Alyosha Karamazov. As the external social fact grows larger, more powerful and more tyrannical, man appears in the novel reduced in will, strength, freedom and scope—until, in Flaubert's *Sentimental Education*, the hero is not even an antihero like Dostoyevsky's, great by reason of his *ressentiment*, but merely a man of no importance, a ridiculous social creature. And if man is of no importance, how is the novel—how, for that matter, is any human activity—justified?

Now we have an anarchy of views in a "free" field. At one end Céline, denunciatory, and at the other someone like Bernanos asserting, but unable to prove concretely, that there are saints still. As for American writers, a good many of them hold before us a decent but exceedingly limited ideal: forbearing, stoical, but of no great capacity, not very passionate, not very strong in thought. This hero is rather abstract, exhibits collective rather than personal traits (I am thinking now of a Steinbeck hero) and shows what is wanted more than what is seen, heard, known. It is almost as though many American writers felt that to confront actuality might be dangerous to our social sympathies, and they do not let the facts gather freely about their superior reality, such as it is.

Many writers have sought justification in the art of writing itself, following Flaubert. For him experience pressed hard against a heroic conception of literature that he felt bound to try to save. Henry James in his criticism of him ideally states the problem for all modern writers. Is one obliged to treat what James calls the "middling" as Flaubert, angry and disappointed, treats it? Because Flaubert, hating common life, displaced his enormous energy from subject matter to style. If literature was a heroic enterprise, it had to be so in spite of the degeneration of life. Flaubert's aim was an aesthetic one: the creation of beauty as a reply to the punishment and pain of degraded existence. Thus for him, and for those who followed him, mastery over language comes to represent mastery over human difficulties, and method in fiction is a symbolic triumph of sense, order and harmony over them. In this way value is supposed to be kept.

James complained that if Flaubert "imagined nothing better for his purpose than such a heroine" (Emma Bovary) "and such a hero" (Frédéric Moreau), "both such limited reflectors and registers, we are forced to believe it to have been a defect of his mind." James understood this difficulty so well because he himself suffered from it and carved out for his work a reality that he controlled too absolutely. It was superior but unchecked; it existed by *fiat*. The way in which he "wrapped" characters was despotic. This despotism brought with it a kind of mercy—the despot's mercy toward his subject. But the system was hermetic, closed to the great disturbances with which Flaubert tried to cope. I do have a great deal of sympathy for James's objection to the "limited reflectors." Why not have, in art, the largest mind available? Indeed, why have any other? Why be middling with the middling subject? Flaubert was not, but he armored himself too greatly in his art to act freely. James shunned it; the largest mind cannot be hermetic to reality.

But what kind of category is "middling experience" and what kind of reality does it denote? In Tocqueville we read, "Nothing conceivable is so petty, so insipid, so crowded with paltry interests, in one word so anti-poetic, as the life of a man in the United States."

I feel, before a statement like this, that the first thing to be said is that "the life of a man in the United States" is, to begin with, "the life of a man." It is not so hard to understand the dislike, even dread, that Tocqueville must have felt before an immense, uncertain new development in human life. Yes, there is pettiness, paltriness, insipidity; there is crime, too; and with these terms the characterization of the life of man in a democracy has not even begun. The truth is deeper, more mysterious and in some ways perhaps even more terrible. The nineteenth century knew Homais but did not yet know Himmler.

This is the problem at the point where the modern novelist must enter it, in a present that is as fearful and as marvelous as presents have always been. The idea that we are at the degenerate dwarf-end of history is one that he must reject as he rejects his own childishness. Writers have a conservative tendency, in the literal meaning of the word, and are hostile toward the future. The future may destroy or ignore their premises, their beliefs, their assumptions, all that they have received from the past. There is a justified hate of the petty, insipid, paltry, but there is this element also to be taken into account, the conservative one.

The task of a novelist is still, as I see it, to attempt to fix a scale of importance and to rescue from styles, languages, forms, abstractions, as well as from the assault and distraction of manifold social facts, an original human value. I do not believe in a hierarchy of feelings descending in a line from aristocracy to mass civilization. Let the aristocratic dead bury their dead and the democratic dead their dead, too. I believe simply in feeling. In vividness. Where feeling is synthetic, ideals of greatness are merely dismal. Only feeling brings us to conceptions of superior reality.

A point of view like mine is not conducive to popular success. I believe with Coleridge that some writers must gradually create their own audience. This is, in the short run, an unrewarding process. The commercial organization of society resists it, and let us face it, there is widespread disgust, weariness, staleness, resistance and unwillingness to feel the sharp edge of life.

We have for hundreds of years had an idolatry of the human image, in the lesser form of the self and in the greater form of the State. So when we think we are tired of Man, it is that image we are tired of. Man is forced to lead a secret life and it is into that life that the writer must go to find him. He must bring value, restore proportion; he must also give pleasure. If he does not do these things he remains sterile himself.

[1951]

Laughter in the Ghetto:
On Sholom Aleichem

The Adventures of Mottel the Cantor's Son, just now translated and published in English at the height of a new vogue for the work of Sholom Aleichem, was the great Jewish humorist's last novel. It was begun in 1907 and Aleichem was writing the last chapter when he died in 1916 at the age of fifty-seven.

This delightful account, given by a boy of his family's emigration from the old-country village to New York, is characteristic of the work of its author. Sholom Aleichem wrote for the family circle and his attitude was that of an entertainer. Hebrew was the language of serious literature among the Jews of the Pale; Yiddish the secular language and the language of comedy. A popular writer, a caricaturist and a sentimentalist, Sholom Aleichem had much more in common with Dickens than he had with Mark Twain, to whom he has often been compared. He was a great ironist—the Yiddish language has an ironic genius—and he was a writer in whom the profoundly sad, bitter spirit of the ghetto laughed at itself and thereby transcended itself.

The Jews of the ghetto found themselves involved in an immense joke. They were divinely designated to be great and yet they were like mice. History was something that *happened* to them; they did not make it. The nations made it, while they, the Jews, suffered it. But when history had happened, it belonged to them inasmuch as it was the coming of the Messiah—*their* Messiah—that would give it meaning. Every male child was potentially the Messiah. The most ordinary Yiddish conversation is full of the grandest historical, mythological and religious allusions. The Creation, the Fall, the Flood, Egypt, Alexander, Titus, Napoleon, the Rothschilds, the sages and the Laws may get into the discussion of an egg, a clothesline or a pair of pants. This manner of living on terms of familiarity with all times and all greatness contributed, because of the poverty and powerlessness of the Chosen, to the ghetto's sense of the ridiculous. Powerlessness appears to force people to have recourse to language. Hamlet has to unpack his heart with words, he complains. The fact that the Jews of Eastern Europe lived among menacing and powerful neighbors no doubt contributed to the subtlety and richness of the words with which they unpacked their hearts.

Mottel the Cantor's Son is a gay, not an oppressive book. Against the grim background of the ghetto and in the presence of death, the small boy continues to play. Almost nothing can take place that he is unable to make into an occasion of happiness; with boundless resilience he tells, after his father's death, how quickly he learns the prayer for the dead, how well everyone treats him now that he is an orphan. When the springs come out of the sofa, he winds them around his neck to see whether he can choke himself. When the last of the furniture is sold, he has more room on the floor for his games. His brother Eli, the new head of the family, is stern with Mottel, but the boy has an inexhaustible power of enjoyment and cannot be affected. He plays in the fields, in the brook, in the filthy yard amid the rich man's stacks of lumber. All places are alike to him. He declines to suffer the penalties the world imposes on him.

The comedy of the book emerges from Mottel's ingenuous descriptions of his elders. Eli, now the support of the family, has concocted a powder for killing mice from directions he found in a book on how to make a fortune quickly. Eli's wife, Brocha—her name in Hebrew signifies Blessing, and she is anything but a blessing—keeps raising the price of this powder.

" 'If you have to eat pork,' she says, 'the lard may as well drip down your beard. And if you've become a rat-chaser, at least take money for it.'

" 'But where is justice? Where is God?' Mother interrupts.

"My sister-in-law replies, 'Justice? It's here!' and points to the oven. 'God? He's there!' and slaps her pocket."

The mouse-powder, containing hellebore, is unusable; it makes everyone sneeze and the victory is with the mice. But the matter must be discussed upon the summits of principle. Gogol would have been intrigued by this idea of a fortune to be made in mouse-powder. Indeed, Sholom Aleichem seems to have learned a great deal from him. Only, Gogol's humor is wilder, more inventive and lavish; Sholom Aleichem's is drier, sadder. His characters have the immediate problem of survival. Poor, hungry and living in fear, they must survive, but not by adapting themselves; adaptation is forbidden and they must remain what they are. Mottel learns early in life to perform difficult feats of equilibrium, and Pinney, one of the immigrants, is quite explicit about this matter of keeping one's balance. Demonstrating balance, Pinney makes himself and the onlookers seasick, but this confidence in the existence of a remedy is typical of them all.

As a novel, *Mottel the Cantor's Son* is not entirely successful; it is loosely constructed and undramatic, but it contains more remarkable characters than any five ordinary novels and it has its pages of incomparable comedy. The translation by the author's granddaughter, Tamara Kahana, is excellent: breezy, free and witty. I suppose any reader who knows Yiddish will mutter to himself in that language as he reads the English; here and there he will come upon a phrase too literally translated, and stiff, and bereft of flavor. He will, however, understand Miss Kahana's difficulties.

[1953]

Dreiser and the Triumph of Art

Dreiser is not very popular now, unfortunately, and the late F. O. Matthiessen's *Theodore Dreiser* will not restore his popularity though it defends him with some real feeling against the usual charges of crude writing, faulty thought and ridiculous prejudices. Part of this biography is disingenuous, the political part; Matthiessen pretends to see no difference between radicalism and communism and refuses to see that communist William Z. Foster is not the heir of socialist Eugene V. Debs. Dreiser understood many things better than he did politics; so probably did Matthiessen. But Dreiser would not have made, in the writing of a novel, an error of the kind Matthiessen tragically allows himself to make in this study. It is true that it was left unfinished but there is no hint in it of a possible different treatment of this political problem; there is only the pitiful obstinacy of a "position," that marvelous dishonesty of modern politics. Through it you sense Matthiessen's confusion and pain.

His admirers grant that Dreiser was a great novelist who wrote badly. But it is very odd that no one has thought to ask just what the "bad writing" of a powerful novelist signifies. Matthiessen says that his groping after words corresponded to the groping of his thought, "but with both words and thought borne along on the diapason of a deep emotion." This is something of a start, but Matthiessen does not attempt to go very deeply into the matter.

Dreiser's novels are best read quickly. You pass rapidly through the pages, almost as if you were reading a newspaper, but great things remain. Occasionally you are arrested by a powerful phrase, but Dreiser is never entirely free from the habits of a feature-story writer, the old-fashioned sort, like Brisbane, who has fed on Gustavus Myers and Ingersoll and on Congressional rhetoric. When he is at his worst he is not even a slick feature-story writer. His passion for the subject failing him, Dreiser can never rest on writing itself; he has not that skill. But there are a few modern writers whose passion for the subject is so steady. And then his journalistic habits are often useful; by means of them he captures things that perhaps could not be taken in other ways—common expressions, flatnesses, forms of thought, the very effect of popular literature itself.

I think it is fair to judge a writer in part by the way he breaks through his first defects, the stiffness of his beginner's manner, his romanticism or sentimentality or modishness, his early thicknesses or thinnesses. In writing, as in personal history, what a man overcomes is a measure of his quality. An individual of any category or class performs an important and a fascinating service when he drives beyond the ordinary limitations of his type. Dreiser is, before our eyes, a newspaperman deepened, serious, finally showing a capacity that unites him with men of a very different sort who started out in a very different way. Each comes to the essential accompanied by all his accidents. A writer in America is likely to be an "irregular."

The majority of modern novelists, with their care for the poetry of detail and in their craving for stability, have not made much progress toward the greatest contemporary facts. How many European novels today have the power of the factual accounts of deportations, camps, escapes, battles, hitherto unknown relations? Considering how hideously life has been shaken, it is remarkable perhaps that any novels are being written at all in, say, France and Italy. And it is understandable that writers should try to preserve the old sort of accomplishments. But how can the *écrivain artiste* keep pace with these phenomena? Even before the war he had fallen far behind. The social meaning of his great skill was conservative; it was an effort to contain, in the military meaning of the word, great disturbances. A very talented novelist, Alberto Moravia, in his recent book, *Conjugal Love*, shows how reality is bound to revenge itself on the writer, the cultivated artist or *écrivain artiste*, when he keeps it at several removes. It will force him to discover the emptiness of his accomplishments, the vanity of his stability.

I often think the criticisms of Dreiser as a stylist betray a resistance to the feelings he causes readers to suffer. If they can say that he can't write, they need not experience these feelings. And I think too that the insistence on neatness and correctness is one of the signs of a modern nervousness and irritability. When has clumsiness in composition been felt as so annoying, so enraging? The "good" writing of *The New Yorker* is such that one experiences a furious anxiety, in reading it, about errors and lapses from taste; finally what emerges is a terrible hunger for conformism and uniformity. The smoothness of the surface and its high polish must not be marred. One has a similar anxiety in reading Hemingway and comes to feel in the end that he wants to be praised for the offenses he does not commit. He is dependable; he never names certain emotions or ideas and he takes pride in that—it is a form of honor. In it, really, there is submissiveness, acceptance of restriction.

Many American novelists, moreover, reveal in their extreme concern with expression that they are greatly oppressed by details. When they lack the strength that can encompass and lift up these details—facts of our American modern reality—they are inclined to put into accomplishments of style what is really a helplessness or recoil. Ugliness and banality growing huge, there is the fear that no poetry can inhabit the same space. So single, isolated perceptions wound the novelist, colors oppress him, factories bear him to the ground, business and advertising make him suffer, cellophane sticks in his throat. He will then "handle" by his writing his various pains. A good example of this sort of "handling" is the trip from West Egg described in F. Scott Fitzgerald's *The Great Gatsby*. Dreiser had no need for this use of language because of his greater lifting power. He depended on principle, not on taste. It was something other than taste that helped him during the crushing years of poverty and near insanity in the New York slums. He returned to sanity and life—disfigured, I believe, but with the important knowledge of how life could be supported, and this was a knowledge that carried fairly easily facts that were too great a burden to other writers.

This important knowledge was not what Dreiser thought it was. When he is writing about his principles in language awkwardly borrowed from Herbert Spencer or Huxley, they are gone the instant he invokes them. They reveal themselves sometimes rather incidentally in a power of lament—"And off he walked, very gay and dapper and as-

There Is Simply Too Much to Think About

sured because of a recent and seemingly durable success of his own." But they are most plain where the line of fate surpasses clearly the confusion of many wishes and efforts and when Dreiser bitterly, grudgingly admits his *amor fati*. This is what is so moving in him, his balkiness and sullenness, and then his admission of allegiance to life. The fact that he is a modern American gives an extreme contour to this allegiance; it is made after immersion in the greatest difficulties and reasons for pessimism and with all the art of which he is capable, art stubbornly insisted upon under the severest discouragements. His history is that of a man convinced, by his experience of "unpoetic reality," of the need to become an artist.

[1951]

Hemingway and the Image of Man

To write a study of a living master must be very difficult and it is especially difficult if that master happens, like Hemingway, to be contemptuous of critics. But Philip Young's *Ernest Hemingway* is an excellent book, neither grudging nor blindly worshipful, free of imitative longings, not in the least academic, serious but not "square," biographical without being snoopy. Hemingway is a glamorous person; his art and his wounds make him respected; his vanity and his peculiar attitudes provoke envy and anger; his fans are often maddening and his detractors include some of the prize goops of our troubled time—Wyndham Lewis, for example. Clearly Hemingway, whether we like it or not, has found out some of the secret places of our pride and trouble.

Is it because he so persistently writes his autobiography that he fascinates us? "There cannot be many writers who stick so rigorously to writing of themselves," says Mr. Young, "and—in a way—for themselves, asking at the same time that an audience take an interest in what they are doing." Undoubtedly Hemingway's self-absorption contributes a great deal to his dramatic power and his success. The fearful struggle of a deaf, isolate self, mutilated and peculiarly ignorant though stubborn and brave, to work out a style of survival is not so very rare. But it is usually an internal struggle and Hemingway stirringly externalizes it. He tests and examines himself like many purely psychological writers, like characters in the novels of Italo Svevo or—if I may go outside of fiction—like Leo Stein, who devoted a lifetime to the daily study of his own psyche. A career of supreme egomania, this may at first appear, until we bethink ourselves and realize how common such desperate self-devotion is. Moreover, there is this to say for Hemingway, that he felt a challenge to master himself in action and that he was not satisfied with arriving at a satisfactory idea of his existence. Goethe once stated that anyone who merely increased his knowledge without at the same time showing himself what to do with it poisoned his life. Only to think is to feel one's powerlessness and that is why Hemingway himself, and his heroes as well, are in extreme need of movement. They are resisting the passivity and impotence that result from the prevalence of thought.

Imagination, like the intellectual process, is also a danger to Hemingway. Mr. Young has approached this problem of the imagination with great insight. "Cowardice," Hemingway has written, ". . . is almost always simply a lack of ability to suspend the functioning of the imagination." Of course the Hemingway characters—with the too many helmets full of brains they have seen, the mothers holding dead babies, the mules drowning in the Greek harbor, the terrifying corpses, the horrible wounds and traumas they themselves have received, and suffering from insomnia and nightmare as they do—have plenty of reason to dread the imagination, particularly if the imagination, instead of going before them to prepare them for the kind of experience they can bear to have, returns always to the memory of its great crises. The happiness that Hemingway courts is often the happiness that comes of the suspension of memory. In "Big Two-Hearted River" the hero feels "good" because his behavior is governed not by thought and imagination but by some mechanism or center in the body on which we can depend but which we generally mistrust. This Mr. Young correctly sees not as anti-intellectualism but on the contrary as a need for liberation from dominance of the mind that only a man who has thought much is likely to feel.

Attempts at psychoanalytic interpretation are generally rather feeble in studies of this kind but Mr. Young, going at it circumspectly and making no pretense of "cracking the case," has found some very relevant and illuminating observations on traumas like Hemingway's in Freud's *Beyond the Pleasure Principle* and in Otto Fenichel's *Psychoanalytic Theory of Neurosis*. Trauma, Fenichel explains, is characterized by "unmastered amounts of excitation." To master these excitations that "flood" him the patient resorts to "a complicated system of bindings and primitive discharges." "And these new ways of adaptation," says Mr.

Young, paraphrasing Fenichel, "have certain consequences, for as a result of the necessary concentration on the crucial task of mastering the 'excitation,' many of the 'higher functions' must go by the board." The personality is necessarily retrenched, and therefore to some degree impoverished, for the purpose of controlling the fear. For this phenomenon Fenichel coins a startling word: "primitivation." This is how Mr. Young deals with the repetitiveness and bare recital of facts in such stories as "Big Two-Hearted River." There is a repetition-compulsion in Hemingway and he is the poet of the crippled state in which men survive the heavy blows of fortune, the mutilations of war, the cruelties of women. Wounded and broken, they somehow mend; the hero establishes an economy of imagination that frees his muscles, his senses and his spirit to accomplish this recovery. There is in Hemingway's style, contributing to its poetry, a tension that comes from the bearing at each moment of the greatest burden he can lift. Does his devotion to purity of style perhaps mean that he will not abandon those "higher functions" and that he tries to retain and carry them in this form? He refuses, I believe, to acknowledge "impoverishment" and intends to win a full victory.

The sixth chapter of Mr. Young's book is devoted to an essay on *Huckleberry Finn,* and here it seems to me that the argument he makes is really cockeyed. He claims that Hemingway and the Hemingway heroes are lineal descendants of Huck Finn. Now he has covered himself somewhat by making a proper distinction between the Hemingway hero and the Code hero. The Code hero is the soldier or the bullfighter or hunter or gambler who has beaten his fear and has learned to live by a rule of honor; the other hero, weaker and defective, like Francis Macomber, envies and imitates the Code hero. In some cases the Code hero initiates the other, bringing him over the threshold of manhood. In time the hero may become Code hero as well. Robert Jordan does so in *For Whom the Bell Tolls* and dies victoriously in the clear. Of course Huck Finn is nothing like this hero of the Hemingway Code, but Mr. Young would have us believe that Nick Adams and the young Hemingway are his twentieth-century embodiment.

"The epic, national hero, call him Huck or Hemingway, is virile and all-outdoors, but he is sick," writes Mr. Young. "He is told that as an

American he does not 'think,' he has no 'mind.' But after what he has been through, mind and thought mean misery; his simplicity is forced on him and he dares not let it go."

This, I think, is the weakest part of Mr. Young's study. The loss of Eden, the vision of death and the birth of knowledge, the beginning of manhood, these things Huck and Nick Adams do have in common. But what about the sense of anxiety and of mental toil that pervades Hemingway's stories? There is nothing like it in *Huckleberry Finn*. Nor is there any self-assignment to ordeals and labors, nor any test of strength like those in Hemingway's books; nor are there Code heroes, nor exclusive definitions of "the right thing." Hemingway has ambitions that Huck never had. Mark Twain was not trying to create in Huck a pattern, whereas Hemingway is forever trying to make his heroes virile and dominant. They are supposed to be cast in the right mold. They are exemplary; Huck is never that.

Democratic poets, Whitman wrote in *Democratic Vistas*, must "create a typical personality of character eligible to the uses of the high average men"—"to endow a literature with great archetypical models." There has been a fierce half-hidden struggle in American society to establish a typical personality and in this struggle the poets have come out poorly. Journalists, soldiers, administrators, movie directors and publicity men have pushed them aside. In the last century many American statesmen and leaders were also literary men. Lincoln was a great writer and his original personality was formed under literary influences. But one of the worst insults in any of Hemingway's books is uttered by a woman in *To Have and Have Not*: "You writer!" she says to her lover. Meaning, of course, "You wrong sort of writer!" or "Mere writer!" The right sort, like Hemingway, emerges in the struggle to establish the great archetypical models, to create the mold of manhood. No mere writer can do this.

It is plain that Hemingway thinks of himself as a representative man, one who has had the necessary and qualifying experiences. He has not been disintegrated by the fighting, the drinking, the wounds, the turbulence, the glamour. He has not gotten lost in the capitals of the world or disappeared in the huge continents. Nor has he been made anonymous with the oceanic human crowd. He keeps the outlines of his personality. This is why his characters are so dramatic: They offer the promise of a strong and victorious identity. But it is strange that Hemingway's standards, unlike Whitman's, should be such exclusive ones. I suppose that, in a game not all can play, only those within the spell and within the rules are eligible. Manhood, as Hemingway views it, must necessarily be the manhood of the few. In *The Old Man and the Sea* a young boy chooses the fisherman as his symbolic father. The actual father is not good enough. He is out. The tourist at the end of the story is out too. He is not one of those who know. (It's strange how Hemingway detests tourists—other tourists. Every traveler, I suppose, has felt the enmity of the American who "hit the place first" and considers himself practically a native.) Now Huck is also initiated by a symbolic father but that is because of his own Pap's cruelty. Nigger Jim qualifies not because he is stoical, enduring, resourceful—a Code hero, in short—but because he loves Huck.

Society does not do much to help the American to come of age. It provides no effective form. That which churches or orders of chivalry or systems of education did in the past, individuals now try to do independently. When the boy becomes a man in an American story, we are asked to believe that his experience of the change was crucial and final; no further confirmation is necessary.

There is one extraordinary exception in American fiction and that is in *The Great Gatsby*. Born James Gatz, Gatsby is ready at the hour of metamorphosis with his new name and new traits. Fitzgerald calls his identity "Platonic." A better term for it is perhaps William James's "twice-born." But whereas the great twice-born, the converted Augustines and Pauls, are reborn in greater reality and become more "themselves," Gatsby's new birth is into illusion and deception. A liar and impostor, he is condemned to a life of anxious vigilance and uneasy adventure. His deepest hope is that love will release him from his false existence, for the man he has made of himself is the *wrong* man. But there is no love forthcoming and it is as the wrong man that he is murdered by a maddened husband.

Where, then, is the right man? Fitzgerald does not pretend that he can produce him and the absence of a right man creates a certain slackness in the novel. The fact that money does not confer manhood seems to have shocked and scandalized Fitzgerald.

Hemingway has an intense desire to impose his version of the thing upon us, to create an image of manhood, to define the manner of baptism and communion. He works at this both as a writer and as a public figure. I find it quite natural that he should want to become an influence, an exemplary individual, and the reason I think it is natural is that he is really so isolated, self-absorbed and effortful. When he dreams of a victory it is a total victory: one great battle, one great issue. Everyone wants to be the right man and this is by no means a trivial desire. But Hemingway now appears to feel that he is winning and his own personality, always an important dramatic element in his writing, is in *The Old Man and the Sea* a kind of moral background. He tends to speak for Nature itself. Should Nature and Hemingway become identical, one or the other will have won too total a victory.

[1953]

Man Underground: On Ralph Ellison

A few years ago, in an otherwise dreary and better-forgotten number of *Horizon* devoted to a louse-up of life in the United States, I read with great excitement an episode from *Invisible Man*. It described a free-for-all of blindfolded Negro boys at a stag party of the leading citizens of a small Southern town. Before being blindfolded, the boys are made to stare at a naked white woman; then they are herded into the ring, and after the battle royal one of the fighters, his mouth full of blood, is called upon to give his high school valedictorian's address. As he stands under the lights of the noisy room, the citizens rib him and make him repeat himself; an accidental reference to equality nearly ruins him; but everything ends well, and he receives a handsome briefcase containing a scholarship to a Negro college.

This episode, I thought, might well be the high point of an excellent novel. It has turned out to be not *the* high point but rather one of the many peaks of a book of the very first order, a superb book. The valedictorian is himself Invisible Man. He adores the college but is thrown out before long by its president, Dr. Bledsoe, a great educator and a leader of his race, for permitting a white visitor to visit the wrong places in the vicinity. Bearing what he believes to be a letter of recommendation from Dr. Bledsoe, he comes to New York. The letter actually warns prospective employers against him. He is recruited by white radicals and becomes a Negro leader, and in the radical movement he learns eventually that throughout his entire life his relations with other men have been schematic; neither with Negroes nor with whites has he ever been visible, real. I think that in reading the *Horizon* excerpt I may have underestimated Mr. Ellison's ambition and power for the following very good reason, that one is accustomed to expect excellent novels about boys, but a modern novel about men is exceedingly rare. For this enormously complex and difficult American experience of ours very few people are willing to make themselves morally and intellectually responsible. Consequently, maturity is hard to find.

It is commonly felt that there is no strength to match the strength of those powers that attack and cripple modern mankind. And this feeling is, for the reader of modern fiction, all too often confirmed when he approaches a new book. He is prepared, skeptically, to find what he has found before, namely, that family and class, university, fashion, the giants of publicity and manufacture, have had a larger share in the creation of someone called a writer than truth or imagination—that Bendix and Studebaker and the nylon division of DuPont, and the University of Chicago or Columbia or Harvard or Kenyon College, have once more proved mightier than the single soul of an individual; he is prepared to find that one more lightly manned position has been taken. But what a great thing it is when a brilliant individual victory occurs, like Mr. Ellison's, proving that a truly heroic quality can exist among our contemporaries. People too thoroughly determined—and our institutions by their size and force too thoroughly determine—can't approach this quality. That can only be done by those who resist the heavy influences and make their own synthesis out of the vast mass of phenomena, the seething, swarming body of appearances, facts and details. From this harassment and threatened dissolution by details, a writer tries to rescue what is important. Even when he is most bitter he makes by his tone a declaration of values and he says in effect: "There is something nevertheless that a man may hope to be." This tone, in the best pages of *Invisible Man*, those pages, for instance, in which an incestuous Negro farmer tells his tale to a white New England philanthropist, comes through very powerfully; it is tragicomic, poetic, the tone of the very strongest sort of creative intelligence.

In a time of specialized intelligences, modern imaginative writers make the effort to maintain themselves as *un*specialists and their quest is for a true middle-of-consciousness for everyone. What language is it that we can all speak and what is it that we can all recognize, burn at, weep over; what is the stature we can without exaggeration claim for ourselves; what is the main address of consciousness?

I was keenly aware, as I read *Invisible Man*, of a very significant kind of independence in the writing. For there is a "way" for Negro novelists to go at their problems, just as there are Jewish or Italian "ways." Mr. Ellison has not adopted a minority tone. If he had done so he would have failed to establish a true middle-of-consciousness for everyone.

Negro Harlem is at once primitive and sophisticated; it exhibits the extremes of instinct and civilization as few other American communities do. If a writer dwells on the peculiarity of this he ends with an exotic effect. And Mr. Ellison is not exotic. For him this balance of instinct and culture or civilization is not a Harlem matter; it is *the* matter, German, French, Russian, American, universal, a matter very little understood. It is thought that Negroes and other minority people, kept under in the great status battle, are in the instinct cellar of dark enjoyment. This imagined enjoyment provokes envious rage and murder and then it is a large portion of human nature itself that becomes the fugitive murderously pursued. In our society Man—Himself—is idolized and publicly worshipped but the single individual must hide himself underground and try to save his desires, his thoughts, his soul, in invisibility. He must return to himself, learning self-acceptance and rejecting all that threatens to deprive him of his manhood.

This is what I make of *Invisible Man*. It is not by any means faultless; I don't think the hero's experiences in the Communist Party are as original in conception as other parts of the book and his love affair with a white woman is all too brief. But it is an immensely moving novel and it has greatness.

So many hands have been busy at the interment of the novel—the hand of Paul Valéry, the hands of the editors of literary magazines, of scholars who decide when genres come and go, the hands of innumerable pipsqueaks as well—that I can't help feeling elated when a resurrection occurs. People read history and then seem to feel that everything has to conclude in their own time. "We have read history, and therefore history is over," they appear to say. Really, all that such critics have the right to say is that fine novels are few and far between. That's perfectly true. But then fine anythings are few and far between. If these critics wanted to be extremely truthful, they'd say they were bored. Boredom, of course, like any mighty force, you must respect. There is something terribly impressive about the boredom of a man like Valéry who could no longer bear to read that the carriage had come for the duchess at four in the afternoon. And certainly there are some notably boring things to which we owe admiration of a sort.

Not all the gravediggers of the novel have such distinction as Valéry's, however. Hardly. And it's difficult to think of them as rising dazzled from a volume of Stendhal, exclaiming "God!" and then with angry determination seizing their shovels to go and heap more clods on the coffin. No, theirs unfortunately isn't often the disappointment of spirits formed under the influence of the masters. They make you wonder how, indeed, they *would* be satisfied. A recent contributor to *Partisan Review*, for instance, complains that modern fiction does not keep pace with his swift-wheeling modern consciousness, which apparently leaves the photon far behind in its speed. He names a few *really* modern writers of fiction, their work unfortunately still unpublished, and makes a patronizing reference to *Invisible Man*: Almost, but not quite, the real thing, it is "raw" and "overambitious." And the editors of *Partisan Review* who have published so much of this modern fiction that their contributor attacks, what do they think of this? They do not say what they think—neither of this piece nor of another lulu on the same subject and in the same issue by John Aldridge. Mr. Aldridge writes: "There are only two cultural pockets left in America; and they are the Deep South and that area of northeastern United States whose moral capital is Boston, Massachusetts. This is to say that these are the only places where there are any manners. In all other parts of the country people live in a kind of vastly standardized cultural prairie, a sort of infinite Middle West, and that means that they don't really live and they don't really do anything."

Most Americans are thus Invisible. Can we wonder at the cruelty of dictators when even a literary critic, without turning a hair, announces the death of a hundred million people?

Let us suppose that the novel is, as they say, played out. Let us only suppose it, for I don't believe it. But what if it is so? Will such tasks as

Mr. Ellison has set himself no more be performed? Nonsense. New means, when new means are necessary, will be found. To find them is easier than to suit the disappointed consciousness and to penetrate the thick walls of boredom within which life lies dying.

[1952]

The 1,001 Afternoons of Ben Hecht

For years after Ben Hecht's departure from Chicago there were legends about him. Before I was out of grammar school I had already read *1001 Afternoons in Chicago* and in high school I combed the secondhand bookstores for his other works, *Erik Dorn, Humpty Dumpty, Gargoyles, Broken Necks* and *Count Bruga*. I have not glanced into any of these for more than twenty years but I remember the stories and the characters and even some of the strange phrases—"a scribble of rooftops along the sky," "the greedy little half-dead."

The garish, breezy, lyrical jargon of the newspaperman who had steeped himself in Remy de Gourmont, Arthur Machen and in the rhetoric of Huneker's *Painted Veils* and H. L. Mencken's *Prejudices* has remained with me. The Great Depression was in full stride and almost all the heroes of Chicago's literary renaissance had departed for New York and Hollywood, but my friends and I had read all about it. We haunted Rush Street and Wells Street under the El, and looked up people who had known Dreiser and Anderson, Hecht and Sandburg and the days of *The Little Review*. Probably we got it all wrong, but it inspired us to think of a Golden Age of drinking bouts, debates, public readings, feuds and great occasions.

What was most marvelous was that people should have conceived of dignifying what we witnessed all about us by writing of it and that the gloom of Halsted Street, the dismal sights of Back of the Yards and the speech of immigrants should be the materials of art. Something could be made of the very things that baffled or oppressed us; the chains of today might become the laurels of tomorrow.

Reading *A Child of the Century*, Ben Hecht's autobiography, I responded as I once had done to his glamour as the poet of the city and remembered that he had once been called "the Pagliacci of the fire-escapes" and that in *1001 Afternoons* he had appeared as the skeptical, sentimental stripling of the city room, talkative, irreverent, romantic, opinionated, not too well informed, not too much of a psychologist and even less of a moralist. He had, moreover, been filled with what he himself calls a "moth-like avidity that kept me beating around the days as if they were shining lamps." This avidity was what we, his youthful readers, loved him for and in his pages about Chicago he again communicated to me.

There is no small amount of O. Henry's Orientalism and of Baghdad on the Subway in Hecht's approach, but the inheritance is primarily stylistic. "He saw people shot, run over, hanged, burned alive, dead of poison, crumpled by age," says the author of himself as a young reporter and this is not the stuff of which O. Henry stories are made.

Much of Hecht's youthful flashiness for its own sake has left him and he is not so clever as he used to be. When he is writing about his family, his newspaper experience and some of his old friends, he is instead wonderfully funny and even touching. Though he also acquits himself better as a thinker, it is his raconteur's gift that has developed most. His studies of his uncles and aunt (evidently he has no cousins to speak of) are among the best things in this lively book of his; these are incomparably the warmest, most spontaneous and generous of his portraits.

Hundreds of characters appear: writers, politicians, actors and other celebrities. Mencken and both Roosevelts are here and Fanny Brice and the Marx Brothers, John Barrymore and Charles MacArthur and humbler people by the score. Hecht does not claim too much in his title. He really is a Child of the Century and has personally experienced some of its deepest crises. I can't quite believe that he actually saw the socialist hero Karl Liebknecht take off his clothes and climb into the Kaiser's bed to signalize the end of Hohenzollern rule. I have an idea that the attitude toward Germans he was later to take in *Guide for the Bedeviled* colors his memories of Germany after World War I. And often I felt that he was passing out tributes to the nightclub characters and newspaper columnists in the grand, florid Hollywood fashion, paying off old debts. But his ability to remember distinctly and with such liveliness is

There Is Simply Too Much to Think About

admirable and significant. He is a man who has passed his life among other people rather than, let us say, one whose career has led him among issues.

I don't mean to say that he has never become involved in issues. He is widely known now as the man who conducted a campaign in behalf of the Irgun movement. I am inclined to accept the reasons that he gives for this. They are unselfish reasons. That the massacre of so many Jews by the Nazis should take place without interference by the great governments and that British and American Jewry should also be silent about it seemed to him an intolerable outrage. His attacks on Jewish leaders and gentile politicians are violent but not baseless.

It is probably an odd thing to say, but some of his radical virtues of the Twenties today have a rather old-fashioned look. When he lambastes Hollywood, when he attacks congressmen, he is very Menckenian: "There are, in fact, no arts. There are entertainments. Our talents, like our waterfalls, have all been harnessed to make life pleasanter for the public. The iconoclastic or anti-public artist exists no more than the anti-public traction company."

Hecht is a rather difficult man to pin down. There are moments when he still seems the rakish and irreverent young newspaperman and others when he is bombastic and Hollywoodian, as inflated and wearisome as one of his own less successful movies. He is one of the creators of that marvelous comedy, *Twentieth Century*, but also of *Specter of the Rose*, a picture I would sooner eat ground glass than see again. His manners are not always nice, but then nice manners do not always make interesting autobiographies and this autobiography has the merit of being intensely interesting. If he is occasionally slick, he is also independent, forthright and original. Among the pussycats who write of social issues today he roars like an old-fashioned lion.

[1954]

The Swamp of Prosperity: On Philip Roth

Goodbye, Columbus is a first book but it is not the book of a beginner. Unlike those of us who came howling into the world, blind and bare, Mr. Roth appears with nails, hair and teeth, speaking coherently. At twenty-six he is skillful, witty and energetic and performs like a virtuoso. His one fault, and I don't expect all the brethren to agree that it is a fault, is that he is so very sophisticated. Sometimes he twinkles too much. *The New York Times* has praised him for being "wry." One such word to the wise ought to be sufficient. Mr. Roth has a superior sense of humor (see his story "Epstein") and I think he can count on it more safely than on his "wryness."

His subject, to narrow it down for descriptive purposes, is Jewish life in suburban New Jersey and New York, the comfortable, paradoxical life of the Jew in prosperous postwar America. Neil Klugman, the hero of the long title story, twenty-three years of age, is different in many ways from the heroes of Jewish stories of the Thirties and Forties. His appetites are more boyish, his thoughts more shrewd. He is strong on observation, a little less strong on affection. His prototypes were far more sentimental. They were more doting and also more combative. Neil is very little concerned with his parents, who have gone for the summer, or with his aunt, who wants to fill him in their absence with pot roast and soda pop. He is something of an outsider; his fictional ancestor was a misfit, a sad sack, pure burlap, weirdly incompetent and extremely unworldly, as incoherent in the face of injustice as Billy Budd himself, a stranger to good manners, but for all of that easily moved, honest and good-hearted. The burlap hero could never keep a job or hold a girl. He was always sure to be shortchanged on the bus and if he went into the Automat for a cup of coffee he would scald himself. On the Jewish side he was descended from the *shlimazl*, obviously; on the Russian, from the poor clerk of Gogol's story "The Cloak"; in American literature he takes his descent from the pure youth (relatively pure) of Anderson's "I'm a Fool"—"Gee whiz! How could I pull such a dumb trick!" The burlap has gone out of fashion now and in the stories of Mr. Roth there are only patches of the grand old fabric. It was during the Depression that burlap had its finest hour. Before our present prosperous and bureaucratic era began, poor Feigenbaum belonged to the Jewish *cafoni*, the Little People. Now our more selfish desires and more complex motives have received a sharp stimulus. Possessions have a new glamour. Even burlap has changed. Madison Avenue people tint it and hang their windows with it, so it must cost more. Probably nylon is no dearer. In any case the hero of Jewish fiction two decades ago knew nothing of Jewish suburbs, country clubs, organized cancer fund drives, large sums of money, cars, mink or jewelry. The burlap hero assumed that the social order was of course wicked, base and harsh. But then the Mammon of Un-righteousness in those days had a smaller wardrobe. He might sometimes appear as Uncle Willie the haughty manufacturer from Riverside Drive, in spats, a cold Upmann cigar in his teeth. But now he wears Ivy League clothes, his hair is cut tight to his head and his name is Legion. The stories of Mr. Roth show the great increase of the power of materialism over us. (I beg leave to remind you that I am neither Karl Marx nor the editorial writer for *Life*.) I don't want to suggest that Mr. Roth simply exchanges the burlap for the nylon, the rugged for the smooth, naïveté for sophistication, only that he has a greater interest in society and in manners and is aware of a great change in the condition of the Jews.

It is entirely clear that he is not satisfied with what Jewish life in the United States has become, and though his criticism is usually made laughingly there are moments when it isn't possible to laugh. A story like "Defender of the Faith," with its portrait of the scheming Private Grossbart, dries up the grin on the reader's face, and "Goodbye, Columbus," the lengthy title story, pleasant and witty as it is, reveals something that is far worse than the corruption of an individual—the vacuity and mindlessness of Pig Heaven. There exist Jewish writers who think that ours are the best of all possible suburbs in the best of all possible Americas. In the final pages of Herman Wouk's *Marjorie Morningstar*, Mamaroneck is glorified. There we are shown a pious and wiser Marjorie, purified of her earlier follies. But to Mr. Roth all is far from well in Mamaroneck. He seems to doubt that the highest prizes of existence have really been moved from the ascetic foundation on which they have always before rested onto the new foundations of money and "normalcy." I think that we must, on the evidence, doubt along with him.

The condition revealed in "Goodbye, Columbus" is really too grave for irony and that is why Mr. Roth's "wryness" appears to me inadequate. There's a lot of mileage to be gotten of our kidding costly Jewish weddings, plastic surgery and similar nonsense, but Mr. Roth wants to go deeper, farther, and the wryness after some time becomes the expression of his discontent with the inadequacy of his method. For, to put it as simply as I can, Mr. Roth wants to make a contrast of spirit and worldly goods.

Neil Klugman and Brenda Patimkin, who are having a love affair during the summer vacation, come down to New York together, she to shop for clothes and to obtain a diaphragm, he to give her his support on such a difficult occasion. "The doctor's office," he says, "was in the Squibb Building, which is across from Bergdorf Goodman's and so was a perfect place for Brenda to add to her wardrobe." While she is being fitted Neil wanders into St. Patrick's and there he makes a little speech to himself: "Can I call the self-conscious words I spoke prayer? At any rate, I called my audience God. God, I said, I am twenty-three years old. I want to make the best of things. Now the doctor is about to wed Brenda to me, and I am not entirely certain that this is all for the best. What is it I love, Lord? Why have I chosen? Who is Brenda? . . . If we meet You at all, God, it's that we're carnal, and acquisitive, and thereby partake of you. I am carnal, and I know You approve, I just know it. But how carnal can I get? I am acquisitive. Where do I turn now in my acquisitiveness? Where do we meet? Which prize is You?

"It was an ingenious meditation, and suddenly I felt ashamed. I got up and walked outside, and the noise of Fifth Avenue met me with an answer:

"Which prize do you think, *shmuck*? Gold dinnerware, sporting-goods trees, nectarines, garbage disposals, bumpless noses, Patimkin Sink, Bonwit Teller—."

Brenda's father is the manufacturer of Patimkin Sinks. A good enough old fellow at home, kindly and hospitable in an empty sort of way, he is formidable at business. He will buy split-level houses and new cars for his children when they marry but he will require Neil, should he become his daughter's suitor, to give up his silly job at the Public Library where he has no prospects and to become capable of giving her garbage disposals and gold dinnerware.

Certainly Neil's meditation is curious. When I had finished the story I went back and read it again. It seems a little too cozy on the third reading. Why should it please God that we are carnal or acquisitive? I don't see that at all. I assume Mr. Roth is saying that it would be a deadly offense to confuse God with Bonwit Teller and garbage disposals, with goods and money. He doesn't say it well; he is confused, nervous, wry and somewhat too aware that this is a shocking way to address God. And in St. Patrick's too, perhaps displeasing the Catholics as well as the Jews. Had Mr. Roth plainly said "worldly goods versus the goods of the spirit" he might have avoided all this wry awkwardness. But now we have grasped his meaning: The world is too much with us, and there has never been so much world. For in the past what could money buy that can compare with the houses, the sinks, the garbage disposals, the Jags, the minks, the plastic surgery enjoyed by the descendants of those immigrants who passed through Ellis Island? To what can we compare this change? Nothing like it has ever hit the world; nothing in history has so quickly and radically transformed any group of Jews. It is this change that is the real subject of "Goodbye, Columbus" and not the love affair. Love, duty, principle, thought, significance, everything is being sucked into a fatty and nerveless state of "well-being." My mother used to say of people who had had a lucky break, in the old Yiddish metaphor, "They've fallen into the *schmaltz-grub*"—a pit of fat. The pit has expanded now into a swamp, and the lucky ones may be those who haven't yet tasted the fruits of prosperity.

The matter becomes even plainer in "Eli, the Fanatic." Into the suburban community of Woodenton comes a school for Orthodox children, refugees; the strange figure of a European Jew in black garments is seen in the supermarket and the Jewish residents are alarmed and angry. Eli Peck, the lawyer, writes to Mr. Tzuref at the school, "Woodenton is a progressive suburban community whose members, both Jewish and Gentile, are anxious that their families live in comfort and beauty and serenity." Eli's friend Teddie says to him about old-fashioned Orthodoxy, "All the place is, is a hideaway for people who can't face life. It's a matter of needs. They have all these superstitions, and why do you think? Because they can't face the world, because they can't take their place in society. That's no environment to bring kids up in, Eli." So, in rhythms that come straight from the Yiddish, Teddie states his case. Peace. Good healthy relationship. Nullity. Eli sends his own best tweed suit to the European Jew in black and then, finding the old garments at his door, puts them on and frightens everyone. The little story is touching and funny and it tells a great deal about the situation of the Jews in the Mamaronecks and Woodentons of this country.

Not all Jewish readers have shown themselves pleased with Mr. Roth's stories. Here and there one meets people who feel that the business of a Jewish writer in America is to write public relations releases, to publicize everything that is nice in the Jewish community and to suppress the rest, loyally. This is not at all the business of Jewish writers or of writers of any kind, and those touchy persons who reproach us with not writing the Jewish *Elsie Dinsmore* over and over again are very like the Russian authorities who created socialist realism. No quantity of Jewish Elsie Dinsmores from Mamaroneck will decrease anti-Semitic feeling. The loss to our sense of reality is not worth the gain (if there is one) in public relations. This is precisely what Mr. Roth is telling us in "Eli, the Fanatic." What plagues Eli is the false image that fear and a hateful spirit of accommodation have created. The tweed suit is no more his than the black garments. He is false to himself in both and it is this falsehood that does him the greatest harm.

My advice to Mr. Roth is to ignore all objections and to continue on his present course.

[1959]

The Writer and the Audience

Eckermann records a statement by Goethe that a writer ought not to pick up his pen unless he intends his words to be read by at least a million readers. None but the crankiest authors would quarrel with this assertion. Naturally a novelist wants to be read. Only, if he is not a popular writer, he is not satisfied to take his million readers as he finds them. He does not want to be conditioned by them but rather to tell them what they ought to be. And he wants them to assume what he and his fictional personages assume. When a character is wounded the reader must feel pain. When a character makes a promise the reader must feel the principles underlying obligation. When Lord Jim leaps into the water the reader must understand that honor has been lost. Lacking a sense of honor, he cannot accept the dramatic moment. The intention of the writer, therefore, is to hold the reader to a sense of the weight of each action. The writer cannot be sure that his million will view the matter as he does. He therefore tries to define an audience. By assuming what it is that all men ought to be able to understand and agree upon, he creates a kind of humanity, a version of it composed of hopes and realities in proportions that vary as his degree of optimism.

Nietzsche declared in *Human, All Too Human* that artists regularly exaggerate the value of personality. Of course exaggeration is a dramatic necessity; and simplification too. If a hero does not matter his fate does not matter. If a single life is of slight importance, deaths are not especially awe-inspiring. In defense of the dramatic element, therefore, the writer has frequently insisted on assigning a definite value to reality. In this respect writers are conservative; they want old agreements and understanding to last. Your villain cannot blackmail your hero if your hero has no reputation to protect. Your heroine cannot expect anyone to die in defense of her chastity if no one appreciates chastity.

Occasionally a novelist is able to furnish and make stable an entire system from his imagination. Balzac, for instance, stands in the very middle of Society, a secular intelligence capable of interpreting everything. His ingenuity is inexhaustible. He is never at a loss for theories, physiological, psychological, political, historical, aesthetic, and explains every occurrence confidently. In order to write fiction Balzac dominates, or pretends to dominate, all of experience. In Thomas Mann we see this encyclopedic method at the stages of exhaustion. In order to validate facts, to make you see them as he does, the writer becomes, or attempts to become, an expert in a score of fields—biology and psychology, philosophy and music, archaeology and history—and all so that we may feel as he feels at any given evocation.

We cannot continue to build in every novel such total systems in order that all may know what, for example, a woman experiences when her husband deserts her, what a man feels on his deathbed. We must take our chances on a belief in the psychic unity of mankind. But of course people—audiences—will not always assume what we assume, as Walt Whitman bids us trust.

Most of the things that all men ought to be able to understand are quite simple, and it is astonishing how much deformity of perception one learns about in the course of writing a book. One learns in the first place how hard it is to get people to pay attention to others in their full complexity. A possible reason for this is that there are so many of us, such a multitude, that it is difficult if not impossible to give every man his due measure of attention. If you demand more you are considered presumptuous and conceited. Therefore most men in their self-presentation to the world settle upon a few simple attributes and create a surface easy to characterize and to understand. Underneath, their real, complex existence takes place, their private affair. The code that protects this privacy is powerful and elaborate. Some emotions are in the course of losing their external form, and because they are not demonstrated they atrophy. With them is atrophied a corresponding sense of reality. Hidden effort, self-sealed activity, huge and sometimes awesome constructions of private fantasy, make the sense of the existence of others not what it once was. I do not say that this is not in itself fascinating but it is obviously different. If you cut Shylock nowadays he will perhaps *not* seem to bleed as others do.

What I am really trying to say is that people do not appear to respond as they once did to the various faces of reality. Innumerable things intervene to cloud or modify reactions. Insults are not given or resented as they were by Shakespeare's Brutuses or Cassiuses or by Mérimée's characters; injustices are not quickly recognized; pains take their time about making themselves felt; likewise pleasures. There is not the same immediacy of response. Analysis and calculation come between. Often we are aware in the modern personality of a system that deals with the majority of situations. This system knows what is appropriate in any given case. For instance: A friend falls sick; our feelings may or may not be touched by this event, but the system knows what ought to be done and socially we behave as though we felt for the sufferer. We have come to consider the functioning of this system as normalcy. If it is suggested that anything else is normal the system shows concern. The system loves abstractions, of course, and is not friendly toward the imagination; it prefers preparedness to impulse; within the minds of Goethe's million, it resists new forms of reality. This is only to say that so much is required of us, that our feelings would be so overtaxed if they had to be immediately involved in all the rapid and complicated transactions confronting us even on an ordinary morning, that the system is indispensable. But it has usurped too large a place.

Beyond this system (or rather, these systems, for in your audience of a million there will be a vast number of such fabrications) the writer must find enduring intuitions of what things are real and what things are important. His business is with these enduring intuitions that have the power to recognize occasions of suffering or occasions of happiness in spite of all distortion and blearing.

[1954]

Distractions of a Fiction Writer

On the one hand literature, tragic as well as comic, belongs in the realm of happiness; on the other hand, writers are often unhappy and distracted. They have never been examined so earnestly before. The writer hasn't often in the past been called upon to give an account of himself. When the poet tries to come between Brutus and Cassius during their quarrel, they throw him out. They don't ask him to give historical reasons for being a poet. He is too unimportant for that. And I believe his unimportance in that day to have been one of his advantages. Now there are people who devote themselves to the study of poets and who badger and investigate them. Poets and other writers are asked—they ask themselves—many serious and weighty questions. Which means either that society has a larger stake in literature than it used to have, or that it can't resist meddling with anything related to happiness, with a view to doing it some damage.

What are some of these questions—or charges or indictments?

Let us say that the writer (in this case a novelist) is in the customary solitude of his room and that he is under a strain and that his writing is not at its best. Today it is hard for him to declare with Joseph Conrad that the world is a temple. He would have to assert, "It *is* a temple." And that would already be a mistake. The feeling of sacredness is beyond price but the assertion has very little value. Therefore the novelist will make no assertion for the sake of strengthening himself. He will rather ask, "Why didn't you choose a different sort of work, something you could do wholeheartedly every day? Why do you write fiction? You can't build a business on inspirations. Besides, what makes you think it's wanted? Maybe it's an unhistorical and superfluous occupation you've chosen. The whole world is in motion, blazing. And what are you doing? Nothing commensurate; only sitting here alone, oddly faithful to things you learned as a boy. They taught you the Palmer Method in school so here you are still covering pages with words. You go on about men and women, families and marriages, divorces, crime and flight, murders, weddings, wars, rises and declines, simplicities and complexities, blessedness and agony and it's all largely imaginary. Who asks you to write such things? What the devil are you doing here? What's all this about dead and nonexistent people—Priams and Hecubas? Who is this Hecuba anyway and what are you to her? You're a foolish busybody," says the writer to himself. "Adding book to book. What for? Aren't there enough books? Even King Solomon was already complaining that there was a 'sufficiency' of them. You are practicing a peculiar and, some say, an obsolete art. You may have an inherited Jewish taste for such things."

Such are the questions or doubts or charges. I believe they can be answered. And though it is sad and possibly harmful that they must be heard, it is not necessarily fatal. Eros manages somehow to survive analysis; and somehow imagination survives criticism. In either case the rising of an imperious need abolishes all the questions. "Do you feel it necessary to do this? Then, for the love of God, do it," says the need. If it argues at all.

As a young man Rilke made a pilgrimage to Russia to see Tolstoy. As I have heard the story, he followed the impatient old man around filling his ears with his problems about writing. Tolstoy couldn't bear it. He had exchanged art for religion and all this seemed very trifling to him. "*Vous voulez écrire?*" he said. "*Eh bien, écrivez donc! Écrivez!*" What else is there to say? Do it if you must and don't fuss so about it.

Nevertheless there are certain distractions.

The novelist is distracted; he writes for someone and that someone is sure to be distracted. The Wedding Guest is distracted when the Ancient Mariner stops him. The Mariner lets the Guest's two companions go and holds him with a glittering eye. Amid the distractions of merrymaking the Bride is led to the altar, ready to forswear all others. The Guest can only tear his hair as he hears the loud bassoon. He is cut off from his beloved distractions by the power of art and he cannot choose but hear. This is the position we are all in: We resist the spell but we also desire it.

"Why should I end my distractions for you?" That is the question asked of the writer. For there are more things that solicit the attention of the mind than there ever were before. The libraries and museums are full, great storehouses with their thousands of masterpieces in every style. Their vast wealth excites our ambition. It can make a Dr. Faustus out of many an educated man. It menaces him with death by distraction. But everyone on every level is exposed to this danger. The giant producers of goods need our defenseless attention. They catch us on the run and through the eyes and ears fill us with the brand names of cars and cigarettes and soaps. And then news and information distract us. Bad art distracts us. Genuine culture is also, as I've already noted, distracting. Lastly there are the inner demands of memory, desire, fantasy, anxiety and the rest. These are perhaps the most tyrannical. The great outer chaos drives us inward and in our own small kingdoms we indulge our favorite distractions.

The following quotation shows the elementary forms of common distraction. It is taken from a popular booklet, *The Handbook of Beauty*, by Constance Hart. The chapter title is "Double-Duty Beauty Tricks": "*While doing your housework*: You can keep your face creamed, your hair in pin curls; you can practice good standing and walking posture; when you're sitting at the kitchen counter peeling potatoes you can do your ankle exercises and foot strengtheners, and also practice good sitting posture. . . . *While telephoning* (at home, of course): You can do neck exercises; brush your hair; do ankle exercises, eye exercises, foot strengtheners, and chin-and-neck exercises; practice good standing or sitting posture; even massage your gums (while listening to the other person). . . . *While reading or watching TV*: You can brush your hair; massage your gums; do your ankle and hand exercises and foot strengtheners; do some bust and back exercises; massage your scalp; use the abrasive treatment for removing superfluous hair."

Here we see basic distraction. Such grim energy can only be drawn from the feeling that life's shortness requires us to combine our activities, combine and combine and multiply the levels of consciousness and those of muscular coördination layer upon layer, on a sandwich principle. We are not perfect. We must perfect ourselves, we must exhaust ourselves. Maybe too there is a perverse desire for freedom in this. Dominated by no single activity, we are free; free but not tranquil; at leisure but not idle since all the while we strive for perfection. No, the face, the neck, the bust, the skin, the mind are not good as they are; we must tirelessly improve them. By so doing we deny the power of death over us, because as long as we're getting better there's no reason why we should die. But I think the ruling principle behind all of this can be stated as follows: Don't give yourself wholly to any single thing. Divide and multiply.

What a fate to marry a woman who follows such instructions! But what shall we say about the fate of the author whose novel she holds in her hand—if she has a hand to spare? How is he to get her attention? Can he hold her with his glittering eye? Why, he himself suffers from such diseases. He, like everyone else, is subject to vanity, not willingly. He also is deafened by the noise of life, by cries and claims and counterclaims and fantasy and desire and ambition for perfection, by false hope and error and fear of death.

But distraction is not necessarily inimical to the imagination. Novels are floated upon distraction. They begin in the midst of it. On the first page of *Anna Karenina* we are told, "All was confusion in the house of the Oblonskys." Distraction is one of the subjects of Tolstoy's masterpiece. Society is in Tolstoy's view a system of distractions. Anna and Vronsky are drawn apart by its disapproval of their union. Vronsky grows bored; he has no proper work or a center of attention, for love, or the purest sort of attention to another, can't be sustained day by day. Love is not an occupation. Therefore Vronsky falls away. Anna's brother Oblonsky makes a last attempt to obtain his brother-in-law Karenin's consent to a divorce. Anna's life depends on this.

"After an excellent dinner with unlimited cognac . . . Oblonsky arrived at the Countess Lydia Ivanovna's," says Tolstoy. In the course of the evening Oblonsky falls asleep and when he awakes he steals out of the house, forgetting the appeal he was to have made to Karenin. Next morning he receives Karenin's final refusal.

I don't see how we can avoid blaming Oblonsky for his sister's suicide. A normally decent man, no worse than most, hearty, *bon vivant*, he loves his sister, yes, but he is unable to keep his attention fixed upon her need. He is not a monster of selfishness—he is distracted. The attention is supplied by Tolstoy in the writing of the novel. His method is one of deliberate slowness and simplification, a contemplative slowness that brings order and unity out of confusion. We never go from distraction to attention (of a certain sort) without experiencing a triumphant emotion. Distractions give force to a work of art by their resolution, and the novelist works more deeply with distractions than any other kind of artist. Many events fall upon us, assail us with claims on our time and our judgment; waves of disintegrative details wash over us and threaten to wear away all sense of order and proportion. The novelist begins at a great depth of distraction and difficulty. Sometimes, as in James Joyce's *Ulysses*, he risks total immersion in distraction. I don't say that the novelist knows what order is; but he relies upon his imagination to lead him toward it. In a work of art the imagination is the sole source of order. There are critics who assume that you must begin with order if you are to end with it. Not so. A novelist begins with disorder and disharmony and goes toward order by an unknown process of the imagination. And anyway, the order he achieves is not the order that ideas have. Critics need to be reminded of this, I think. Art is the speech of artists. The rules are not the same as those in science and philosophy. No one knows what the power of the imagination comes from or how much distraction it can cope with. We are now told that it has reached its limit. The distraction is supposed to be too broad for love and too deep for beauty and too agonizing for any order. And so we are told by critics that the novel is dead. These people can't know what the imagination is or what its powers are. I wish I could believe in their good-natured objectivity. I can't. I should like to disregard them, but that is a little difficult because they have a great deal of power. Not real power, perhaps, but power of a sort. They can be very distracting.

And the deadly earnestness with which they lower the boom! On what, after all? On flowers. On mere flowers. It occurs to a man that he is a writer. He doesn't obtain a certificate like a doctor or take the bar examination like a lawyer; nor does he apprentice himself like a tool-and-die maker or get into a union like a bricklayer. A novel is written

There Is Simply Too Much to Think About

by a man who thinks of himself as a novelist. Unless he makes such an assumption about himself he simply can't do it. The thing is impossible. He has to encounter the world in a particular way. He lives within a sort of tissue that floats about the mind when he is well or collapses upon it when he isn't. It's hard to say exactly where this tissue comes from or what it is, but it is a sign of his autonomy. He has called himself out and anointed himself. No prophet picked him. And so he has neither supernatural nor social assistance. Now aren't we Americans fond of self-made men? Of some of them, yes. And to this peculiar self-election of the man who goes about calling himself a novelist there is no visible barrier, at least. Well then, let's say that the anointee is carried away by the force of his imagination; he gives utterance to the images it brings him and with a certain arrogance he assumes that what he writes needs to be read and will be read. The origin of this arrogance, if arrogance is what it is, is rather mysterious too. In fact, from any sensible, rational point of view the whole thing is bewildering. Still, as it begins privately and harms no one, there are no objections. None will be heard so long as the interests of power are not touched.

Society doesn't do much to encourage this self-elected man; on the contrary it subjects him to many negative pressures. Is it angry with the imagination? Does it perhaps hate it? That may well be. At any rate it holds the imagination under suspicion. For there are always leading activities that society needs and sponsors. Sometimes it is the lawgiver who is in the highest place and sometimes the priest and sometimes the general. With us it is the businessman, the administrator, the political leader, the military man. These have the power; they are the representative men; in them manhood is mirrored. They honor themselves and are universally honored and imitated as the possessors of power and virtue. They rule armies and industries and publishing empires and build atomic reactors and legislate for us all. A modern writer, when he comes to speak of their powers, is forced to speak vaguely because he doesn't really know what they're doing. Any connection between art and authority has for some time been broken.

Well then, if it is true that the writer has no actual connection with power, and that he is separated from the main current of things not only by the lack of certain dignities but also because he is compelled by his self-authorization to live in a manner different from most other men, why doesn't he by the daring of his imagination alone make a leap into the councils of state or into the Pentagon or a cabinet meeting? Oddly enough he doesn't even expect it of himself. He accepts timidly all the restrictions of the rule of experience. The demons of firsthand knowledge, documentation and naturalistic accuracy have seized him. *The Red Badge of Courage* was probably the last American novel to be taken wholly from the imagination and there are indignant letters in the old *Dial* by Civil War veterans denouncing Crane for the technical errors that, not then experienced in war, he had made. We are a nation devoted to facts and we don't like to waste time with books that give the wrong dope about shipwrecks on the coast of Bohemia. We like to get things straight. Otherwise we feel that we are wasting valuable time. And if a man writes a book we think we are justified in asking him, as though we were about to hire him, about his qualifications and his experience. For we really feel that experience is intrinsically valuable and we have the same acquisitive attitude toward it as toward other things of value. Experience can never be bad, we seem to believe; the more one has had, the better. While this attitude may be justified in some respects, I think it ought to be pointed out that the disorder of experience is distraction. Imagination may do with experience or with nonexperience precisely what it likes. By refusing to write anything with which he is not thoroughly familiar, the American writer confesses the powerlessness of the imagination and accepts his relegation to an inferior place.

"All the qualities of a man acquire dignity when he knows that the service of the collectivity that owns him needs him," wrote William James in his essay "The Moral Equivalent of War." Well, the writer certainly must think that if the collectivity knew what its best interests were it would see that it needed him as much as it does—let's not go so far as to say the Secretaries of State or Defense—but as much as it needs psychiatrists, who deal also with the confusions of experience, or television directors. But since the writer of novels has found the oil and anointed himself he need not deceive himself about the "collectivity." He can't feel that it needs him. Not unless he creates a sensation or makes a great fortune. For of course money will turn the trick. "If proud of the collectivity," continues William James, "his own pride rises in proportion." There doesn't seem to be much of this pride around. In modern times the feelings and thoughts of writers have gone counter to the general direction. If they have gone with the collectivity—the mass—it has been on the terms of the mass and not their own.

American writers have often described themselves as loafers, vagabonds, beggars and bums. Thoreau sits apart from the economy in idleness beside Walden Pond. Walt Whitman describes himself as one of the "roughs." Vachel Lindsay wrote *A Handy Guide for Beggars* out of his experiences as a preacher of his Gospel of Beauty. Writers have stood aside from the ordinary duties of their fellow citizens. I don't perhaps so much mean duties as I mean the routines of the mill towns, the mining towns and the great cities. Others get up in the morning and ride in crowds to their work. Not the self-anointed writer. He sits up in his room writing, a freer man. Or is he freer? Is he free? Perhaps he feels a weak and treasonable fear in his soul at doing something so hard to explain to the others, the early morning passengers on the Milwaukee Avenue streetcar.

"I loaf and invite my soul," said Walt Whitman. Well, perhaps his counterpart today does too. Perhaps. I hope so, because his imagination requires the tranquil attitude. But chances are that he is working, bitterly working, in an effort to meet his brothers of the office and factory sympathetically. The odds are good that he is literally a brother and comes out of the same mass. And now for some strange reason he is trying to throw a bridge from this same place, from a room in Chicago to, let us say, Ahab, to Cervantes, to Shakespeare, to the kings of the old Chronicles, to Genesis. For he says, "Aren't we still part of the same humanity, children of Adam?" So he invites his soul away from distractions.

But sometimes he can feel in the very streets that the energies of the population have been withdrawn to mass activity, industry and money. At midday in an American city you are aware of a certain emptiness about the houses. You hear the organ groaning in dissolution as the scenes of the soap opera change in the kitchen below, beneath the table where you sit writing. And sometimes the suspicion arises that maybe the Studebaker, maybe the Bendix have absorbed man's highest powers.

Can the intellectual, aesthetic, moral genius of the human race have come to a stop? That's impossible. Aeronautical engineers have just shown that the globe can be circumnavigated in a forty-five-hour non-stop flight. That is genius—to lift man and metal from the ground and send them around the face of the earth. Before such an achievement nobody ought to be bored and no one ought to feel isolated. The shuddering of the organ, the vacant dullness of a world that is (temporarily) not a temple, have no great importance. The smell of beer on the dark stairs is nothing. The absence of a human contact is merely temporary. The page in the typewriter describing a certain conversation that never actually took place is an offering placed on the altar of certain gods who—who aren't around just now. But they'll be back, for in time everyone will miss them. Remember Thoreau sitting beside his pond. The industry of his neighbors failed to sever his connection with nature. "You are," the writer may tell himself, "joined with your fellows in a better way. For in actual fact how well are they joined to one another? They form a very loose, friable mass. The comradeship of the assembly line isn't very thick; nor that of the bowling alley, community club, tavern, package store. Camps and barracks were different. But there you drew sneers and hatred if you read books or spoke in your own style. Remember your loyalty to the human spirit and don't drag after the mob protesting that you're not a writer at all but a fisherman or farmer. It would be fear only that made you say such things; the shame of being divorced by difference from other men, and also the fear of the savage strength of the many."

Thus the fiction writer may talk to himself—when he's distracted. For when he is actually at work the excitement of the imagination carries him and he does not need the justification of the vagabond or dedicated idler who by his example will recall his money-chasing brethren to sit down with him and feel their hearts and tell sad tales and be tranquil before the beauty of the external world and all the rest of it. No, for then he is too busy.

But once in a while he is visited by the thought that he is sitting still in the midst of the most widespread destruction. Man's hatred of himself has led in this century to the wildest of wars and demolition of the human image in camps and jails built for that purpose. Bodies stacked like firewood we have seen; and the bodies of the massacred exhumed for the gold in their teeth. And even the so-called years of peace have been years of war. The buying and consumption of goods that keep the economy going, the writer sitting in his room may envision as acts of duty, of service, of war. By our luxury we fight too, eating and drinking and squandering to save our form of government, which survives because it produces and sells vast quantities of things. This sort of duty or service, he thinks, may well destroy our souls. They are taken from us and put to strange uses. Perhaps under it all, he reflects, is a hatred of individual being. "Let it be obliterated" is the secret message we hear. And many in their hearts answer, "Yea, so be it." It may be that this is the hidden purpose of the frantic distraction to which we are exposed. If that is the case, the writer, like the minister of a religion, feels that perhaps he is anachronistic.

"The priest departs, the divine literatus comes," said Whitman. He felt that the office of the poet absorbed the sacerdotal one. In *Democratic Vistas* he gave the poet the responsibility of creating a type of man, an archetype he called it, and he offered himself as a model or representative. We have to begin somewhere. Touch me, he said, and you touch a man. I am not different from others; they are not different from me. What I assume you shall assume. This is not always understood for the act of love that it was. Between the radically unlike there is no love. So the creation of an archetype was to belong to the poet— and the humanist, the scholar. Well now, where are these people? You can see them around the country in various places, most commonly in colleges and universities. They are different, though many of them try not to be. They are powerless. The universities are the warehouses of culture. Let us imagine a man who lives in Akron, Ohio, and teaches the history of the Italian Renaissance. It is dreadful to think what he has to reconcile. Or he teaches ethics and takes part in departmental politics. He behaves shabbily and his own heart cannot bear the contrast. What I am trying to say is that certain ideas can't be held idly. Attempted containment of them is ruin. Lying in his bed in his impoverished attic, Raskolnikov is ashamed of the thoughts of mastery that come into his head; this shame, like a radioactive material, eats through the wall of moral restraint and issues destructively.

He commits a double murder. But it is not only ideas of evil that become destructive. Ideas of good, held in earnest, may be equally damaging to the passive thinker. His passivity puts him in self-contempt. This same contempt may estrange him from the ideas of good. He lives below them and feels dwarfed. On certain occasions a hero in thought, he has become abject in fact and cannot be blamed for feeling that he is not doing a man's work. He reads about man's work in the paper. Men are planning new bond issues, molding public opinion, solving the crisis of the Suez Canal. Men are active. Ideas are passive. Ideas are held in contempt. Literature in these circumstances is contemptible. Of course it is pleasant to have some poets around. All great empires have had them. We are a great empire and need some too. And so Herod sits in his vast palace of advertising and publicity, and once in a while he hears the voice of John from the dungeon. He doesn't even bother to cut off his head.

The writer has no connection with power and yet he keeps thinking about it. I offer a few eighteenth- and nineteenth-century declarations in evidence: "Poets are the unacknowledged legislators of the world." "Give me the making of the songs of a nation and I care not who makes its laws." "Above all previous lands a great original literature is surely to become the justification and reliance (in some respects the sole reliance) of American democracy."

But I should like to point out that impotence has received more attention from modern writers than any other subject. I use the word *impotence* rather loosely to include the loss or defect of the sympathetic power, the failure of feeling (what Elizabeth Bowen has called "the death of the heart") as well as literal incapacity. Here is a brief list:

Oblomov: He spends his life in bed.

Frédéric Moreau in Flaubert's *Sentimental Education*: a life spent on trifles, utterly spoiled.

Captain Ahab: "I have lost the low enjoying power." He means that he is distracted. Natural beauty is recognized by his mind but it doesn't move him.

Clym Yeobright in *The Return of the Native*: empty of the feeling that Eustacia desires.

Dostoyevsky's hero or anti-hero in *Notes from Underground*: His

There Is Simply Too Much to Think About

spite, his coldness, his venom, combined with the largeness of his mind, give him an exceptional stature.

Leopold Bloom: the distracted and impotent man.

I could add hundreds more to this list, from Lawrence or Proust or Hemingway and their innumerable imitators. They all tell the same story. The dread is great, the soul is small; man might be godlike, but he is wretched; the heart should be open but is sealed by fear. If man, wretched by nature, is represented, what we have here is only accurate reporting. But if it is man in the image of God, man a little lower than the angels, who is impotent, the case is not the same. And it is the second assumption, the subangelic one, that writers generally make. I don't know whether *exaggeration* is quite the word, but what it suggests we can certainly agree with. Why should wretched man need power or wish to inflate himself with imaginary glory? If this is what power signifies, it can only be vanity to suffer from impotence. On the nobler assumption, he should have at least sufficient power to overcome ignominy and to complete his own life. His suffering, feebleness, servitude then have a meaning. This is what writers have taken to be the justification of power. It should reveal the greatness of man. And if no other power will do this the power of imagination will take the task upon itself.

"That undisturbed, innocent, somnambulatory production by which alone anything great can thrive, is no longer possible," said Goethe to Eckermann. "Our talents at present lie before the public. The daily criticisms which appear in fifty different places, and the gossip that is caused by them among the public, prevent the appearance of any sound production. . . . He who does not keep aloof from all this, and isolate himself by main force, is lost."

So if the writer is wise he will avoid certain books and papers and magazines and social circles. But perhaps wisdom won't help. Everybody talks. The cat is already out of the bag. You go to a party and a psychiatrist tells you that *his* analyst believes literature is dying. This is an act of aggression. But how can a novelist be expected to stay away from parties? He must go and he must inevitably hear the worst, exposing his somnambulatory innocence to grave dangers. Once more the boom is lowered on the flowers. But they will grow again. There is man's own greatness and then there is the greatness of his imbecility—both are eternal.

It's only natural that writers should have their enemies. It's the rule of life, among writers as among snakes, mice and lice. The subtler creatures have subtler enemies. The subtlest of enemies are those who get you over to their own side. You read the authoritative words of an eminent critic; they sound reasonable; you half agree and then are distracted and stiflingly depressed.

Finished! We have heard this from Valéry and from T. S. Eliot, from Ortega and from Oswald Spengler and most recently from the summit of Morningside Heights. We are supposed to be done for. The great dinosaurs are gone; only vestigial Gila monsters remain. Oh, to have once more the unimportance of that poor poet whom Brutus and Cassius threw out! For every poet now there are a hundred custodians and doctors of literature and dozens of undertakers measuring away at coffins. If only, says D. H. Lawrence in a poem, man were as much man as the lizard is lizard! If only the novelist, thought merely a degenerate Gila monster, were at least a true Gila monster! He would sit in the sun undistracted and catch flies.

The novelist has been trained to take words seriously and he thinks he is hearing words of high seriousness. He believes it is the voice of high seriousness saying, "Obsolete. Finished." But what if it were to prove to be the voice of low seriousness instead?

Scholars and critics are often curiously like property owners. They have their lots surveyed. Here the property begins and there it ends. A conservative instinct in them—which every lover of order will recognize and respect—resists extension, calls for limits. And why not? Besides, it's awfully fine to be an epigone. It tickles one so in the self-esteem. But how odd it is that these words *obsolete* and *finished* should never be spoken with regret or pain. The accent is rather one of satisfaction. And this is all the more strange because if the critics are wrong, their opinions will do harm. They are certain to be destructive.

The students of literature line up with the epigones. "Thank God!" they say. "It's over. We have a field. We can study." Well, it does seem logical that the thing should have an end. The libraries and the second-hand stores are very full, as I've already observed. Isn't it enough that the physical universe overwhelms us with its immensities; must the works of man flood us as well? But I wonder whether novels can be studied with much profit or even read if we don't continue to write them. Not professional study but imagination keeps imagination alive. Samuel Butler offers a theory to which I subscribe: "All things which come to much," he says, "whether they be books, buildings, pictures or living beings, are suggested by others of their kind." I wonder what historical reasons there are for this process of suggestion to stop. And what will happen to *Anna Karenina* or to the *Iliad* if they are never read by those to whom they may suggest others of their kind? Literature, all of it, will then be extinct.

"The novel has died a victim to the loss of an agreed picture of the Universe, which has faded with the stifling of Christianity by nondogmatic idealism and crude materialism." Thus writes Mr. J. M. Cohen in his recent *History of Western European Literature*. His is the bluntest, flattest, most Spartan statement of the position and I like it because there is something wonderfully bureaucratic about it. It reminds me of the textbooks I studied in college. "The Crusades were begun because . . ." "The following developments made possible the beginning of the Renaissance in Italy. . . ." It is always like that, blunt, plain and positive. Textbooks told us what the prerequisites were for a flourishing literature. The end of feudalism, the rise of the burghers, the Reformation, the Age of Reason, the growth of science (et cetera) made possible the great century of the novel. The method has worked so well (obviously) in explaining the past that now scholars have decided to project it into the future. This is a new branch of the historians' art—*made* history. Ever since M. Jourdain, the bourgeois gentleman, discovered that his everyday speech was Prose, writers have written Literature, painters have painted Art, musicians have composed Music and now culture-historians create Culture epoch by epoch, past, present and future.

An agreed picture of the Universe? What is that? And when we have come to know what it means, if we can, must we believe that novels have become poor because they lack it? It has recently been well argued by Jacob Bronowski in *The Nation* that the imagination of the scientist is not vastly different from that of the artist. Does the scientific imagination also have need of an agreed picture of the Universe? Science quickly changes the agreed pictures. And why does it survive so well the stifling of Christianity?

The argument that the novel is dying or dead is made by men who shut the door on multiplicity and distraction. They suppose the distraction to be too great for the imagination to overcome. When they speak of an agreed picture what they mean is that we are a mass civilization, doomed to be shallow and centerless. Question: "And what if the soul doesn't accept?" Answer: "It had better. Its acceptance is historically determined." But this smells of bars and prisons. And we started out to talk of literature and happiness! How busy the grimmer impulses are!

Why were we born? What are we doing here? Where are we going? In its eternal naïveté the imagination keeps coming back to these things. It does this when we have an agreed picture and when we haven't. For it isn't an agreed picture that makes man interesting to himself. It isn't history and it isn't culture; the interest is intrinsic. And it's not unfair to ask those literary people who argue that the novel is dead whether their own feelings are fresh or tired. Life quickly wears us out; there is good reason to be tired. But this is not a matter for the tired to settle.

We are living in what they call an eschatological age. Whole worlds have become as light as Ping-Pong balls. At lunch we talk about good and evil, death and immortality, and over cocktails metaphysical questions are raised as if the world, like the bottles, might be empty by dinnertime. Then why should so minor a thing as The Novel escape its moment of question?

A lot of things have been called obsolete. I brooded over Spengler in college. As a Jew I was, in his vocabulary, a Magian and therefore obsolete. Toynbee, unless I am mistaken, has a similar view of Jews, that they are a sort of fossil. Marx and Engels too were prophets of obsolescence. For Stalin the kulaks were obsolete; for Hitler, all the inferior breeds of men. In the dustbins of various reform movements are found numerous orthodoxies called obsolete. And we all know—what else does Mr. Cohen mean when he speaks of the stifling of Christianity?—that God has been called obsolete. I don't mean to say that there is no such thing as obsolescence. I merely wish to show that the term *obsolete*,

There Is Simply Too Much to Think About

derived from evolutionary thought, has a place of some importance in the history of modern persecution. Far, far down in the scale of power, far from Rome and Berlin and Leningrad, in certain academic and critical circles, we hear it said that a particular kind of imagination is now obsolete. The objective conditions necessary for its existence are supposedly gone. I've never heard it stated in these circles that money is obsolete or that social advancement and distinction are obsolete. Apparently these things are hardier and don't require the same agreement as to the nature of the Universe.

Well, such an issue can never be settled in debate. Neither the denials of academic people nor the affirmations of writers can make much difference. "To believe in the existence of human beings as such is love," says Simone Weil. This is what makes the difference. It is possible—all too possible—to say when we have read one more modern novel, "So what? What do I care? You yourself, the writer, didn't really care." It is all too often like that. But this caring or believing or love alone matters. All the rest, obsolescence, historical views, manners, agreed views of the Universe, is simply nonsense and trash. If we don't care, don't immediately care, then perish books both old and new, and novelists and governments too. If we do care, if we believe in the existence of others, then what we write is necessary.

The writer asks himself, "Why shall I write this next thing?" It is still possible, despite all theories to the contrary, to answer, "Because it *is* necessary." A book, any book, may easily be superfluous. But to manifest love—can this be superfluous? Is there so much of it about us? Not so much. It is still rare, still wonderful. It is still effective against distraction.

[1957]

Deep Readers of the World, Beware!

Interviewed as he was getting on the train for Boston, E. M. Forster was asked how he felt on the eve of his first visit to Harvard. He replied that he had heard that there were some particularly deep readers of his books to be found in Cambridge. He expected to be questioned closely by them and this worried him. The reason is perfectly understandable.

In this age of ours serious people are more serious than they ever were and lightness of heart like Mr. Forster's is hard to find. To the serious a novel is a work of art; art has a role to play in the drama of civilized life; civilized life is set upon a grim and dangerous course—and so we may assume if we are truly serious that no good novelist is going to invite us to a picnic merely to eat egg salad and chase butterflies over the English meadows or through the Tuscan woods. Butterflies are gay, all right, but in them lies the secret of metamorphosis. As for eggs, life's mystery hides in the egg. We all know that. So much for butterflies and egg salad.

It would be unjust to say that the responsibility for this sort of thing belongs entirely to the reader. Often the writer himself is at fault. He doesn't mind if he *is* a little deeper than average. Why not?

Nevertheless deep reading has gone very far. It has become dangerous to literature.

"Why, sir," the student asks, "does Achilles drag the body of Hector around the walls of Troy?" "That sounds like a stimulating question. Most interesting. I'll bite," says the professor. "Well, you see, sir, the *Iliad* is full of circles—shields, chariot wheels and other round figures. And you know what Plato said about circles. The Greeks were all made for geometry." "Bless your crew-cut head," says the professor, "for such a beautiful thought. You have exquisite sensibility. Your approach is both deep and serious. Still, I always believed that Achilles did it because he was so angry."

It would take an unusual professor to realize that Achilles *was* angry. To many teachers he would represent much but he would not *be* anything in particular. To be is too obvious. Our professor, however, is a "square" and the bright student is annoyed with him. Anger! What good is anger? Great literature is subtle, dignified, profound. Homer is as good as Plato anytime; and if Plato thought, Homer must surely have done so too, thought just as beautifully circle for circle.

Things are not what they seem. And anyway, unless they represent something large and worthy writers will not bother with them. Any deep reader can tell you that picking up a bus transfer is the *Reisemotif* when it happens in a novel. A travel folder signifies Death. Coal holes represent the Underworld. Soda crackers are the Host. Three bottles of beer are—it's obvious. The busy mind can hardly miss at this game and every player is a winner.

Are you a Marxist? Then Herman Melville's *Pequod* in *Moby-Dick* can be a factory, Ahab the manager, the crew the working class. Is your point of view religious? The *Pequod* sailed on Christmas morning, a floating cathedral headed south. Do you follow Freud or Jung? Then your interpretations may be rich and multitudinous. I recently had a new explanation of *Moby-Dick* from the young man in charge of an electronic brain. "Once and for all," he said. "That whale is everybody's mother wallowing in her watery bed. Ahab has the Oedipus complex and wants to slay the hell out of her."

This is deep reading. But it is only fair to remember that the best novelists and poets of the century have done much to promote it. When Mairy (in James Joyce's *Ulysses*) loses the pin of her drawers she doesn't know what to do to keep them up; the mind of Bloom goes from grammar to painting, from painting to religion. It is all accomplished in a few words. Joyce's genius holds all the elements in balance.

The deep reader, however, is apt to lose his head. He falls wildly on any particle of philosophy or religion and blows it up bigger than the Graf Zeppelin. Does Bloom dust Stephen's clothes and brush off the wood shavings? They are no ordinary shavings but the shavings from Stephen's cross.

Deep Readers of the World, Beware!

What else? All the little monkish peculiarities at which Robert Browning poked fun in the "Soliloquy in a Spanish Cloister," crossing knife and fork on the platter at the end of a meal and the rest of it, have become the pillars of the new system.

Are we to attach meaning to whatever is grazed by the writer? Is modern literature Scripture? Is criticism Talmud, theology? Deep readers of the world, beware! You had better be sure that your seriousness is indeed high seriousness and not, God forbid, low seriousness.

A true symbol is substantial, not accidental. You cannot avoid it, you cannot remove it. You can't take the handkerchief from *Othello* or the sea from *The Nigger of the "Narcissus"* or the disfigured feet from *Oedipus Rex*. You can, however, read *Ulysses* without suspecting that wood shavings have to do with the Crucifixion or that the name Simon refers to the sin of simony or that the hunger of the Dubliners at noon parallels that of the Laestrygonians. These are purely peripheral matters; fringe benefits, if you like. The beauty of the book cannot escape you if you are any sort of reader, and it is better to approach it from the side of naïveté than from that of culture-idolatry, sophistication and snobbery. Of course it's hard in our time to be as naïve as one would like. Information does filter through. It leaks, as we have taken to saying. Still the knowledge of even the sophisticated is rather thin and even the most wised-up devils, stuffed to the ears with arcana, turn out to be fairly simple.

Perhaps the deepest readers are those who are least sure of themselves. An even more disturbing suspicion is that they prefer meaning to feeling. What, again about the feelings? Yes, it's too bad. I'm sorry to have to ring in this tiresome subject but there's no help for it. The reason the schoolboy takes refuge in circles is that the wrath of Achilles and the death of Hector are too much for him. He is doing no more than most civilized people do when confronted with passion and death. They contrive somehow to avoid them.

The practice of avoidance is so widespread that it is probably not fair to single out any group for blame. But if nothing is to be said or done, we might as well make ready to abandon literature altogether. Novels are being published today that consist entirely of abstractions, meanings, and while our need for meanings is certainly great our need for

There Is Simply Too Much to Think About

concreteness, for particulars, is even greater. We need to see how human beings act after they have appropriated or assimilated the meanings. Meanings themselves are a dime a dozen. In literature humankind becomes abstract when we begin to dislike it. And . . . Interruption by a deep reader: Yes, yes, we know all that. But just look at the novels of the concrete and the particular, people opening doors and lighting cigarettes. Aren't they boring? Besides, do you want us to adopt a program to curtail the fear of feeling and to pretend to *like* the creature of flesh and bone?

Certainly not. No programs.

A pretty pass we have come to!

We must leave it to inspiration to redeem the concrete and the particular and to recover the value of flesh and bone. Meanwhile, let Plato have his circles and let the soda crackers be soda crackers and the wood shavings wood shavings. They are mysterious enough as it is.

[1959]

A Talk with the Yellow Kid

I have always affected a pearl stickpin upon my neckwear," says Yellow Kid Weil. The Kid, who is now in his eighties, is an elegant and old-fashioned gentleman; he likes round phrases and leisurely speech. One of the greatest confidence men of his day, he has publicly forsworn crime and announced his retirement. A daughter of his in Florida urges him to pass his remaining years with her, but he prefers Chicago. He will tell you that he knows of no better place and he has lived in many places. Chicago is his city.

As we stood talking in the lobby of the Sun-Times Building not long ago, a young photographer came running up to the famous criminal, threw an arm about his narrow old shoulders, and said affectionately, "Hi ya, Kid. Kid, how's it goin'?" At such moments his bearded old face is lit with a smile of deepest pleasure and looks of modesty and of slyness also steal over it. Bartenders, waitresses, reporters know him. The vanishing race of old intellectuals in the neighborhood of Bughouse Square respects him. Real estate men, lawyers, even judges and bankers will sometimes greet him. Why should he live elsewhere? He was born in Chicago, his career began there.

It was Bathhouse John Coughlin, Chicago's primitive alderman and illustrious boss, who named him the Yellow Kid. Bathhouse had started out in life as a masseur in the old Brevoort Hotel. When he attained great power he was not too proud to talk to a young fellow like Joe Weil, as the Kid was then known. Weil came often to Coughlin's saloon. An early comic strip called "Hogan's Alley and the Yellow Kid" was then appearing in the *New York Journal*, to which Coughlin subscribed. Weil followed it passionately and Bathhouse John saved the papers for him. "Why, you're the Kid himself," Coughlin said one day, and so Weil acquired the name.

The Kid is now very frail and it becomes him. His beard very much resembles the one that the late Senator James Hamilton Lewis, a great dandy, used to wear. It is short, parted in the middle and combed into two rounded portions, white and stiff. Beneath the whiskers the Kid's chin is visible, an old man's chin. You think you have met with a happy old quack, a small-time charlatan who likes to reminisce about the wickedness of his past, until you become aware of the thin, forceful, sharp mouth under the trembling hairs of old age. It is the mouth of a masterful man.

He must once have been very imposing. Now there is a sort of fallen nattiness about him. His shoes are beautifully shined, though not in top condition. His suit is made of a bold material; it has gone too often to the cleaner but it is in excellent press. His shirt must belong to the days of his prosperity for his neck has shrunk and the collar fits loosely. The cloth has a green pattern of squares within squares. Tie and pocket and handkerchief are of a matching green. His little face is clear and animated. Long practice in insincerity gives him an advantage; it is not always easy to know where he is coming from.

By his swindles he made millions of dollars, but he lost as many fortunes as he made and he lost them always in legitimate enterprises. This is one of his favorite ironies and he often returns to it. His wife was forever urging him to go straight. He loved her—he still speaks touchingly of her—and for her sake he wanted to reform. It never worked. There was a curse on any honest business that he tried, whether it was giving pianos away as a coffee premium or leasing the Hagenbeck-Wallace circus. An inner voice seemed to warn him to stay crooked and he did not ignore it.

The years have not softened his heart toward the victims of his confidence schemes. Of course he was a crook, but the "marks" he and his associates trimmed were not honest men. "I have never cheated any honest men," he says, "only rascals. They may have been respectable, but they were never any good." And this is how he sums the matter up: "They wanted something for nothing. I gave them nothing for something." He says it clearly and sternly; he is not a pitying man. To be sure, he wants to justify his crimes, but quite apart from this he believes that honest men do not exist. He presents himself as a Diogenes whose lifelong daylight quest for absolute honesty ended in disappointment. Actually he never expected to find it.

He is a thinker, the Kid is, and a reader. His favorite authors seem to be Nietzsche and Herbert Spencer. Spencer has always been the favorite of autodidactic Midwestern philosophers, that vanishing species. During the 1920s the Kid belonged to a bohemian discussion group on the Near North Side called the Dil Pickle Club. Its brainy and colorful fleet of eccentrics—poets, painters and cranks—have long been dispersed by vulgar winds. Once Chicago promised to become a second London, but it was not to be; bowling alleys and bars increased, bookshops did not. New York and Hollywood took away the artists. Death did the rest. Herbert Spencer also was destined for the dustbin.

But the Kid is still faithful to him; he spends his evenings at his books—so at least he says—mediating upon the laws of society, the sanctioned and the unsanctioned, power and weakness, justice and history. I do not think the Kid loves the weak and he dislikes many of the strong, especially politicians and bankers. Against bankers he has a strong prejudice. "They are almost always shady," he says. "Their activities are usually only just within the law."

The twilight borderlands of legality attract the Kid's subtle mind. Not long ago he was picked up in the lobby of the Bismarck Hotel on suspicion. He had merely been chatting with one of the guests, he told me, but the manager was worried and phoned the confidence squad. The Kid is used to these small injustices and they do not offend him or disturb his tranquillity. In court he listened attentively to the case preceding his own, that of a bookie.

"Why should this man be fined and punished?" said the Kid when his turn came at the bar. "Why should he be punished for betting when betting is permitted within the confines of the track itself?" The judge, to hear the Kid tell it, was very uneasy. He answered that the state derived revenues from the track. "I would gladly pay revenues to the state," the Kid said, "if I could rent a building within which confidence games would be legal. Suppose the state were to license me. Then confidence men operating outside my building could be arrested and imprisoned. Inside the door, licensed operatives would be safe. It makes the same kind of sense, Your Honor." According to the Kid, the judge offered "no cogent reply."

Perhaps the Kid's antagonism toward bankers rests on an undivulged belief that he would have made a more impressive banker than any of them. In his swindles he often enough pretended to be one. With phony Wall Street credentials he would take in the president of some country bank who would be only too eager to give him permission to make use of his premises. Often the Kid would find a pretext to sit in the president's own office. Entering, his victims would see him seated behind the great mahogany desk and take him for the president.

At one time the Kid was actually the legitimate officer of a bank, the American State Bank on South La Salle Street in Chicago. He and Big John Worthington, a confidence man who closely resembled J. Pierpont Morgan, together paid some seventy thousand dollars and obtained a controlling interest. The Kid became a vice president. He started a racket in phony letters of credit by which he made about three hundred thousand dollars. He was not caught. On another occasion the Kid rented an empty bank building and filled it with his stooges. The stooges made it look busy; they arrived with bogus currency for deposit and bags full of lead slugs. Taken in by this activity, the mark was swindled easily by the Kid. Once, he took a suite of offices in the heart of Chicago's financial district. Girls from secretarial schools were hired to look busy. They typed names from the telephone directory.

Sometimes the Kid posed as a doctor, sometimes as a mining engineer or a professor or a geologist. Or, during World War I, as a financial representative of the Central Powers. He put magazines and books into circulation from which original photographs were removed and pictures of himself inserted. All his life long he sold nonexistent property, concessions he did not own, and air-spun schemes to greedy men.

The Kid's activities landed him in jail now and then—he has served time in Atlanta and Leavenworth—but he says, and not unbelievably, that there were not many dull days in his life. His total gains are estimated by the "police and the daily press" at about eight millions. Most of this money he lost in bad investments or squandered in high living.

He loved wild parties, showgirls, champagne suppers, European trips. He had his clothes made in Bond Street or Jermyn Street. The English wardrobe is still good; real quality doesn't go out of fashion. But almost everything else is gone.

"Before I reached the years of maturity," the Kid said, "I fell in love with a young woman of the most extraordinary pulchritude. I brought her home one night to dinner. My mother," he said with a bluster of his whiskers and looking gravely at me with the thin diffused blue of his eyes, "was renowned for her perfection in the culinary art. We had a splendid meal and later my mother said to me, 'Joseph, that is a most beautiful young woman. She is so lovely that she cannot be meant for you. She must have been meant for some millionaire.' From that moment I determined that I, too, would be a millionaire. And I was." The sexual incentive to be rich, the Kid told me, was always very powerful with him.

"I was of a very fragile constitution, unfit for the heavier sort of manual labor. I knew I could not toil like other men. How was I to live? My power lay in words. In words I became a commander. Moreover, I could not lead a tame life of monotony. I needed excitement, variety, danger, intellectual stimulus.

"I was a psychologist," he went on. "My domain was the human mind. A Chinese scholar with whom I once studied told me, 'People always see themselves in you.' With this understanding, I entered the lives of my dupes. The man who lives by an idea enjoys great superiority over those who live by none. To make money is not an idea; that doesn't count. I mean a real idea. It was very simple. My purpose was invisible. When they looked at me they saw themselves. I only showed them their own purpose."

There are no longer such operators, says the great confidence man, perhaps jealous of his eminence. Where are they to come from? The great mass of mankind breeds obedient types. They express their protests in acts of violence, not ingeniously. Moreover, your natural or talented confidence man is attracted to politics. Why be a robber, a fugitive, when you can get society to give you the key to the vaults where the greatest boodle lies? The United States government, according to the Kid, runs the greatest giveaway program in history.

There Is Simply Too Much to Think About

The Kid at one time tried to found an independent little republic upon a small island made of fill, somewhere in Lake Michigan. His object was to make himself eligible for foreign-aid grants.

A prominent figure, something of a public man, a dandy and a philosopher, the Kid says that he now frequently does good works. But the confidence squad still keeps an eye on him. Not so long ago he was walking down the street with a certain monsignor, he tells me. They were discussing a fund drive in the parish. Presently the con squad drew alongside and one of the detectives said, "What you up to, Kid?"

"I'm just helping out the monsignor here. It's on the level."

The monsignor assured him that this was true.

The detective turned on him. "Why, you so-and-so," he said. "Aren't you ashamed to be wearin' the cloth for a swindle?"

The thought so enraged him that he took them both to headquarters.

The Kid laughed quietly and long over the copper's error; wrinkled, bearded, wry and delighted, he looked at this moment like one of the devil's party.

"They refuse to believe I have reformed," he said. The psychology of a policeman, according to the Kid, is strict, narrow and primitive. It denies that character is capable of change.

So much for the police, incurably, hopelessly dumb. But what about the criminals? The Kid did not think much of criminal intelligence either. And how does the underworld see the confidence men? I asked. Gangsters and thieves greatly dislike them, he said. They never trust them, and in some cases they take a peculiar and moral view of the confidence swindler. He is too mental a type for them.

"The attitude of the baser sort of criminal toward me is very interesting," he said. "They have always either shunned or behaved with extreme coldness to me. I never will forget a discussion I once had with a second-story man about our respective relations to our victims. He thought me guilty of the highest immorality. Worst of all, in his eyes, was the fact that I openly showed myself to dupes in the light of day. 'Why,' he said to me with an indescribable demeanor, 'you go right up to them. *They see your face!*' This seemed to him the worst of all deceits. Such is their scheme of ethics," said the Kid. "In their view, you should sneak up on people to pick their pockets, or break and enter to burglarize their houses, but to look them in the eyes, gain their confidence, that is impure."

We parted on noisy Wacker Drive, near the Clark Street Bridge. No longer listening to the Kid, I heard the voice of the city. Chicago keeps changing, amazing its old-timers. The streetcars, for instance, are different. You no longer see the hard, wicked-looking, red, cumbrous, cowlike, trampling giant streetcars. The new ones are green and whir by like dragonflies. Glittering and making soft electrical sounds, one passed the Kid as he walked toward the Loop. Spruce and firm-footed, with his beard and wind-curled hat, he looked, beside the car, like the living figure of tradition in the city.

[1956]

The Sixties

———◆•◆•◆———

The Sealed Treasure

A few years ago I traveled through the state of Illinois to gather material for an article. It was brilliant fall weather; the corn was high and it was intersected by straight, flat roads over which it was impossible not to drive at top speed. I went from Chicago to Galena and then south through the center of the state to Cairo and Shawneetown. Here and there, in some of the mining counties and in the depopulated towns along the Mississippi, there were signs of depression and poverty, but these had the flavor of the far away and long ago for the rest of the state was dizzily affluent. "Pig Heaven," some people said to me. "Never nothing like it." The shops were filled with goods and buyers. In the fields were the newest harvesting machines; in the houses washers, dryers, freezers and refrigerators, air conditioners, vacuum cleaners, Mixmasters, Waring blenders, television and stereophonic hi-fi sets, electrical can openers, novels condensed by *Reader's Digest* and slick magazines. In the yards glossy cars in giddy colors, like ships from outer space.

. . . For the most part, everything was as new as possible. Churches and supermarkets had the same modern design. In the skies the rich farmers piloted their own planes. The workers bowled in alleys of choice hardwood where fouls were scored and pins reset by electrical devices. Fifty years ago the Illinois poet Vachel Lindsay had visited these towns preaching the Gospel of Beauty and calling on the people to build the New Jerusalem.

Except for the main stem the streets were boringly empty and at night even the main stem was almost deserted. Restless adolescents gathered in the ice cream parlors or loitered before the chain saws, vibrating recliners, outboard motors and garbage disposal units displayed in shop windows. These, like master spirits, ruled the night in silence.

Some important ingredients of life were conspicuously absent.

I had been asked to write about Illinois, but how was I to distinguish it from Indiana, Michigan, Iowa or Missouri? The houses were built and furnished in the same style, the cows were milked by the same machines, the programs broadcast by CBS and NBC were alike in Rockford, Illinois, and Danbury, Connecticut, and Salt Lake City, Utah. The magazines, the hairstyles, the salad dressings, the film stars were not merely American but international. What but slight differences in the menu and the cut of the clothes distinguished the comfortable life of middle-class Illinois from that of Cologne or Frankfurt?

I asked, "What do people do hereabouts?" "They work." "And when they don't work?" "They watch TV. They play a little poker or canasta or gin." "What else?" "They go to club meetings. Or to the drive-in movie. They pitch a little. They raise a little hell. They bowl. They drink some. They tinker around the place, fool with power tools. They teach the kids baseball in the Little League. They're den mothers over at the Cub Scouts." "Yes, but what do they *do*?" "Well, mister, I'm telling you what they do. What are you getting at?" "You see, I'm writing an article on life here." "Is *that* so! Gosh, you're barking up the wrong tree. There ain't nothing here to write about. There's nothing doing here or anywhere in Ellenois. It's boring." "You can't have millions of people and nothing doing." "I tell you, you want to write about Hollywood or Las Vegas or New York or Paris. That's where they've got excitement."

I had a score of conversations like this one.

Was the vitality of these people entirely absorbed by the new things? Had a superior inventive and productive power taken them over, paralyzing all the faculties it did not need? Or had the old understanding of reality been based on the threat of hunger and on the continual necessity for hard labor? Was it possible that what people complained of as boredom might in fact be an unbearable excitement caused by the greatness of the change?

I went to the public libraries and was not surprised to learn that good books were very much in demand and that there were people in central Illinois who read Plato, Tocqueville, Proust and Robert Frost. I had expected this. But what I did not understand was what use these

There Is Simply Too Much to Think About

isolated readers were making of the books they borrowed. With whom did they discuss them? At the country club, the bowling league, sorting mail at the post office, or in the factory, over the back fence, how did they bring up Plato's Justice or Proust's Memory? Ordinary life gave them little opportunity for such conversation. "You can't have millions of people and nothing doing." I was dead sure of that. But the intelligence or cultivation of a woman in Moline, Illinois, would necessarily be her secret, almost her private vice. Her friends at the bridge club would think it very odd of her to think such things. She might not reveal them to her sister or perhaps even to her husband. They would be her discovery, her treasure ten times sealed, her private source of power.

"The language, the dress, and the daily actions of men in democracies are repugnant to ideal conceptions," said Tocqueville. He said more but this is text enough for the moment. Let us set beside it the fact that these men, or some of them, will read *The Divine Comedy*, *The Tempest* and *Don Quixote*. What will they make of these works? They will, some of them, mix them up with television productions. Others will scale them down. Our understanding of them (it is time to drop the third person) will certainly be faulty. Nevertheless they move us. That is to say, human greatness can still be seen by us. And it is not a question of the gnat who sees the elephant. We are not members of a different species. Without a certain innate sympathy we could not read Shakespeare and Cervantes. In our own contemporary novels this power to understand the greatest human qualities appears to be dispersed, transformed or altogether buried. A modern mass society has no open place for such qualities, no vocabulary for them and no ceremony (except in the churches) that makes them public. So they remain private and are mingled with other private things that vex us or of which we feel ashamed. But they are not lost. The saleswoman in Moline, Illinois, *will* go to the library and borrow *Anna Karenina*. This society, with its titanic products, conditions but cannot absolutely denature us. It forces certain elements of the genius of our species to go into hiding. In America these hidden elements take curiously personal secret forms. Sometimes they corrupt people; sometimes they cause them to act with startling generosity. On the whole they are not to be found in what we call our Culture.

They are not in the streets, in the stores, at the movies. They are the missing ingredients.

The greatest danger, Dostoyevsky warned in *The Brothers Karamazov*, was the universal anthill. D. H. Lawrence believed the common people of our industrial cities were like the great slave populations of the ancient empires. Joyce was apparently convinced that what happened to the ordinary modern man, his external life, was not interesting enough to chronicle. James Stephens in his preface to *Solitaria* by the Russian philosopher Rozanov said that novelists were trying to keep alive by artificial means feelings and states of being which had died out of the modern world, implying that we were only flattering the dwarfs by investing them with the passions of dead giants.

Mind manipulation, brainwashing and social engineering are only the newest developments in an evolution long understood by writers of the civilized world. When we read the best nineteenth- and twentieth-century novelists we soon realize that they are trying in a variety of ways to establish a definition of human nature, to justify the continuation of life as well as the writing of novels. Like it or not, says Dostoyevsky, it is our nature to be free and, under the sting of suffering, to choose between good and evil. And Tolstoy says of human nature that it contains a need for truth that will never allow it to rest permanently in falsehood or unreality.

I think the novelists who take the bitterest view of our modern condition make the most of the art of the novel. "Do you think," Flaubert replies to a correspondent who has complained of *Madame Bovary*, "that this ignoble reality, so disgusting to you in reproduction, does not oppress my heart as it does yours? If you knew me better you would know that I abhor ordinary existence. Personally, I have always held myself as aloof from it as I could. But aesthetically I desired this once—and only once—to plumb its very depths."

The writer's art appears to seek a compensation for the hopelessness or meanness of existence. By some occult method the writer has connected himself with the feelings and ideal conceptions of which few signs remain in ordinary existence. Some novelists, the naturalists, have staked everything on ordinary existence in their desire to keep their connection with the surrounding world. Many of these have turned themselves into recording instruments at best, and at worst they have sucked up to the crowd, disgustingly. But the majority of modern novelists have followed the standard of Flaubert, the aesthetic standard. The shock caused by the loss of faith, says Professor Erich Heller in *The Disinherited Mind*, made Jakob Burckhardt adopt an aesthetic view of history. If he is right, a sharp sense of disappointment and aestheticism go together. Flaubert complained that the exterior world was "disgusting, enervating, corruptive and brutalizing . . . I am turning toward a kind of aesthetic mysticism," he wrote.

I am sticking to Flaubert because the connection between Yonville in Normandy and Galesburg in Illinois is constantly growing closer; because Flaubert believed that the writer by means of imagery and style must supply the human qualities that the exterior world lacked. And because we have all been schooled in his method we are like the isolated lady in Moline whose sensitivity is her ten-times-sealed treasure.

Disappointment with its human material is built into the contemporary novel. It is assumed that society cannot give the novelist "suitable" themes and characters. Therefore the important humanity of the novel must be the writer's own. His force, his virtuosity, his powers of poetry, his reading of fate are at the center of his book. The reader is invited to bring his sympathies to the writer rather than to the characters, and this makes him something of a novelist too.

The insistent aesthetic purpose in novelists like Flaubert and Henry James and Virginia Woolf and James Joyce is tyrannical at times. It overconditions the situation of the characters. We are greatly compensated with poetry and insight, but it often seems as though the writer were deprived of all power except the power to see and to despair. In reality, however, he has a very great power. Is it likely that westerns, thrillers, movies, soap operas and true confessions can usurp that power and permanently replace it? Not unless human nature is malleable without limits and can be conditioned to do without its ancient bread and meat.

A work of fiction consists of a series of moments during which we are willingly engrossed in the experiences of others. Or, as a recent article in *The Hudson Review* puts it, "the exuberant conviction that the individual life of *somebody else* holds all human truth and human potentiality" must be shared by the novelist and his reader. Let us say, putting it as mildly as possible, that modern society does not often inspire this exuberant conviction. We have learned to lie to ourselves about this. Americans, softly optimistic, do lie about the love they bear one another. My informant in Illinois was telling the truth when he said his life was boring, but he would have turned awfully pious if I had asked him whether he loved his neighbor. Then he would have stood on the creed and answered that he felt a boundless love for him.

The matter was put as strongly as possible by D. H. Lawrence. "The sympathetic heart is broken," he said. "We stink in each other's nostrils." That is, we cannot easily accept our own creaturely existence or that of others. And that is the fault of modern civilization, he tells us. We must in part agree, but the matter is so serious that we should be careful not to exaggerate. Our lives depend on it. Yes, there are good reasons for revulsion and fear. But revulsion and fear impair judgment. Anxiety destroys scale and suffering makes us lose perspective.

One would have to be optimistic to the point of imbecility to raise the standard of pure Affirmation and cry, "Yea, yea," shrilly against the deep background of nays. But the sympathetic heart is sometimes broken, sometimes not. It is reckless to say "broken"; it is nonsense to say "whole and unimpaired." On either side we have the black and white of paranoia.

As for the novelist, he must proceed with care and modesty. He should deplore no general evil on purely literary grounds. The world owes him nothing and he has no business to be indignant with it on behalf of the novel. He must not expect life to bind itself to be stable for his sake or to accommodate his ambitions. If he must, let him, like Flaubert, "abhor ordinary existence." But he should not fall into despair over trifles. One of his legacies from romanticism is a sensitivity to banality and ugliness, in which originates much of the small change of

There Is Simply Too Much to Think About

modern fiction—the teeth that are crooked, the soiled underclothes, the clerk with carbuncles. From this comes a conventional unearned wretchedness, a bitterness about existence that is mere fashion.

The enormous increases in population seem to have dwarfed the individual. So have modern physics and astronomy. But we may be somewhere between a false greatness and a false insignificance. At least we can stop misrepresenting ourselves to ourselves and realize that the only thing we can be in this world is human. We are temporarily miracle-sodden and feeling faint.

[1960]

On Jewish Storytelling

The religion of the Jews has appeared to the world as divinely inspired history. The message of the Old Testament, however, cannot be easily separated from its stories and metaphors. Various commentators, unrestrained by orthodoxy and looking at the Bible with the clear or cold eye of the twentieth century, have spoken of the books of both testaments as novels. The late Ernest Sutherland Bates edited a Bible "to read as living literature" and D. H. Lawrence spoke of the patriarchs and King David as though they were fictional characters. Thomas Mann, in one of his Joseph novels, suggests that in having a story to tell, the nearly tragic account of the envy of his brethren (how he was given a coat of many colors; how his brothers were angry; how he was sold into Egypt by them; how his father mourned him; how he was molested by Potiphar's wife and imprisoned; how he interpreted dreams and rose to greatness; how there was a famine in the land and his brothers came to buy grain; how he revealed himself at last to them)—that in having such a story to tell, Joseph may have been a greater man than the Pharaoh, his master. For there is power in a story. It testifies to the worth, the significance of an individual. For a short while all the strength and all the radiance of the world are brought to bear upon a few human figures. Hamlet, dying, says to his friend: "O good Horatio, what a wounded name, Things standing thus unknown, shall live behind me! If thou didst ever hold me in thy heart, Absent thee from felicity awhile, And in this harsh world draw thy breath in pain, To tell my story." In defeat, a story contains the hope of vindication, of justice. The storyteller is able to make others accept his version of things. And in the stories of the Jewish tradition the world, and even the universe, have a human meaning. Indeed, the Jewish imagination has sometimes been found guilty of overhumanizing everything, of making too much of a case for us, for mankind, and of investing externals with too many meanings. To certain writers Christianity itself has appeared to be an invention of Jewish storytellers whose purpose has been to obtain victory for the weak and the few over the strong and the numerous.

To such accusations Jews would apply the term *bilbul*. A *bilbul* is a false charge; literally, a confusion. For the previous generation of East European Jews, daily life without stories would have been inconceivable. My father would say, whenever I asked him to explain any matter, "The thing is like this. There was a man who lived . . ." "There was once a scholar . . ." "There was a widow with a son . . ." "A teamster was driving on a lonely road . . ." "An old man lived all alone in the forest. He was the last of his family and he was so sick and feeble that he could hardly cook his gruel. Well, one cold day he had no more firewood and he went out to gather some. He was stooped and old and he carried a rope. In the woods he spread the rope on the snow and laid his fuel on it and tied a knot, but he was too weak to lift the bundle. This was too much for him. He lifted his eyes and called to Heaven. 'Gott meiner, send me Death!' At once he saw the Angel of Death coming toward him. And the Angel said to him, 'You sent for me, what do you want?' And the old man thought quickly and said, 'Yes, as a matter of fact I did. I can't get these sticks up on my back and wonder if you'd mind giving me a hand.'"

"So, you see, when it comes to dying," my father said, "nobody is really ready."

Three Jews were boasting of their rabbis and one said, "My rabbi's faith is so great and he fears the Lord so much that he trembles day and night, and he has to be belted into his bed at night with straps so that he doesn't fall out." The second said, "Yes, you have a marvelous rabbi, but he really can't be compared to my rabbi. Mine is so holy and so just that he makes God tremble. God is afraid of displeasing him. And if the world has not been going so well lately, you can figure it out for yourselves. God is trembling." The third Jew said, "Your rabbis are both great men. No doubt about it. But my rabbi passed through both stages. For a long time he trembled too, and in the second stage he made God tremble. But then he thought it over very carefully and finally he said to God, 'Look—why should we both tremble?'"

I would call the attitudes of these stories characteristically Jewish. In them, laughter and trembling are so curiously mingled that it is not easy to determine the relation of the two. At times the laughter seems simply to restore the equilibrium of sanity; at times the figures of the story, or parable, appear to invite or encourage trembling with the secret aim of overcoming it by means of laughter. Aristophanes and Lucian do not hesitate to involve the Olympian gods in their fun, and Rabelais's humor does not spare the heavens either. But these are different kinds of comic genius. Jewish humor is mysterious and eludes our efforts—even, in my opinion, the efforts of Sigmund Freud—to analyze it. Recently, one Jewish writer (Hyman Slate in *The Noble Savage*) has argued that laughter, the comic sense of life, may be offered as proof of the existence of God. Existence, he says, is too funny to be uncaused. The real secret, the ultimate mystery, may never reveal itself to the earnest thought of a Spinoza, but when we laugh (the idea is remotely Hasidic) our minds refer us to God's existence. Chaos is exposed. . . .

Quite understandably, to the writer in the Russian Pale it seemed most important to present Jewish life as sympathetically as possible. Because the Jews were remorselessly oppressed, all the good qualities of Jewish life were heaped up in the foreground of their stories. Raw things—jealousies, ambitions, hatreds—were frequently withheld. The Jewish slums of Montreal during my childhood, just after the First World War, were not too far removed from the ghettos of Poland and Russia. Life in such places of exile and suffering was anything but ordinary. But whatever it was, ordinary or extraordinary, harsh or sweet, it was difficult to recognize it in the work of most modern Jewish writers. These writers generally tended to idealize it, to cover it up, in prayer shawls and phylacteries and Sabbath sentiment, the Seder, the matchmaking, the marriage canopy; for sadness the Kaddish; for amusement the *schnorrer*—the village beggar; for admiration the bearded scholar. Jewish literature and art have sentimentalized and sweetened the ghetto; their "pleasing" pictures are far less interesting than the real thing. In this century, so agonizing to the Jews, some people think it wrong to object to such lack of realism, to insist on maintaining the distinction

There Is Simply Too Much to Think About

between public relations and art. It may appear that the survivors of Hitler's terror will benefit more from good publicity than from realistic representation or that posters are needed more urgently than master-pieces.

Admittedly, say some people, Leon Uris's *Exodus* was not much of a novel, but it was extraordinarily effective as a document and we need such documents now. We do not need stories like Philip Roth's that expose unpleasant Jewish traits. The Jews are much slandered, much threatened, greatly sinned against—should they for these reasons be unfairly represented in literature, to their alleged advantage? The question is a very ticklish one. It could be shown, I think, that the argument based on need is also the one used by Khrushchev. The Russian oligarchy approves only of what it quaintly calls "socialist realism." It would prefer to have us read Simonov rather than Pasternak. Paradoxically, therefore, the American Jewish public buys Uris and Pasternak for entirely different reasons—*Exodus* because it is good for us, and *Doctor Zhivago* because it is bad for them. In literature we cannot accept a political standard. We can only have a literary one. But in all the free countries of the world Jewish writers are able to write exactly as they please, in French (André Schwarz-Bart), in Italian (Italo Svevo), in English, or in Yiddish and Hebrew.

In Jerusalem several years ago I had an amusing and enlightening conversation with the dean of Hebrew writers, S. Y. Agnon. This spare old man, whose face has a remarkably youthful color, received me in his house, not far from the barbed-wire entanglements that divide the city, and while we were drinking tea he asked me if any of my books had been translated into Hebrew. If they had not been, I had better see to it immediately because, he said, they would survive only in the Holy Tongue. His advice, I assume, was only half serious. It was his witty way of calling my attention to a curious situation. I cited Heinrich Heine as an example of a poet who had done rather well in German. "Ah," said Mr. Agnon, "we have him beautifully translated into Hebrew. He is safe."

Mr. Agnon feels secure in his ancient tradition. But Jews have been writing in languages other than Hebrew for more than two thousand years. The New Testament scholar Hugh J. Schonfield asserts that parts of the Gospels were composed in a sort of Yiddish Greek "as colorful in imagery and metaphor as it is often careless in grammatical construction." With less wit and subtlety than Mr. Agnon, other Jewish writers worry about using the languages of the Diaspora. They sometimes feel like borrowers, compelled by strange circumstances to use a tongue of which their ancestors were ignorant. I cannot recall that Joseph Conrad, a Pole, ever felt this to be an intolerable difficulty. He loved England and the English language. I do remember that James Joyce, an Irishman, did feel such a difficulty. Stephen Dedalus in *A Portrait of the Artist* somewhat envies an old English Jesuit, perfectly at home in his own language. But then, young Dedalus was at this period of his life still rather parochial. In a story by Meyer Levin one character exclaims: "I was a foreigner, writing in a foreign language . . . What am I? Native, certainly. My parents came to this country . . . they were the true immigrants, the actual foreigners. . . . But I, American-born, raised on hot dogs, I am out of place in America. Remember this: Art to be universal must be narrowly confined. An artist must be a perfect unit of time and place, at home with himself, unextraneous. Who am I? Where do I come from? I am an accident. What right have I to scribble in this American language that comes no more naturally to me than it does to the laundry Chinaman?"

Theories like those expressed by Mr. Levin's character, as Mr. Levin is at pains to show, about the "perfect unit of time and place" seldom bring any art into the world. Art appears, and then theory contemplates it; that is the usual order in the relations between art and theory. It cannot be argued that the stories of Isaac Babel are not characteristically Jewish. And they were written in Russian by a man who knew Yiddish well enough to have written them in that language. Before he disappeared from view during one of Stalin's purges, Babel had been put in charge of publishing the works of Sholom Aleichem in Yiddish. Why should he have chosen, therefore, to write his own stories in Russian, the language of the oppressors, of Pobedonostsev and the Black Hundreds? If, before writing, he had taken his bearings, he could not have found himself to be "a perfect unit of time and place." He wrote in Russian from motives we can never expect to understand fully. These stories have about them something that justifies them to the most grudging inquiry—they have spirit, originality, beauty.

Who was Babel? Where did he come from? He was an accident. We are all such accidents. We do not make up history and culture. We simply appear, not by our own choice. We make what we can of our condition with the means available. We must accept the mixture as we find it—the impurity of it, the tragedy of it, the hope of it.

[1964–65]

Up from the Pushcart: On Abraham Cahan

The founder and editor of the New York *Jewish Daily Forward*, Abraham Cahan (1860–1951), belonged to the generation of Eastern European Jews who started out in the Talmudic seminary and ended by making a considerable place for themselves in the great world. Cahan became a socialist, a student of literature, a social theorist and a novelist. He began to write fiction with the encouragement of William Dean Howells and *The Rise of David Levinsky* (first published in 1917) is in many ways typical of the "social criticism" novel of the period—the novel that turned inside out the smooth garment of that success story tailored for boys with such pathetic optimism by Horatio Alger.

Cahan, too, inverts the old and well-loved formula with its odd sums in commercial arithmetic—the eager beginner finding himself in the Bowery with $4.83; Dreiser also had a passion for this sort of elementary account-keeping. But *The Rise of David Levinsky* is, as John Higham in his admirable and intelligent introduction to the new Harper Torchbooks edition correctly claims, more than a merely good specimen of its class. Cahan was a gifted writer.

I confess I began rather skeptically to reread *David Levinsky* after many years. I remembered the sentimental novels of East Side Jewish life serialized in the Yiddish dailies thirty years ago—romances like *Die Unglückliche Kalle fun Suffolk Street*, over which my mother wept. I expected to find a certain nostalgic softness. I found instead that Cahan was a tough-minded man and that David Levinsky was anything but an ingenuous hero. About his mother's death at the hands of hooligans from whom she was trying to defend him, Levinsky says astonishingly little. He merely accepts the benefits of pity and sympathy and does quite well by himself as the poor orphan. But he is by no means a self-seeking scoundrel. And he is anything but stupid. He says, shortly after his arrival in New York, when he has gone on the streets with a push-cart: "I saw the cunning and meanness of some of my customers, of the trades people of whom I bought my wares, and of the peddlers who did business by my side. Nor was I unaware of certain unlovable traits that were unavoidably developing in my own self under these influences. And while human nature was thus growing smaller, the human world as a whole was growing larger, more complex, more heartless and more interesting."

David Levinsky's night-school English teacher gives him a copy of *Dombey and Son*; he reads it so avidly and passionately that his pushcart business falls apart. He is now ambitious to become an intellectual; he longs to take his college entrance examinations. "University-bred people were the real nobility of the world," he says with feelings very much like those of Hardy's Jude the Obscure. "A college diploma was a certificate of moral as well as intellectual aristocracy." City College on Lexington and Twenty-third Street becomes "the synagogue of my new life."

He tries to get Gussie, an unattractive garment worker, to marry him and put him through college on her savings. She is far too intelligent to be taken in. Then in a touching passage of great psychological shrewdness he tries to get her to invest her money with him and offers to love her. With dignity she refuses this second and almost heartfelt proposal. The needs of Levinsky's practical life frustrate his intellectual ambitions. Or perhaps they are not needs after all; perhaps Levinsky, who at times has kept to his room for days studying mathematics and reading Darwin and Spencer, has powerful instincts for money and position which he attempts to justify by invoking the struggle for survival.

Today's dress manufacturers will smile at Levinsky's description of his shop on Division Street and his adventures as a salesman. Modern business complexity makes these small deals amusing. But the description of Levinsky's rise in the cloak business is perfectly straightforward. Cahan had a remarkably good head about self-interest, snobbery, social climbing, money and the Americanization of Jews; he is not a doctrinaire socialist; he is never simpleminded. He was not a great literary artist and his book is more interesting as a social history than as literature. Nevertheless he had the instincts of a fine novelist and one finds in him none of the false piety of later generations of Jewish writers.

[1961]

There Is Simply Too Much to Think About

Where Do We Go from Here?
The Future of Fiction

We know that science has a future, we hope that government will have one. But it is not altogether agreed that the novel has anything but a past. There are some who say that the great novelists of the twentieth century—Proust, Joyce, Mann and Kafka—have created sterile masterpieces and that with them we have come to the end of the line. No further progress is possible.

It does sometimes seem that the narrative art itself has dissolved. The person, the character as we knew him in the plays of Sophocles or Shakespeare, in Cervantes, Fielding and Balzac, has gone from us. Instead of a unitary character with his unitary personality, his ambitions, his passions, his soul, his fate, we find in modern literature an oddly dispersed, ragged, mingled, broken, amorphous creature whose outlines are everywhere, whose being is bathed in mind as the tissues are bathed in blood and who is impossible to circumscribe in any scheme of time. A cubistic, Bergsonian, uncertain, eternal, mortal someone who shuts and opens like a concertina and makes a strange music. And what has struck artists in this century as the most amusing part of all is that the descriptions of self that still have hold of us are made up of the old unitary foursquare traits noted according to the ancient conventions. What we insist on seeing is not a quaintly organized chaos of instinct and spirit but what we choose to call "the personality"—a presentably combed and dressed someone who is decent, courageous, handsome, or not so handsome but strong, or not so strong but certainly generous, or not so generous but anyway reliable. So it goes.

Of all modern writers it is D. H. Lawrence who is most implacably hostile toward this convention of unitary character. For him this character of a civilized man does not really exist. What the modern civilized person calls his personality is to Lawrence figmentary: a product of civilized education, dress, manners, style and "culture." The head of this modern personality is, he says, a wastepaper basket filled with ready-made notions. Sometimes he compares the civilized conception of character to a millstone—a painted millstone about our necks is the metaphor he makes of it. The real self, unknown, is hidden, a sunken power in us; the true identity lies deep—very deep. But we do not deal much in true identity, goes his argument. The modern character on the street, or in a conventional story or film, is what a sociologist has recently described as the "presentation" self. The attack on this presentation self or persona by modern art is a part of the war that literature, in its concern with the individual, has fought with civilization. The civilized individual is proud of his painted millstone, the burden that he believes gives him distinction. In an artist's eyes his persona is only a rude, impoverished, mass-produced figure brought into being by a civilization in need of a working force, a reservoir of personnel, a docile public that will accept suggestion and control.

The old unitary personality that still appears in popular magazine stories, in conventional best-sellers, in newspaper cartoons and in the movies is a figure descended from well-worn patterns and popular art forms (like the mystery novel and the western) continue to exploit endlessly the badly faded ideas of motives and drama or love and hate. The old figures move ritualistically through the paces, finding now and then variations in setting and costume, but they are increasingly remote from real reality. The functions performed by these venerable literary types should be fascinating to the clinical psychologist who may be able to recognize in these stories an obsessional neurosis here, paranoid fantasy there, or to the sociologist, who sees resemblances to the organization of government bureaus or hears echoes of the modern industrial corporations. But the writer brought up in a great literary tradition not only sees these conventional stories as narcotic or brainwashing entertainments, at worst breeding strange vices, at best performing a therapeutic function. He also fears that the narrative art we call the novel may have come to an end, its conception of the self exhausted and with this conception our interest in the fate of that self so conceived.

It is because of this that Gertrude Stein tells us in one of her lectures that we cannot read the great novels of the twentieth century, among which she includes her own *The Making of Americans*, for what happens next. And in fact *Ulysses, Remembrance of Things Past, The Magic Mountain* and *The Making of Americans* do not absorb us in what happens next. They interest us in a scene, in a dialogue, a mood, an insight, in language, in character, in the revelation of a design, but they are not narratives. *Ulysses* avoids anything resembling the customary story. It is in some sense a book about literature and offers us a history of English prose style and of the novel. It is a museum containing all the quaint armor, halberds, crossbows and artillery pieces of literature. It exhibits them with a kind of amused irony and parodies and transcends them all. These are the things that once entranced us. Old sublimities, old dodges, old weapons, all useless now; pieces of iron once heroic, lovers' embraces once romantic, all debased by cheap exploitation, all unfit.

Language too is unfit. Erich Heller in a recent book quotes a typical observation by Hugo von Hofmannsthal on the inadequacy of old forms of expression. Hofmannsthal writes, "Elements once bound together to make a world now present themselves to the poet in monstrous separateness. To speak of them coherently at all would be to speak untruthfully. The commonplace phrases of the daily round of observations seem all of a sudden insoluble riddles. The sheriff is a wicked man, the vicar is a good fellow, our neighbor must be pitied, his sons are wastrels. The baker is to be envied, his daughters are virtuous." In Hofmannsthal's *A Letter* these formulas are present as "utterly lacking in the quality of truth." He is unable, he explains, "to see what people say and do with the simplifying eye of habit and custom. Everything falls to pieces, the pieces to pieces again, and nothing can be comprehended any more with the help of customary notions."

Character, action and language then have been put in doubt, and the Spanish philosopher Ortega y Gasset, summing up views widely held, says the novel requires a local setting with limited horizons and familiar features, traditions, occupations, classes. But as everyone knows, these old-fashioned local worlds no longer exist. Or perhaps that is inaccurate. They do exist but fail to interest the novelist. They are no longer local societies as we see them in Jane Austen or George Eliot.

Our contemporary local societies have been overtaken by the world. The great cities have devoured them and now the universe itself imposes itself upon us; space with its stars comes upon us in our cities. So now we have the universe itself to face, without the comforts of community, without metaphysical certainty, without the power to distinguish the virtuous from the wicked man, surrounded by dubious realities and discovering dubious selves.

Things have collapsed about us, says D. H. Lawrence on the first page of *Lady Chatterley's Lover*, and we must each of us try to put together some sort of life. He offers us a sort of nature mysticism, love but without false romanticism, an acceptance of true desire as the first principle of recovery. Other writers have come forward with aesthetic or political or religious first principles. All the modern novelists worth mentioning aim at a point beyond customary notions, customary dramas and customary conceptions of character. The old notion of a customary self, of the fate of an all-important Me, displeases the best of them. We have lived now through innumerable successes and failures of these old selves. In American literature we have watched their progress and decline in scores of books since the Civil War, from buoyancy to depression. The Lambert Strethers, the Hurstwoods and Cowperwoods, the Gatsbys may still impress or please us as readers, but as writers, no. Their mental range is no longer adequate to these new circumstances. Those characters suit us better who stand outside society and, unlike Gatsby, have no wish to be sentimentally reconciled to it. Unlike Dreiser's millionaires, we have no more desire for its wealth; unlike Strether, we are not attracted by the power of an old and knowing civilization.

This is why so many of us prefer the American novels whose characters are most nearly removed from the civil state—*Moby-Dick* and *Huckleberry Finn*. We feel in our own time that what is called the civilized condition often swings close to what Hobbes calls the state of nature, a condition of warfare in which the life of the individual is nasty, brutish, dull and short. But we must be careful not to be swept away by the analogy. We have seen to our grief in recent European and especially German history the results of trying to bolt from all civilized

There Is Simply Too Much to Think About

and legal tradition. It is in our minds that the natural and the civil, autarchy and discipline, are most explosively mixed.

But for us here in America discipline is represented largely by the enforced repressions. We do not know much of the delights of discipline. Almost nothing of a spiritual, ennobling character is brought into the internal life of a modern American by his social institutions. He must discover it in his own experience, by his own luck as an explorer, or not at all. Society feeds him, clothes him, to an extent protects him, and he is its infant. If he accepts the state of infancy, contentment can be his. But if the idea of higher functions comes to him, he is profoundly unsettled. The hungry world is rushing on all continents toward such a contentment, and with passions and desires frustrated since primitive times, and with the demand for justice never so loudly expressed. The danger is great that it will be satisfied with the bottles and toys of infancy. But the artists, the philosopher, the priest, the statesman are concerned with the full development of humanity—its manhood, occasionally glimpsed in our history, occasionally felt by individuals.

With all this in mind, people here and there still continue to write the sort of book we call a novel. When I am feeling blue I can almost persuade myself that the novel, like Indian basketry or harness-making, is a vestigial art and has no future. But we must be careful about prophecy. Even prophecy based on good historical study is a risky business and pessimism, no less than optimism, can be made into a racket. All industrial societies have a thing about obsolescence. Classes, nations, races and cultures have in our time been declared obsolete, with results that have made ours one of the most horrible of all centuries. We must, therefore, be careful about deciding that any art is dead.

This is not a decision for a coroner's jury of critics and historians. The fact is that a great many novelists, even those who have concentrated on hate, like Céline, or on despair, like Kafka, have continued to perform a most important function. Their books have attempted, in not a few cases successfully, to create scale, to order experience, to give value, to make perspective and to carry us toward sources of life, toward life-giving things. The true believer in disorder does not like novels. He follows another calling. He is an accident lawyer or a promoter, not a novelist. It always makes me sit up, therefore, to read yet another scolding of the modern novelist written by highly paid executives of multimillion-dollar magazines. They call upon American writers to represent the country fairly, to affirm its values, to increase its prestige in this dangerous period. Perhaps, though, novelists have a different view of what to affirm. Perhaps they are running their own sort of survey of affirmable things. They may come out against nationalism or against the dollar, for they are an odd and unreliable lot. I have already indicated that it is the instinct of the novelist, however, to pull toward order. Now this is a pious thing to say but I do not intend it merely to sound good. It should be understood only as the beginning of another difficulty.

What ideas of order does the novelist have and where does he get them and what good are they in art? I have spoken of Lawrence's belief that we must put together a life for ourselves—singly, in pairs, in groups—out of the wreckage. Shipwreck and solitude are not, in his opinion, unmixed evils. They are also liberating, and if we have the strength to use our freedom we may yet stand in a true relation to nature and to other men. But how are we to reach this end? Lawrence proposes a sort of answer in *Lady Chatterley's Lover*, showing us two people alone together in the midst of a waste. I sometimes feel that *Lady Chatterley's Lover* is a sort of *Robinson Crusoe* for two, exploring man's sexual resources rather than his technical ingenuity. It is every bit as moral a novel as *Crusoe*. Connie and Mellors work at it as hard and as conscientiously as Robinson and there are as many sermons in the one as in the other. The difference is that Lawrence aimed with all his powers at the writing of this one sort of book. To this end he shaped his life, the testing ground of his ideas. For what is the point of recommending a course of life that one has not tried oneself?

This is one way to assess the careers and achievements of many modern artists. Rimbaud, Strindberg, Lawrence, Malraux, even Tolstoy can be approached from this direction. They experiment with themselves and in some cases an artistic conclusion can come only out of the experimental results. Lawrence had no material other than what his life— that savage pilgrimage, as he called it—gave him. The ideas he tested,

There Is Simply Too Much to Think About

and tested not always by an acceptable standard, were ideas of the vital, the erotic, the instinctive. They involved us in a species of nature mysticism that gave, as a basis for mortality, sexual gratification. But I am not concerned here with all the particulars of Lawrence's thesis. I am interested mainly in the connection between the understanding and the imagination, and the future place of the intelligence in imaginative literature.

It is necessary to admit, first, that ideas in the novel can be very dull. There is much in modern literature, and the other arts as well, to justify our prejudice against the didactic. Opinion, said Schopenhauer, is not as valid as imagination in a work of art. One can quarrel with an opinion or judgment in a novel, but actions are beyond argument and the imagination simply accepts them. I think that many modern novels, perhaps the majority, are the result of some didactic purpose. The attempt of writers to make perspective, to make scale and to carry us toward the sources of life, is of course the didactic intention. It involves the novelist in programs, in slogans, in political theories, religious theories and so on. Many modern novelists seem to say to themselves "what if" or "suppose that such and such were the case" and the results often show that the book was conceived in thought, in didactic purpose, rather than in the imagination. That is rather normal, given the state of things, the prevalence of the calculating principle in modern life, the need for conscious rules of procedure and the generally felt need for answers. Not only books, painting and musical compositions, but love affairs, marriages and even religious convictions often originate in an idea. So that the *idea* of love is more common than love and the *idea* of belief is more often met with than faith. Some of our most respected novels have a purely mental inspiration. The results are sometimes very pleasing because they can so easily be discussed, but the ideas in them generally have more substance than the characters who hold them.

American literature in the nineteenth century was highly didactic. Emerson, Thoreau, Whitman and even Melville were didactic writers. They wished to instruct a young and raw nation. American literature in the twentieth century has remained didactic, but it has also been unintellectual. This is not to say that thought is lacking in the twentieth-century American novel, but it exists under strange handicaps and is much disguised. In *A Farewell to Arms,* Hemingway makes a list of subjects we must no longer speak about—a catalog of polluted words, words ruined by the rhetoric of criminal politicians and misleaders. Then Hemingway, and we must respect him for it, attempts to represent these betrayed qualities without using the words themselves. Thus we have courage without the word, honor without the word, and in *The Old Man and the Sea* we are offered a sort of Christian endurance, also without specific terms. Carried to this length, the attempt to represent ideas while sternly forbidding thought begins to look like a curious and highly sophisticated game. It shows a great skepticism of the strength of art. It makes it appear as though ideas openly expressed would be too much for art to bear.

We have developed in American fiction a strange combination of extreme naïveté in the characters and of profundity implicit in the writing, in the techniques themselves and in the language. But the language of thought is banned; it is considered dangerous and destructive. American writers appear to have a strong loyalty to the people, to the common man. Perhaps in some cases the word for this is not *loyalty*; perhaps it might better be described as *fealty*. But a writer should aim to reach all levels of society and as many levels of thought as possible, avoiding democratic prejudice as much as intellectual snobbery. Why should he be ashamed of thinking? I do not claim that all writers think or should think. Some are peculiarly inept at ideas and we would harm them by insisting that they philosophize. But the record shows that most artists are intellectually active and it is only now in a world increasingly intellectualized, more and more dominated by the productions of scientific thought, that they seem strangely reluctant to use their brains or to give any sign that they have brains to use.

All through the nineteenth century the conviction increases in novelists as different as Goncharov in Russia and Thomas Hardy in England that thought is linked with passivity and is devitalizing. And in the masterpieces of the twentieth century the thinker usually has a weak grip on life. But by now an alternative, passionate activity without ideas has also been well explored in novels of adventure, hunting, combat and eroticism. Meanwhile miracles born of thought have been

There Is Simply Too Much to Think About

largely ignored by modern literature. If narration is neglected by novelists like Proust and Joyce, the reasons are that for a time the drama has passed from external action to internal movement. In Proust and Joyce we are enclosed by and held within a single consciousness. In this inner realm the writer's art dominates everything. The drama has left external action because the old ways of describing interests, of describing the fate of the individual, have lost their power. Is the sheriff a good fellow? Is our neighbor to be pitied? Are the baker's daughters virtuous? We see such questions now as belonging to a dead system, mere formulas. It is possible that our hearts would open again to the baker's daughters if we understood them differently.

A clue may be offered by Pascal, who said there are no dull people, only dull points of view. Maybe that is going a little far. (A religious philosophy is bound to maintain that every soul is infinitely precious and therefore infinitely interesting.) But it begins perhaps to be evident what my position is. Imagination, binding itself to dull viewpoints, puts an end to stories. The imagination is looking for new ways to express virtue. Society just now is in the grip of certain common falsehoods about virtue—not that anyone really believes them. And these cheerful falsehoods beget their opposites in fiction, a dark literature, a literature of victimization, of old people sitting in ash cans waiting for the breath of life to depart. This is the way things stand; only this remains to be added, that we have barely begun to comprehend what a human being is and that the baker's daughters may have revelations and miracles to offer to keep fascinated novelists busy until the end of time.

I would like to add this also, in conclusion, about good thought and bad thought in the novel. In a way it doesn't matter what sort of line the novelist is pushing, what he is affirming. If he has nothing to offer but his didactic purpose, he is a bad writer. His ideas have ruined him. He could not afford the expense of maintaining them. It is not the didactic purpose itself that is a bad thing, and the modern novelist drawing back from the dangers of didacticism has often become strangely unreal, and the purity of his belief in art for art in some cases has been peculiarly unattractive. Among modern novelists the bravest have taken the risk of teaching and have not been afraid of using the terms of religion, science, philosophy and politics. Only they have been prepared to admit the strongest possible arguments against their own positions.

Here we see the difference between a didactic novelist like D. H. Lawrence and one like Dostoyevsky. When he was writing *The Brothers Karamazov* and had just ended the famous conversation between Ivan and Alyosha in which Ivan, despairing of justice, offers to return his ticket to God, Dostoyevsky wrote to one of his correspondents that he must now attempt, through Father Zossima, to answer Ivan's arguments. But he has in advance all but devastated his own position. This, I think, is the greatest achievement possible in a novel of ideas. It becomes art when the views most opposite to the author's own are allowed to exist in full strength. Without this a novel of ideas is mere self-indulgence and didacticism is simply ax-grinding. The opposites must be free to range themselves against each other and they must be passionately expressed on both sides. It is for this reason that I say it doesn't matter much what the writer's personal position is, what he wishes to affirm. He may affirm principles we all approve of and write very bad novels.

The novel, to recover and flourish, requires new ideas about humankind. These ideas in turn cannot live in themselves. Merely asserted, they show nothing but the goodwill of the author. They must therefore be discovered and not invented. We must see them in flesh and blood. There would be no point in continuing at all if many writers did not feel the existence of these unrecognized qualities. They are present and they demand release and expression.

[1962]

At the Movies

THE ART OF GOING IT ALONE

For the past eight or nine years Morris Engel of New York has been producing his own motion pictures with the assistance of his wife, Ruth Orkin (a leading still photographer in her own right), and a few collaborators. 'Independent moviemaking' generally refers to the combination of a group of experts—writers, cameramen, editors—who have broken away from one of the colossi of Hollywood and gone into business for themselves. With a little luck, they may create a new colossus of their own. This does not describe the situation of Engel, whose independence is of a different sort.

What we now call the New Wave originates with him. It was Engel who first went into the streets with a moving-picture camera and photographed whatever moved past the lens, making no attempt to avoid the peripheral activity in the neighborhood or to bring the space about his actors under control. Accidental sounds and motions enter into his pictures as they will. After him have come the French *nouvelle vaguistes* and an increasing number of low-budget moviemakers in New York. In an age that has witnessed the triumph of collective effort or team spirit, in backward China as in mechanical Detroit, Engel has tried to recover the mobility and adaptability possible only to individuals. It is hard to describe his peculiar virtue. He has grasped the idea that the progress of technology may make large, cumbersome, joint efforts obsolete in films. He has designed his own equipment to give the cameraman flexibility and free him from sets and soundstages, from creation by conference and consultation. As a producer-director—an entrepreneur in his own right—Engel writes scenarios, raises capital (few will envy him that), recruits actors, elects settings and finally edits his own rushes. Then when the films are ready he still has to go out and find distributors; he proceeds, that is, without prior guarantees from outside producers or distributing organizations. Every art depends for its progress on the courage (and sometimes on the obstinacy) of such innovators. But they cannot expect to have an easy time. Completing a film on one's own is a costly and wearing business; subsequently persuading distributors to "place" it may prove even harder.

Engel has made three full-length pictures, one of which, *The Little Fugitive* (1953), has been shown throughout the United States and widely overseas. Of the two others, *Lovers and Lollipops* (1955) has also been exhibited in this country (though with less financial success than *The Little Fugitive*) and *Weddings and Babies* (1959) had a preview showing at one theater in New York City but has not been seen elsewhere.

The director gives the reasons for this neglect with great calm and forbearance. The exhibitors are not scoundrels, but their theaters are valuable properties and they are obliged to run them at a profit. If they are going to exhibit films that depart from the reliable Hollywood pattern they want them to be moneymakers like *La Dolce Vita* or *Never on Sunday*. Not by so much as a murmur did Engel, when I spoke to him, offer to criticize either of these films. He is perhaps more concerned to forge ahead with several new projects of his own.

Starting out as a still photographer, Engel was for many years on the staff of the New York newspaper *PM*, working mainly in the city, occasionally going on distant assignments, covering strikes and murders but also recording the daily lives of families he lived with for weeks at a time. From journalism he turned to films.

The scene of his movies is New York. Their subject is ordinary life, the life the late Billy de Beck used to describe as "Parlor, Bedroom, and Sink." Engel works in the Manhattan streets, in West Side and Greenwich Village interiors, on Coney Island, in the harbor, in parks and zoos and at the top of the Empire State Building.

Lovers and Lollipops, for example, has more city than story in it and strikes the viewer as being a tour of what a social worker might call Community Resources. The photography is superb and Engel's expert work with the camera—his taste in the choice of lights and angles—

provides the main interest of the film and its unity. The images themselves are required to make up for the absence of a story. The visible and the audible are intended to propose fresh, contemporary meanings. The look of a summer street, the appearance of a child in a doorway at night, the rows of cars in the parking lot at Rockaway Beach—these things demand that we discover for ourselves the principles that connect them.

The honesty of *Lovers and Lollipops* has a certain shock value; we begin to see what a film might be and how we are treated by conventional movies with their dressed-up and painted figures, spiced and sexualized, placed in expensive and luxurious settings, glamorized on Park Avenue, glamorized in the Far West and even in the slums and the underworld. To see things as they really are, as we meet them daily, unthinkingly, is curiously startling. It becomes clear at least that what is familiar is in any number of ways made abstract by our avoidance, by the conclusions we refuse to draw from the sight of the well-known sofa, the corner table, the familiar look. We discover the power of the hard and succinct fact—of a woman's face wan with disappointment, of the bristles of a man's beard, of muffled words and random gestures, of the closeness of summer on the stoop of a brownstone house.

In *Lovers and Lollipops* the interest is almost entirely in the recording of these facts, for the human material is rather poor and bleak, threadbare, lacking depth and shading. The lovers are a widow and a young man home on a holiday from his job in South America. The widow has a little daughter whose feelings, now that marriage is in prospect, must be given very special consideration. There, in the child, is the *problem*— the problem of psychology, or liberal pedagogy, of patience and decency. The couple worry about her. But she is spirited and impulsive while they are harassed and wooden. There is, it appears, more sorrow than love between them; the woman is enveloped in a sourceless anxiety or sadness. In an empty new house that she and her young man have gone in a holiday mood to look over, the woman waits alone while her lover goes on a brief errand in a rented car and for no apparent reason her dread grows. She hears bells and sirens and fears the worst, yielding to her habitual mood. Hardly anything she does is free from it and we are afraid for her. Even when she is laughing her substance is so meager and her happiness so fragile. To look at ordinary life like this—Engel himself seems to feel, judging by the changes he has made in his more recent work—is rather depressing. One would have to believe fanatically in plain people to think that a formless realism could justify itself by the implicit merit or dignity of plainness. The plainness of plain people is not a thing that is simply thrust on them. They themselves help to achieve it.

If Engel were nothing but an extraordinary cameraman, we would have to say that he had laid out some very sharp instruments but had as yet performed no operation. *The Little Fugitive*, however, the story of a small boy straying on Coney Island—curious, frightened, avid, sad, touching—is a charming film. *Weddings and Babies* is even better. Engel is not bucking the system merely to be obstinate. He has his own very definite ideas of what a film should be, is capable of realizing them, and the progress he makes in each successive picture is astonishing. It occurred to me after I had seen only *The Little Fugitive* that he held advanced theoretical notions or prejudices such as flourish in France today among novelists like Robbe-Grillet who dismiss narrative interest altogether and consider character and personality to be based on an obsolete psychology. Because of Engel's photographic passion for things shown literally, I guessed that he had an up-to-date theory of his own. My guess, however, was wrong.

The story of *Weddings and Babies*, Engel's latest picture, which was filmed with portable camera and sound equipment—a novel synchronized sight-and-sound process that was developed by Engel himself— starts off a little lamely with a woman who wishes to marry the man and the man, a photographer, resisting naturally enough, pleading that he must support his old mother. The woman, Viveca Lindfors, turns in a stunning performance. The man, John Myhers, is a capable actor. But the anonymous old Italian immigrant who plays the mother breaks through every contrivance of the plot with smashing immediacy. There she is, stout and old, a sinking, squarish frame of bones, tireless, with hairs on her chin and a toothless mouth, talking to herself in Italian. She is at least partly senile but has enough sense and dignity to be more than merely pitiable. Viveca Lindfors wants to marry and have babies while there is still time. She feels she is cheapening herself in an endless love affair. The photographer wants a new camera to build a sounder future and make something of himself. (Weddings and babies are the mainstay of the dreary trade he wants to get away from in order to attempt something more important.) The old mother wants shelter (with the aid of Social Security money) and an angel affixed to her tombstone. She escapes from a home for the aged and the care of its nuns to go out to Queens on the subway. In the stonecutter's yard she stops to marvel at the face of the angel. Then she goes to a cemetery not far away. What happens there is as impressive as anything I've ever seen on the screen. News of his mother's disappearance has broken up the birthday party at which the photographer has given Viveca Lindfors an engagement ring (the result, alas, of pressure applied by Viveca). Looking for his mother among the graves, the photographer begins to feel that he cannot give up his freedom and his opportunities to distinguish himself, to be something.

Here we begin to realize more definitely what we have already sensed in earlier frames of the picture: that when the situation is clear, when the feeling is right, Engel can penetrate the hard surfaces of appearance, make the stones eloquent, cause subways and pavements to cry out to us and the millions of dead in clumsily marked rows to influence us. The lesson of the dead, as the photographer reads it, is that he must act before it is too late. He must fulfill himself before he is overtaken by the grave. A bit of psychiatry now creeps in to dim the effect of the great city cemetery. Viveca pronounces her lover not yet free from Mama and walks off. But at film's end the photographer, alone in his melancholy and empty studio, is dialing his Viveca on the telephone, and the signs are that he will recover her. No other resolution seems possible. In the face of old age and death, weddings are still performed and brides hunger for children.

Morris Engel, going it alone, is proving that the quality of a picture filmed independently is different from the results of collective effort. A large team must inevitably have a leveling effect on the imagination of any single member of it. Besides, there is the pressure of money. The thought of several million dollars invested in a film is enough to change the giddy artist into a sober bureaucrat. Engel seems to be asking whether there is not some way to free the filmmaker from the complexities of organization and the power of the dollar.

[1962]

BUÑUEL'S UNSPARING VISION

In recent months the Spanish-born director Luis Buñuel has startled moviegoers with the ferocious imagery of a film called *Viridiana*. This has been, commercially, Buñuel's most successful effort, though he has been making powerful films in France, Spain, America and above all Mexico for more than thirty years—among them *Le Chien Andalou* (1929), *Land Without Bread* (1932), *The Young and the Damned* (1951), *Robinson Crusoe* (1954), *The Roots* (1957), *Nazarin* (1959), *The Young One* (1960), *Stranger in the Room* (1961) and *The Exterminating Angel* (1962), the latter still unreleased in this country.

Buñuel—like Ingmar Bergman, Federico Fellini and Michelangelo Antonioni—is one of the film directors whose views of the human condition must now be granted considerable importance. Movies have become subtler than they once were; and the film director has joined the poet, the philosopher, the theologian, the scientist and the historian to spin with them in the great vortex of explanations of our world. The film director enjoys a noticeable psychological advantage over the others. Because discussions of the human condition fatigue the mind and strain the will, we welcome views that can be assimilated in the darkness of the theater by a relaxed and diverted consciousness. We may agree or disagree with stated opinions but we rarely quarrel with images: These are immediately persuasive.

Thirty years ago film was considered a vulgar art or no art at all but a source of sensations for the masses. For the most part film directors were satisfied merely to make obvious, heavy references to the modern condition. In pictures like Chaplin's *City Lights* the comedy and pathos were primary and we were left to form our own conclusions about tender tramps and drunken millionaires. Chaplin's later films, however, are intellectually ambitious—his thinking becomes primary, and Monsieur

There Is Simply Too Much to Think About

Verdoux being led to execution says, "Numbers sanctify." The state may slaughter men in quantities but private enterprise in death leads to the gallows and the guillotine. The thought is not original; what is new is the appearance of a larger intellectual ambition in the movies.

Buñuel's work is certainly ambitious and intellectual. It is also truly impressive. He views himself as a sort of poet and he is a radical and uncompromising thinker. Since *Le Chien Andalou*, the short surrealist picture he made with Salvador Dalí in the late Twenties, his social and religious concerns have been plainly visible. In a typical sequence from that film a lover whose face is strained with desire pursues a woman who understandably, even in surrealist fantasy, shrinks from him because he has a halter about his neck and is pulling a load that consists of two grand pianos, two dead donkeys, decomposing and slimy, and two priests in full clerical garb. These same elements—passion, terror, religion, death, bourgeois culture (the pianos)—are still present in Buñuel's latest work though in richer, more mature form.

Buñuel's films have been shot in many countries and always deal with poverty. In almost all of them the starving, the crippled, the sick, the blind, the dead are shown vividly and violently after the manner of the anonymous author of Lazarillo de Tormes and of García de Quevedo and Pérez Galdós, Spanish masters who are famous for their hardness. Buñuel's *Land Without Bread*, which must be the most naked record of death by starvation ever made, was banned in Spain not, as I had imagined, by Franco but by the Republican government. Buñuel spares us nothing—nor himself, I must suppose—for there is nothing resembling sentimental manipulation in any of these films, no effort to exploit easy sympathies or to prick the heart and make it bleed a bit: a pleasant enough thing for an audience, in careful moderation. Unlike Fellini, who, in *La Dolce Vita*, hovers over his horrors and often betrays an Italianate softness in the presence of blood and death, Buñuel strikes his blows in quick succession and does not linger over his effects.

Buñuel's views of Christianity have made him a controversial figure in Spain, of course, but also in France and in Catholic Germany and in the United States. Invited by the Franco government, in line with its policy of conciliating its famous exiles, to make a film in Spain, Buñuel made *Viridiana*. Too late the government learned it had been deceived. One version of *Viridiana* was confiscated but the other got out, won a prize at Cannes and was condemned by a Vatican critic for anticlericalism.

The beauty of this picture is miraculously inseparable from its horrors. The lovely Viridiana, about to take final vows, is sent away from her convent to pay a brief final visit to an uncle by marriage whom she scarcely knows. This uncle, an odd sort of recluse, lives on a neglected estate, plays Bach and Handel on the parlor organ and with provincial Spanish innocence—soft-eyed, round-faced, touchingly unaware of his own perversity—dreams continually of the bride who died in his arms years ago, still in her wedding gown and veil. He occasionally wraps himself in her corset and fondles her things and when Viridiana appears he immediately recognizes her to be the image of the dead bride. She, during her brief visit, never for an instant relaxes her ascetic discipline; she rejects the bed to sleep on nails and cherishes her crown of thorns. The eccentric Spanish gentleman, narcotized by his queer solitary life and his erotic devotion to the dead, is almost too remote from life to discern any wickedness in his desires. He does everything he can to prevent the return of the girl to the convent. He goes so far as to beg her to wear her dead aunt's wedding dress, as a very particular favor, and then with the assistance of his housekeeper drugs her and carries her sleeping to her bed. There he begins to unbutton the gown but cannot bring himself to take advantage of her. In the morning, desperate over her impending departure, he tells her she is no longer pure and cannot take her vows. Believing his lie, she leaves the house in horror but is stopped at the railway station by the police and brought back. Her uncle has hanged himself with the jump rope of his housekeeper's little daughter. By the terms of the will, made just before his suicide, Viridiana inherits half her uncle's estate. The other half goes to his natural son, Jorge.

Penitent, Viridiana tries to expiate her sin of withholding forgiveness from her wretched uncle by filling the estate with as ugly a crew of paupers and beggars as she can gather and to these nasty sinners she devotes herself with saintly piety; but we quickly understand, as does Viridiana's mother superior, that she is a proud, rebellious girl, a kind of Protestant who gives supreme authority to her own conscience. This

There Is Simply Too Much to Think About

second, Franciscan phase of her saintliness is shattered by the beggars and by her cousin Jorge. Jorge is a brisk, modern, masterful young man from the big city who brings his mistress to the estate with him but is willing to ditch her for Viridiana (if he can get her) and for his house-keeper in either case. When the master leaves the estate briefly with Viridiana the beggars get into the house and give themselves a banquet, which turns into an orgy of drunkenness, gorging and copulation. They have themselves "photographed," in a travesty of *The Last Supper,* by a gypsy who snaps the "camera" by lifting up her skirts. When Viridiana and Jorge return unexpectedly to the house he is caught and bound while Viridiana barely escapes being raped by two of her poor, one of them a syphilitic. Her second venture into sainthood thus ended, Viridiana exchanges her piety for a sensual life with Jorge, whom she will have to share with the housekeeper. All three sit down to play cards to the loud banging of rock-and-roll music. This last scene suggests the room in Sartre's *Huis Clos* in which two women and a man are shut up in an eternal hell.

The transition from medieval Spanish Christianity to rock-and-roll requires about eighty minutes but the thing is done with so much vigor and truthfulness, with such poetry and insight, that I do not think Buñuel can be accused of irresponsible brightness or muckraking or village atheism or shallow anticlericalism. The barrenness of the modern condition can give little satisfaction to so passionate an artist. Nothing is "exposed." Buñuel is not an admirer of tough operators. He remains, as he shows again in another recent movie, *Stranger in the Room*, an enemy of the bourgeois.

In *Stranger in the Room* a sleek industrialist with a little beard is first shown peeping into the clinic of his factory on a barren island where a worker is being treated for burns. What catches his eye, however, is not the unconscious victim, nor even the doctor, but a pretty little nurse whom he proceeds to pick up. The doctor's young bride is the spoiled daughter of a French businessman. She can't bear the suffering, "dull" poor and urges her husband to come back to Nice and lead a comfortable life. The industrialist fires and evicts a worker and is thus responsible for the death of the man's wife. The worker, crazed with grief, comes to the industrialist's house to kill him. There is a priest present who tries to reason with him, but what can a suffering worker have to do with clergy who eat dinner in the homes of the rich? He shoots the industrialist and later commits suicide.

In this film, as in *Viridiana* and in his earlier Mexican movie, *Nazarin*, Buñuel addresses the same question: What is good in human life? Viridiana the would-be saint and the young priest in *Nazarin* apply their Christian measure to the realities of human nature and the facts of money and power. Violent truth sobers the priest; it sends Viridiana spinning into sensuality. The poor and the humble are not invariably good but Buñuel rarely finds any virtue or even firmness of character among well-to-do people. Charity, courage and friendship he discovers in the hard-pressed worker; in the peasant woman who offers a piece of fruit to a thirsty prisoner; in a girl capable of honorable love; or in the doctor of *Stranger in the Room* who serves the poor disinterestedly. But among those seeking sainthood or martyrdom in traditional form he sees only illusion; not sacrifice but a perverse desire for pain; not love but self-will.

It would probably be correct, however, to say that Buñuel is even more concerned with reality than with virtue and vice. Sin and goodness seem to him to have become irrelevant categories. But the wages of selfishness is perdition. If we cannot have religion we can have reality, the acceptance of our true condition. But reality is social and collective and Buñuel wishes to deal, as he himself says, "with the fundamental problems of today's man, taken not as a particular case, but in his relation to other men." In Buñuel's eyes reality is supreme and reality is authentically derived not from "particular cases" but from an entire society. The old story of the individual is exhausted and was exhausted a century ago. Buñuel tells us: "Lack of work, insecurity in life, fear of war, social injustice are things that, because they affect all men of today, also affect the spectator; but that Mr. X is not happy at home so, to amuse himself, he looks for a girl friend whom he will eventually leave to return to his wife, is undoubtedly moral and edifying, but leaves us completely indifferent." The comfortable man, self-concerned, attempting to embrace more comfort, bores us stiff. And what Buñuel is telling us is also what Tocqueville forecast in *Democracy in America*. The scope of the individual has shrunk so that we can be interested only by looking at mankind as a whole. In the films of Buñuel the old self pursuing the old goals is unreal. The great question seems to me to be: When will we see new and higher forms of individuality, purged of old sicknesses and corrected by a deeper awareness of what all men have in common? Buñuel has not yet shown us what these forms might be. But neither, on the other hand, has anyone else.

[1962]

THE MASS-PRODUCED INSIGHT

American films were slow to catch up with psychology. Quite early, the Germans caught the modern psychological fever. *The Cabinet of Dr. Caligari* (1919), a strange and powerful picture on the theme of mental aberrations, brought together the expressionist innovations of Strindberg and the atmosphere of Central European psychiatry. But the American moviemakers of the Twenties did not care for that sort of thing. They were curiously, even obstinately, old-fashioned. It is odd to think that Freud's *Interpretation of Dreams* (1900) and the nickelodeon are approximately contemporary. And in the Twenties, while Mary Pickford and Lillian Gish were thriving on the screen, so were Jung and Ferenczi in psychology, James Joyce in literature, Klee and Picasso in painting. Evidently the moviemakers of that not-so-remote time were dragging their feet. Perhaps they correctly interpreted the desire of the public not to be hurried at the same rate of speed along every level of development.

Whatever the reasons, Hollywood continued for a long time to make action films. Cowboys, Indians, pioneers, cops and robbers, doughboys and Krauts, rags and riches gave it all the material it needed. But slowly the movies became psychological. Plain goodness, blunt badness, the honor of strong silent men, simple love and classical jealousy went out of fashion. Hollywood went on making action pictures, of course, but significant actions became harder to find as we entered this present age of upheaval and disarray. We could no longer take the old virtues straight. It was necessary to be reconciled to them indirectly and for this purpose Hollywood created a popularized Freudianism. A new kind of "insight," used at first as an ornament or gimmick, presently became the main reliance of the movie scriptwriter.

For richer or for poorer, as the marriage service goes, in health but especially in sickness, we are now wedded to this new movie psychology. About ten years ago a shrewd and gifted movie critic, Manny Farber, noted the change in an article called "Movies Aren't Movies Any More" and subtitled "The Art of Gimp Takes Over." The Gimp was a mechanical device used by Victorian lady golfers. It lifted their skirts for one flashing instant to enable them to hit the ball. "Something like this device has now been developed in Hollywood," wrote Farber. "Whenever the modern film-maker feels that his movie has taken too conventional a direction and is neglecting 'art,' he need only jerk the Gimp string, and behold!—curious and exotic but psychic images are flashed before the audience, pepping things up at the crucial moment, making you think such thoughts as 'The hero has a mother complex,' or 'He slapped that girl out of ambivalent rage at his father image which he says he carried around in his stomach.'"

Since Farber wrote this article the psychological revolution has been completed. The public has been thoroughly trained. It can be depended upon to take up every cue given by the filmmaker. *Insight*, a proud word for things that millions of people have learned by rote, stands now in the very center of the entertainment industry. Often the plot and all the actions of a movie are derived from a nucleus of psychological illumination. Heroes are those who struggle heroically with neuroses while villains are afflicted with sadistic or sadomasochistic difficulties that we are invited to understand sympathetically, with Hollywood insight. Even the action film—the western, the spectacular, the thriller—is now constructed on this principle.

Ten years ago Alfred Hitchcock's *Psycho* would have been simply *The Mad Murderer*—tried and true Grand Guignol. The old tricks still work: The blood of the murdered woman swirls in the drain of the shower stall, the slaughtered detective struck by his unseen assailant falls backward down a flight of stairs. The effects are so broad that we smile as we shudder. We have come to be kidded by a master and he does not let us down. But how different things are now! Our murderer is the victim of an unhealthy Oedipal love. He keeps his mummified mother in the coal cellar and commits his crimes dressed in her clothes. When the mystery is solved and the criminal apprehended, the action moves to a mental hospital. A psychiatrist invites us to view the murderer as a clinical subject; there are no more punishments, only explanations.

So we sit patiently as the psychiatrist lectures us. His confident, rather ignorant and platitudinous words conclude the picture. The poor transvestite murderer is left looking quietly psycho in his mother's very unstylish clothes. In a cruder day he would have fallen from the roof or failed to beat a train to the crossing. *Nous avons changé tout cela*. Young Perkins is even shown as a wholesome, winsome, sincere-looking American youth—a type that Hollywood has taught us to mistrust. There *are* no handsome, winsome Johnnies anymore: Their corruption has been exposed to our insight.

It is utopian to expect Hollywood movies without this sort of thing. In *Spartacus* the Roman jailers are voyeurs. In *Butterfield 8* the distress of Elizabeth Taylor is caused by a wicked old friend of the family who corrupted her when she was a little child. In *The Hustler* the young lovers are clearly stamped, face and form, with the psychological Hollywood look. Brave soldiers of fear, they seek, in skill with a pool cue, in drink and in love, to free themselves from neurosis. But there is an evildoer who perversely envies the pair and destroys them with psychological poisons. In *The Misfits* each portion of the action is followed instantly by an appropriate insight. On one side are ranged, thematically, aperçus into beauty and love, happiness, instinct, liberty and creativity, and on the other side stand the opposing vices—misery, hate, the impoverished imagination, money and death. A movie so intensely instructive in purpose might more effectively have been presented as an old-fashioned morality play with each abstraction clearly labeled. As it is, the realism of *The Misfits* simply gets in the way. We have to wait nearly an hour, watching a laborious accumulation of evidence, to discover that the young divorcée (the late Marilyn Monroe) represents It—the Life Force itself. The difficulty is that movie problems, movie insights, have come to be more interesting by far than the characters they preoccupy or afflict. The actors in a movie occasionally remind us of the models in a fashion magazine. The models have no human qualities: They merely wear the merchandise.

Consider *Summer and Smoke*, adapted from the play by Tennessee Williams. Its characters can never really convince us that they are human beings; they are animated postulates, figures in a plight—they are showing off the goods. The heroine is a repressed Southern girl. Her glaucous eyes, in brilliant color, reveal all in a single glance. Her mama is a kleptomaniac, much attached to the bottle. She too is a familiar figure. She has been going strong ever since *The Little Foxes* when she was known as Aunt Birdie. But now we have more insight into the type. We understand how it is with people who tipple and steal hats from the milliner: Anyone who steals compulsively suffered a deprivation of love during the crucial years of development.

The hero too is a psychological type. He is mixed up with some wild, dionysiac bayou folk, rather drearily put together from the leftovers of an old Mexican picture. The young doctor's brilliant red roadster is a welcome sight, a far more dynamic object than any of the young ladies who are chasing Laurence Harvey, its driver. But we know that the car is something else too. And so we wait, seasoned veterans of boredom that we are, for the real thing. That is revealed to us when the young doctor pulls down an anatomical chart and says to our heroine, whose gaze is desperately thickened by the drugs she has been swallowing to help her bear her unrequited love: "Do you know what this is? This is a man!" Or, in the dialect of the region, "a ma-un!"

It is now that we know we are about to transact the real business of the evening and this business has nothing to do with the South or with cars or with alleged bayou people. It has to do mainly with psychological issues. The occasion is one for "insight." It is didactic. We have come to learn something. Perhaps it would be more correct to say that we have come to rehearse a lesson and this lesson is that puritanical repression is an evil, that the instincts are not to be mocked, that the body is a sacred object and that sex, properly understood, is a form of holy worship.

Such beliefs, held in the past by radical artists and thinkers, are now offered daily to mass audiences by the large-circulation magazines and the television industry and other molders of public opinion. The public is being taught new standards and it is *this,* the liberalization of opinion, that has become the dramatic event in the movie house. This liberalization has developed its own form of piety. People feel about these popular insights that they are moral, and movie psychology thus turns out to be a popular sort of moralizing.

What André Malraux rather bitterly calls "the arts of delectation"—he classes the popular novel with the movies—are being used for Improvement (a Victorian term for Upgrading). Americans are in general sensitive to their responsibilities and when they confront the great public they feel a very particular responsibility to instruct it. And they have instructed it. But somehow the new excitement of Hollywood's psychological morality is not as great as the old excitement of the action film. This new excitement is the excitement of belonging to the vanguard of enlightenment, a triumphant private sense of being in the know, of the confirmation of judgments we believe to be our own. It gives us the illusion that we are thinking seriously about life.

[1963]

ADRIFT ON A SEA OF GORE

Spiritual themes are the occasion for the goriest and most violent scenes in the movies today. Moviemakers, when they have an obviously good thing on hand, like Liberty (*Spartacus*), Chivalry and Honor (*El Cid*) or Our Lord (*Ben-Hur* and now *Barabbas*), can really pour it on; they drench us in blood and blame the barbarous past for it. But the Roman crowds whose heartlessness makes us shudder didn't have the best seats in the house. We do.

The cunning work of the camera in close-ups allows us to watch these torments in privileged intimacy. Under the stands, after the chariot race, we see Messala shivering cruelly as he dies. We watch the face of Jack Palance as he begs the crowd for mercy just before Anthony Quinn (Barabbas) and his sword put an end to his sufferings. We derive some gratification from this violence *and* we are able to congratulate ourselves on our superiority to these frightful pagans. We are invited to enjoy the passions of the murderer and the blessings of innocence and enlightenment at the same time. We can't lose. No one can lose. All impulses can be gratified at once and the thing is profitable as well. This can only be called all-purpose spiritual materialism. Here is a phenomenon not restricted to movies; in our public life religious and quasi-religious personalities have concocted dismal mixtures of piety and opportunism. We have been asked to swallow many a queer dose.

Dino De Laurentiis, who produced *Barabbas*, Richard Fleischer, who directed it, and Christopher Fry, who adapted it from the novel *Barabbas* by the Nobel Prize–winning author Pär Lagerkvist, have commemorated the release of the movie in an illustrated book, *Barabbas: The Story of a Motion Picture*. Here they tell us solemnly how it all happened. It seems that the making of this picture greatly affected them spiritually and gave them as artists an unforgettable experience, like the experience of Barabbas himself after he had witnessed the Crucifixion. Do they really believe this? Apparently they do. "*Barabbas*," explains De Laurentiis, "offered more than the usual problems of transferring a novel to the visual medium of the screen, for it is the story of one man's search for faith and truth laid against the most spectacular period in history. We had to combine these two vastly different elements but we believe we have succeeded in producing what might be called the first 'intimate spectacle' in motion picture history."

All the principals—Messrs. Fleischer, Fry, Quinn and De Laurentiis—make many bows and obeisances before the creative superiority of Pär Lagerkvist. De Laurentiis bends so hard that we begin to have orthopedic fears for his back. He quotes the pronouncement of the historian Giovanni Papini, author of a book about Jesus, on Lagerkvist's novel: "It is not a historical novel, nor is it a romantic novel; it is an intellectual poem." Trembling, De Laurentiis accepts this intellectual poem as a business risk. And he tells us that no one but Christopher Fry, a devout Christian playwright of great refinement (*A Sleep of Prisoners*; *The Boy with a Cart*; *Thor, with Angels*), could possibly have done the script.

At this point one is tempted to say this enterprise is simply high-minded bunk, pious cheating, the same old racket. But then reading over the statements of De Laurentiis and the others, one detects no evidence of deliberate cheating. Throughout, the attitudes of producer, director and writer are consistently earnest, respectful, serious, humble without exaggeration. There is something extraordinarily touching about such evident good faith. Could it be that the producer and his associates have confused what they set out to do with what they have done?

The critic Lucien Maury says of Lagerkvist's novel that it is austere and "of a form that has been pared down to essentials." According to the description of Lagerkvist, this ruffian Barabbas, in whose place Jesus died, was a stubborn man, a creature entirely of this world, a rudimentary rationalist whose heart was closed to awe. Divine mystery would not let him alone but followed him through his life. Barabbas died in Rome, on a cross, saying to the darkness, "To thee I deliver up my soul."

De Laurentiis, Fleischer and Fry have made sure they would not fall into similar error. The darkness they work in is, to be sure, the darkness of the theater, but they have taken particular care to give their souls a better orientation. They do not resist the allure of "the most spectacular period in history" and there is nothing restrained or austere about their "intimate spectacle." The idea of an intimate spectacle goes down a little hard. Still, we have been trained in our time to get down all sorts of stuff. We know it is the usual thing for modern artists, particularly in the motion picture industry, where great wealth and technical resources afford original means for deranging the senses, to teach us new tricks and realign our sensibilities. For this, after our first resistance has been overcome, we are often grateful. If they tell us, in this era of eighty-minute circumnavigations of our planet, that they are about to put Golgotha and the Circus Maximus in our laps, we had better not object. Reserving judgment, therefore, we go on to see what De Laurentiis and his company have wrought.

We see first what they have done with the novel. There is not much blood in this book. (Lagerkvist's imagination is not stirred to extremes by "the most spectacular period in history." A reflective, private man, undevoted to the acquisition of money, he no doubt prefers the Greeks.) But there are lakes of blood in this picture, just as in the less "intimate" spectaculars. The extras, selected from the cast of thousands, die horribly, covered with *salsa di pomidoro* (the picture was made in Italy). In addition to all the blood, the producers have added an intimate mine disaster and set off an intimate series of sulfurous explosions. The slaves stagger, scream as they are burned, are buried alive or succumb bleeding under fallen beams. This last episode is not very different from that of the sea battle in *Ben-Hur*, a movie adapted from the far less austere novel by General Lew Wallace. In the matter of sex the producers of *Barabbas* have also allowed themselves several liberties. The humble harelipped girl who appears in the novel is transformed into the beautiful Rachel (Silvana Mangano) and forced to submit to the rough embrace of Anthony Quinn.

But Quinn, whose testimony is added to the rest in the publicity book, seems highly satisfied with the way things have been done. He had had his doubts about biblical films, he says: "Too often, I had found, they were simply an excuse for illustrating sin and sex in a lurid manner." And he had been about to turn down the invitation of De Laurentiis when he learned that the script would be written by Christopher Fry, a writer who could be trusted to deliver a great spiritual message to an international public. Well, a picture without a beautiful woman or two is hardly imaginable and the woman, once introduced, can't very well be ignored. Miss Mangano is ill used only once and this—as spectaculars, intimate and otherwise, go—shows remarkable restraint. She is stoned to death in a pit.

But Quinn was on to something. Everything that we are spared in lasciviousness, we are given in violence. Christopher Fry has, for instance, expanded the part of Sahak, the Christian slave (Vittorio Gassman) who suffers an obscure martyrdom in the novel. In the movie he and Barabbas are brought to Rome and enrolled in the gladiatorial school. Fleischer explains that he used "the spectacle of the arena and the gladiators simply as a means of developing the character of Barabbas, not as an end in itself. It would have been silly," he says, "to ignore such things for they were a part of the life and times of ancient Rome."

That the Circus was there all the while is perfectly true. Still, a good many people did manage to stay out of it. Saint Paul, who encountered some of the worst evils of the Empire, did not have to attend the gladiatorial college; nor did Pär Lagerkvist seem to feel the omission foolish.

Perhaps it is nearer the truth that many pictures rich in spiritual content also get in far larger amounts of pain and bloodshed than they require to float the message.

No one would dream of scolding a movie for being a movie. There is nothing new about the passive pleasure of virtue when it beholds the wicked in hell—a very ancient form of entertainment many centuries older than colored films and caramel corn. Therefore *let* this martyr Rachel have lovely legs. *Let* the effects-people have a field day with a genuine eclipse as noonday darkens on Calvary. *Let* the mine blow up and burn and bury the slaves. *Let* us have the gladiators at school training with the swinging spiked ball, the trident and the net. *Let* Jack Palance show his white teeth in sadistic glee à la Richard Widmark as he rides down poor clods in his chariot. *Let* the Italian extras fall down, gushing tomato paste. We are used to all this and find it easy to understand.

What is difficult to explain, however, is the sincerity of the company, the spiritual purpose, the reverence, the dedication. And the lump in the throat. Do these people believe what they are saying? Are they aware of any hypocrisy? Perhaps De Laurentiis and the company are and yet *are not* being truthful. Just as the spectator enjoys both the cruel act and the purity of innocence, so it is possible that the artists are able to combine spiritual intentions with hokum.

Like their entertainment, their problem has a long and ancient pedigree; it is the problem of reconciling religious and practical activities. Practical people are often enraptured by the idea of a spiritual enterprise and are so carried away by the declaration of their high aims that what they actually do scarcely matters. Many people nowadays are too sophisticated to be caught in an obvious hypocrisy and have learned instead to put out a sort of aromatic fog of purple vapor in which everything seems honest and nothing need be definitely untrue.

[1963]

On Shakespeare's Sonnets

I love theories about the sonnets," cries the narrator of Wilde's "The Portrait of Mr. W. H." Mr. R. P. Blackmur calls his essay "A Poetics for Infatuation," and apparently the sonnets also infatuate their readers. I find *The Riddle of Shakespeare's Sonnets* a fascinating critical collection. "With the possible exception of Hamlet, no other work of Shakespeare's has called forth more commentary and controversy than the sonnets, and on no other work has more nonsense been written," says Mr. Edward Hubler in his admirably clear introduction. He tells us also, or rather warns us, that the Shakespeare industry produces books, articles and essays at the rate of almost one thousand a year.

Perhaps the pleasure this collection gives me is in part the pleasure of seeing modern critics working hard in the early seventeenth century. It is like having mischievous children at last out of the house. But really the air of the Renaissance does them a lot of good; their cheeks glow and their talents look fresh. Leslie Fiedler, for instance, whose homoerotic interpretation of *Huckleberry Finn* has vexed so many readers, is on firm ground with the poet and Mr. W. H.; and Mr. Blackmur, whose critical reflections on Thomas Mann I had occasion to read recently, can at least be understood in this volume.

Now for a look at some of the theories, starting with the most extreme, which is, predictably, that of Mr. Fiedler. His approach, almost entirely from the sexual side, is justified or at least explained by the daintiness or queasiness of generations of commentators who have tried to clean the sonnets up and to keep them looking "normal." Very likely these have greatly provoked Fiedler, not the most patient of scholars. Unsatisfied with the conclusions he reaches about homoerotic elements in the sonnets, he ranges also through the plays, discovering masculine

relationships that can be revealed only by his dark light. I was somewhat taken aback by the swiftness with which he caught *Julius Caesar*
in his critical ray. I thought at first that he was referring to homosexual
overtones that may be detected in the relations between Cassius and
Brutus (they quarrel in a camp)—but no, the allegation is against Caesar himself, less irreproachable than his wife. "In Shakespeare's imagination, the older lover does not escape unscathed but is condemned, as
in *Julius Caesar*, to be stabbed to death; or destined, as in *Henry IV*, to
be cast off to die of a broken heart." Such statements are not made
carelessly, *de gaieté de coeur*. Mr. Fiedler is genuinely learned and is able
to find allusions and buried references that would escape the untrained
reader. He establishes, for instance, that the word *hell* refers also to the
vagina of the Dark Lady, that *fire* attributes to her both "the power to
damn and venereally infect the youth," that in Sonnet 129 "the expense
of spirit in a waste of shame" refers also to the emission of semen, and
that *waste* is also to be read *waist*, and that *Will* means carnal desire as
well. "The poem," he says, speaking of Sonnet 129, "rapidly becomes a
typical Renaissance palinode, a vehement Christian denial of the flesh."
In his view, the excoriation of the Dark Lady is to be understood as
Shakespeare's attempt to escape the ancient cult of Woman that dominated the poetry of Europe for long centuries. The sonnets should therefore be approached not so much as a personal narrative but as an
interpretation of love, "of love itself as understood in Western Europe
toward the end of the sixteenth century. The sonnets, that is to say, record one man's attempt to reconcile certain contradictions inherent in
courtly love codes as well as certain difficulties arising where those
codes confronted Christianity." What Mr. Fiedler argues is that Shakespeare invests a man with the mysterious powers that in the tradition of
courtly love always belonged to Woman. To him the difficulties that
arise between the code and Christianity appear sharper than they do to
Mr. Northrop Frye in this volume. I myself am on the sidelines with
the common reader, but I balk somewhat when Fiedler attributes a
homoerotic character to the figure of Dante's Beatrice. "Love as grace
is attached to the homoerotic Beatrice," he says. Because she is identified with Christ? That is a little steep!

With Stephen Spender we find ourselves in a milder climate. He is sensible, studious, a bit predictable perhaps, but reliable as well. His concern is not so much for "what happened" as for "the feeling involved." He speaks of a "dark and guilty side of the relationship between the two men, perhaps on account of certain acts with one another, perhaps through the moral involvement which made the poet suffer the friend's guilt as his own." Mr. Spender, less arbitrary and opinionated, is—like Oscar Wilde—far more absorbed in the Platonics of the matter and cares more for the philosophy and the account of love given in the sonnets than for the psychiatric aspect of things. He recommends that the poems be read as one half of a dialogue and not as a monologue. The beauty of the young man evidently is translated into other qualities—inner truth, virtue, poetry—and these in turn mingle in a conception of aristocracy. This is defined by Spender as "original being which has purity and integrity. It is perhaps the result of birth, but at any rate contains intrinsic virtue (symbolized by the rose) which he who *is* must not corrupt or betray. Original virtue is planted truth and where there is external beauty its only value is to correspond to this. There is the idea of continuity that runs from root, through bough, to flower and fruit, through the seasons, through history, through individual life. 'Ripeness is all.'" In this is expressed whatever religion is to be found in the sonnets, and Shakespeare draws from Christianity or from paganism whatever best suits his poetry.

A good deal of Mr. Spender's effort is devoted to the young man, of whom he draws a psychological portrait to explain the changes of Shakespeare's attitudes. He attributes to him a cold narcissism that forces the poet-lover to become also a preceptor:

> *They that have power to hurt and will do none,*
> *That do not do the thing they most do show,*
> *Who, moving others, are themselves as stone,*
> *Unmoved, cold, and to temptation slow,*
> *They rightly do inherit heaven's graces*

For Spender this is the poet warning his frigid beauty. Such frigidity has its proper virtue, but its defects are more terrible than the defects of warmer, more impulsive natures. These have a regenerative power. The

There Is Simply Too Much to Think About

cold have their own form of perfection. Missing it, however, they are doomed to a horrible decay. "Lilies that fester smell far worse than weeds."

Spender and Northrop Frye are both interested in the place of the sonnets in Shakespeare's development as a dramatist. Spender calls attention to Keats's notion of negative capability. "A poet," writes Keats, "is the most unpoetical of anything in existence; because he has no identity—he is continually in for—and filling some other body—the Sun, the Moon, the Sea and Men and Women who are creatures of impulse and poetical and have about them an unchangeable attribute—the poet has none; no identity—he is certainly the most unpoetical of God's creatures." Spender is inclined to accept the designation for Shakespeare of "camelion poet," the being of negative capability who enters into the existence of others, the hand that takes color from the medium in which it works, "the dyer's hand" of Sonnet III:

> *And almost thence my nature is subdued*
> *To what it works in, like the dyer's hand.*

There is a sense therefore in which the poet is at the mercy of existence, subjugated by its miraculous character, giving back miraculous words:

> *What is your substance, whereof are you made,*
> *That millions of strange shadows on you tend?*

This for Spender should lead us to reduce the importance of the purely autobiographical element in the sonnets.

Northrop Frye's essay I found the most valuable in the collection. For him the theme of love is best interpreted in relation "to the training of the poet." In the Renaissance, he tells us, "anyone who wanted to be a serious poet had to work at it. He was supposed to be what Gabriel Harvey called a 'curious universal scholar' as well as a practical expert in every known rhetorical device. . . . But learning and expertise would avail him little if he didn't, as we say, 'have it.' Have what? Have a powerful and disciplined imagination, to use the modern term, which, by struggling with the most tempestuous emotions, had learned to control them like plunging horses and force them into the service of poetry. . . . Love was for the Renaissance poet a kind of creative Yoga, an imaginative discipline, in which he watched the strongest possible feelings swirling around sexual excitement, jealousy, obsession, melancholy, as he was snubbed, inspired, teased, ennobled, forsaken, or made blissful by his mistress." This is not to say that the Renaissance poet set out to gain "experience" in the modern sense, but he was accustomed to open his mind and spirit in the manner that would complete his discipline, setting him in a certain relation to experience. "Poetry," Mr. Frye argues, "is not reporting on experience, and love is not uncultivated experience; in both poetry and love, reality is what is created, not the raw material for the creation."

Frye agrees with Spender and perhaps exceeds him in the matter of negative capability. Shakespeare has a capacity for subduing his nature to what it works in, he says, "unrivaled in the history of culture, a career which leaves him not only without a private life but almost without a private personality." But two statements by Frye struck me as extraordinarily relevant. One has to do with the selfish young man of the winter-and-absence sonnets who is transformed by the poet into "the radiant godhead of Sonnet 105. . . . But what relation does the youth have, if any, to the 'marriage of true minds'? There is little enough in the sonnets to show that the youth had a mind, much less a true one. We can hardly answer such a question: even Christianity, with all its theological apparatus, cannot clearly express the relation of whatever it is in us that is worth redeeming to what we actually are." And in conclusion Mr. Frye characterizes the sonnets as a "poetic realization of the whole range of love in the Western World." Perhaps, he says, Shakespeare has not unlocked his heart in these poems. He has remained somehow anonymous. But he has opened our minds and shown us "that poetry can be something more than a mighty maze of walks without a plan."

[1962]

The Writer as Moralist

I t is hard to know what is meant by a moral novelist or what people think they are talking about when they ask for commitment, affirmation or messages. The view attributed to Ernest Hemingway is "If you're looking for messages, try Western Union." Writers, oppressed by the popular demand for messages, can readily appreciate Hemingway's feelings on this subject. But the fact is that the American writer himself has been brought up to take messages seriously. Americans are a sententious people and are taught at an early age to moralize. They learn it in Sunday school. They learn it from Poor Richard—at least they did so in my time. In Chicago during the Twenties we were filled up with Poor Richard: "Little strokes fell great oaks." "Plow deep while sluggards sleep." These formulas seemed true and sound. Longfellow, whom we had to memorize by the yard, was also strongly affirmative: "Life is real! Life is earnest! And the grave is not its goal." And finally there was "The Chambered Nautilus": "Build thee more stately mansions, O my soul."

But while this was happening the Chicago papers reported gangland killings almost daily. Dion O'Banion was murdered in his flower shop, Hymie Weiss died violently on the steps of a church, the Capone headquarters was shot up by machine guns, Jake Lingle was murdered, Jake the Barber was abducted. To survive such events the moral teachings of literature had to be very strong. It might have occurred to schoolchildren as they passed from the pages of the *Tribune* to those of *Elson's Reader* that perhaps literature didn't have too much to do with life. "Give all to love," they read in Emerson. But in City Hall there were other ideas on giving and we had to learn (if we could) how to reconcile high principles with low facts.

Americans who care for this line of work need never be unemployed.

Emerson devoted his life to it. Thoreau, after he has directed our attention to some fact of nature, cannot rest until he has extracted a moral significance from it. Whitman, of course, is a persistent moralist. At times the moral purpose of these great writers of the nineteenth century tires us, their sermons seem too long—naïve. The crudity, disorder, ugliness and lawlessness of commercial and industrial expansion which scandalized them have been our only environment, our normalcy. And sometimes we are a little impatient with their romantic naïveté. When Emerson tells us, "Drudgery, calamity, exasperation, want, are instructors in eloquence and wisdom," we can't help wondering what he would have made of some of the sinister intricacies of a modern organization.

Walt Whitman in *Democratic Vistas* exhorted the poets of democracy to create archetypes, images of the American citizen, and charged writers with the highest of moral duties. "The priest departs, the divine literatus arrives," he wrote in a prophetic spirit. This particular brand of romanticism held the poet (the writer) to be the new spiritual leader and teacher of a community freed from slavery and superstition. Very often, and this was certainly true in Whitman's case, the poet offered himself as a model. In effect he said: If you want to know what an American of this democracy might be like—here I am. What I assume you shall assume and whoever touches me touches a man.

Ideas, when they achieve a very high level, can easily be accepted by a busy, practical people. Why not? Sublimity never hurt anyone. I have heard a worldly character, discussing the place of history in a curriculum, saying, "Well, why shouldn't the kids know about them kings? That's OK." Our national holdings in moral grandeur are OK too.

The teachings of Horatio Alger reached a wider audience than those of Whitman. Several generations of American read *Sink or Swim, Phil the Fiddler, Mark the Match Boy* and *From Canal Boy to President*, records of achievement that rewarded personal goodness with happiness and goods. Alger had a potent message—the message that worldly asceticism leads to capitalistic success—which was violently repudiated by many of our best novelists. The realists and naturalists in their anger and moral zeal turned Horatio Alger inside out. Norris and Dreiser and James T. Farrell give us a very different account of American life. Fitzgerald tells us in *Gatsby* of the "foul dust" that has a way of trailing youthful dreams of fulfillment. Nathanael West in *A Cool Million* tears the gospel of success to shreds.

The history of American literature can be described as a succession of encounters between rival claimants. The opposing parties have been variously described. Philip Rahv has said that American writers are either Palefaces or Redskins. We know that there was a genteel tradition, challenged by roughnecks. We know, too, that the regionalists were ranged against the cosmopolites, that certain agrarians insisted that roots and traditions were what we wanted and that their claims were disputed by novelists of urban class struggle. Visionaries disagreed with practicals, and writers of sensibility with social historians.

At the present time there is a sort of struggle going on between the squares and some other shape considered better. Or as I prefer to call it, between Cleans and Dirties. The Cleans want to celebrate bourgeois virtues. At least they *seem* to respect them—steadiness, restraint, a sense of duty. The Dirties are latter-day romantics and celebrate impulsiveness, lawless tendencies, the wisdom of the heart. The Cleans are occasionally conservative and sometimes speak for the Anglo-Saxon majority. The John P. Marquands and James Gould Cozzenses are Cleans of this latter type. Mr. Cozzens is a conscious ideologist of the Cleans. Henry Miller, a man whose talent is beyond dispute, is the father of the Dirties. His crudities can be explained by the excesses of the opposition, for it is the unfortunate result of this progress by contrasts in American literature that it always produces exaggeration. The hypocrisy of the apologists begot a hunger for scandal in the muckrakers that was exactly proportionate. Certain upper-class idiocies are answered by growling from the swamps. The snooty Puritanism of Mr. Cozzens calls forth the sexual Katzenjammers of William Burroughs. The sighing of Henry Adams in his club window as he laments the passing forever of precious qualities makes the immigrants more clamorous at Coney Island and Atlantic City.

But in many cases the differences are superficial, and Cleans and Dirties are remarkably similar. Not unpredictably, the Cleans express destructive feelings while the Dirties, when they become intelligible, are often sentimental moralists; their Prometheanism at times amounts to little more than the demand that preschool sexual explorations be publicly accepted as an adult standard. The Dirties are convinced that scandal is good for what ails us. And they try to make a sensation. But it is not easy to scandalize people. Everyone has seen and heard so much.

It's not easy to be a writer in the United States. Many people are worn out before they have picked the right clothes for the job. Even Whitman paid particular attention to his negligent appearance, feeling that the American singer should look the part. He was and was not one of the Roughs. His very presence, however, must have conveyed a moral intention. No less than Whitman, our Dirties, the Beats, offer themselves to their countrymen as exemplary types. They want their brethren, especially of the middle class, to express themselves more freely, more truthfully, to widen their horizons, to resist the drudgery of vacant duties and rebel against the servitude of banal marriage and unpleasurable sex. But similar improvements are suggested in the advice columns of ladies' magazines. They are not in themselves so frightfully revolutionary. Innocent of any wrongdoing, many of the middle-class brethren of the Beats have gone far beyond Kerouac, Mailer and Burroughs. They behave as they think writers should. The public is happy with their antics; it likes to read of their doings in the gossip columns, is tickled by the dirty words and consumes the writers like food, whiskey, tobacco or publicity, indifferent to the earnestness that is the source of these excesses.

Essentially the Dirties want us to be what we truly are, to be self-accepting, to cease to be horrified by our sexual impulses, however they may manifest themselves. They teach the honor of what is natural. Thus they make us ask, "Well, what is natural? Is it myself under the influence of junk, putting on a nightclub show at upward of $3,000 a week?" If this be nature, dear friends, it will not only redeem us morally but send us to a first-class loony bin. (We can afford it at three G's a week.)

The public never hesitates to demand an inordinate amount of goodness from writers. It considers clergymen, schoolteachers and novelists its moral servants. This is not an altogether unfair conception of things. But there are certain inconsistencies in the situation, which often produce strange effects.

Imagine that the managing editor of a large American daily who is under the influence of liquor is riding in his goat cart about his estate and that he falls and injures his hip and is taken to the hospital and put in traction. Imagine further that a friend (or flunky) has sent him a gift of three or four recent novels and that the bedridden editor reads these novels and is outraged by their immorality. The case is made more interesting if the great daily has, among other things, distorted the political news, reported its opponents with miserable unfairness and glaring prejudice, tried to goad the government into declaring war on Cuba, lowered the mental level of life in the community, debased the language, filled its pages with vast ads for pork butts, storm windows, undergarments, dollar sales, antiperspirants, failed to inform the public on matters of great importance, fought medical care for the aged and so forth. Such a daily might, to a reasonable judge, seem immoral. But the great man, outraged by some novelist's account of the life of the poor in his city, picks up the phone to chew out his book editor and to order him never again under any circumstances to mention the book, never to advertise it.

Great corporations seem at times to be intrinsically moral. No one asks a big company to affirm anything. It may, if it is public-spirited, hire an advertising firm to explain how much good it is doing and it spends tax-exempt money on quotations from Emerson and Walt Whitman. But its balance sheets are not published and discussed in hundreds of journals by high-minded critics. Thus the moral duties of business organizations are simpler and less burdensome than those of a poor lone novelist in the solitudes of Nebraska. Perhaps this is as it should be. The great corporation is guilty of a certain vaingloriousness but it doesn't make sweeping moral claims. It simply says: Capitalism is good for you. We are tough energetic realists and that is as God and the Founding Fathers meant it to be.

The writer, however, is bound by tradition to live under a different standard. Even if he is an avowed immoralist, even if he calls himself an anti-artist, a rebel, a hater of life, a desperate enemy of society, he is invariably motivated by a desire for truth. Clarification, deepening, illumination are moral aims even when the means seem to readers anarchic or even loathsome. The "wild" writings of Dadaists and surrealists were intended to shock the reader into a new, more vivid wakefulness and not to fill him with disgust. They execrated conventional literature and the bourgeois profession of authorship and were largely justified in so doing, but when the noise of cries and curses had died away it became quite clear that they were moralists, and romantic moralists at that. Among our Dirties a similar purpose is discernible. They have to my mind often splashed in filth for its own sake, have adored brutality for its own sake and been carried away by sickness for sickness's sake, but even William Burroughs, who has surpassed them all in bloodiness and perversity, seems to feel that it must all have a purpose and offers his *Naked Lunch* as a warning against narcotics. "The junk habit is public health problem number one of the world today," he says.

Of course, the more difficult things become, the more intensely the demand for affirmation is repeated. The dimmer, the grayer, the drearier they are, the louder the call for color and variety; and the more people cheat, the more they ask to hear about goodness. It must be in the course of nature. But it seems equally to be in the course of nature that the writers must try to honor such demands. Some with childlike earnestness, others more thoughtfully, try to suggest how what we all need so badly may be found: that sense of order, those indispensable standards that in other ages did not originate with novelists or playwrights.

Where are novelists and others to find these standards? What will they offer to the morally indigent public that asks for affirmation? If a novelist is going to affirm anything, he must be prepared to prove his case in close detail, reconcile it with hard facts, and he must even be prepared for the humiliation of discovering that he may have to affirm something different. The facts are stubborn and refractory and the art of the novel itself has a tendency to oppose the conscious or ideological purposes of the writer, occasionally ruining the most constructive intentions. But then, constructive intentions also ruin novels.

A good example of this sort of mutual destruction may be seen in a recent book by Graham Greene, *A Burnt-Out Case*. The theme of this novel is the spiritual aridity that begins with the self-disgust and self-rejection of a successful architect who is tired of the world and who comes to Africa in an effort to lose himself. He settles in a leper colony, vaguely drawn to the sick and to the medical missionary order, the priests and the doctor. At first he feels no genuine desire to help. He accepts death in himself and has no incentive to rid himself of the weight of purposeless existence, but presently he is drawn into the struggle with the disease and begins to make himself useful. We never get beyond this beginning in the novel, however, for it now breaks up. The young wife of one of the colonists, neurotic and silly, enters the story and with unconvincing histrionics causes the unlamented destruction of our burnt-out architect. What remains is a dubious affirmation of the necessity to desist from such devotion to our own suffering and to live and act for others. This, we must all grant, is a good thing to affirm; if Mr. Greene had been able to illustrate it passionately in his novel, we would all have been boundlessly grateful. As it is, we are indebted to him for his impressive description of the arid condition. But the novel itself, or the conscience of the artist, would not permit an affirmation to be forced and the book itself could therefore do nothing but disintegrate.

There was a carefree time in the history of the novel when the writer had nothing to do but to tell us what had happened. Experience in itself then pleased us; the description of experience was self-justifying. But nothing so simple now seems acceptable. It is the self, the person to whom things happen, who is perhaps not acceptable to the difficult and fastidious modern consciousness.

Writers of genius in the twentieth century (Paul Valéry, D. H. Lawrence, James Joyce among others) have made us question the stability of the experiencing self, have dissolved it in intellect or in instinct, in the common life of the species, in dream and in myth, and all together have made us aware that the sovereign individual, that tight entity whose fortunes, passions and moral problems filled the pages of novels (and of historical studies as well) was simply a fabrication, the product of a multitude of interests and influences and of our ignorance of physics, psychology and our social class divisions.

Whatever the objective results, the nihilistic passions produced by this revaluation have not worn off. If anything, the demand for radicalism in literature grows louder. We have recently been told by Leslie

Fiedler that it is the responsibility of novelists to be in the opposition, to say no, always no, no in accents of thunder. Mr. Fiedler reminds us that the negative tradition in literature, the tradition of prophetic denunciation, claims our loyalty.

Well, prophecy is nice work if you can get it. By this I mean that the prophet must be genuine. If, in place of the word of God that he *must* utter, he should have a literary program in his back pocket, his prophecies can never be accepted. Two warnings are necessary. First, the idiocy of orthodox affirmation and transparent or pointless optimism ought not to provoke an equal and opposite reaction. Second, no one should found his nay upon the study of literature. Literature may show, as some have argued, that from Sophocles to Shakespeare and from Shakespeare to Tolstoy, the greatest geniuses have cursed life. But the fact that a writer similarly curses it proves absolutely nothing. The deliberate choices of writers in such matters can never be interesting. We have had our bellyful of a species of wretchedness that is thoroughly pleased with itself. In France the wretched, angry, fulminating hero has come to be as common in bookshops as *choucroute garnie* in restaurants—despairing sauerkraut, a side dish to the knackwurst of middle-class Prometheanism. Really, it's about time everyone recognized that romantic despair in this form, naggingly conscious of the absurd, is absurdly portentous, not metaphysically "absurd." There is grandeur in cursing the heavens, but when we curse our socks we should not expect to be taken seriously.

The poets who continue the tradition of romantic pessimism that began so richly with Byron, Pushkin and Gérard de Nerval are now simply trifling. The optimism of the bourgeois that inflamed poets in the nineteenth century is no longer so proud and confident. It began to totter several generations ago and by now has fallen on its face several times and has a dusty discredited look. If optimism were not so poor and shaky it would not solicit affirmation continually.

Most writers agree that their art is moral. Tolstoy held that a novelist should have a moral relation to his subject matter and his definition of morality was passionate. The writer should either love or hate his subject. Tolstoy condemned neutrality or objectivity therefore as inartistic. He was contradicted by the "art for art's sake" novelists who explicitly rejected moral purpose. Probably Flaubert is the most significant of these. He, and Joyce following him, felt that anything that might be described by us as a moral commitment would be a serious error. The artist, said Joyce, should have no apparent connection with his work. His place is in the wings, apart, paring his nails, indifferent to the passions of his creatures. Such aesthetic objectivity was an imperative with Joyce and in *A Portrait of the Artist* he explicitly rejected anything in art that excited desire or a need for action. The feeling a work of art should arouse is in his view static, beyond desire, too pure to be involved in judgments, contemplative.

This is a rather lofty attitude in a novelist. It would seem more appropriate to a poet or a musician, for the novel meets life at a commoner level where confusion is inordinate. The art for art's sake novelist believed in pure form, classical order. Order of this sort is seldom available and in chaotic conditions such beliefs must inevitably lead to disappointment.

A novelist of this sort will not agree to love or hate as Tolstoy says he should. He reserves comment. He refrains from holding an opinion. He believes, as Erich Auerbach writes of Flaubert, "that every event, if one is able to express it purely and completely, interprets itself and the persons involved in it far better and more completely than any opinion or judgment appended to it could do. Upon this conviction—that is, upon a profound faith in the truth of language responsibly, candidly and carefully employed—Flaubert's artistic practice rests." Professor Auerbach calls this "objective seriousness" and makes the following observation: "Objective seriousness, which seeks to penetrate to the depths of the passions and entanglements of human life, but without itself becoming moved, or at least without betraying that it is moved—this is an attitude which one expects from a priest, a teacher or a psychologist rather than from an artist. The priest, teacher and psychologist wish to accomplish something practical, which is far from Flaubert's mind."

Thus it apparently makes no difference what the artist should decide about his commitment, whether he considers himself a moralist or a purely objective artist. The writer in any case finds that he bears the burdens of priest or teacher. Sometimes he looks like the most grotesque of priests, the most eccentric of teachers, but I believe the moral function cannot be divorced from art.

This means that the artist had better not strain so to be didactic. To look for elaborate commitments is vain. Commitments are far more rudimentary than any "position" or intellectual attitude might imply. I should like to suggest that commitment in a novel may be measured by its power to absorb us, by the energy it contains. A book lacking in power cannot be moral. Dullness is worse than obscenity. A dull book is wicked. It may intend to be as good as gold, as nice as pie, as sweet as can be, but if it is banal and boring it is evil.

What we sense in modern literature continually is not the absence of a desire to be moral but rather a pointless, overwhelming, vague, objectless moral fervor. The benevolent excitement of certain novelists and dramatists is not an isolate literary phenomenon. What is obscurer in them than in political leaders or social planners is what they are going to be benevolent about and how they are going to be benevolent or constructive. In this sphere we see a multitude of moral purposes in wild disorder. For as long as novelists deal with ideas of good and evil, justice and injustice, social despair and hope, metaphysical pessimism and ideology, they are no better off than others who are involved cognitively with these dilemmas. They can only go the same ways: The liberal way, the way of nature, the Promethean way, the way of socialism—the list is almost endless. From it the writer may make his choice and proceed to affirm his truth. It is then scarcely possible for his art to avoid the fate of his ideas. They triumph together or fall together. Novelists as different as Camus, Thomas Mann and Arthur Koestler are alike in this respect. Their art is as strong as their intellectual position—or as weak.

For this reason an art that is to be strong cannot be based on opinions. Opinions can be accepted, questioned, dismissed. A work of art can't be questioned or dismissed.

One last thing. Not too many people will disagree if the proposition is put as follows—either we want life to continue or we do not. If we don't want to continue, why write books? The wish for death is powerful and silent. It respects actions; it has no need of words.

But if we answer yes, we do want it to continue, we are liable to be asked how. In what form shall life be justified? That is the essence of the moral question. We call a writer moral to the degree that his imagination indicates to us how we may answer naturally, without strained arguments, with a spontaneous, mysterious proof that has no need to argue with despair.

[1963]

Beatrice Webb's America

The Sidney Webbs came to the United States in 1898 to have a look at American institutions; they had already published their study, in fifteen volumes, of local government in England. Crossing the continent they continued westward to Australia and New Zealand on a trip around the world. Beatrice Webb kept a daily record of her impressions, a document that might have been left to us by one of Shaw's bluestocking heroines. Mrs. Webb, gently bred, daughter of a railway magnate, rejected the life (was it a life?) of a leisured Englishwoman and scorned the idea of a conventional and proper marriage. "When I turned to social investigation as my craft in life," she wrote in *My Apprenticeship*, "it was just my experience of London Society that started me with a personal bias effectually discounting, even if it did not wholly supersede, my father's faith in the social value of a leisured class."

Judging by the diary, Mrs. Webb never quite succeeded in changing her social complexion. Congressional leaders in Washington, bosses in New York, Chicago, Denver and San Francisco, she described with a note of patrician condescension, a sort of socialistic snobbery. She reminds me often of Tolstoy as he is described in Gorky's memoirs—the grand seigneur in peasant garb. Faultfinding, humorless, self-important, she was still a shrewd and observant woman with a quick grasp of new and complicated situations. After a week in Boston she concludes a brilliant discussion of the political scene there with the following summary: "Boston is administered by public spirited and well-informed brains, and corrupt and inefficient hands. The city of Boston is in fact governed by its aristocracy working through a corrupt democracy."

How she must have astonished the bosses, who thought they were entertaining—or giving the brush-off to—a pretty English visitor and found the glad hand ignored by this formidable inquisitor who demanded information about the police, the voters, patronage, sewage and paving.

She quickly discerned the inordinate powers of Congressional committees, the dangers of bureaucracy, the complacency of the public toward graft, the power of business in government. She noted "the American contempt for the vested interest or 'established expectations' of the individual citizen. Private enterprise is permitted to trample on the individual." She was shrewd too in her observations of the businessman and manager. She noted in Pittsburgh ("a veritable Hell of a place") the militant arrogance of the people who got things done at the Carnegie mills, the "brainworkers." Carnegie himself she thought a "reptile." Her portraits of such types have nothing old-fashioned about them. The attitudes of "private power" are evidently little changed.

But she was not more flattering in her estimates of a man like labor-friendly Governor John Peter Altgeld of Illinois, who immediately seemed to her "a cross between a working man and a dissenting minister," who lacked "personal dignity and a certain 'savoir faire.'" Mrs. Webb intended to judge the intellectual and moral qualities of people by the polish of their social harness. Woodrow Wilson pleased her, Teddy Roosevelt made her enthusiastic—he was "deliciously racy." Thomas Reed, Speaker of the House, she thought would make a "fairly good cashier." "He is said to be pious; he may be honest: but he does not matter." Idle American women she described as painfully dull creatures, hardly worth one's notice, "without intellectual curiosity or public spirit."

A word about her style. On the whole it is precise and sharp: Cornell students are "well-mannered but somewhat unhealthy looking youths, bad teeth, spotty complexions, narrow chests and sloping shoulders." Robert Lincoln "floated on his father's reputation into a position of importance. He had the ill-humor of continuous over-feeding and over-drinking: the hard uninspired intelligence of a complete materialist." Joseph W. Bailey, House minority leader, "to English eyes, looks a cad of the worst description, a strange combination of a low-class actor and rowdy stump orator."

Her explanations of the American political setup are invariably lucid and to the point. The diary contains a memorable description of San Francisco, a brief history of Hawaii and a lively, spirited and interested report of a meeting with one of the wives of a Mormon elder, herself a doctor by profession and running against her husband in an election for the state senate. Mrs. Webb allows the lady to tell her own story, a fascinating one, and concludes that she was a "pure-minded little soul" but probably had no political ability and only a fragmentary medical knowledge. Mrs. Webb's high-mindedness here is redeemed only by her remark about polygamy: "Only one bull is required for twenty cows."

It would seem that the farther west Mrs. Webb traveled, the greater was her freedom from the self-imposed obligation to compare everything she saw with the English experience. Insular and provincial as she was, the crossing of the Rockies seems to have liberated her mind and her style. West of the Rockies, too, the Webbs were relieved of their single-minded pursuit of the facts of local government in the United States (Washington was something of a disappointment: "An unfortunate time to be at Washington, seeing that all the politicians to whom we have introductions are completely absorbed in Cuba") and Mrs. Webb could relax a little. Viscount Bryce and Alexis de Tocqueville looked more penetratingly into American institutions. Mrs. Webb was not a generous observer; what her journal does not lack, however, is intelligence and charm.

[1963]

Recent Fiction: A Tour of Inspection

T he individual in his peculiarly modern form first appears in literature with Montaigne, to take an arbitrary starting point. Montaigne in his *Essays* presents himself as quite a plain and ordinary man
but one in whom everything essential may be seen: "I desire . . . to be
viewed as I appear in mine own genuine, simple, and ordinary manner,
without study and artifice: for it is myself I paint." Shunning extremes,
he concentrates upon the average. This, however, he investigates in
depth, and fixing his attention on matters entirely human he emerges
with a new conception of the scope and meaning of a personal existence. Man lives on this earth, his life is fragile, his time is short; still,
he enjoys many remarkable powers and he may acquire a profound
skeptical wisdom. The essays of Montaigne are a personal document,
parts of an extensive confession that, unlike the *Confessions* of Saint
Augustine, does not have a spiritual character. For Montaigne the human condition is secular. The facts, all of the facts, though many of
them are sure to be trifling, belong in his description of the human
creature. The whole sum of the facts is necessary. Mixed though they
be, they do not prevent the individual from attaining his own sort of
human grandeur. Thus Montaigne is able to pass with ease from kitchen
matters to metaphysics. This mixture of things high and low is peculiarly modern.

Romantic individualism two centuries later, in Rousseau, proclaims
the uniqueness of the Self and, much more aggressively and ambitiously
than in Montaigne, contrasts the individual and the surrounding world.
Nineteenth-century romanticism celebrates the individual, his natural
and intuitive qualities, and sees in civilization his great enemy. It awaits
a new and broader freedom and prefers human life to have an aesthetic

character. But these brave expectations have, in fact, a very brief career. In the modern world (and romanticism is a modern phenomenon) the excited sense of the exceptional is required to bear the experience of the commonplace. An industrialized mass society cannot accommodate any sizable population of Prometheans and geniuses. The century of Shelley's Prometheus is also that of Emile Zola's near-primate peasants and proletarians. The large claims made for the self in the early period of romanticism begin to sound foolish in the modern age of large populations. To men of acute intelligence, by the second half of the nineteenth century, romantic individualism began to appear fraudulent. Dostoyevsky shows (in the figure of Miüsov in *The Brothers Karamazov*, for instance) how easy it is for comfortable, indolent people, thoroughly bourgeois in spirit, to think of themselves as romantic idealists. As romantic feeling becomes vulgarized and debased, literature begins to treat the romantic hero with sharp hostility.

Early realism, in the novels of Balzac, makes much of the individual. Though it examines life in a contemporary and ordinary setting, the Balzacian novel grants full dignity to people from the lower ranks of society. Romanticism in the last years of the eighteenth century began to see great virtue in the humble life. The plowboy, the cotter, the simple country girl charmed Burns and Wordsworth. Far less attractive, however, was the ordinary civilized urban man who appeared in the realistic novels of the nineteenth century. Examined with great and even tragic seriousness by Balzac, he proved to be a creature of deep and distorted passions. Old Goriot, Grandet, Vautrin—the monomaniac father, the genius of avarice, the inspired criminal—are great figures taken from common life. That common life is, in eighteenth-century novels like *Tom Jones*, still the material of comedy. Serious realism belongs to the nineteenth century.

It soon appears that the degradation of the common life is plainer to nineteenth-century writers than its heroic possibilities. Hawthorne, in a prefatory chapter to *The Scarlet Letter* called "The Custom House," tells with gentle but bitter irony why he was obliged to write a romance. He draws a deadly picture of the customhouse at Salem, its sluggishness and dullness, and of the old men, originally slow-witted or decaying, who make up the staff. This to him is modern Salem. The "dim and dusky grandeur" of the old town and its colonists who came with sword and Bible, the pious but fierce Puritans who persecuted Quakers and burned witches—all of that has ended in this modern dreariness. The writer must seem to his magnificent ancestors to be shamefully insignificant. "'What is he?' murmurs one gray shadow of my forefathers to the other. 'A writer of story-books! What kind of business in life—what mode of glorifying God, or being serviceable to mankind in his day and generation—may that be?'"

In an effort to save himself—mind and spirit threatened by the torpor and emptiness of the customhouse—Hawthorne writes his romance: "It was a folly, with the materiality of this daily life pressing so intrusively upon me, to attempt to fling myself back into another age, or to insist on creating the semblance of a world out of airy matter, when, at every moment, the impalpable beauty of my soap-bubble was broken by the rude contact of some actual circumstance. The wiser effort would have been to diffuse thought and imagination through the opaque substance of today, and thus to make it a bright transparency; to spiritualize the burden that began to weigh so heavily; to seek, resolutely, the true and indestructible value that lay hidden in the petty and wearisome incidents, and ordinary characters with which I was now conversant. The fault was mine. The page of life that was spread out before me seemed dull and commonplace only because I had not fathomed its deeper import. A better book than I shall ever write was there."

We cannot be sure that Hawthorne was completely in earnest, since he is in effect apologizing for a masterpiece. He is not alone, however, in his dissatisfaction with ordinary life or with the writer's incapacity to deal with it. "Nothing conceivable is so petty, so insipid, so crowded with paltry interests, in one word so anti-poetic, as the life of man in the United States," wrote Alexis de Tocqueville in 1840. He added, "But among the thoughts which it suggests there is always one which is full of poetry, and that is the hidden nerve which gives vigor to the frame."

Novelists of the nineteenth century, nourished on romantic individualism, find that they are obliged to cope with the results of industrial collectivism. Cultivated inwardness, a rich private life, becomes possible for a fairly large number of people. But at the same time the individual, the single, separate self, feels severely limited, oppressed by the weight of numbers, by nature, by the conditions of life—his distinction rendered valueless by the lack of true power. In every direction the romantic individual sees injustice, the threat of debility, sickness, senselessness and ruin. The typical hero of the later nineteenth-century novel has been robbed of his vitality by Christian idealism (in Thomas Hardy), is spoiled or destroyed by the arrangements of civilized society (in Tolstoy), decides not to get out of bed (in Goncharov) or lives under elaborate restraints (Henry James). Emma Bovary, the heroine of Flaubert's great novel, is an altogether insignificant person who belongs to the petty bourgeoisie of the provinces. But *Madame Bovary* is something more than the record of a wretched life. It is a very special sort of aesthetic creation, immensely influential, which gives to the performance of the artist, his virtuosity and discipline, his reading of fate, an importance that belonged formerly to the subject of the novel. In *Madame Bovary* art itself makes up for lack of mind or heart in the characters. The pettiness of the heroine is granted. It is the art that is exalted. The aim of the Flaubertian novelist is to immerse himself in his subject, self-forgetfully. Flaubert, says Erich Auerbach in one of his superb critical studies in *Mimesis*, "believes that the truth of the phenomenal world is also revealed in linguistic expression."

The world is, however, in the novelist's view, an incredibly complicated and frightful thing. It is in reality a multitude of private worlds without connection, explains Auerbach, where "each is alone, none can understand another, or help another to insight; there is no common world of men, because it could only come into existence if many should find their way to their own proper reality, the reality which is given to the individual—which then would be also the true common reality." Individualism thus finds sanctuary in the artist himself, but only very briefly, for twentieth-century literature does not tolerate this. It assails the older sort of romantic individualism fiercely. The Christians (T. S. Eliot) attack it as strongly as the Marxists (Bertolt Brecht). In *The Cocktail Party,* Edward Chamberlayne cannot believe in his own personality; in Brecht's *The Measures Taken*, a zealous young Communist organizer is liquidated by his comrades because he is an individual, hence dangerous to the Party. From still another point of view D. H. Lawrence declares the nullity of civilized personalities. He finds, for

There Is Simply Too Much to Think About

instance, in his essay on Melville (in *Studies in Classic American Literature*), that in his "human self" Melville is "almost dead. That is, he hardly reacts to human contacts any more: or only ideally: or just for a moment. His human-emotional self is almost played out. He is abstract, self-analytical and abstracted. And he is more spellbound by the strange slidings and collidings of Matter than by the things men do." Melville's is an "isolated, far-driven soul, the soul which is now alone, without any real human contact." Ordinary and conventional conceptions of the self are to Lawrence "painted millstones." He thought that we were witnessing the ghastly end of a false "social" and slavish selfhood. Enduring the horror of this death, we may expect to be reborn. This, as modern attitudes go, is comparatively optimistic. Lawrence expects rebirth and regeneration, a new and greater victory for the instincts, to occur. A statement made in the early 1920s by Hugo von Hofmannsthal, the Viennese poet, frequently quoted by critics, expresses a far more nihilistic attitude: "Our time is unredeemed; and do you know what it wants to be redeemed from? . . . The individual. . . . Our age groans too heavily under the weight of this child of the sixteenth century that the nineteenth fed to monstrous size . . . We are anonymous forces. Potentialities of the soul. Individuality is an arabesque we have discarded. . . . I should go so far as to assert that all the ominous events we have been witnessing in the last twelve years are nothing but a very awkward and longwinded way of burying the concept of the European individual in the grave it has dug for itself."

Such a position, as the critic Lionel Abel points out in his highly original book *Metatheatre*, must make "moral suffering absurd," and morality itself, in the words of the Symbolist poet Arthur Rimbaud, a "weakness of the brain," for if man is an "anonymous force" then morality may be one of the historical costumes it has pleased him to wear during several millennia. For moral ideas, whose focus is the individual, the present tendency is to substitute ideas of class, nation or breed. In the political sphere, classical liberalism holds that the sovereign Many ought to be guided by the gifted One or Few. "The initiation of all wise or noble things comes and must come from individuals; generally at first from some one individual," said J. S. Mill in *On Liberty*. The political significance of the anti-individualism of Occidental literature in the twentieth century is, however, far from clear. The Many would be celebrated in the literature of a democracy, Tocqueville prophesied, as the One grew insignificant. Modern literature has not fulfilled this prophecy. Writers of great power, even of genius, express their disgust and hatred for the Self. They cry out for the demolition of that false god. They often admire the hardness, even the brutality, of the man of the people or of the crowd; but on the whole the indictment of romantic individualism, itself romantic, and the dislike of humanism, itself of humanistic origin, suffices them. None has gone so far as to summon us to enter what Dostoyevsky's Grand Inquisitor called the "unanimous and harmonious ant-heap," the final form of collectivity.

Two recent novels, Alexander Solzhenitsyn's *One Day in the Life of Ivan Denisovich* and James Jones's *The Thin Red Line*, show, the one by describing life in a Soviet prison camp, the other in an account of the American infantryman as he advances against the Japanese on Guadalcanal, what the submergence of the individual can be like. There are immense differences, of course, between a combat soldier and a slave laborer, but these differences make the similarities all the more curious. Both books deal with the struggle for survival and with attitudes toward authority and, consequently, toward the Self, on which survival depends. Bread and warmth are what Ivan Denisovich mainly needs; these and the occasional luxury of tobacco incessantly occupy his thoughts as he labors in the arctic darkness. The man who breaks the camp rules cannot live. Confinement in a cold cell will destroy his health. But the man who does not break its rules cannot live either. He must take every opportunity to pick up what may be useful; he must learn how to conceal a broken bit of useful metal from the searching guards, how to sew a piece of bread into his mattress. He cannot afford, even for a moment, to feel unwell. Because he is feverish and steals a few moments of rest in his bunk, Ivan Denisovich is penalized by the Tartar guard. He asks, "What for, citizen chief?" (Prisoners are not allowed to use the word *comrade*.) Solzhenitsyn notes that this question is asked "with more chagrin in his voice than he felt." Ivan knows, however, that he cannot plead with the Tartar and he protests merely

There Is Simply Too Much to Think About

for the sake of form. The very thought of appealing to sympathy or expecting justice is ruled out. Any such thought or expectation would weaken the will to survive and must therefore be a betrayal of that will. Prisoners like the ex-naval officer who do not quickly forget their past dignity and have not learned to check their tongues will eat cold food in jail and they will die of it. At twenty degrees below zero, thinly clad and underfed, a man cannot live. Ivan Denisovich reflects, "There wouldn't be a warm corner for a whole month. Not even a doghouse. And fires were out of the question. There was nothing to build them with. Let your work warm you up, that was your only salvation." And elsewhere he observes, "Real jail was when you were kept back from work." He is therefore grateful to the Tartar for imposing a work penalty.

Spartan self-discipline and rugged peasant cunning have enabled Ivan to endure years of labor in the taiga. He will not think about the authorities, about government, about rights, about his own unjust imprisonment, about the sufferings of the other prisoners, about home and family—all this would vex his heart needlessly and waste energy. His thoughts are all of bread, sugar, fish stews, boots, and of being the sort of man who will make the grade. Of the meek virtues of Platon Karataev in *War and Peace*, whose simple wisdom Pierre Bezukhov learns in captivity, there is scarcely a hint. Though Ivan Denisovich is not without a rudimentary religious faith, this faith is as meager as his diet. At the day's end he thanks God for survival. "Glory be to Thee, O Lord, Another day over. Thank you I'm not spending tonight in the cells. Here it's still bearable." Alyosha, a religious prisoner in the next bunk, overhears the whispered words and urges Ivan Denisovich to pray. Ivan Denisovich, however, replies that prayer, like hope, is dangerous. "Prayers," he says, "are like those appeals of ours. Either they don't get through or they're returned with 'rejected' scrawled across them." Faith will neither move mountains nor shorten the prisoner's sentence. But the Baptist Alyosha is horrified by the mere thought of freedom. "In freedom," he says, "your last grain of faith will be choked with weeds. . . . Here you have time to think about your soul." If it be God's will that Alyosha should sit in prison, somehow it works out all right for him. "But for whose sake am *I* here?" says Ivan Denisovich. "Because we weren't ready for war in forty-one? For that? But was that *my* fault? But these theoretical considerations are not very important and the religious naïveté of Alyosha the Baptist may be intended to satisfy the antireligious demands of Soviet literary policy.

Ivan Denisovich has greater factual, or documentary, than literary interest. It is pedestrian work, lacking in color and passion, in dramatic vision. The facts themselves, however, are strangely eloquent and the very modesty or flatness with which they are stated is suited to the subhuman grimness of the camp and to Ivan's almost deindividualized desire to endure.

Such animal endurance, the entire object of Ivan's struggle, represents in itself a positive or heroic activity to certain modern writers. For Bertolt Brecht, to whom the individual is really the so-called individual, and in whose view all human realities must undergo a radical review, the truth should be sought in illusionless endurance. His Galileo says, "I don't understand a man who doesn't use his mind to fill his belly." The purpose of such a statement is not to debase the mind but to elevate the body, as Mr. Abel in his *Metatheatre* argues. Whatever we wish to assert about mankind must be squared with the commonest facts of human conduct, and the interpretation of those common facts offered by authority and tradition is not acceptable to Galileo.

Such issues are present, though seldom so clearly stated, in most modern books. They are quite explicit, however, in *The Thin Red Line*. That war makes men of boys is of course old stuff. What interests James Jones is the civilian society that sends forth the boys and the kind of brutality that shapes them into manhood. The slack codes of family and community collapse in situations of primitive violence, and conventional beliefs are exposed as impositions which an illusionless man will never take as his own again, though the wisdom of convenience, the wisdom of the survivor, may counsel an apparent acceptance. The boy still imagines that he has the value of an individual and that his survival is a matter of great concern to someone, somewhere. The hardened man has realized that the truth is otherwise; he has been thrust into the path of destruction by the people at home and the sooner he grasps what this means the better. It matters little in the greater scheme of things whether he stands or falls. The older, wiser, tougher men, the professionals, understand this. Someone like First Sergeant Welsh believes it with absolute or metaphysical conviction. Of those who do not understand, he is intolerant and he waits with a certain eagerness for reality to punish the ignorant, the credulous, the naïve and the immature. Welsh's toughness and harshness is more than a personal attitude; it is also his rudimentary wisdom. He drives away a young soldier in the combat area who wants permission to dig a slit trench near his. To cling to someone else is miserable; it betrays an unformed character, for which the seasoned combat soldier has an intuitive contempt. The word that expresses for Welsh all that a sensible man, a real man, can care about in this world is *property*. He has no clear idea what he means by it and mutters the word to himself like an incantation—"Property." The wise have it; the rest are suckers. But even Sergeant Welsh has irrational impulses of generosity. He crawls out under fire to bring back a wounded man. The effort is wasted, the man is dying and Welsh returns to cover. "Sobbing audibly for breath, he made himself a solemn unspoken promise never again to let his screwy wacked-up notions get the better of his common sense."

In these circumstances a "fact" is whatever brings men to a common level. Terror, bloodlust, greed and sexual excitement are the main facts. One of Jones's characters, not ordinarily given to reflection, goes so far as to wonder whether the craving for a peculiar sort of sexual gratification may not be an ineradicable cause of wars. Under threat of death and liberated from ordinary selfhood, these soldiers are subject to fierce bursts of cruelty and perversity. A mythologist might say, in the terms of which modern thought has grown so fond, that the presiding god is not Apollo, god of individuation, but Dionysus, who represents the instincts, the species.

J. F. Powers, in *Morte D'Urban*, observes life in a very different sphere. Father Urban, the hero of his novel, belongs to the imaginary order of St. Clement. He is an active worldly priest, much in demand as a speaker, a sociable, charming man, fond of food and sports and company. Urban serves his order well in Chicago and the decision of his superior to transfer him to a remote part of Minnesota is, to say the least, trying his patience. He finds it incomprehensible. He obeys, of course, but with dragging feet. His impression of the country north of Minneapolis, as he views it from the train window, is that it is "flat and treeless, Illinois without people. It didn't attract, it didn't repel. He saw more streams than he'd see in Illinois, but they weren't working. November was winter here. Too many white frame farmhouses, not new and not old, not at all what Father Urban would care to come to for Thanksgiving or Christmas. Rusty implements. Brown dirt. Gray skies. Ice. No snow. A great deal of talk about this on the train. Father Urban dropped entirely out of it after an hour or so. . . . The Voyageur arrived in Duesterhaus a few minutes before eleven that morning, and Father Urban was the only passenger to get off."

Father Wilfred, whom Urban had known during their novitiate as Bunny Bestudnik, is head of the Clementine Foundation in Duesterhaus. The property is in poor shape, the means of the Fathers are limited, and Wilfred is trying to make things go as efficiently as possible. He thinks of little besides tile, hardware, paint, machinery, fuel and free rides on the railroad. The interests of the Fathers are approximately those of any group of Midwesterners who have a place to run. Urban, as his name hints, is something of a sophisticate, and he sniffs at these hicks. He is far from humble, as he himself is aware. Wilfred is poky, unimaginative and bumbling. Urban is knowledgeable and worldly, charming and proud.

Mr. Powers's theme is the religious life of practical, average Americans and he develops it with a fine talent for wry comedy. He avoids strong contrasts and emphatic statements and, at times, follows this method of restraint to the verge of vagueness or passivity. In *Morte D'Urban* Roman Catholicism meets the American Way of Life, and the results of this encounter are not quite clear because the spiritual qualities of Urban, though there is no question of the genuineness of his calling, are very dimly outlined.

The Clementine Order has a wealthy patron named Billy Cosgrove, who is fond of Father Urban's company. Billy is generous but erratic; he is in fact a spoiled, bullying, idle man whose life is one ferocious, unending holiday. He is a big spender, and he likes doing things for the Church. Urban is half amused by willful, playful Billy, pardons his vulgarity and his insolence and rather enjoys the good meals and the fine cars—Urban has a weakness for sports and for automobiles. Partly because he enjoys it, partly for the good of the order, Urban accompanies Billy on a fishing trip to the North Woods. There Billy's temper becomes ugly. He has had bad luck with the fish at Bloodsucker Lake, and seeing a stag swim by he decides that he must have the antlers. He tries to drown the animal by holding its head under water. Such cruelty is more than Urban can bear. He speeds up the outboard so that Billy falls into the water. When he is rescued, Billy then dumps Father Urban into the lake and speeds off. The effect of this is by no means comic.

Urban has been thinking, in the boat before these events, about the matter of living or dying for the Faith and he has made a comparison between Billy and William the Conqueror, "mild to good men of God and stark beyond all bounds to those who withsaid his will." This parallel is mildly amusing. Billy could never give a damn about history. He is a completely contemporary American phenomenon, bent utterly on having his own way, violently pursuing his happiness and losing none of his strength in thought. Of the two it is he who has the more passionate character. Urban's religion is far from intense. It too is perhaps American—liberal, relaxed, nice, comfortable, unobtrusive, rather unfocused. The book concludes with two highly significant changes in the life of Urban. After he has been struck in the head by a golf ball he has tormenting headaches and fits of dizziness. It is at this time that he is appointed Father Provincial and returns to Chicago. As Provincial he disappoints everyone but it presently becomes clear that he is unwell. To hide his attacks from callers he turns aside and pretends to read his breviary, gaining a reputation for piety "which, however, was not entirely unwarranted now." The concluding pages of the novel are written without irony and are, I think, intended to show a changed Urban, martyred by sufferings and brought to the fulfillment of his religious destiny. Actually they show us very little; they attempt, rather, to tell us that we cannot expect to follow the progress of Urban's soul. Its condition is incommunicable.

Mr. Powers adheres to the convention accepted by most realistic writers. He does not give his characters thoughts or emotions they are not "realistically" likely to have. It is odd that religious novelists like

Powers, or like Graham Greene and Evelyn Waugh, with whom he obviously agrees, should be unwilling to offer a specifically religious psychology in their books. Anything deeper than the ordinary circumstances of life permit us to see may only be hinted at and since we are confined by these ordinary circumstances in corruption, in states of boredom and in egotism, the most spiritual person is the one who suffers most through the human condition. The heroes of these novelists are thus for the most part scarcely articulate martyrs. The realities of the world are more terrible than the darkest inventions of the imagination. Mr. Powers describes those realities as ably as François Mauriac or Graham Greene or Eliot or any other Christian writer and he is just as reticent in describing spiritual experience. But what, after all, *is* a spiritual life in the twentieth century? These writers refuse to enlighten us. Perhaps the fault is ours for demanding enlightenment with our usual positivistic assurance that a spiritual life ought to be a reality within our grasp. But we are reading novels or witnessing plays by writers who have accepted the challenge of a play or novel and ought to show us the actualities of a religious life. In almost every case the choice of a spiritual course results not in correction but in death, and the Christianity of the modern religious novel is the Christianity of the Passion and the Cross; its religious life turns out to be a saintly death. These writers see our choice, as the philosopher Gabriel Marcel puts it, lying between "the termite colony and the Mystical Body." Such a view perhaps expresses Romantic Disappointment more than it does Christian Faith.

Gabriel, the hero of Philip Roth's *Letting Go*, has been brought up to lead a comfortable life but also to think of "higher things." These "higher things" interfere somewhat with his happiness. But though the shadow of pain may pass over him as he eats and drinks, there is light enough to find the spoon. He is aware that it is somewhat degrading in a world like this to be a vulgar epicurean, a petty bourgeois creature. He reads (Gabriel is a graduate student) of noble feelings, great enterprises, sublime sensibilities and he feels it is faintly ridiculous to pursue his private ends so aggressively and ambitiously, but this does not alter his cast-iron selfishness. He has just enough self-awareness or "unhappy

There Is Simply Too Much to Think About

consciousness" to consider himself sensitive in his love affairs and he can be pleased with his insightfulness while he does what young men of his class generally do. As in Lewis Carroll's "The Walrus and the Carpenter," tears are shed, but the little oysters are eaten anyway. Gabriel wants to behave well. He tries to obtain a baby for adoption by an unhappy couple and the pages dealing with the pregnant waitress who is prepared to give away her child are among the liveliest in the book. But the personal life with its problems of personal adjustment and its pursuit of personal happiness cannot be as interesting to us as it is to Mr. Roth and Gabriel. Mr. Roth is evidently not aware that he is strengthening the case of the antipersonalists by being so solemn about Gabriel's troubles. We know from our first meeting with Gabriel that he is a rather tough young man who in basic matters—food, shelter, money, advancement—will always make out. There is nothing to be said against a prudent hero or against any hero whose case is clearly and interestingly stated. The difficulty is that Gabriel expects to fascinate everyone though there is no one who fascinates *him*.

Peter, in John Updike's *The Centaur*, is a youthful hero of a slightly different sort. He presents us with a case of what modern critics, with regrettable ponderousness, call sensibility. Here are some of the typical thoughts and impressions of a sensibility: "I had been admiring a section of lavender shadow under the walnut tree in my painting of the old yard. I had loved that tree; when I was a child there had been a swing attached to the limb that was just a scumble of almost-black in the picture. Looking at this streak of black, I relived the very swipe of my palette knife, one second of my life that in a remarkable way had held firm. It was this firmness, I think, this potential fixing of a few passing seconds, that attracted me, at the age of five, to art. For it is at about that age, isn't it, that it sinks in upon us that things do, if not die, certainly change, wiggle, slide, retreat, and, like dabs of sunlight on the bricks under a grape arbor on a breezy June day, shuffle out of all identity?"

This passage offers several illuminating curiosities to our study. These are the words and ideas of a high school boy. At fifteen he already has a nostalgia for early childhood. He remembers with a tone of elegy and elderly wisdom the beginning of his aesthetic development. Jonathan Swift in old age was said to have congratulated himself on having written so well in his youth, but Mr. Updike's adolescent hero is moved by the artistic triumphs he had at the age of five. This deeply subjective musing requires a careful choice of words, rhythms and images. A poet might have written this paragraph, if he had thought it worth his while. A student of literature can detect in it echoes of Henry James and of Virginia Woolf and of the James Joyce who wrote *Dubliners* and *Portrait of the Artist as a Young Man*. Sensibility is for the most part youthful. It owes that to romanticism, which celebrated early life—the feeling heart of childhood, the emotions of adolescence. Early romanticism, when it dethroned Zeus, welcomed the advent of Prometheus. Mr. Updike's Peter plays Prometheus to his father's Chiron but the author does not succeed in making this myth take in the Pennsylvania countryside.

He has more success in his stories. "When they moved to Firetown," Mr. Updike writes in the title story of his new collection, *Pigeon Feathers*, "things were upset, displaced, rearranged." David, a sensitive and only child, is frightened when he picks up H. G. Wells's *Outline of History* and reads that Jesus was something of a communist, "an obscure political agitator, a kind of hobo in a minor colony of the Roman Empire." He cannot accept the answers given by his mother and by the pastor, the Reverend Dobson, in Sunday school, to his questions about death and immortality. Nature itself fails to give him comfort. He is puzzled by the pleasure it gives his mother to take long walks. "To him the brown stretches of slowly rising and falling land expressed only a huge exhaustion." "What do you want Heaven to be?" his mother asks. "He was becoming angry, sensing her surprise at him. She had assumed that Heaven had faded from his head long ago. She had imagined that he had already entered, in the secrecy of silence, the conspiracy that he now knew to be all around him." Since David is a little hero of sensibility, it might have been predicted that he would resolve his difficulties aesthetically. After he has shot some pigeons in the barn he contemplates their feathers and is enchanted and consoled. "The God who had lavished such craft upon these worthless birds would not destroy His whole Creation by refusing to let David live forever." Reflectiveness makes Mr. Updike's children precocious, almost elderly. He does not leave David without a touch of irony. The boy has killed these inoffensive birds but sees the proof of his immortality in their feathers. The story itself reveals that the writer has great faith in craftsmanship. The religion of the writer of sensibility is, of course, the religion of art.

That the world of the mature should be described as a conspiracy to conceal ignorance and resignation is to be expected in any American story of adolescence. The theme goes back at least as far as Sherwood Anderson's "I Want to Know Why" and some students of literature find it also in Fenimore Cooper and Mark Twain. In J. D. Salinger's *Catcher in the Rye* and in his more recent chronicles of the Glass family the horror of an adult society is also recognized by boys on the threshold of maturity. These adolescents are often described as deeply and naturally intuitive; they still possess what a Chinese philosopher once called "the first heart" and in this world of corruption and compromise they are the only ones in whom democratic and liberal values, mercy and generosity, may be found. In the nineteenth century, too, maturity is often portrayed as either villainous or sad. Butler's *The Way of All Flesh* describes the liberation of youth from the tyranny of the elders and Butler observes elsewhere, perhaps only half jestingly, that it might be best for a child to come into the world with no parents to bring him up but with a twenty-thousand-pound note pinned to his swaddling clothes. The parental figures who dominate nineteenth-century literature are craggy, whiskered types who personify discipline, renunciation, order, hypocrisy, control. Even so balanced a person as J. S. Mill cannot conceal a certain bitterness in his *Autobiography* when he describes how his father, with the best of intentions, drilled all feeling out of him. What Mill lost—lost temporarily—when he was plunged into despair was his conviction that he had before him a useful and meaningful life; when he had slowly recovered that conviction, the crisis was over. Ivan Karamazov tells his brother Alyosha in a mood of rebellion that while he does indeed love life, loves the sticky little leaves of spring, he expects and prefers an early death, possibly foreseeing that with maturity he will lose his rebellious spirit and become merely comfortable and cynical. Since he believes that God has created an unjust world he respectfully offers to return his "ticket." By the end of the century, however, another sort of romantic youthfulness is in evidence that refuses to make itself responsible for the world. It seems no longer necessary to weigh the world and find it wanting; one can find it wanting without going to the trouble of weighing it. The writers most admired in the twentieth century are either intensely subjective or nihilistic or both. For them traditional authority does not exist. State, family, religion are regarded as phantoms. The authority of art itself has been declining among artists, although literature continues to flourish even where the idea of literature is treated with contempt by those calling themselves anti-artists.

The reason immaturity makes so great an appeal to American writers, or to those postwar European writers who have come under American influence, is perhaps not too difficult to discover. The enforced passivity of the individual confronted by the huge power of modern organizations resembles the impotence of childhood. Those who say yea to these combinations of power are not children but adults. There occurs, consequently, a clinging to childhood and youth, which may explain certain middle-aged and even elderly Beats and superannuated and gaily wrinkled Peter Pans.

> *Heaven lies about us in our infancy!*
> *Shades of the prison-house begin to close*
> *Upon the growing Boy,*

wrote William Wordsworth and his point of view, supported by psychoanalytic explorations and discoveries about infancy and by popular sentiment as well, has many lively exponents.

Of these J. D. Salinger, a brilliant performer, is easily the best. He gives his allegiance mainly to children and to the young in heart and writes of them with great warmth and purity. *The Catcher in the Rye* perhaps argues too closely his romantic theory that the child, in Wordsworth's words, is "still Nature's Priest." Holden Caulfield has some vatic moments that make him sound very unlike a schoolboy. Mr. Salinger's stories, less ambitious and ideological, are more successful than his novel. But his theme is always the same. In "For Esmé—with Love and Squalor" a soldier enjoys a very special and privileged communion with a little girl and her small brother. In "A Perfect Day for Bananafish"

There Is Simply Too Much to Think About

Seymour Glass, in Florida with his bride, commits suicide, but not before he has played in the water with a little girl and told her his tale of the bananafish. In "Raise High the Roof Beam, Carpenters" Salinger tells of an odd wedding party in New York on a hot day during World War II and exposes the imbecility of "normal" social conduct. He describes a different war, the one carried on by the regular against the irregular or exceptional members of society. The absent hero is Seymour Glass, who has ideas of his own about love, weddings and wedding parties. The ladies of the wedding party, and especially the matron of honor, are angry at the fancied humiliation of the bride by the groom. Salinger turns a clear, not altogether kindly light on the code of the outraged women. The matron of honor is described as "a hefty girl of about twenty-four or -five, in a pink satin dress, with a circlet of artificial forget-me-nots in her hair. There was a distinctly athletic ethos about her, as if, a year or two earlier, she might have majored in physical education in college. In her lap she was holding a bouquet of gardenias rather as though it were a deflated volley-ball." Her husband chucklingly refers to her as a "bloodthirsty wench," apparently familiar with her deflationary powers. The other lady, Mrs. Silsburn, is treated more sympathetically. The perspiration has seeped through her heavy pancake makeup but she holds her patent leather purse "as though it were a favorite doll, and she herself an experimentally rouged and powdered, and very unhappy, runaway child." Mrs. Silsburn's childishness earns her Salinger's indulgence; she is not a part of the solid aggressive union of mature females. The groom's brother, who tells the story, brings a little band of wedding guests, including the belligerent matron of honor, to a small apartment shared by the young Glasses. There he mixes a pitcher of drinks and defends his brother ardently when the matron accuses Seymour of being a freak who doesn't know how "to relate" to people. "He's absolutely unfit for marriage or anything halfway normal, for goodness' sake," she says. The angry brother replies that he doesn't give a damn what Seymour's mother-in-law "or, for that matter, any professional dilettante or amateur bitch had to say." Seymour is a poet. "A poet, for God's sake. And I mean a *poet*." Neither matrons nor mothers-in-law nor psychiatrists will ever see him for what he really is. After this outburst the brother sits on the edge of the bathtub, alone, reading in Seymour's diary. Seymour, it appears, sees everyone about him with saintly tolerance and love, somehow interpreting banalities as divine miracles. A dessert of frozen cream cheese and raspberries served by his bride-to-be makes tears come to his eyes. He observes of Mrs. Fedder that she is a woman "deprived, for life, of any understanding or taste for the main current of poetry that flows through things, all things. She might as well be dead, and yet she goes on living, stopping off at delicatessens, seeing her analyst, consuming a novel every night, putting on her girdle, plotting for Muriel's health and prosperity. I love her. I find her unimaginably brave." "Oh, God," Seymour says at last, "if I'm anything by a clinical name, I'm a kind of paranoiac in reverse. I suspect people of plotting to make me happy."

The contrast of purity with social villainy and decadence is continued and expanded in "Seymour: An Introduction." This memoir is touching but becomes somewhat prolix, a common fault in hagiography. The vulgarity of a brazen, unfeeling world is tirelessly condemned. The saint forgives, but there is so much to forgive. He is enraptured by everything ordinary, though that might appear to other eyes frightful, and he kills himself at the height of his ecstasy. Now as all writers know, it is hard to make a virtuous character look real. Readers want hard proof of every claim made for him. The Children of Darkness long perhaps to see the Children of Light, but they examine their credentials with great suspicion. Nowadays they are too sophisticated to sneer at virtue, however. They are more inclined to say, "Well, isn't this nice, really—sweet. We need more of this endearing romantic childishness." In this way a writer like Salinger can be widely appreciated while the feelings he deals with remain on an adolescent level. I doubt whether the naïveté of "the first heart" can win out against sophisticated judgment. It is not easy to confound the wise for they grow wiser and wiser with time. Nevertheless Salinger does what a writer should do; he stubbornly clings to his fragile idealism. There is a nobility of feeling in his stories that is, unfortunately, rare in contemporary literature. Perhaps such nobility can only belong to innocence or be appreciated only within a small circle. The children of the Glass family are a very small community of the elect. They have their Oriental Buddhist connections but their strongest local sympathies are with one another. It commonly happens in American writing (in Hemingway and Fitzgerald among others) that the best things can be appreciated by the initiates alone, by the most *in* people. In this case, the young and the pure of heart are *in*.

Samuel Butler declared, nearly a century ago, that he could bear lying but hated inaccuracy. John O'Hara, too, has a passion for correctness and as a social historian tolerates none but precise facts. He knows that in 1926 a lady with a sweet tooth would eat Lowney's chocolates (or Samoset, Page and Shaw's or Whitman's); he knows exactly what it would mean to be chosen for Walter Camp's Second All-America team; how far the bullet of a .30-06 would carry; how a man might have founded a black-market fortune during World War II; how often a garage mechanic in Trenton, New Jersey, will need to change clothes. His information seems inexhaustible; it is offered, with some pride, as the real thing and it is almost always fascinating. In reading the twenty-three stories of his new collection, *The Cape Cod Lighter*, one can feel the strength of facts when they are recorded by a writer who loves them to fanaticism. In his line of work Mr. O'Hara is a master. His ear for dialogue is faultless. In stories set in the Twenties like "The Engineer," no character will be heard using the slang of a later period. In this avoidance of false notes and of excesses in dialogue, there is an evident pridefulness. It is pardonable but it is also noticeable. Weeks, the engineer, moving into a hotel, makes his arrangements with Jimmy the Negro porter in a conversation that covers five pages. He settles laundry prices with him, he tells him he wants his suits pressed without creases in the sleeve, he ascertains whether, in shining shoes, Jimmy takes out the laces. Jimmy answers,

> "When they ask. I run them under the tap and rinse 'em out to
>   look nice and fresh. I do it right. But some don't ask."
> "Well, I ask."
> "Yes, sir, I seen that."
> "I like to have my things just so."

It is not Weeks alone who wants things to be just so. O'Hara is just as cunning and penetrating in matters of detail. His fullest admiration goes to those who know their jobs, and although the engineer himself turns out to be a bad egg, O'Hara nevertheless records his accomplishments with a relish and energy that amount to sympathy. Realistic writers follow a method—traceable to Montaigne—of circling over random facts, awaiting their opportunity to pounce on the essential. O'Hara shows how useful that method remains. But there are times when the essences he comes up with are not very essential. Certain of his stories run like little trolleys, bright and glittering but without a passenger. "Sunday Morning," for instance, has almost no content. "Justice" makes an unsuccessful attempt to deal with problems of conscience that trouble a man in the autumn of his life, visited unexpectedly by sexual desires: "How can I explain to myself what happened to me? I came to life again, as I had before, but this time it was the tin chill of a distant autumn and not the recollected pressure of a real woman against me that brought me to life so desperately. I hardly even thought of her; I thought of myself. And then I began thinking that this new life would remain incomplete if I did not go back again to that hideous house. This new life I was feeling was hideous too, but I had lost any sense of beauty that I had ever had. Yes, I thought, killed by an early frost, and to hell with it. One thing killed, another thing come to life; and what was gone was truly gone and better gone and useless. Only this hideous new life was not dead." This sort of lapse from clarity and good judgment is rare in O'Hara. He seldom comes at sensitive feelings from the front. For obvious reasons, he does better when he approaches them indirectly.

On the whole he prefers people who are honest, blunt and plain, stoical and decent. Ernest Pangborn in "The Professors," discovering that he has judged his colleague Jack Veech wrongly, considers whether he should say anything. "A compliment would be rejected, and a word of pity would be unthinkable. Indeed the compliment was being paid to Pangborn; Veech honored him with his confidence and accorded him honor more subtly, more truly, by asking no further assurances of his silence." These are the quiet virtues O'Hara likes. They remind one of Kipling. Here the "sovereign self" of romanticism is exchanged for the more reticent and undemonstrative decent self. This decent self de-

There Is Simply Too Much to Think About

rives great satisfaction from belonging to a class of initiates who have a feeling for the right thing. The romanticism of an elaborate and possibly self-indulgent inner life is rejected by O'Hara as it was by his master, Hemingway.

Another Country by James Baldwin should perhaps be judged as a document and not a novel. It is hard to believe that Baldwin, with his talents, could himself take it seriously as a piece of fiction. Its characters have a fitful reality; on the same page they can be in one phrase genuine and, in the next, false and lifeless. The style is alternately fierce, free, dramatic or arty, foolish, empty. The scenes of lovemaking, and they are many, are very bad, rhetorical in an inferior Lawrentian manner, a kind of seedy nature mysticism of rivers, tides, jungles and cosmic events laid on in the thrill-language of "instinctual fulfillment." It is undoubtedly well meant and perhaps serves the interests of social progress but it is very poor stuff, falsely sensitive, made up entirely of phrases and almost devoid of feeling. Baldwin is genuine and admirable when he expresses rage or indignation and not at all convincing when he writes of love and tenderness. In this novel all the important questions, and they are many, are translated into sex. Truth and honor, indignation, love and hate, the injustices of American society, the menacing and explosive racial conflicts for which there is no acceptable apology—the situation of the Negro in America is a scandal—all these matters are connected by Baldwin to the sexual theme. Civilized white sexuality is pitilessly denounced and damned. Everything the ordinary white citizen of this country would accept as average and normal, his "square" values, Baldwin angrily tears to shreds. "All that jazz about the land of the free and the home of the brave," says a Negro woman in *Another Country*. "Some days, honey, I wish I could turn myself into one big fist and grind this miserable country to powder. Some days, I don't believe it has a right to exist." "Wouldn't you hate all white people," she asks elsewhere, "if they kept you in prison here?" She is speaking of the Harlem slums in all their filth, ugliness and wretchedness. "Kept you here, and stunted you and starved you, and made you watch your mother and father and sister and lover and brother and son and daughter die or go mad or go under, before your very eyes? And not in a hurry, like from one day to the next, but every day, every day, for years, for generations?" The anger is just. As a document, therefore, *Another Country* has great importance; but it does very little for the progress of the novel.

George Orwell in 1940 wrote an essay in praise of Henry Miller ("Inside the Whale") in which he noted that a significant change had occurred in literature. It had, in Miller, dropped what Orwell called "the Geneva language of the ordinary novel" and was dragging "the *realpolitik* of the inner mind into the open." In Miller's case, he said, "this is not so much a question of exploring the mechanisms of the mind as owning up to everyday facts and everyday emotions. For the truth is that many ordinary people, perhaps an actual majority, do speak and behave in the way that is recorded here. The callow coarseness with which the characters in *Tropic of Cancer* talk is very rare in fiction, but it is extremely common in real life; again and again I have heard such conversations from people who were not even aware that they were talking coarsely." Orwell is quite right about Miller. He brought into literature things that had never been there before. The question for the writer, as he advances ever deeper into the formlessness of everyday facts, is what he is to do with them, whether he simply wants us to be shocked or has some other purpose. Miller has always been an artist but those writers who have learned from him, like Baldwin, have not in every case believed that to be necessary. Some have felt it obligatory to go shuddering and naked through chaos or to experience disintegration because disintegration is *there*. Art, too, must submit to this annihilation. Many writers are strongly opposed to an art that triumphs while in every other sphere of life mankind suffers. Baldwin must be one of these for he could very easily write better novels if he believed they served his moral aims effectively. He is a writer who, for reasons not difficult to appreciate, will not take literature as such seriously. Still, he cannot let it go, either, for he *is* a writer and a rather fashionable writer at that. He has a following, largely white and liberal, for which he performs a significant moral, but a dubious artistic, function. As for his morality, both in the novel and in his recent *New Yorker* essay (now published in book form under the title *The Fire Next Time*), it is fiery but formless. Baldwin believes intensely but with considerable vagueness in love and freedom. White America is shocked to find itself so hated but it is also attracted by angry denunciation, by the exposure of its failures, and in some cases fascinated by the freer and deeper sexuality often attributed to the Negro. Baldwin accepts the popular thesis that moral soundness and the capacity for sexual gratification are connected. In many modern novels sexual impotence and wickedness go together and (in Lawrence's *Lady Chatterley's Lover*, for instance) the desexualized or instinctually crippled are the most devoted servants of a heartless industrial civilization. Baldwin implicitly relies on these Lawrentian ideas, ultimately traceable to psychoanalysis, and shows the Negro, insulted and disfigured as he has been, truer to his instincts, closer to reality, better and more human than his white oppressors: "You must consider what happens to this citizen, after all he has endured, when he returns—home: search, in his shoes, for a job, for a place to live; ride, in his skin, on segregated buses; see, with his eyes, the signs saying 'White' and 'Colored,' and especially the signs that say 'White Ladies' and 'Colored *Women*'; look into the eyes of his wife; look into the eyes of his son; listen, with his ears, to political speeches, North and South; imagine yourself being told to 'wait.' And all this is happening in the richest and freest country in the world, and in the middle of the twentieth century."

The bourgeois has been providing the comedian with material since he appeared on the stage of world history; he still does so, even though his historic career, it is often said, is ending. In Molière's *Bourgeois Gentilhomme* he is fresh and ludicrous; in Shaw's *Heartbreak House* he is already stale; Mr. Mangan's very wealth is a fiction, a joke, and his prudence is the cause of his death. It is not so much the full-fledged bourgeois who is the theme of modern comedy as the little man—the little man who apes the dignity and refinements of the leaders of society. In the nineteenth-century novel the subject of the ambitious man or woman, one generation removed from the rural laborer or peasant, like Hardy's Jude or Flaubert's Emma Bovary, the obscure provincial whose head is turned by bad books and who dreams of romantic delicacy and erotic happiness, is treated with high and even tragic seriousness. Shaw treats it later in a mixed manner in *Pygmalion*, where the poor Doolittle girl, taken from the dust heap by the Professor and taught to speak like a woman of the upper classes, also acquires a new spirit and is capable of feeling and suffering in a different fashion. The common man, like Hardy's Jude, who falls in love with learning and religion, civilization and all the higher forms of thought and feeling, discovers after an ambitious and heartbreaking struggle only the snobbery of the learned, the hollowness of beliefs and a moribund civilization. He is rewarded for his efforts by the pain of insight and an agony of spirit.

The comedian of the twentieth century has made much of the private, shabby person who plays the gentleman. Joyce's Leopold Bloom in *Ulysses* is one such figure—"How grand are we this morning!" In the movies the type is represented by Charlie Chaplin and by the *clochard* of René Clair's *À Nous La Liberté* who becomes a bourgeois tycoon but finds it all too much and hits the road again. Artists and poets themselves have enjoyed playing the role of the respectable person, disguising themselves as bank clerks or insurance executives, making subversive fun of the romantic conception of the artistic personality as well as of the petty individualist of common origins and gentlemanly pretensions. An appearance of "dignity" is still good for a laugh, as J. P. Donleavy has recently proven in *The Ginger Man*. Sebastian Dangerfield, who is allegedly studying law in Dublin, is continually on his dignity, patronizes shopkeepers and the "peasantry" but is a very funny scoundrel and unscrupulous sensualist. Private life, inner life, worthy and even laudable sensibility—these too have become the materials of comedy now. More than a century ago Stendhal was already becoming bored with the first-person singular and complained that it was very trying to be writing "I" continually. The exploration of consciousness, introspection, self-knowledge and hypochondria, so solemnly conducted in twentieth-century literature, is treated ironically and humorously in books like *The Confessions of Zeno* by Italo Svevo. The inner life, the "unhappy consciousness," the management of personal life, "alienation"—all the sad questions for which the late romantic writer reserved a special tone of disappointment and bitterness—are turned inside out by the modern

There Is Simply Too Much to Think About

comedian. Deeply subjective self-concern is ridiculed. *My* feelings, *my* early traumas, *my* moral seriousness, *my* progress, *my* sensitivity, *my* fidelity, *my* guilt—the modern reader is easily made to laugh at all of these. Perhaps the population explosion makes such forms of self-concern seem funny. Perhaps the political and scientific revolutions, the wars, the difference between practice and doctrine in all modern countries, the failures of religion, et cetera—the explanations are many, endless—have made the prevailing forms of individualism obsolete.

To guide us in our observations, a comparison between Thomas Mann's *Death in Venice* and Vladimir Nabokov's *Lolita* may be useful. Both are stories of older men who fall in love with someone much younger. The parallel is really very close. Humbert Humbert is Gustav von Aschenbach in his comic form. In Nabokov the Nietzschean, Freudian theme is mocked. Humbert is not impressed by sickness, nor does he associate it with genius; perversity is a concept from the whiskered past with its notions of normalcy. Nor does he show the theme of Apollo-Hyacinthus, which Mann develops with such earnestness. Questions of world destiny do not move him in the good old grave Germanic style. He falls in love without classical allusions and murders his rival in a grotesque parody of the jealous lover. Quilty, the rival, will not hold still and die becomingly but makes fun of himself and of his murderer and of the grand passion—of the value of life.

It was not merely the dull solemnity of the Eisenhower era, its fatty piety and the lack of wit in high places, that discouraged comedy in America. The Kennedy administration, though it likes wit better, does not give us much to laugh about. The dignity of the citizen of a democracy has been humorlessly insisted upon by minorities who were in their powerless days the subject of rude unfeeling satire. It does not matter that *Huckleberry Finn* is a classic and that the runaway slave, Jim, is a great character. He is called Nigger Jim and for this reason organized Negro opinion is for burying the book. Other minorities in their struggle for equality have behaved no better and the effect has been a bogus rhetorical "respect." The touchiness or hypersensitivity of various classes that develops in the course of their social ascent unfortunately results in pompousness, hypocrisy and tyranny. We begin to understand what this may mean when we hear Premier Khrushchev cry out that the younger generation of poets and painters in the Soviet Union "eat the bread of the people" and repay them with "horrible rot and dirty daubs." This is what comes of the policy that art must serve the political and social aims of any regime or class directly. Every despot, George Bernard Shaw once wrote in his airy way, must have a disloyal subject to keep him sane. He, the comedian, was that disloyal subject whose dangerous duty it was to remind the despot of the truth. It is somewhat old-fashioned to assume that the truth will always be clear enough to make the aim of the comedian plain to everyone. The severity of the tyrant who is obviously mad and who murders or imprisons millions of people makes the truth most painfully, horribly clear. Luckily we have had nothing so terrible to cope with; our own forms of tyranny are incomparably milder. But we ought not to spend too much time in self-congratulation. We have problems enough of our own.

For reasons that seem peculiarly American, pretensions of many kinds have to be taken very seriously. Faced with people who in another context might be figures of satire or caricature, the writer has felt obliged to clear his throat respectfully and to address them as Mr. Boor or the Honorable Mr. Idiot. As a shrewd critic, Mr. Harold Rosenberg, has observed on the subject, the writer "loves his neighbors too much, in being so disturbed at their weaknesses." That is to say, he approaches them all with the earnestness they are theoretically entitled to. And either from lack of courage or lack of candor, or because he does not trust his instincts or has failed to develop his understanding, he brings a great deal of solemnity to intrinsically comic themes. "With a little less love and solidarity on the part of their scribes, the braves of Long Island's North Shore or of Mississippi county seats might have supplied some living grotesques as solid as those of Dickens or Gogol," writes Rosenberg. "Fitzgerald and Faulkner, however, hesitate to throw to the dogs of comedy these citizens upon whom they depend for 'values.'"

This situation is gradually changing. The comedian is not more willing to attack power at its source, but he has begun to exploit comically the romantic theme of the precious, unique self. Romantic sensibility

There Is Simply Too Much to Think About

has always had satirists to mock it. Thomas Love Peacock was one of the first. Dostoyevsky made marvelous fun of the exquisite romantic personality in *The Possessed*. But on the whole the modern movement in literature represents a victory for wretchedness and even in the recent "absurd" plays and novels there is still more metaphysical despair than laughter. However, a small handful of writers, among them the best talents of the present generation, have offered us, in comedy, our only relief from the long-prevalent mood of pessimism, discouragement and low seriousness (the degenerate effect of the ambition for high seriousness). Let us hope that, superfluity and solemn nonsense having been laughed and hooted away by the comic spirit, we may see the return of a genuine moral seriousness in literature. Regardless of what we may ultimately decide on the basis of existential metaphysics, modern psychology, Marxism or symbolic logic about the meaning of an individual life, it is only proper and sensible to remember that there are now more individual lives than ever and that certain revolutions in production have made these lives possible. Free public education has given the power of expression and a new understanding (in that order) to the grandsons and granddaughters of laboring illiterates. It has made them able to deplore their civilized condition. A mighty and universal spirit of grievance, long in abeyance, is uttering its first words, releasing what was perhaps to have been expected—the cry that the world is an oppressor and that existence is absurd. In this situation, the comic spirit is also the spirit of reason opposing the popular orgy of wretchedness in modern literature.

As for the future, it cannot possibly shock us since we have already done everything possible to scandalize ourselves. We have so completely debunked the Self that we can hardly continue in the same way. Perhaps some power within us will tell us what we are, now that the old misconceptions have been laid low. Undeniably the human being is not what he commonly thought a generation ago. The question nevertheless remains. He is something. What is he? This question, it seems to me, modern writers have answered poorly. They have told us, indignantly or nihilistically or comically, how great our error is, but for the rest they have offered us thin fare. The fact is that modern writers sin when they suppose that they *know* as they conceive that physics *knows* or that history *knows*. The subject of the novelist is not knowable in any such way. The mystery increases, it does not grow less, as types of literature wear out. It is, however, Symbolism or Realism or Sensibility wearing out and not the mystery of mankind.

[1963]

Barefoot Boy: On Yevgeny Yevtushenko

The photographs of Yevtushenko in his *Precocious Autobiography* show a slender young man, hair combed forward à la Bert Brecht, reciting poetry under spotlights, uninhibited by crowds and micro phones. His gestures, hands on his breast as though to lay bare his heart, remind us that Diaghilev, Stanislavsky, Chaliapin did not issue from a void. Russian movements, Russian eloquence are still alive. Patricia Blake in *Encounter* describes Yevtushenko as "marvelously handsome and engaging. Dressed in a wildly patterned American sports shirt under a gray silk suit . . . he waved familiarly at the audience." Yevtushenko is a star. Fans seek his autograph. The world press covers his activities. His autobiography appears in *The Saturday Evening Post* with an introduction by the retired head of the CIA, Mr. Allen Dulles. He is bad for Them, good for Us. Premier Khrushchev is annoyed. Comrade Ilychev, chief propagandist under Stalin, is furious. In the Soviet Union, Yevtushenko has been described as "Russia's chief juvenile delinquent." In Miss Blake's account he is shown leading the poet's life, adored by the young, enthusiastic, drinking wine and eating chocolates. Photographed with cosmonaut Yuri Gagarin or waving his arms with attractive recklessness, pressing his own pants, flaunting fur neckties, what Yevtushenko satisfies, apparently, is the need of a large public, in Russia and abroad, for the figure of a Russian poet who speaks out boldly on matters of conscience, a civic poet of the kind as badly needed in the West as in the East, a symbol of the free spirit.

He must be a courageous young man. The world is such that to write a poem mourning the massacre of ten thousand Jews by the Nazis in the ravine of Babi Yar, near Kiev, is to earn a rebuke from the premier of the USSR. At a special Kremlin meeting of intellectuals and artists on March 8, 1963, Khrushchev declared: "Events are depicted in the poem as if only the Jewish population fell victim to the fascist crime, while at the hands of the Hitlerite butchers there perished no few Russians, Ukrainians and Soviet people of other nationalities. It is apparent that its author did not display political maturity and showed ignorance of the historical facts. For whom, and why, was it necessary to present the matter as if the population of Jewish nationality in our country were being harried?" There are certain common facts of the modern world that the mind does not readily accept; they have to be knocked into one's head with a mallet. Why, eighteen years after the destruction of Hitler, should Russia continue to persecute Jews? And why should the Soviet premier compel a poet to rewrite his lines? For Yevtushenko has since put into "Babi Yar" references to Russians and Ukrainians. A *whole* poem on a Jewish subject? That the Russian government cannot allow.

In their English version Yevtushenko's poems seem entirely inoffensive, made of milk, butter, arrowroot, eggs—the most innocent ingredients. Nor does Yevtushenko sound fiercely revolutionary in his autobiography. "Man is an idealist by nature . . . man has a need to dream. . . . The most important thing in life is human kindness." It is no easy matter for an outsider (no Kremlinologist) to understand why anyone should risk censure for publishing such benevolent sentiments in *L'Express* of Paris. But the fact is that in the official Russian view this was an extraordinarily provocative act. Even Gagarin rebuked Yevtushenko for saying "in the foreign press such things about our country and our people . . . I feel ashamed of you."

Yevtushenko writes, "I love my fellow countrymen not only as a Russian but also as a revolutionary. I love them all the more because in spite of everything they have never lost their faith in the original purity of the revolutionary idea in spite of all the filth that has since desecrated it." His rhetoric is in part derived from slogans. These slogan fragments he recombines to criticize Stalinism, bureaucracy, dogmatism, purges, concentration camps, all the while protesting the purity of his patriotism, his loyalty to Communist ideals. It is as though an American poet were to try to wrest Americanism from the Birch Society in the language of Fourth of July oratory. "'Communist' and 'disinterested'

There Is Simply Too Much to Think About

mean the same thing," says Yevtushenko, as the authorities scowl and he himself perhaps trembles. He must feel it necessary to press forward as far as he dares to secure the gains of the Russian Thaw or Spring. But his "autobiography" is a brief political act of 124 pages rather than a personal document. Yevtushenko himself remains no more than a phantom at the end of it. And the fact that Sargent Shriver has decided to provide copies to members of the Peace Corps indicates that this sort of political seltzer water is now as palatable in the West as in the East.

Yevtushenko's followers in Russia are the young, the university students, and very probably his appeal is great among the intellectuals, the technical intelligentsia indispensable to the dictatorship—physicists, chemists, industrial designers. Odd fellows at poetry readings arise and identify themselves as "Engineer So-and-So." In his autobiography Yevtushenko introduces his friend the physicist Tarasov with "the forehead of a Martian and the chessboard under his arms" who helps and encourages him. No modern society can function without these intellectual technicians and it is probable that in the Soviet Union the Yevtushenkos express the demand of this new class for more freedom. To Communist leaders trained in the rugged, brutal days of Stalinism, the mild defiance of a Yevtushenko and his insistence on a few elementary decencies must seem an outrage. Such "effrontery" twenty years ago would have been punished with a pistol shot in the head under the Lubyanka prison. The party leaders apparently recognize that those days are now past. Yevtushenko himself is said to have reminded Khrushchev that the grave is not a perfect remedy for all evils. Let us hope the premier can stand being sassed a bit. He cannot continue to terrorize the technical intellectuals in the old way, and these appear to be great patrons and lovers of poetry.

[1963]

My Man Bummidge

In America few novelists in fact write plays, but almost all are perfectly sure that they could easily become dramatists. For them to have such confidence is quite natural. A writer must consider himself equal to any demand in his line. He is traditionally the antispecialist. Though he has felt the universal pressure to limit himself to a single profession, a belief in his versatility, often forced to conceal itself in fantasies, survives in poems or other inspired utterances jotted down in old address books.

I myself was quite prepared to become a dramatist and was not taken by surprise when, about five years ago, Lillian Hellman suggested that I write a play. In a short time my play was ready. Miss Hellman found it amusing and estimated it would run about eight hours without Wagnerian orchestration. She offered valuable advice, much of which I could not use because it required the collaboration of experts, the serious interest of a theater. So I put my utopian project away and turned again to fiction.

About two years ago I was invited by a group, the Theater of Living Ideas, to give a reading. This group, to which Robert Lowell, Lionel Abel, Robert Hivnor, Eric Bentley, Mary Otis, Shirley Broughton and other writers and artists give their support, attracts good audiences on Sunday afternoons. I studied my manuscript and cut several hours from it. The performance was still very long. I took all the parts, reading as fast as I could. Wildly excited, I began to lose my voice before I reached Act II. My own virtuosity exhausted me and the first victim of my invention was myself.

Ask a writer what he thinks of the American theater and he will tell you that it has no language, that it lacks rhetoric or gesture. Ask any professional in the theater what is wrong with plays written by novelists and he will answer that they don't know the difference between the page and the stage. On this matter it's still a bit early for me to express any opinion worth considering. What I am aware of now is the limit placed on the authority of the writer by the theater. It intrigues and amuses me to recognize how independent the habits of a novelist are.

Alone with his page, between four walls, he is compensated for his solitude by a high degree of autonomy. In the theater he discovers the happiness of collaboration. The late Georges Bernanos complained that the isolated labor of writing deprived novelists of essential human contacts. This is indeed a bitter and painful privation, even if it is in some instances a temperamental preference of novelists. But in the theater you see living faces, you feel yourself part of a company, your heart opens to the actors, even to the squalor of West Forty-fourth Street. The very bums sleeping in doorways are like cretinous angels. The price of all this delight is a reduction in one's exclusive powers.

There are certain obvious resemblances between Broadway and Washington, D.C. In both, progress is made by compromise. In both, one may see checks and balances at work. Both conduct public business by means of mysterious political arrangements. The dramatist writes the legislation, the director gets the bills through committee, and after much negotiation and alteration they are enacted.

This is no idle analogy. A novelist speaks intimately to his reader. The theater audience is not a collection of readers. The novel has democratic origins but in its later development takes on an aristocratic coloration. The theater is for the millions. A French writer speaks of the drama as *un art grossier.* Its requirements are certainly more primitive than those of the novel; whether it is necessarily coarser is another question.

In any case, I have tried to put ideas on the stage in what is possibly their most acceptable form at this time, the farce. Some will perhaps take my play *The Last Analysis* for a spoof of psychoanalysis, as in part it is. But what I really wanted to reproduce was the common modern mixture of high seriousness and low seriousness. I am attracted to autodidacts, those brave souls who rise to encounter ideas. We are all of course molested by ideas in a world so mentalized, so transformed by thought as ours is, and we must all, without exception, educate ourselves.

I have been especially stirred by jazz musicians, prizefighters and television comics who put on the philosopher's mantle. I find them peculiarly touching. In the tumult of Birdland they are thinking of Kierkegaard. When they turn away from the microphone their painted smiles grow pensive. They are often preoccupied with Freud and Ferenczi, with Rollo May and Erik Erikson, and their private conversation is very rich in analytic concepts. The self-absorption of people who never tire of exploring their depths is the source of our comedy.

Bummidge, my hero in *The Last Analysis,* is, as another character says, "like a junky on thought." But is it thought? Metaphor is more like it, perhaps, and I am concerned with the influence of metaphors on the human mind. Any powerful interpretation of human destiny—the Fall of Man, Apollo versus Dionysus, History as Class Struggle, the Dialectic of Eros and Death—so fixes or hypnotizes the imagination that it can see no alternatives.

Philip Bummidge has been carried away by the metaphors of psychoanalysis and in this farce he is looking for firm ground on which to stand. *The Last Analysis* is what he is seeking. Or as people, joking, called out to each other in Greenwich Village a generation ago, "Off the couch by Christmas!" Our comedian, Bummidge, does manage to burst the bonds of metaphor by certain peculiar means, to "get off the couch," to stand on his own feet and even to dance a bit.

[1964]

The Thinking Man's Waste Land

The fact that there are so many weak, poor and boring stories and novels written and published in America has been ascribed by our rebels to the horrible squareness of our institutions, the idiocy of power, the debasement of sexual instincts and the failure of writers to be alienated enough. The poems and novels of these same rebellious spirits, and their theoretical statements, are grimy and gritty and very boring too, besides being nonsensical, and it is evident now that polymorphous sexuality and vehement declarations of alienation are not going to produce great works of art.

There is nothing left for us novelists to do but think. For unless we think, unless we make a clearer estimate of our condition, we will continue to write kid stuff, to fail our function; we will lack serious interests and become truly irrelevant. Here the critics must share the blame. They too have failed to describe the situation. Literature has for generations been its own source, its own province, has lived upon its own traditions and accepted a romantic separation or estrangement from the common world. This estrangement, though it produced some masterpieces, has by now enfeebled literature.

The separatism of writers is accompanied by the more or less conscious acceptance of a theory of modern civilization. This theory says in effect that modern mass society is frightful, brutal, hostile to whatever is pure in the human spirit, a Waste Land and a horror. To its ugliness, its bureaucratic regiments, its thefts, its lies, its wars and its cruelties, the artist can never be reconciled. This is one of the traditions on which literature has lived uncritically. But it is the task of artists and critics in every generation to look with their own eyes. Perhaps they will see even worse evils, but they will at least be seeing for themselves. They will not, they cannot permit themselves, generation after generation, to hold views they have not examined for themselves. By such willful blindness we lose the right to call ourselves artists; we have accepted what we ourselves condemn—narrow specialization, professionalism, snobbery and the formation of a caste.

Unfortunately the postures of this caste, postures of liberation and independence and creativity, are attractive to poor souls dreaming everywhere of a fuller, freer life. The writer is admired, the writer is envied. But what has he to say for himself? Why, he says, just as writers have said for more than a century, that he is cut off from the life of his own society, despised by its overlords who are cynical and have nothing but contempt for the artist, without a true public, estranged. He dreams of ages when the poet or the painter expressed a perfect unity of time and place, had a real acceptance and enjoyed a vital harmony with his surroundings—he dreams of a Golden Age. In fact, without the Golden Age there is no Waste Land.

Well, this is no age of gold. It is only what it is. Can we do no more than complain about it? We writers have better choices. We can either shut up because the times are too bad or continue because we have an instinct to make books, a talent to enjoy, which even these disfigured times cannot obliterate. Isolate professionalism is death. Without the common world the novelist is nothing but a curiosity and will find himself in a glass case along some dull museum corridor of the future.

We live in a technological age that seems insurmountably hostile to the artist. He must fight for his life, for his freedom, along with everyone else—for justice and equality, threatened by mechanization and bureaucracy. This is not to advise the novelist to rush immediately into the political sphere. But in the first stage he must begin to exert his intelligence, long unused. If he is to reject politics he must understand what he is rejecting. He must begin to think, and to think not merely of his own narrower interests and needs.

[1965]

Cloister Culture

We can't master change. It is too vast, too swift. We'd kill ourselves trying. It is essential, however, to try to understand transformations directly affecting us. That may not be possible either but we have no choice.

The changes on which I would like to comment are those in the relations between the writer and the public in the English-speaking countries. I shall begin with the sort of description of these relations an avant-garde writer might have given thirty years ago.

He would certainly have referred to himself as highbrow. Not without irony, but seriously nevertheless, he would have distinguished himself from the middlebrow, the ape of culture, and from the lowbrow or no-brow, that philistine hater of all that was good and beautiful in the modern tradition. This is not to say that the highbrow writer invariably loved his isolation and that he rejected the great public out of pride or decadent class-feeling. On the contrary, the division of cultures into high and low caused much bitterness and was considered by many highbrows to be dangerous to society and to civilization as a whole.

Perhaps overlooking the humiliations of the poet under patronage, the vanguardist of the Thirties was often nostalgic for the eighteenth century and the small, refined and aristocratic public of that age of masterpieces. In his view the nineteenth-century public was already fully vulgarized—enthusiastic perhaps but coarse-grained, an audience of shopkeepers. The weaknesses of this public were aggravated by commercial exploitation, by promoters who made great fortunes in cheap novels, bringing mass culture into the world. The vanguard minority, by this vanguard account, grew smaller and smaller. The specialist now appeared, the technician, a new sort of intellectual with little or no understanding of art and small sympathy for the life of the mind.

Finally, in the twentieth century, to state the case as it was stated by a brilliant critic and observer, the late Wyndham Lewis, an authentic highbrow, civilization cut itself in two, driving into pens and reservations all that was most creative and intelligent. The vanguard artist, like the American Indian, was shut up in barren places, sequestered in the ivory tower, deprived of human contact and influence. Probably all this would end in the total liquidation of intellectuals. Only a few twilight masterpieces by men like Joyce or Paul Klee would remain and we would reach the stage of final degradation, the era of brutal unrelieved stupidity.

This in some ways resembles the description of the bourgeois situation given by the nineteenth-century romantic, not wholly unjustified but containing certain exaggerations. The romantic saw himself cut off from society, held in contempt by its rulers, separated from the people and longing to be reunited with them.

Wyndham Lewis was a thoughtful and original observer, but it is apparent that he made any number of wrong guesses. Intellectuals have not been liquidated. On the contrary they have increased in number and in influence. They are now spoken of with respect, even with awe, as indispensable to the government, as makers of educated opinion, as sources of symbolic legitimacy—replacing the clergy. Old Walt Whitman announcing, "The priest departs, the divine literatus arrives," does not sound as unhinged as he did thirty years ago.

I speak not of the quality of these literati (that is another matter; they are still a little remote from divinity) but of the growth of their power.

On the eve of World War II the highbrow public was indeed very small. This is no longer the case. We now have a growing class of intellectuals or near intellectuals. There are millions of college graduates. A college degree may not mean much. It does, however, indicate exposure to high culture. And the literary culture to which these students are exposed was the creation of highbrow geniuses—disaffected, subversive, radical. The millions who go to art museums today admire there the strangely beautiful, powerful paintings of artists who worked in

There Is Simply Too Much to Think About

what Lewis called the thickening twilight of modernism. The millions who take courses in literature become acquainted with the poems and novels of men who rejected the average preferences of their contemporaries.

The minority public is no longer that handful of connoisseurs who read *Transition* in the Twenties or discussed "significant form." We have at present a large literary community and something we can call, *faute de mieux*, a literary culture, in my opinion a very bad one.

For one thing, the universities have now embraced modern literature. Stony old pedants two generations ago refused to discuss anyone newer than Browning, but their power was broken in the Thirties and all universities permit the study of contemporary writers. Thousands of teachers turn out millions of graduates in literature. Some of these teachers, a very small minority, are quite useful; others are harmless enough, textual editors, antiquarians and fuddy-duddies. Others are influential interpreters. Or misinterpreters.

It is in the universities that literary intellectuals are made, not on Grub Street, not in bohemia. The mass media and the university-sponsored quarterlies have between them swallowed up literary journalism. The salaried professor will supply literary articles cheaply and has all but wiped out his professional competitors. Bohemia too has been relocated in new quarters, near to university campuses.

The university therefore is producing quantities of literary intellectuals who teach, write or go into publishing houses. So far as I can see, this new group, greatly influenced by the modern classics, by Joyce, Proust, Eliot, Lawrence, Gide, Valéry, et cetera, have done little more than convert these classics into other forms of discourse, translating imagination into opinion or art into cognitions. What they do is to put it all differently. They redescribe everything, usually making it less accessible. For feeling or response they substitute acts of comprehension.

Sometimes they seem to be manufacturing "intellectual history," creating a sort of subculture more congenial to them and to their students than art itself. Sometimes I think they are trying to form a new model of the civilized intelligence for the twentieth century, an intelligence to which a more worthy art will one day be offered—the *Zeitgeist* permitting. Perhaps the "dehumanization of art" of which Ortega spoke reflects the demands made upon art by literary intellectuals. It may in part be a result of the pressure they put upon it for meanings.

Redescription can be intriguing and useful and succeeding generations must, like Adam and Eve in the Garden of Eden, rename their beasts. Molière revealed the comic possibilities of this when M. Jourdain discovered that all his life he had been speaking Prose. We Americans take great satisfaction in this comedy of terms. We pay psychologists to penetrate our characters and redescribe them to us scientifically, rationalizing consciousness on the verbal level at least. We are delighted to hear that we are introverted, fixated, have a repression here, a cathexis there, are attached to our mothers thus and so. Such new accounts seem valuable in themselves, worth the money we pay for them.

Yet what our literary intelligentsia does is to redescribe everything downward, blackening the present age and denying creative scope to their contemporaries. They assume themselves to be the only heirs of the modern classical writers. Our most respected men of letters identify themselves with Joyce, Proust, et cetera, and present themselves as the distinguished representatives, indeed the only representatives, of these masters. The agents, managers or impresarios (popularizers) of James or the French Symbolists consider themselves the only successors of these writers. Thus they enjoy a certain genteel prestige. They are the happy few. And they are not unlike the old praetorians faithful to the remains of poor Browning. But the scale of operations is much greater.

There are clear signs that intellectuals in what American universities call the humanities are trying to appropriate literature for themselves, taking it away from writers. These intellectuals are like the British princess who said to her husband during the honeymoon, "Do the servants do this too? Much too good for them." Literature is too good for contemporary novelists, those poor untutored drudges.

And what do these intellectuals do with literature? Why, they talk about it; they treasure it; they make careers of it; they become an élite through it; they adorn themselves with it; they make discourse of it. It is their material, their capital. They take from it what they need for their own work in culture history, journalism or criticism of manners, producing hybrid works, partly literary, sometimes interesting in themselves but postulating almost always the decadence or obsolescence of contemporary literature. They want to use the literature of the modern tradition to make something far better; they project a higher, more valuable mental realm, a realm of dazzling intellectuality.

Let me direct your attention to other consequences of the teaching of modern literature. In his essay "Beyond Culture," Professor Lionel Trilling tells us that we now have a sizable group of people in the United States educated in the modern classics. He thinks they have not turned out very well. One sees his point.

They seem to have it both ways. On the one hand these teachers, editors or culture-bureaucrats have absorbed the dislike of the modern classic writers for modern civilization. They are repelled by the effrontery of power and the degradation of the urban crowd. They have made the Waste Land outlook their own. On the other hand they are very well off. They have money, position, privileges, power; they send their children to private schools; they can afford elegant dental care, jet holidays in Europe. They have stocks, bonds, houses, even yachts, and with all this, owing to their education, they enjoy a particular and intimate sympathy with the heroic artistic life. Their tastes and judgments were formed by Rimbaud and D. H. Lawrence. Could anything be neater?

Yet this may be the way things are in the modern world, a consequence perhaps of the decline in belief or of certain doubts about the value of human actions. Thus in a short life one feels free to combine all things of value. People pursue luxury but try to keep, by some means, values conceived in austerity. They combine private security with rebellious attitudes, monogamy with sexual experiment, conventional family life with bohemian attitudes, the *dolce vita* with the great books. Vice presidents during the working day, they may be anarchists or utopians at cocktail time. In the higher income brackets, insulated from the dirt and danger of New York, they retain as a matter of course all the sentiments of alienation, honor bound to be sullen, ungrateful, dissatisfied, suspicious and theoretically defiant of authority.

There is nothing very new in this. Dostoyevsky observed that people who recited Schiller's odes with tears in their eyes were also very good at managing their bureaucratic careers. No wonder Professor Trilling is upset. He sees that a literary education may be a mixed blessing and that the critics, writers and executives sent into the world by English departments have not turned out very well.

What important function might they be performing? That question is answered by Irving Kristol in a number of *The Public Interest.* He points out that the literary intellectuals help shape the opinions of the educated classes and play a crucial role in defining the moral quality of our society. He says, "There is surely no more important task than to question or affirm the legitimacy of a society's basic institutions, to criticize or amend the original assumptions on which political life proceeds. How well equipped are our literary intellectuals for this job? Not, it must be confessed, as well equipped as they ought to be."

This then is the situation. Critics and professors have declared themselves the true heirs and successors of the modern classic writers. They have obscured the connection between the contemporary writer and his predecessors. They have not shaped the opinions of the educated classes. They have done nothing to create a new public. They have miseducated the young. They are responsible for a great increase in what Veblen called "trained incapacity."

Furthermore, they have projected the kind of art and literature that suits them and have the power to recruit painters and novelists who will meet their requirements. Novels are written that contain attitudes, positions or fantasies pleasing to the literary intelligentsia. These are of course given serious consideration, though they may be little more than the footnotes of fashionable doctrines.

Literature is becoming important for what one can do with it. It is becoming a source of orientations, postures, lifestyles, positions. These positions are made up of odds and ends of Marxism, Freudianism, existentialism, mythology, surrealism, absurdism *und so weiter*—the debris of modernism, with apocalyptic leftovers added.

I am speaking of educated and indeed supercivilized people who believe that a correct position makes one illusionless, that to be illusionless is more important than anything else and that it is enlightened to expose, to disenchant, to hate and to experience disgust. Wyndham Lewis had an excellent term for this last phenomenon—he spoke of the vulgarization of once aristocratic disgust by the modern romantics. One might add that the skepticism of the Enlightenment has also been

There Is Simply Too Much to Think About

vulgarized, and that it is at present thought blessed to see through to the class origins of one's affection for one's grandfather or to reveal the hypocritical weakness and baseness at the heart of friendships.

Nevertheless there are friendships, affinities, natural feelings, rooted norms. People do not on the whole agree, for instance, that it is not wrong to murder. And even if they are unable to offer rational arguments for this, they are not necessarily driven to commit gratuitous acts of violence. It seems to me that writers might really do well to start thinking about such questions again. Evidently they will have to do this without the aid of the critics. The critics are too romantic to deal with these problems.

A final word about the avant-garde. To labor to create vanguard conditions is historicism. It means that people have been reading books of culture-history and have concluded retrospectively that originality is impossible without such conditions. But genius is always, without strain, avant-garde. Its departure from tradition is the result not of caprice or of policy but of an inner necessity.

As for the highbrow public of an earlier time, it has now been assimilated by our literary culture and transformed into something else. For the time being the writer will have to do without it. He will have to believe that what he writes will evoke a public, that the new forms he creates will create a new public, summoned up by the force of his truth.

[1966]

Israel: The Six-Day War

IN ISRAEL'S EYES, IT'S A CRAZY WORLD

Tel Aviv, 12 June 1967—Day and night the armored columns came down the main street of Tiberias, turned left at the Lake of Galilee and continued northward past the Mount of the Beatitudes, where Jesus preached.

From the mountains on the Syrian side, the road was often shelled at night. One could see the fields blazing, set afire by artillery, and hear the deep growling bombs. Tiberias was blacked out. People sat by the water and listened to the news, exchanging rumors and predictions.

Nasser had resigned, the Egyptian announcer had sobbed, but the Egyptians were free weepers. Nasser had not resigned, said someone else. By then he no longer mattered; his army had been torn to pieces in the Sinai Desert. It was the Syrians who mattered now. The invasion had begun that morning. The Israeli armies appeared to be on their way toward Damascus. The Russians were threatening to break off diplomatic relations. No one seemed much disturbed by this.

Apparently Israelis decided that they need not concern themselves with the great powers since the great powers had apparently decided to let the Arabs have their way.

The great powers had allowed Nasser, Hussein and the Syrians to mobilize and to threaten to run the Israelis into the sea, to drown them like rats, to annihilate everyone. Now Nasser, one Israeli told me, was clearly a lunatic. Yet the Americans had given this lunatic wheat and the Russians had given him arms and military advice. The French courted him; the Yugoslavs believed that he headed the progressive elements of the Middle East; the Indians sympathized with him. Though shrewd, he was perhaps also crazy. Therefore these leaders who let him lead the world to the brink of a wider war shared his dementia.

These views at this moment do not appear to be far-fetched. On Saturday morning northern Israel was filled with troops, armor and artillery. The tanks were decorated with flowers and photographs, captured flags, and female dummies modeling the latest Arab fashions. In the mountains the shelling and bombing continued. The jets screamed by invisibly, and shortly afterward one heard the thump and saw the smoke on the mountaintops. But in the kibbutzim, parents now felt that it was safe to bring their kids out of the shelters where they had been kept for days.

The Syrians had been shelling the frontier settlements heavily on Friday. The kibbutz I visited had also been attacked. The attackers had left some of their dead in the orchards. But now Israeli troops were here and the settlers carried their kids up from the shelter. At seven in the morning Kibbutz Resem resembled a community-service working-class camp in New Jersey, with baby buggies and playthings in the shabby sandy yard and small children in Denton pajamas and fleece slippers. But there are shell holes and corpses in the woods and now and then one smells explosives and burned oil; and just below the trees there is an armored column. The soldiers are picking apples from the trees and this—soldiers, apples, kids in sleepers, tricycles—is what the war looks like on a Saturday morning.

The soldiers want to chat with foreign journalists. One, with studious thick specs, fought the Jordanians two days ago. With another, to my surprise, I find myself speaking in Spanish. He comes from Málaga, has lived eleven years in "the land," is a welder by trade and at present is slightly wounded. His head is bandaged.

With great satisfaction the Israeli-Spaniard points below to the first Syrian prisoners. They are squatting in a gravel pit, slight brown men in high boots looking up at their guards. "The first," says my Jewish Spaniard. He spoke of them as though they were minnows, the big fish yet to come.

Then, grinning at my seersucker coat, he said I must be an American. Who else would be so oddly gotten up at the front? Some of the European correspondents were in full jungle camouflage. My seersucker was like the Denton sleepers, but it has all been like that. From the comfortable veranda and the smooth grounds of the King David Hotel in Jerusalem, guests watched the violent fighting last Monday in the Old City. One eyewitness told me that he had just finished his breakfast when he went to look at the battle. He saw an Israeli serviceman hit by a mortar, blown out of his boots; just a moment before, the man had been reading a newspaper.

Later, within sight of Mount Hebron, I stood with a party of journalists looking down into the valley where armored columns maneuvered. We could hear artillery and heavy machine guns and see the bombs exploding. Accompanying one of the foreign cameramen was an English chick in purple slacks, Carnaby boots gladdening her feet. It was of course no fault of hers that men were being killed below. The boyfriend had said, "Come along," and so she came.

In Tel Aviv there are ultramodern buildings but in Gaza, within a few miles, there are Arab tents that look like the molted husks of dung beetles. They are patched with dirty sheets of plastic and pieces of cardboard. One rides through rich orchards and suddenly the irrigation ends. Waves of sand gush across the road. One leaves a tourist hotel with every modern luxury and an hour later sees Egyptian soldiers swollen in death along the roads of the Sinai Peninsula, black and stinking in the desert sun, and all about them are the most modern machines—Russian—burned out and useless. But these puzzling contrasts will not affect an Israeli at this moment. To him the questions are clear. His existence was threatened and he defended himself.

SINAI'S SAVAGE SUN FITS ITS SCENERY

Somewhere in Sinai, 13 June 1967—A concrete emplacement built by the Egyptians in the square of Gaza is now manned by an Israeli with a machine gun. Tanks control the main avenue and from the rooftops soldiers are watching.

Hot. Dull. The streets stink with fermented garbage. Corrugated roofs are weighted with rocks and old truck tires. Elderly women in black cover their somber, mannish faces with black veils and some of the men go about in striped pajama trousers suggesting sleep. The Arab

There Is Simply Too Much to Think About

music, too, induces torpor with its endless sweetish winding and its absurd insinuations and seductions. One not only hears it but feels it distressingly in the bowels, like a drug.

The rubble is being swept from the sidewalks near Israeli headquarters by men in drooping white trousers, and an Egyptian doctor tells us that he has been given plenty of food and medical supplies by the army. He has a Nasserish look, even the Nasser mustache, and he smiles, but his mouth turns down at the corners and when he is silent his face is heavy.

Leaving Gaza, we see the first of the tanks, vehicles, guns and supplies abandoned by the Egyptians—some smashed and burned but most of them intact. The lettering on the new trucks informs you that they were made in Gorkovsky Avtozavod. A fine investment for the Russians. It gives you confidence in the judgment of great powers when you see the Sinai Peninsula filled with millions of dollars' worth of machinery run off the roads into the sand and the dead bodies of Egyptians alongside.

Many of the dead are barefooted, having thrown off their shoes in flight. Only a few have helmets. Some wear the headdress. After leaving Gaza I saw no live Egyptians except for a small group of captured snipers lying bound and blindfolded in a truck. The tent dwellers had run off. Their shelters of old sacking and tatters of plastic were unoccupied, with only a few dogs sniffing about and the flies, of course, in great prosperity. The jackals would be along presently, someone said.

A veteran of the 1956 Sinai campaign told me that the Egyptians had done much better this time. They had prepared their positions skillfully. They had extensive trenches. Their Russian or Nazi teacher—for there are, said my informant, a good many Germans in Egypt who settled down to a useful life after World War II—had some reason to feel encouraged, but without air cover the Egyptian army was helpless and Israel had knocked out the Arab airfields, even those supposedly out of range, blasting the runways, then returning to shoot up the planes. If they had not done this the war would have been long and bloody.

No military expert, I know nothing of the caliber of guns or the thickness of armor. What I am aware of is the enormous scale of the victory and the wreckage, the heavy strength of the sun and the heavy odor of death. Burned trucks overturned, artillery shells spilling from boxes, clothing, shoes, bedsprings, smashed furniture, letters, Arab newspapers, stretchers, bandages, duffel bags and a scattering of gas masks.

I particularly observed the destruction of automobiles. For an American the car is something of an icon and the fate of cars in war therefore has a singular interest. The hood and the trunk of a struck car flap open as if in surrender and what is left of the glass becomes opaque. Some of the grayish cars left behind by the UN forces are flattened and dismembered.

The Egyptian dead lie where they have fallen. No attempt has been made to gather them. The first dead Egyptian I saw was on his belly, raised from the ground by bloat. Legs spread taut, the swollen bodies resemble balloon figures in a parade. Faces blacken and are obliterated by the sun. Corruption is rapid in this heat and the skull soon stares through. One feels the bristling of horror, not pity. The sour-sweet, decayed-cardboard smell becomes a taste in the mouth.

For once, as a nonsmoker, I am glad to have people about me who are puffing cigarettes. Some of the corpses lie charred and curled up near their tanks. Others, in groups, are seen in the trenches on hillsides, in the hollows. Presently one stops looking. You simply know by the slant of the figures that they are there.

Near the airport of Al Arish the Israeli boys are playing soccer, performing calisthenics, resting. Two have found easy chairs and are lounging, chatting, eating rye bread. Behind them at a siding are burned-out railroad cars. Black metal plates loosened from their rivets and springing out. One looks, trying to find relief from omnipresent death.

A LOOK O'ER JORDAN

16 June 1967—You pass from the Israeli sector of Jerusalem to the Jordanian along improvised corridors of brown Jerusalem dust; through coils of figure-eight barbed wire, steering around oil-drum barriers at the checkpoint where the fighting was heavy.

There Is Simply Too Much to Think About

New Israeli apartment buildings were shelled. From some windows, inexplicably, dangle baby strollers and tricycles. Out in the dry weeds, soldiers in bush hats are digging up mines. They prod the ground lightly with metal rods and mark out safe lanes with white tapes.

This is touchy work. The Arabs were generous with their mines in this neighborhood around the United Nations relief warehouse. The UN building was shot up but the roof and walls are intact and so are the sacks and cases of U.S. flour and rice, Swiss powdered milk, the cakes of soap, the beans, the Argentine corned beef and the blended ground vegetable matter sent from America for Arab refugees. The dried milk is labeled "Gift of the Swiss Confederation."

We—that is, Sydney Gruson, the representative of *The New York Times*, the Israeli liaison officer, the driver and myself—are going down into the Jordan valley, territory taken last week. We are bound for Ramallah and will be going as far as Nablus, which the Bible calls Shechem. In Shechem a passionate prince fell in love with Dinah, the daughter of Jacob, and took advantage of her. In revenge, her brothers killed all the young men of the town. Someone briefly mentions this piece of ancient history as the convoys pass.

Tanks and cannons are still going down toward the river. ("I looked o'er the Jordan, an' what did I see?") Toward us come trucks, heavily loaded. The day is hot: The parching dusty wind, the *khamsin*, is blowing. New automobiles damaged by shrapnel and crumpled by tanks are a common sight. The trucks coming up the road carry British and American munitions. Enormous quantities of these have been found in storage dumps cut into Jordanian mountainsides. No one is surprised.

We Americans examine these exports curiously. The wooden cases, containing more than a hundred tons of munitions, are quite new. They bear a proud sticker—stars, stripes, red, white and blue—coming from the Anniston Army Depot in Alabama. On the U.S.A. sticker two strong hands are joined in a heartening symbol of unity and friendship. One of the friends is unnamed. It might be anybody—anybody, that is, able to use 4.2-inch mortars or 106-mm ammunition for recoilless rifles, capable of launching W-20 grenades or of firing artillery shells.

The caves in which this stuff was stored are two miles from biblical Shiloh and are very spacious, cool and airy. Ventilators are visible on the cliff above.

A soldier, British by birth, bare head, bare dusty chest streaked with sweat, says a few things to us about our country and our President, which I cannot reproduce. He says, "You bastards are awfully nice to us. You let us have tractors. And you give the peaceful natives all this other stuff." In fairness, it should be added that some of the supplies are British.

There are also large cans of potatoes from Poland, neatly peeled, there are peas from Holland and there is canned meat from Nigeria. Over the meat an Orthodox sergeant raises his arms in interdiction. The Israeli army keeps a kosher diet. Some of the soldiers, however, fix a hungry eye on the cans. But who knows, says someone, what the Nigerians are canning?

In Ramallah, before curfew, the Arab population is in the streets, the shops are open and although one informant tells us there is nothing to eat, nothing to drink, we see meat in the butcher shops, bananas on the carts. Crews are repairing electrical lines.

The military governor here is Colonel Orial, a reserve paratroop officer. There are twin cities here, he tells us. Fibira is largely Moslem. Ramallah's Arabs are Christians. In addition to the combined population of 32,000 there are 25,000 Palestinians in the refugee camp. Several thousand Jordanian villagers took refuge in the town when the fighting began. There are two mayors, one from each community, who are cooperating with the colonel. Water will be in short supply until the electrical repairs are completed. The pumping is staggered, but no one is dying of thirst. There is no danger of epidemics. The Jordanian casualties are being buried. An Israeli medic supervises public health. The UN Relief and Works Agency for Palestine Refugees in the Near East continues to feed refugees.

Colonel Orial says that we will probably be interested as Americans in the plight of eighty or ninety American citizens of Arab birth visiting here and caught by the war. Since they are now in Israeli territory but

There Is Simply Too Much to Think About

with passports showing no Israeli entrance stamp, they are temporarily unable to leave. Himself a lawyer, Colonel Orial thinks this a nice point in law. "But we will solve it," he says. The colonel does not appear to be the sort of man who finds it hard to solve problems.

Going down, we meet an elderly couple from Chile visiting their old Ramallah home and have a Spanish chat with them. We have in common the western hemisphere and are soaring above all local questions. The itinerary they show us ranges from Cairo to Spitzbergen. The old gentleman wears Arab cloth on his head, bound with a braided plush cord, but he is quite an American in spirit. He is in his seventies. About the neck he is somewhat crumpled but he does not seem weak or frightened.

Others, waiting to talk to the colonel, are near tears. Two soldiers in a jeep, leading us to the large refugee camp, lose their way and ask us to wait at the Ramallah Hilton while they make inquiries. There we talk with other soldiers and prowl about the empty hotel.

The Ramallah is not one of the classier Hiltons. It has a truncated look, as if severed from something much grander.

I get into the kitchen—always drawn to kitchens—and admire the great saucepans and cleavers, grinders, the chopping block a piece of tree trunk with the bark still on it. Nothing edible here—not that one has much appetite in the Holy Land while the *khamsin* blows and the hot mountains glitter. Shade and water count much more. Investigation, not hunger, is my motive.

I look into old gravy in a sauceboat covered with a crust of mutton fat. The deep freeze, unfrozen, is empty and smelly. A lily-pad pool has a coat of slime. "Our garden," the hotel's publicity reads, "6,800 sq. meters, is a relaxation to all. And during summer, Oriental delicious with the local 'arak' is served in folkloric presentation—an experience not to be missed. The cuisine blending west and eastern food will satisfy the most exacting appetite."

We are informed also that the hotel is five minutes from the airport. That is indeed so. The terminal and the runways are now in the hands of the Israelis. They seemed from the road to be intact. We drive up to the Kalandia camp and are at once surrounded by Arabs.

Young men in shirtsleeves come running from all directions. Two soldiers with submachine guns stand apart. Five deep, the stocky young men crowd in on us. At the center is someone speaking English. Three or four days unshaven, he has large fillings in his front teeth. Arms crossed, his nose eager and his eyes dilated, he is here to deliver the goods to the foreign press, the goods being a tale of hunger and grief.

The claim that people are starving is a little hard to support. We see bread everywhere and know that there is plenty of flour. The UN may not offer a varied diet but there is no hunger. In tiny corners of soil near their stone warren, the refugees have tomato plants, squash vines and a few small fig trees.

Less propaganda-conscious, the older people, the men in their pillow-ticking coats and the wives busty and comfortable in coarse white, ask us into their houses with elaborate courtesy. The tiny, sunken, windowless rooms have a few scraps of carpet, a stool, a bedroll, a piece of broken mirror. I look into the latrine—the cement floors with slots for the feet are washed down. There is water.

The men study trades at the UN schools but do little with them. It was impossible to find out how many of these Palestinian refugees had actually fought against Israel. Some—a considerable number, probably—had taken off and crossed the Jordan.

Israelis say that the Jordanians armed the entire population two days before the war. Guns are now being surrendered. Some sniping has occurred in Ramallah. But snipers are far more active in Gaza, where the refugee problem is acute. In Gaza the UN is trying to feed 300,000 people who are in an explosive state. I have been told that not even UN officials are safe among the Gaza refugees.

A Jordanian report says that 70,000 people who fled from Jericho and from the Syrian borders are in the Zerka area, near Amman. The Jordanians are now supposedly turning refugees back. And defeated Egyptians in the Sinai Desert are trying to make it back to Suez without food or water. Nasser does not want these survivors to spread details of the disaster. In rumor-happy Tel Aviv people are saying that Egyptian soldiers emerging from the Sinai have been shot on Nasser's orders, and a French newspaper this morning has put this in print.

That Nasser, endorsed by Marxist leaders like Tito as a Progressive and by the Russians and the Chinese as a true enemy of imperialism, might order a massacre of the survivors is not inconceivable. In any case, more men are dying at this moment of hunger, thirst and exposure than were killed in battle.

An editorial in the London *Times* urges the great powers to send emergency help. Their fleets are still in the eastern Mediterranean. It seems to have taken Israel some time to realize that in disarming the Egyptians and allowing them to go free "they were in fact sentencing them to death," says the *Times*.

Obviously the refugee problem requires an international solution. No one can reasonably claim that right is entirely on the Israeli side, and although some Arab leaders exploited the misery of the refugees to intensify hatred of Israel, the Israelis might have done more for the Arabs. It should have been possible, for instance, to set aside money for indemnity and reconstruction. Part of the money paid to Israel by West Germany might have been used for this purpose. Now the number of refugees has increased enormously, and if the old system is followed the UN will be supporting more dozens of rotting slums in which demoralized, idle young men can concentrate on "politics."

Only Arab extremists can profit from this. A negligible percentage of the oil royalties of Kuwait would have paid for the rehabilitation of the Palestinian Arabs. So would the billions spent on two campaigns in the Sinai. So would the Suez Canal tolls.

A big Arab crowd in Nablus waits for gas or kerosene rations. Curfew has been advanced to 6:00 P.M. according to the military authorities. It is now 2:00 P.M. The streets are filled. The light comes down sharply with a stony glitter from the Judean hills. Under this parching heat I begin to sag somewhat.

I am glad to sit down in the thick-walled HQ building. An Israeli sergeant pours us a slug of whiskey. When we get our second wind we venture into the heat again. The sun hits you at the back of the neck and you get an odd thickening sensation in the skull.

We go down the street, looking into shops. We can buy nothing. Israeli currency is not accepted. Half a dozen Arabs stare at us from a barbershop and seem to be inviting us to enter. All the customers but one wear Western clothes. The exception, an elderly gentleman, has a tarboosh covering his head down to the sad brows. His chin is puckered with many emotions, but it is curiosity that wins out. He stands near us listening, a hookah tube (as near as I can make out) hanging from his pocket like a stethoscope.

The mirror is straight from a Coney Island funhouse. We all look very wide, with squash noses, split grins and distorted eyes. Here too there is a spokesman. Very handsome, dark-browed, he has a furious nonsmile, and as the old barber, engrossed and even doting, cuts steadily at his black hair, the spokesman tells us, to begin with, that the Americans are spies. No, he does not believe that the Americans flew air cover for Israel. But Americans did spot the Egyptian airfields for the Israelis. Come, come, says the *New York Times* representative.

The hair snipping continues and the spokesman tries to be pleasant but has too many passions to manage. His grin is bitter. Still, he wants to talk. Speaking to correspondents, he feels that his truth will reach the world. He is a dairy farmer, he says. He has sixty cows to milk. He can't get the gas to go to the relief of his suffering cows. They need their hay, and the children need milk. It occurs to me that the job might be done with donkeys. There are plenty of people here listening to music, being shaved, passing the time of day, and the farm is only two miles up the road.

Instead we go on about the future, Arab unity, hints of vengeance. "But you declared war on Israel," says the *Times*. "We had a treaty," says the gentleman dairy farmer. He adds, "King Hussein was pushed, outsidely, and pulled, insidely." Then he is silent and looks at us from under his brows, like the late John Gilbert playing an Arab role.

It is instructive to see what Middle Eastern poster artists do with the faces of Hollywood stars, the feelings they impart to them. Robert Mitchum Arabized is strong, honorable, but his features are twisted with foreknowledge of defeat. Fate is dead against him. We know that he is not going to make it. Our gentleman farmer is like that.

Now, having his neck trimmed with a Schick electric razor, he sits with stilted suffering pride. I am unable to give a T. E. Lawrence/Freya

Stark interpretation to this look. In my cruder, Midwestern judgment it seems all wrong. What good are these traditional dignities? No good at all if they lead to the Sinai roads with their blasted Russian tanks, the black faces of the dead dissolving and the survivors fighting for a sip of ditch water.

Skepticism and the Depth of Life

For a young man it is probably easier to become a writer than it was thirty years ago, but perhaps it is harder now to *be* a writer. Until recently American society was so raw that it was difficult for the artist to explain his presence in it. Because writers felt foreign anyway, they often went abroad to live.

The first writer I ever met was an elderly neighbor in Chicago, a tool-and-die maker who turned out pulp stories. He had an ugly little bungalow and typed in the attic. His house was beautifully kept; he had much time to give it, painting, watering, pruning. He said to me once, "People see me hanging around and they think I'm sick or loafing. But I'm not a loafer, I'm a writer." The streets in this working-class neighborhood were empty during the day. To be free from labor, from factory routine, made the old writer acutely guilty. A man's duty was to get up in the night, wait on the corner at daybreak for the streetcar, go to the plant. During the day it was the wife who should be seen about the house, not the husband.

My neighbor wrote for *Argosy* and *True Confession*. I dreamed of contributing to *The American Mercury* or *Transition*. Obviously, however, one could not write in the attic on an old typewriter no longer fit for business correspondence, looking down into streets deserted by all decent people, by men earning their bread, as men should, in the sweat of their brows. Not long before, Coolidge had told us through his New England nose that the business of America *was* business. We might despise him for saying such a thing, but no one could prove that the proposition was false. We were living in those days, as for the most part we still live, in vast industrial compounds. American cities, even New York, are formed by the necessities of business and work.

But since the Twenties considerable changes have occurred. Writers feel somewhat less foreign, and the family of a would-be novelist will now accept the announcement of his calling with greater composure. Art and literature are okay. They can be profitable. And the common man is far more emancipated than my old tool-and-die maker. Idleness no longer makes him so uneasy. He has himself acquired some bohemian traits. Truck drivers may now be observed sipping martinis while listening to the sophisticated songs of transvestites. Policemen discuss psychology and checkers in supermarkets read John O'Hara and Thomas Altizer and watch cultural TV programs about LSD and religion.

Still, the main facts of American life are productive. The overwhelming fact is that of a manufacturing and business civilization. Money, production, politics, planning, administration, expertise, war—these are what absorb mature men. This is what society as a whole is manifestly about. Most writers cannot expect to get easily into the minds of people absorbed in such matters—a public, one should add, influenced by the mass media.

So the young writer does not expect to have any great number of readers. A small discriminating public would suit him well enough. But to begin with, he has trouble getting people to admit that he is any sort of writer at all. He has a self-anointed look. He is without proper credentials. His first task is to legitimize himself.

Fifty or sixty years ago the would-be novelist from Sioux Falls or Lincoln, Nebraska, headed for St. Louis, New Orleans or Chicago. If he had the gift of words he could become a newspaper reporter and live in a little bohemia on the banks of the Mississippi or the Near North Side of Chicago. He became a writer. But such opportunities no longer exist. The gathering and dissemination of news have been rationalized, mechanized, electronified. Most American papers are thick with advertisements for meat and plastics, underpants and used cars. They haven't much space for writing. They carry certain canned news items and syndicated columns. There is no more reflective, personal reporting. The old and easy informality has gone. No more idling and scribbling in saloons. No more *Front Page* razzle-dazzle. Real and earnest life has caught up with us. World destiny, et cetera.

By the end of the Twenties, writers had abandoned New Orleans and Chicago for Hollywood, New York or Paris. Today, New York is generally thought to be the literary capital of the United States. But is it really that? What can a young writer expect to find in New York? When he arrives from Paducah or Topeka he has the feeling of having escaped at last from the barren periphery. He has reached to the center. But the center of what? Of new literary ideas, new impulses? Has he indeed any reason to believe that he will find such things here?

New York is a publishing center, the business center of American culture. Here culture is prepared, processed and distributed. Here the publishers with their modern apparatus for printing, billing, shipping, editing, advertising and accounting, with their specialized personnel, wait for manuscripts. Their expenses are tremendous so they cannot afford to wait too long; they must find material somewhere, attract writers or fabricate books in their editorial offices. New York, of course, includes Washington and Boston. Some of its literary mandarins actually live in Cambridge, in New Haven, Bennington, New Brunswick, Princeton; a few are in London and Oxford. These officials of high culture write for the papers, sit on committees, advise, consult, set standards, define, drink cocktails, gossip—they give body to New York's appearance of active creativity, its apparently substantial literary life. But there is no substance. There is only the *idea* of a cultural life. There are manipulations, rackets and power struggles; there is infighting; there are reputations, inflated and deflated. Bluster, vehemence, swagger, fashion, image-making, brain-fixing—these are what the center has to offer.

What one can do, coming from Topeka or Dallas or Denver, is to lead the *life* of a poet or a novelist. One can get a pad, go to the bars, wear the clothes and make the scene. This is to poetry what an ad for bread is to nourishment. It is merely the picture of the thing. But some people ask for nothing better. The idea of being a writer or of leading the art-life is far more attractive than the perfection of an art. The art is difficult. Artists are beset by detractors, challenged by change and threatened with obsolescence by the prophets of electronics and by snooty college professors who want to pick up the marbles of tradition and break up the game. Also we seem to have reached a stage at which

There Is Simply Too Much to Think About

any moderately educated man already has all the literature he needs and is not really interested in the novels of his contemporaries. These are often indeed irrelevant to his real concerns, derivative feeble things. But literary life and the art life in New York and San Francisco can look very desirable. Freed from the cultural guilt and the dread of idleness that afflicted the tool-and-die maker, the young, emancipated from the work ethic, though sometimes wearing the clothes of the poor working stiff of forty years ago, invest their liberty and leisure in the art life. And the public approves of this. It wants poets or people who look like poets. A great civilization has always had, and must have, poets. And ours is a great civilization. One does not necessarily read poetry. Influential men have others read it for them. But it is important that all the positions should be occupied.

Writers of talent do occasionally manage to make a beginning in New York, but their tendency is to compensate themselves too handsomely and too fully for the hardships they endured on the way up. They are often transformed into Major Literary Figures and for the rest of their lives do little more than give solemn interviews to prestigious journals or serve on White House committees or fly to the Bahamas to participate in international panel discussions on the crisis in the arts. Often the writer is absorbed by the literary figure. In such cases it is the social struggle that has been most important, not the art.

New York, then, is not the literary capital of America. It is simply the center of the culture business. It manufactures artistic lifestyles for the American public. The literary activity of the country is concentrated mainly in the universities. The university has come to be in the Sixties what Paris was to Fitzgerald and Hemingway in the Twenties. Ann Arbor and Iowa City are not Paris. But then Paris isn't Paris either. The old glamour is used up. Gertrude Stein is gone. Joyce and Gide are gone. The great national capitals of culture have passed away. So where is one to turn for asylum? Where can the young man from Georgia or Minnesota find a protective, spiritually nutritive environment? Not in Paris. Today the art-fostering city can be claimed by no country. New York City for painters perhaps, though even the painters have fled the galleries, the directors, the journalists and art-speculators. The young writer wants to withdraw from life in discredited shapes, from communities that will not allow him to declare himself an artist or tend to see him (if they do grant that one of their own may become an artist) as genteel, unmanly—queer. No wonder young men from Minnesota want to find the "good place," the "true center." In behaving like artists and substituting art-behavior for art, people are trying to create the conditions associated with the charmed life. To obtain these conditions they are prepared, if necessary, to grind up art and strew it underfoot like sand. Another way of saying this is that the role of artist—the role itself—absorbs too much energy. Many writers give to this image of the artist the strength they might be giving to their art. Now writers have been given asylum in universities, but they are not quite comfortable there. Most of them bring into the university their romantic, populistic and anti-intellectual attitudes. I think I am justified in saying that there have been few new literary ideas in the last decades. Writers have taken their social attitudes from the modern classics and held to them stubbornly—the Eliot view, the Joyce view, the Lawrence view. The main current of cultural criticism of the twentieth century has run without much change for some fifty years. Few people are dissatisfied with modernist orthodoxy. This orthodoxy rules the English departments, which have become the Paris-substitutes of young literary men.

Of the changes in American life that for better or for worse have conferred a sort of revolutionary power on the universities, giving university-trained intellectuals a tremendous role to play in the organization of industry, in education, in politics, in the replanning of cities, in the use of leisure (or in planning the "reconstruction" of Vietnam, a project of Michigan State), writers have only the dimmest understanding. I am not terribly optimistic about the uses the university-trained scientists and intellectuals will make of these new powers. But at the moment I limit myself to the disgrace felt by writers in accepting the protection of universities seen by them, quite falsely, as the old-fashioned academy. Human life is being radically transformed in university laboratories, but novelists are still thinking of action in terms of the jeep, the gun, the whiskey bottle, the bullfight. Most American writers accept the American anti-intellectual traditions that see professors, clergymen, artists and all males in "genteel" occupations as women, not men. And the writer in the university has not discovered the intellectual

There Is Simply Too Much to Think About

life of universities. This may be because universities have no such thing as a unified intellectual life. They have dispersed specialties. Under ideal conditions a common culture might coalesce about university-sheltered artists. The conditions do not, however, seem to me favorable. And in any case writers in English departments have little access to any science except psychoanalysis, the favorite science of such departments. And psychoanalysis itself is greatly indebted to literature and is by some people thought to be a German systematization of romantic literary insights into the realm of dreams and unconsciousness.

But suppose writers were to interest themselves in the modern sciences. What would they do with them? In the nineteenth century science gave writers—from Edgar Allan Poe to Paul Valéry—certain exciting or sinister ideas. They were delighted with the masquerade of precision, deduction, exact measurement and experiment. But then it was possible to think that one could master the sciences. In the twentieth century writers cannot expect mastery. They feel somewhat awed. They are timid. They advance opinions, they have impressions. They have lost confidence and hesitate to claim knowledge. And what is knowledge now? Even last year's specialist is not a genuine specialist. Only today's specialist may be said to know something, and he must move quickly if he is not to be overwhelmed by ignorance.

Indeed, some writers have argued that information is now the only muse. But we are all beginning to understand, confronting *The New York Times* on Sunday mornings, that being fully informed may also be an illusion. We must wait for art to produce figurative equivalents of information—objects or symbols of knowledge and consciousness transcending mere fact. At the moment, however, the writer feels a certain inferiority. He inherits a realistic tradition in which the writer deals in *facts* and seems to *know*. But what sort of knowledge does he actually have? What has he to offer to the mature judgment, to the serious interests of people who are trying to understand what goes on? What has he to say about the "crisis of our civilization?" How can he compete with those whose knowledge seems so "objective," so "real"?

Writers cannot simply continue in the old way. Even the old way, if chosen, would have to be chosen anew. What can be said now? What is truly relevant? What can art signify? What core of significance endures through all the changes we have experienced? Those who read fiction are sometimes more aware of these things than those who write it. A man in Washington recently said to me that he did not think writers ought to try to describe political realities. That was hopeless. They ought rather to concentrate on internal and subjective states. I answered that they had already done quite a lot of this. But he said that organizational America was swallowing him up and that he was beginning to feel lost in corporate conceptions. Even his imagination of death was affected. At times he thought of the soul as an interchangeable part. Perhaps he exaggerated. But we do fear for our freedom. And the apparatus of organization is immense. Can we allow ourselves to continue fiddling on the old strings, in the old gypsy style?

Writers have been backward and slow, reluctant to reconsider. They have met the crisis by repeating their routines—doing the Symbolist bit, the man-of-action bit, the rogue bit, the extremist bit, et cetera. The disorder and confusion of middle-aged writers is sad to see. Their transforming moment is twenty-five years behind them. Few people follow their first revolution with a second and a third. One must understand what is happening. And populist orthodoxy never encouraged them to use their heads. On the contrary it made them feel that they owed it to the people, to the democratic average, to be dumb. Now the universities have hired them. But not to think. The universities want them to train professional writers. Also they would rather like them to bring the art-life to the campus. Bohemia. Not the vices. Just the color of bohemia. Arriving with his typewriter on campus, the writer finds the modern lit profs, and some of the philosophers and theologians, already behaving like writers. Should he compete? He would be better advised to sit down, apart, and think things over quietly.

There are, generally speaking, two types of lit prof. The first type is concerned with the classics; he is an antiquarian, a custodian of the cultural valuables. These valuables have been edited and cataloged, sufficiently described, and there is little more to do about them. Except, with modest pride, and a feeling of being separated from the unseemly, thrashing, boring, dangerous world, to hand them over to qualified curators in the next generation. The second type of lit prof deals with the moderns and often takes them as models. When I was an undergraduate there were teachers of literature who looked Tennysonian, Browningish, Swinburnian, pre-Raphaelite or Celtic Twilight. Later they were influenced by Hemingway, a very popular model. Many who grew up in the Twenties copied the Fitzgerald style of the sad young man who drank too much and had a nutty wife. (Many wives obliged.) Now we have Lawrentian profs, Dylan Thomas profs, Becketts, Ionescos and Mailers, wood-demons, sons of Pan, Dionysians, LSD godseekers.

We seem to have come to a time when the main problem for culture is to make it personally applicable. We have been trained to consume good things, to make them our own. One can see this happening in the literary quarterlies, which have also been drawn into the universities. Like other American magazines they are now mainly attitude-sources. They do for graduate students and young intellectuals what *Vogue* and *Glamour* do for working girls and housewives. They instruct them in the in-things and the out-things. They replace art with art-discourse and supply ideas for dress or discussion—ready-made advanced views. Perhaps the role of the modern lit profs who fill the quarterlies is to prepare young intellectuals to occupy the positions an expanding culture (billions for education; federal funds for art) is making ready for them. The point is, perhaps, to have nothing new in literature but rather to exploit what we already have.

No, new literature really does not interest these people much. They themselves, the literary intellectuals, are what is new. They are the brilliant event, the great result of modern creativity. They are, as it were, clad in art and literature. They wear them as young ladies wear their plastic Mondrian raincoats.

The pantheon of the university-vanguard world is already full. New applicants are not welcomed. Contemporary writers serve mostly to remind us of what is good or bad in the great tradition, as defined by literary intellectuals. This attitude toward living writers makes the criticism of university-trained intellectuals violent, vindictive and harsh. There is a taste for Roman holidays, for bloody entertainment, in universities and intellectual circles. Novelists and poets are prodded into gladiatorial fights. Literature is acquiring a sporting color, like hockey or prizefighting. Editors of literary magazines or professors who arrange

the visiting lecture or annual symposium often behave like fight promoters. I have more than once been invited by Professor X to confront
Professor Y who has called me (the text is usually quoted) a sellout, a
flunky, a faker or a fink. The invitation reads, "I am sure you would like
an opportunity to reply to this from the same platform, in public." A
fine old Irish saying is relevant here, from Archie Road, Chicago, in the
golden age of Mr. Dooley: "Joe said you wasn't fit to live with pigs. But
I stood up for you. I said you was."

A poet, it is assumed, should be willing to reveal his soul under the
glare of great lights, to assure the public that it is getting full value, that
he really is a poet. More or less.

This, too, is living the life—the art-life, I mean. There are many
artists and painters who see nothing wrong with this. The painters and
sculptors seem especially willing to perform various art-stunts and to
promote themselves. Inventing novelties, they themselves become news
and they keep up the level of art-excitement for those who are, by status,
privileged to enjoy it. What suffers in the process is art itself, which
cannot be the source of such excitements. These evidently have an extra-
aesthetic function—social, psychological, barbarous, tribal—involving
people in group activities that have the color of art. They do something
with literature or with painting.

The late Wyndham Lewis wrote in the early Fifties that the artist
offered his work primarily to the community of artists. The audience
most competent to evaluate a novel is an audience of novelists, he believed. The writer writes for somebody. "In our day," he said, "that
somebody is almost infallibly another writer. . . . It will appear from
this what a tragic matter it is if other writers (intellectuals) begin to fail
in those integrities upon which good workmanship depends and the act
of creation itself." Lewis believed in what used to be called the Republic
of Letters. (He included as citizens of this Republic scholars and members of the teaching profession.) The Republic of Letters must, he
thought, "somehow acquire a better sense of corporate responsibility . . .
if it did so it would as far as it is able secure for its members that unim-
peded latitude of expression which it knows to be a condition of the best
work. It would also seek to provide some master prophylactic against
obsessional contagions."

There Is Simply Too Much to Think About

Nothing like this is happening at present. The community of writers (scholars, critics, teachers) does not secure any sort of latitude for its members; on the contrary, it constricts them more and more. Criticism tries to control the approaches to literature. It confronts the reader with its barriers of interpretation. A docile public consents to this monopoly of the specialists—those "without whom literature cannot be understood." Critics, speaking for writers, succeed eventually in replacing them. The integrities upon which good workmanship depends, and the act of creation itself, interest critics and scholars very little. They seem unaware of the fundamental fact that the tradition cannot exist unless contemporary artists continue to do what artists have always done. The critic who does not understand this has no more feeling for the great tradition than a dog can have for a cathedral.

There is no sense of corporate responsibility. Our literary intellectuals shun all such ideas. The very thought of a Republic of Letters makes them flinch. They have curious notions about their artistic and intellectual freedom. They seem to think freedom for literary intellectuals to be a kind of barbarism made possible by civilization. They hate that civilization as only its subtlest, most pampered children can hate. They appear to believe that their loyalty to the highest human standards or ideals (ideals unformulated but nevertheless pervasive) is expressed by the most radical destructiveness. This assumption about the necessity of destructiveness is seldom examined. It has been around for a long time. Since the end of the nineteenth century it has been particularly influential.

"Car l'Homme a fini! l'Homme a joué tous les rôles!" Man is finished! Rimbaud wrote. Man has played all the parts! And at noonday, tired of smashing his idols, he will come to himself, free from those old gods. There is something very stirring in this, certainly. Or in D. H. Lawrence's image of the phoenix rising from the flames of universal destruction and purification. But the optimism contained in these images is considerable. Iconoclasm clears the way for the living god within. We go down into hell, but in the myth we come out again, all the better for it. Fortified by a secret optimism, the pessimistic critic does not have to bother his mind with such stuff as corporate responsibility or the Republic of Letters. He may in fact think that wicked old Wyndham Lewis went soft in the head

toward the end of his life. But in reality this radical destructiveness is largely gesture and play. It keeps up the level of art-excitement in journals, in seminars, in art galleries and at Happenings. This extremism is handsomely subsidized by universities and other benevolent institutions. What lies beneath, it seems to me, is the notion of a widespread sharing of "the aesthetic." Art, atomized and dispersed, is absorbed into the lives of individuals and the general level is thought to be raised thereby.

A curious aspect of this is that the modern classics themselves have contributed to the development of these attitudes. One does not simply read *A Portrait of the Artist as a Young Man*. The reader is aesthetically retrained by the novel. What can he do but become an artist? He is obliged to follow Joyce into the world, feeling as he felt, seeing as he saw, finding the same internal standard, using the power of words, images and rhythms to transform an otherwise ordinary, wretched life. This may be one reason why critics are today independently "artistic." They have spent many hours at the controls of powerful machines, working "aesthetically" on the materials of common experience. Their teachers were the master-monopolists who created new types of consciousness. They led their readers (or students; or subjects) also into art history. They instructed them in revolutionary attitudes and revolutionary techniques. And if one thinks oneself a Joyce or a Lawrence, an artist of some sort, ideas of corporate responsibility and the Republic of Letters are a bit beside the point.

So then, with the air about us filled with small Stephen Dedaluses who teach literature, edit magazines and write critical articles and who can be seen swarming far from Crete or Dublin, we turn our attention again to the young man from Topeka whose literary gifts give him no rest. He will of course have to leave home. New York has little to offer him. As for the university, its influence on him may be bad, may depress him. But literary activity in America is mainly there. All the higher mental activities of the country are there, for better or worse. Even radicalism has, at the moment, no other home.

Ortega y Gasset, I remember, criticized Goethe for settling down in Weimar. A poet should, Ortega thought, accept shipwreck and consent with all his heart to be homeless. That may be. Poets are a little hard to prescribe for. Critics dearly love to have their hearts wrung by the disasters of the great artist. Is the university simply Weimar in another

There Is Simply Too Much to Think About

more disgusting and intensely more bourgeois form? In Ortega's view it might be just that.

In the radical attitudes of many writers there is evidence of such Weimar fears. Hostile to institutions, anti-authority by tradition, they are not likely to be tranquil in their university sanctuary. Bad conscience leads them to take exaggeratedly radical attitudes. But this radicalism of gesture turns out to be immensely popular. A large and growing public shares the uneasiness of artists and welcomes this show of radicalism. The feelings of organization men, of lawyers or Madison Avenue professionals, of civil servants at the higher levels—intelligent but powerless people—are not very different, at this moment, from those of writers on whom the shades of the universities have fallen. Such people, often thwarted, resentful, perplexed and fatigued by the incessant demands on the intellect and feelings, respond to the vivid gesture of emancipation, defiance, illusionlessness, the spirit of skepticism and dissent. But it is only the *manner* that is radical. Few things can be safer, more success-assuring, than this nonthreatening radicalism, dangerous to no one and relying, at bottom, on the stability of institutions.

Then what is to be done? An intelligent and learned friend of mine suggested to me recently, more than half in earnest, that perhaps possession was the answer, that writers should be more shamanistic in these times. The shamans, primitive Siberian priests given to trances, dream-utterances—androgynous, creatures of mystery, uninhibited, antinomian—I don't suppose he was seriously proposing that writers in civilized countries should be exactly like that. But when things are tough, when the knowledge needed for realistic analysis is out of reach, some form of intuitive daring may seem best. After all, Rimbaud was a sort of Druidic figure and D. H. Lawrence with his Dionysian apocalyptic insights was something of a shaman. Shamanism is accredited to the modern temper by its connotations of squalor, neurotic sexuality, mesmerism, charlatanism and so forth. To people resisting the glib poster-world of packaging and public relations, blood, spittle, excrements and swoons seem to offer a healthy antidote. Defacement and smearing appear to be called for. Blasphemy, if you can still find things sacred enough to blaspheme. Shamanism would attract people who must live within elaborate systems of compromise, holding out the promise of a magical penetration of the fortifications of organization, tyranny, established falsehood and dullness. The suggestion that what we need in American literature is some of this shamanism implies a tremendous longing that someone should be free enough to tell off the State and all its organizations, the ruling industries and the enormous apparatus of persuasion, information-misinformation, manipulation and control. It implies that there is a considerable need for defiance and even subversion among people who are fairly prosperous and in many respects free. It implies also a turn toward the sacred, if only in the shaggy, dubious, inferior form of shamanism. It means, perhaps, that the artist must pray to be possessed by spirits so that he may utter in his rapture the truth that patient reason can no longer hope for.

A century ago, when the Christian clergy began to feel certain doubts, poets and novelists moved into the center of the spiritual crisis and assumed spiritual obligations. Walt Whitman announced that the priests were departing, the divine literati arriving. Henry James said that "the author's paramount charge was the cure of souls, to the subjugation and if need be the exclusion of the picturesque." Writers have by no means given up the cure of souls. Some of them have descended to a lower sphere of practical orientation, attitude-teaching. Some prefer the primitive shamans to the divine literati. But the feeling of responsibility somehow remains. There are few writers who really deny the right of the species to exist. Jonathan Swift, a clergyman in good standing, was not convinced that our species should prevail and endure. But such pessimism is quite rare, even in our radical and reckless times and despite the efforts of nihilistic writers to scandalize us and to frighten us with visions of the void. On the whole writers have not given up the cure of souls. But what have most of them to offer? Good-natured assurances? Liberal confidence that it will "all work out"? Retread morality? Retread Christianity? In America the cure of souls has dwindled away to sex advice and other useful but minor forms of instruction. Perhaps the young writer may profit from his association with the university to think about these matters. He had better prepare to do his thinking alone. For the old lit profs he doesn't really exist. The modern lit profs may make him wish that *he* didn't. The philosophers and theologians will perhaps include what he writes in their diagnoses of the disorders of the modern spirit. He will add to their "existential" proofs. But that he will learn much from them is not probable.

In this period of vague and shifting outlines, when the public is half artist, the artist is not clear as to his function. Everything familiar is considered dull and degrading. Certain forms of life appear to be self-discrediting. There is great uneasiness and shame at the unworthiness and the unaesthetic quality of existence. An extraordinary sense of dulling and leveling drives people to extremes in their quest for what is interesting. The rule of rational organization is so thorough that belief in the power of our contemporaries to enchant us is dwindling. We long for enchantment but our skepticism is too great. It is hard for modern readers to believe in an added dimension or quality of existence. The credentials of writers, of would-be enchanters, are examined more thoroughly than those of the Joint Chiefs or of candidates for the Presidency. The public, though it still has the same great hunger for the fascinating, for expression, the same immortal longing for meaning, has no confidence in the power of its writers to put it under a marvelous spell. So instead it takes from them ideas of behavior, suggestions for a lifestyle, practical orientations or self-descriptions.

Well, we have come through many transformations. Simply to think of these will tire strong men. In the twentieth century writers have emphasized, for the most part unconsciously, the necessary liberation of mankind from ancient restraints and taboos. We now enjoy much that was forbidden in the past. This mounting atmosphere of emancipation has thrilled the twentieth century. Traditions, like weights, may be picked up and moved aside. But having moved them out of the way, what have we achieved? People are beginning to see that many of these old obstacles are somehow still significant. In literature we have reached such a degree of liberation that we are threatened by nudity, barrenness, weightlessness and nonexistence-in-existence.

Looking back to the beginning of the century, we can make out the following literary tendencies:

1. The tendency of that group which believed it could restore enchantment to human life by means of revolutionary ideology.
2. Romantic sexual theories, like those of D. H. Lawrence, of-

fering to save mankind from repression, sterile rationalism and soul-destroying industrial ugliness, and calling for the restoration of the gods of nature, of ancient mythic truths, et cetera.

3. The rejection of sentiment and the antagonism to human qualities that seemed to interfere with the supremacy of consciousness. This is the tendency best represented by Paul Valéry, and it is one, I believe, which has the support of many contemporary psychological developments. I quote the following sentence from one of his essays: "The acme of the human is that man has come to enjoy it: a search for emotion, fabrication of emotion, desire to lose one's head, to make others lose theirs, to disturb and be disturbed."

In speaking of a degree of liberation in which we approach weightlessness and final detachment, I was thinking of Valéry's dislike of the demonstrative, of his rejection of character traits, of his opposition, shared by many, to the theater of the soul, the drama of personality, the exaggeration and overvaluation of eccentricities—the being tired, in short, of our own human carrying-on.

It seems that intelligence has reached a point of extreme skepticism about this human carrying-on. It is with this skepticism that the writer today has to deal. It gives readers and spectators great satisfaction to see these old dramas of personality, love, duty, beauty, family, "heroic will" exposed by the ironies of pop art or absurdist theater. Since the First World War we have seen these traditional ideas subverted by any number of artists. The modern public has developed a curious spectator-passivity and detachment from things formerly felt and believed. It contemplates its own humanity, uncommitted, from a position of security and immunity. A withdrawn, musing antiself watches the emotion circus. It is objective; it is busy divorcing itself from innumerable falsehoods, errors. The desire to get away from so many human states may arise from a desire to purify the conscious intellect, to increase its power. But it may also contain an element of self-dislike. It may be the most contemporary form of misanthropy.

The skepticism I have spoken of assumes that it can "see through

There Is Simply Too Much to Think About

things." It seems to feel, unhappily, that things are shallow enough to be "seen through." In other words, it feels that "the depth of life" is gone.

If it is no longer where it used to be, where has it gone? Where can it go? If you drain a lake, the water must run somewhere. If some wicked engineering genius invented a way to steal Lake Michigan, he would have to find a place to store it. And it may be so also with the significance of human existence and action. If it is not where we were accustomed for ages to see it, where is it? Art will have to deal with this question. Perhaps it will turn out to be an unreal question. Nothing should be allowed to prevent the imagination from reexamining the evidence.

It was for such reasons that I began by saying that it was not too difficult today to become a writer but perhaps it was harder than ever to be one. It is easier to lead the life than to be the thing. The picture of the bread cannot nourish our bodies.

[1967]

The Seventies

On America: Remarks at the
U.S. Cultural Center in Tel Aviv

First of all, I would like to say that I am not here as an expert in American history. I am just a writer. Occasionally, especially in a foreign country, a writer finds himself as a spokesman of his people; I doubt that I would receive their nomination or their vote.

The United States is the most advanced of modern capitalist democracies and it finds itself now in terrible crisis; and the real question is whether it can survive the role that it is playing today as a great world power, and also whether two hundred million people can live in a capitalist democracy without losing their liberties and without poisoning themselves out of existence. This seems to me the real question: whether a democratic mass society can remain a free society; whether it is capable of dealing with this crisis and whether it will have the will to prevent itself from degenerating into something like Huxley's *Brave New World*.

We are all of us the children of immigrants who grew up in the U.S., committed to certain democratic ideals which I for one to this day am not willing to give up and by which I still live. There is such a thing as a liberal faith. There is, however, a great deal of difference among people as to how one realizes this liberal faith. There is at one and the same time a sense of increased participation by the public in current events, in public affairs, and a sense of individual helplessness or impotence, so that people are very much afraid of being depoliticized in the U.S. But at the same time they find themselves in the center of events and they've never been as active as they are at the moment, one way or another, in public events.

Is there a gap between the generations in the U.S.? I object to any kind of categorization that interferes with the humanity of its members. I don't like to say that any particular group or generation, in the U.S. or elsewhere, is less human than another group. When I hear that there is some sort of ideological line between the old and the young, I get rather worried. For one thing I recall—because I'm old enough to recall—that the totalitarian movements in Europe in the Twenties and Thirties were also youth movements.

Now, insofar as this movement is an intellectual movement, perhaps it ought to be mentioned that the intellectuals in the U.S. have always been separatists. That is to say, they have always considered themselves to stand outside the power arrangement of the country. In the nineteenth century they felt very much outside. It is the tendency of intellectuals generally to dissent from authority and to take a stand apart from organized power. There have been times when intellectuals have been involved in government service or in politics in a rather significant way, but that is not really the tendency in the U.S. It's very unlike the British idea of democracy, according to which government service was not considered a sellout of or treason to intellectual principles. Many of the greatest Englishmen of the nineteenth century were men who served their government, like James Mill or Disraeli. For American intellectuals to become involved in government or in the direction of social affairs seems to be considered a form of treason. This presents a very peculiar difficulty since the society can now no longer function without its intellectuals.

The universities are not the ivory towers they once were, and if the intellectuals feel that they are selling out when they accept a government position this makes life in the U.S. very difficult—both for the intellectuals and for the governments. How a technological society and a world power with a population of two hundred millions is going to function when the intellectuals consider that it is their moral duty to be estranged from it, I don't know.

These children come from middle-class families, most of them; and the accusation they make against the middle class is quite a justified accusation—that the middle class did not produce any values by which these young people can live. The fact, of course, that the middle-class parents, like all groups in society, were also caught by surprise in a society continually being transformed and without precedent is not accepted as an excuse or justification. The fact is that they did concentrate on material success and that they offered their children a kind of prosperity and special care but without any particularly spiritual or moral element. The fathers behaved as though there was some sort of illicit life outside the family, that business life was corrupt, that they were engaged in some kind of racket but that they would keep a sort of purity at home, if possible. This is what Charlie Chaplin satirized in *Monsieur Verdoux*—the idea that you go out and murder but that you can have a perfectly well-balanced and respectable bourgeois family life. Insofar as the children are protesting against this, they are perfectly justified; insofar as their protests are self-destructive, we must try to do something to prevent them from destroying themselves.

Middle-class parents in the U.S.—and I speak particularly of Jewish parents but I think they were all in on the act—had the feeling that they had emerged from a terrible nightmare, that their own upbringing was faulty, that parents did not understand, that they were cruel and repressive but that their children were going to be free and were going to enjoy every privilege of life. The children took this quite seriously. They believed what the parents told them—that everything was for them, that the middle-class parents were a lost generation, but that they, the youth, were the meaning of it all, and that society was entitled to purity, and that they were exempt from the conditions of life. The young really feel that there is no scarcity of anything in life, that everything is present in abundance because everything always has been present in abundance and therefore the solutions to life's problems must also be there upon demand. And they make the demand; and they are astonished when the solutions are not forthcoming.

The youth ideology is romantic, and people have romantic sentiments about the youth ideology, and that's a very nice thing—poetically speaking; but practically speaking, I think it becomes rather harmful.

Students know that they are at the university for four years or five years or six years and after those years are over the system is going to swallow them up—that is to say, their last chance to make a change in society will disappear; they will become specialists or professionals; and this is really what happens. Many of the protesters, of course, when their student life is over, enter the ranks of the professions and the whole thing is over and done with, so this is their last opportunity to register a protest against the system. But the students are attacking the universities and the universities are not the principal sinners. The universities are the only and perhaps the last centers of free exchange and discussion in the U.S., and if you destroy the universities, if you choose the universities as your primary target, what is going to happen to free institutions in the U.S.?

The universities are the most vulnerable of all institutions. Like the churches or the synagogues, they never had any system of defense prepared. Now if the students attack the universities, they are attacking the whole society; and they are identifying the universities with the society. But I think this is a mistake because the universities are by no means the society; nor is the society the universities. . . .

American society is in a state of siege. Who is going to solve its problems? Are they going to be solved in the streets, are they going to be solved by some kind of authority or by some kind of organized power taking thought? Students don't want to recognize any sort of authority. Now, what proposals do they have for a substitute for authority in the U.S.? What you often hear from the New Left is, well, we'll burn everything down and we'll shoot all the old guys and then we'll have an inspiration. I don't really trust that kind of inspiration, and I don't really believe that if you burn things to the ground a phoenix will arise. . . .

Of course, in the United States as in all countries—in Israel too—we all live in the midst of a great deal of public noise and the events of the times have a very strong claim on us. There is hardly any way in which we can avoid them. Israel has the advantage at least of having to face a visible and real crisis every day, but in the U.S. these things come to us through the media and they are more often than not in the form of fantasies. That is to say, political realities that in the minds of individuals acquire a kind of fantastic character, as when people at breakfast, children and parents, having turned on the television set, see men fighting and dying in the jungles of Vietnam . . .

I don't really know whether art can exist without a certain degree of tranquillity or spiritual poise; without a certain amount of quiet you can have neither philosophy nor religion nor painting nor poetry. And as one of the specialties of modern life is to abolish this quiet, we are in danger of losing our arts together with the quiet of the soul that art demands.

So when you ask whether I am *engagé*, of course I am *engagé* insofar as I have to meet this challenge. It is not the challenge of moral considerations—that is, I don't say to myself that I am a teacher or a leader or a prophet who has to bring a moral lesson to the American public. I have the calling of a writer, of a novelist, and not necessarily of a moralist. I suppose that every writer feels there is an implicit morality in what he is doing, that he does not have to bother with an explicitly moral definition of what he is doing. But I say everyone is unwillingly *engagé*, that's the real answer; and the question is, How do you overcome this noise?

Every writer who reaches a certain level of prominence in the U.S. has the choice of belonging to the jet set or not. It's really up to him. Many years ago I read the Russian critic and philosopher Lev Shestov, who said that the public wants writers to be gladiators. The public *does* want to see the writers fight and bleed prominently in the Colosseum; of course, nobody bleeds real blood nowadays except humble people who can't avoid it, but if I look around at many American writers who I am willing to name by name—like Norman Mailer, Truman Capote and Gore Vidal—I see that they really enjoy performing for the mass media and they like very much becoming public figures. Now, that's not necessarily a bad thing. A great many writers in the past have been public figures and have managed to do something very good with it. Voltaire was a public figure and Victor Hugo was a public figure. None of these things are in themselves necessarily bad as long as there is some grain of truth or passion in what the writer is doing, even if other writers find it disagreeable. So if Norman Mailer wants to be a clown on television or things of that sort, I have no objection to it, provided always that it produces interesting literature—and many times it does. There is no reason why one should take an ideological approach to these questions; and I don't.

[1970]

New York: World-Famous Impossibility

How do Americans think of New York? That is perhaps like asking how Scotsmen feel about the Loch Ness monster. It is our legendary phenomenon, our great thing, our world-famous impossibility. Some seem to wish that it were nothing more than a persistent rumor. It is, however, as human things go, very real, superreal. What is barely hinted in other American cities is condensed and enlarged in New York. There people feel themselves to be in the middle of things. That is certainly true and it is certainly odd.

In New York, as in all great capitals, people often behave symbolically and try to express the spirit of the place. A visiting diplomat writes a letter to express gratitude to the anonymous person who discovered his wallet and returned it intact to lost and found. Off Times Square a blind man has been assaulted, his seeing-eye dog stolen; he is bleeding and weeping. A cop mutters, "This could only happen in New York." Impulses can be released here that in calmer environments are restrained. On every street people are taught "what life is like."

New York is stirring, insupportable, agitated, ungovernable, demonic. No single individual can judge it adequately. Not even Walt Whitman could today embrace it emotionally; the attempt might capsize him. Those who want to contemplate the phenomenon are well advised to assume a contemplative position elsewhere. Those who wish to *feel* its depth had better be careful. For fifteen years I lived in and with New York. I now reside in Chicago.

In other cities and regions local pride has subsided. The old naïve self-confidence is gone. After the events of the last decade, Texas no longer brags, Mayor Daley's Chicago does not boast. At the turn of the century Chicago was a regional capital. In 1893 it dreamed of being a world city. Scholars, architects, poets, musicians came up from Indiana, down from Wisconsin, east from Nebraska, but by the end of the Twenties the cultural life of the Midwest was dying. Trains leaving Chicago carried poets as well as pork and the city rapidly sank into provincialism.

Several generations of young Americans, seeking a broader and deeper life, abandoned Main Street to the businessmen and yokels and went to Paris or Greenwich Village. The country's great aim was not, after all, the encouragement of painters, philosophers and novelists. To live as a painter or an intellectual one had to go somewhere else, out of Detroit, Minneapolis or Kansas City. As bohemians and expatriates these emigrants hoped to find the dream-states and special atmospheres on which art thrives.

Bohemian life in the Village was, in the Twenties, quite elegant—even patrician, for it attracted the rich as well as writers, painters and radicals. The old Village was a grand success and for a time New York really was the center of the country for certain rare and valuable qualities. Its free-versers, free-lovers and elegant boozers, its rich ninnies and eccentrics, its artists and revolutionists charmed and heartened the younger generation, strengthening their resistance to the ugliness and philistinism of the hometown.

All that, of course, is over. New York is now the business center of American culture, the amusement or frivolity center, the excitement center, perhaps even the anxiety center. But it has no independent and original intellectual life. It provides no equilibrium, it offers no mental space to artists. Ideas are no longer discussed here. Meeting an old Village intellectual, now gray-bearded and hugely goggled, I find him as densely covered with protest buttons as a fish is with scales. He has become a former intellectual.

For better or for worse, the intellectual life of the country has moved into its universities. Bohemian manners and notions have also spread over the continent. New York is the principal producer and distributor of the mental goods consumed by this large new public. The present leaders of culture in New York are its publicity-intellectuals. These are college-educated men and women who have never lived as poets, paint-

There Is Simply Too Much to Think About

ers, composers or thinkers but who have successfully organized writing, art, thought and science in publishing houses, in museums, in foundations, in magazines, in newspapers (mainly *The New York Times*), in the fashion industry, in television and in advertising. All these things have been made to pay and pay handsomely.

No less an authority than Mr. Jason Epstein of Random House has told us in *The New York Review of Books* that New York can be a splendid place—if you're making fifty thousand dollars a year. He might have added that what Mr. Theodore Roszak has called the "counterculture" and Professor Lionel Trilling the "adversary culture" is the Dick Whittington's cat that brings in this sort of wealth, that the sale of radical ideas (some of them quite old, but many Americans have not found the opportunity to read Baudelaire, Proudhon or Marx for themselves) is profitable, and that criticism or even open hatred of society is no impediment to success in this glittering city.

But I do not think that anyone will fly in today from Boise, Idaho, eagerly seeking other writers in New York whose love of poetry is pure, or who are waiting on the steps of the Public Library like Athenians to discuss existence or justice. The publicity-intellectuals have little interest in such matters. They read little and they don't talk much about literature. Cultural New York founds its prosperity upon the former presence of these great things and keeps up the illusion that they are still about. New York is a great marketer of echoes. The past is translated even into Village rentals and real estate values, into meal prices and hotel rates. New York seems to thrive also on a sense of national deficiency, on the feelings of many who think themselves sunk hopelessly in unsatisfactory places, in the American void where there is no color, no theater, no vivid contemporaneousness, where people are unable to speak authoritatively, globally, about life.

We have no holy places in America so we make do with the profane. Inquire in Rockford, Illinois, what is happening there. The commonest answer will be: "Nothing. The action is all in San Francisco, Las Vegas and New York." When you return to Chicago from a trip to New York you are asked: "What did you see? Of course you went to the theater." But what can one see in the New York theater now? People's sexual organs. The aim is perhaps to celebrate one's emancipation from puritanism and to mark our redemption from sexual bondage. But *Oh! Calcutta!* is really a play within a play, for New York itself is the theater of the nation, showing strange things. Outsiders—the rest of the nation—do not tire of watching.

[1970]

There Is Simply Too Much to Think About

Machines and Storybooks:
Literature in the Age of Technology

Nineteenth-century writers disliked or dreaded science and technology. Edgar Allan Poe, discovering that scientific attitudes could be richly combined with fantasy, created science fiction. Shelley experimented romantically with chemicals and Balzac thought himself a natural historian or social zoologist. But for the most part science, engineering, technology horrified writers. To mechanical energy and industrial enterprise, mass production, they opposed feeling, passion, "true work," artisanship, well-made things. They turned to nature, they specialized in the spirit, they valued love and death more than technical enterprise. Writers then preferred, and still do prefer, the primitive, the exotic and the irregular. These romantic attitudes produced masterpieces of literature and painting. They produced also certain cultural platitudes. The platitude of dehumanizing mechanization formed on the one side. Equally platitudinous, the vision of a new age of positive science and of rational miracles, of progress, a progress that made art as obsolete as religion, filled up the other horizon. The platitude of a dehumanized technology gives us, today, novels whose characters are drug-using noble savages, beautiful, mythical primitives who fish in the waters dammed up by nuclear installations.

Now as power-minded theoreticians see it, the struggle between old art and new technology has ended in the triumph of technology. The following statement, and it is a typical one, is made by Mr. Arthur C. Clarke in a book called *Report on Planet Three*. "It has often been suggested," he says, "that art is a compensation for the deficiencies of the real world; as our knowledge, our power and above all our maturity increase, we will have less and less need for it. If this is true, the ultra-intelligent machine would have no use for it at all. Even if art turns out to be a dead end, there still remains science."

This statement by a spokesman of the "victorious" party is for several reasons extraordinarily silly. First, it assumes that art belongs to the childhood of mankind and that science is identical with maturity. Second, it thinks art is born in weakness and fear. Third, in its happy worship of ultra-intelligent machines it expresses a marvelous confidence in the ability of such machines to overcome all the deficiencies of the real world. Such optimistic rationalism is charming, in a way. Put it into rhyming verses and it may sound a lot like Edgar A. Guest. Edgar felt about capitalism and self-reliance precisely as Arthur C. Clarke feels about the supertechnological future. They share a certain expansiveness, the intoxication of the winner, the confidence of the great simplifier. Mr. Clarke says in effect, "Don't worry, dear pals—if art is a dead end, we still have science. Pretty soon we won't need Homer and Shakespeare, Monteverdi and Mozart. Thinking machines will give us all the wisdom and joy we want, in our maturity."

I have chosen a different sort of theorist to put the question from another angle. Writing in *The Atlantic* of July 1972, Theodore Roszak takes issue with Robert J. Good, a professor of chemical engineering. In a letter to the magazine Professor Good, of the party of science and technology, says that it is sad to see modern intellectuals "cutting off their own root in rationality." Mr. Roszak tries to deal gently with the professor. He says with a pious tremor, "What can one do, even in radical dissent, but handle with affectionate care so noble and formidable a tradition within our culture—even knowing it is a tragic error and the death of the soul?" Mr. Roszak goes on, "It is not primarily science I pit myself against in what I write. Rather, the wound I seek to heal is that of psychic alienation: the invidious segregation of humanity from the natural continuum, the divorce of visionary energy from intellect and action. What Professor Good disparages as the irrational . . . is a grand spectrum of human potentialities. When rationality is cut away from that spectrum, then the life of Reason becomes that mad rationality which insists that only what is impersonal and empirical, objective and quantifiable is real—*scientifically* real. Believe that and you are not far from tabulating the tragedies of our existence by way of body counts

There Is Simply Too Much to Think About

and megadeaths and chemical imbalances within our neural circuitry." Of course such issues cannot be discussed without invoking the most monstrous topic of the day. For ideologists in all fields the political question is always hugely, repulsively, squatting behind a paper screen. But when we have cited the argument that ultra-intelligent technology has no need of art, and the counterargument that creativity is needed to heal psychic alienation and keep us from criminal wars, we have not altogether exhausted our alternatives. There is a third alternative, which has nothing much to do with compensation for the deficiencies of the world or with society's health. This alternative holds that man is an artist and that art is a name for something always done by human beings. The technological present may be inhospitable to this sort of doing, but art can no more be taken from humankind than faces and hands. The giving of weight to the particular and the tendency to invest the particular with resonant meanings cannot be driven out by the other tendency—to insist on the finitude of the finite and to divest it of awe and beauty. . . .

I have been told by a famous progressive psychiatrist that in future ages, with sexual jealousy gone, Othello will be incomprehensible. Scientism dearly loves to speak of the childish past, the grave future. When I hear people invoking the maturity of future generations, I think of a conversation in the *Anti-Memoirs* between Malraux and a parish priest who joined the Resistance and later died fighting the Germans:

> "How long have you been hearing confessions?"
> "About fifteen years."
> "What has confession taught you about men?"
> ". . . First of all, people are much more unhappy than one
>   thinks . . . and then . . . the fundamental fact is that
>   there's no such thing as a grown-up person."

Anyway, romantics hold that it is very dangerous to sanity to deny the child within us, while scientism says that technological progress is about to carry us for the first time into the adult stage. On both sides intellectuals take positions on what art can or cannot add to human happiness. In most discussions the accent falls on health, welfare, progress or politics—anything but art. About art itself most intellectuals know and care little.

Malraux begins his *Anti-Memoirs* with the wise chaplain of the Maquis. He then goes immediately into the subject of memoirs and confessions and discusses the "theatrical self-image" in autobiography. "Once," he says, "man was sought in the great deeds of great men; then he was sought in the secret actions of individuals (a change encouraged by the fact that great deeds were often violent, and the newspapers have made violence commonplace)." Malraux then concludes, "The confessions of the most provocative memorialist seem puerile by comparison with the monsters conjured up by psychoanalytic exploration, even to those who contest its conclusions. The analyst's couch reveals far more about the secrets of the human heart, and more startlingly too. We are less astonished by Stavrogin's confession [in Dostoyevsky's *The Possessed*] than by Freud's Rat Man [in "Notes Upon a Case of Obsessional Neurosis"]: genius is its only justification."

The genius, I take it, belongs to Dostoyevsky. I am not quite sure what Malraux means, but I think he is saying that what a clinical psychologist learns about the human heart is far deeper and more curious than anything the greatest novelists can reveal. Perhaps he hints even that the madman is more profoundly creative in his rat-imaginings or grotesque fantasies than the writer, who can only compensate us for the ordinariness of his "vile secrets" or "frightful memories" by the power of his mind—"genius is [his] only justification." But even if we do not push the matter so far, we can legitimately take Malraux, a novelist, to be saying that in the field of facts the writer is "puerile." He cannot compete there with the clinical expert.

So novelists once gave "information" to the public. But when people now really want to know something they turn to the expert. Universities and research institutes produce masses of experts and governments license them. The dazzle of expertise blinds the unsure, the dependent and the wretched. It is not the novelist alone who has lost ground. Expertise has made all opinion shaky and even powerful men are reluctant to trust their own judgment. In totalitarian countries where facts are suppressed, writers of exceptional courage still tell the truth in the old

There Is Simply Too Much to Think About

way. (Why was it not a Soviet expert who told the world about the Gulag Archipelago?) But in the free world novelists seldom instruct the public in the old way.

Artists were great and highly visible monuments in the nineteenth century. The public listened deferentially to its Victor Hugo and its Leo Tolstoy. But Shaw and Wells were the last of these prestigious literary spokesmen. In the postwar period only Bertrand Russell and Jean-Paul Sartre appeared before the world in this role, and even if these two had been more consistent and sensible they would not have affected the public as their greater predecessors had done. The era of the writer as public sage and as dependable informant has ended.

A single standard has been set for novelists and for experts— the fact-standard. The result of this strict accountability has been to narrow the scope of the novel, to make the novelist doubt his own powers and the right of his imagination to range over the entire world. The authority of the imagination has declined. This has had two remarkable results. Earlier in the century certain writers rejected the older novel with its more modest objectives. The Dickens sort of novel—*Great Expectations*, say—was replaced by the more comprehensive novel, nothing less than an aesthetic project for encompassing the whole world. Proust's *Remembrance of Things Past* and Joyce's *Ulysses* do not draw the real world so much as replace it by aesthetic fiat.

Joyce was, perhaps unintentionally, an aesthetic dictator. The century needed a book? He provided one. It was a book that would make other books unnecessary. It had taken about twenty years to write *Ulysses* and *Finnegans Wake* and it should take just as long to read them. This was one result of the weakening of the authority of writers and of the power of the literary imagination to command attention—overassertiveness. A more recent result has been surrender. Writers have capitulated to fact, to events and reportage, to politics and demagogy. Modern art has tried to create power for itself on arbitrary terms and has also pursued and worshipped power in its public forms.

Until recent times the artist's dream-sphere was distinctly separate from the practical or mechanical realm of the technician. But in the twentieth century, as Paul Valéry recognized, a change occurred. "The fabulous," he wrote in an essay, "is an article of trade. The manufacture of machines to work miracles provides a living to thousands of people. But the artist has had no share in producing these wonders. They are the work of science and capital. The bourgeois has invested his money in phantoms and is speculating on the downfall of common sense."

Yes, technology is the product of science and capital, and of specialization and the division of labor. It is a triumph of the accurate power of innumerable brains and wills acting in unison to produce a machine or a commodity. These many wills constitute a fictive superself astonishingly effective in converting dreams into machines. Literature, by contrast, is produced by the single individual, concerns itself with individuals, and is read by separate persons. And the single individual—this unit of vital being, of nerve and brain, which judges, knows, is happy or mourns, actually lives and actually dies—is unfavorably compared with the fictive superself acting in unison and according to plan to produce jet planes, atom-smashers, computers, rockets and other modern technological wonders. Glamorous, victorious technology is sometimes considered to have discredited all former ideas of the single self.

To theorists of the new, a thing is genuine only if it manifests the new. Valéry in the essay "Remarks on Progress," from which I have just quoted, illustrates this attitude remarkably well. "Men," he says, "are doubtless developing the habit of considering all knowledge as transitional and every stage of their industry and their relations as provisional. This is new." And again, "Suppose that the enormous transformation which we are living through and which is changing us continues to develop, finally altering whatever customs are left and making a very different adaptation of our needs to our means; the new era will soon produce men who are no longer attached to the past by any habit of mind. For them history will be nothing but strange, incomprehensible tales; there will be nothing in their time that was ever seen before—nothing from the past will survive into their present. Everything in man that is not purely physiological will be altered, for our ambitions, our politics, our wars, our manners, our arts are now in a phase of a quick change; they depend more and more on the positive sciences and hence less and less on what used to be. *New facts* tend to take on the importance that once belonged to tradition and *historical facts*."

There Is Simply Too Much to Think About

This is the quintessence of the tradition of the new. By attaching itself to technology "newness" achieves a result longed for by those thinkers of the last century who were oppressed by historical consciousness. Karl Marx felt in history the tradition of all the dead generations weighing like a nightmare on the brain of the living. Nietzsche speaks movingly of the tyranny of "it was" and Joyce's Stephen Dedalus also defines history as a nightmare from which he is trying to awaken. The vision of freedom without conditions—a state of perfect and lucid consciousness into which we are released by technological magic from all inertias—is a sort of romance, really, a French intellectual's paradise. But Valéry does not neglect the painful side of this vision. "One of the surest and cruelest effects of progress," he says, "is to add a further pain to death, a pain increasing of itself as the revolution in customs and ideas becomes more marked and rapid. It is not enough to perish; one has to become unintelligible, almost ridiculous; and even a Racine or a Bousset must take his place alongside those bizarre figures, striped and tattooed, exposed to passing smiles, and somewhat frightening, standing in rows in the galleries and gradually blending with the stuffed specimens of the animal kingdom."

So at the height of technological achievement there blazes the menace of obsolescence. The museum, worse than the grave because it humiliates us by making us dodos, waits in judgment on our ambitions and vanities. Of course no one wants to suffer the double doom of obsolescence—to be dead and also to be a fossil. Everyone wants to be the friend and colleague of history. Consciously or not, intellectuals try hard to be what Hegel called Historical Men or World-Historical Individuals, those persons through whom truth operates and who have an insight into the requirement of the time, who divine what is ripe for development, the nascent principle, the next necessary thing. They may denounce the nightmare past but they have also an immortal craving to be in the line of succession and to prove themselves to be historically necessary. It is these people, lovers of the new, who derive from technological progress a special contempt for the obsolete. The enemies of pastness, even though they tell us that we will depend more and more on the positive sciences and hence less and less on what used to be, insofar as they seek the next necessary development, make their own kind of historical judgment. Intellectuals, when they sense the cruel effects of technological progress, try not only to escape oblivion themselves by association with the next necessary thing but also to impose oblivion on others—condemning those writers who fail to recognize that the human condition has been, or will be, completely transformed by science and the revolution of customs and who, in the old-fashioned solitude of old-fashioned rooms, continue to consider the destinies of old-fashioned individuals and follow their old-fashioned trade (a home industry of the seventeenth century), unaware that the World Spirit has abandoned them just as it abandoned the walled city and the crossbow.

Unlike Huxley's *Brave New World* or George Orwell's *1984*, Joyce's *Ulysses* is not directly concerned with technology. It remains nevertheless the twentieth century's most modern novel—it is *the* account of human life in an age of artifacts. Things in *Ulysses* are not nature's things. Here the material world is wholly man's world and all its objects are human inventions. It is made in the image of the conscious mind. Nature governs physiologically, and of course the unconscious remains nature's stronghold, but the external world is a world of ideas made concrete. Between these two powers, nature within, artifacts without, the life of Mr. Leopold Bloom is comically divided. The time is 1904. No one in Dublin has seen Mr. Arthur C. Clarke's ultra-intelligent machine even in a dream, but the age of technology has begun and *Ulysses* is literature's outstanding response to it.

Now what is *Ulysses*? In *Ulysses* two men, Dedalus and Bloom, wander about the city of Dublin on a June day. Mrs. Bloom, a singer, lies in bed, reading, misbehaving, musing and remembering. But nothing that can be thought or said about human beings is left out of this account of two pedestrians and an adulteress. No zoologist could be more explicit or complete than Joyce. Mr. Bloom first thing in the morning brews the tea, gives milk to the cat, goes to the pork butcher to get meat for his breakfast, carries a tray up to his wife, eats a slightly scorched kidney, goes out to the privy with his newspaper, relieves himself while reading a prize-winning story, wipes his bottom with a piece of the same paper, and then goes out to the funeral of Paddy Dignam. Matters could not be more real.

Now realism in literature is a convention, and this convention postulates that human beings are not what everyone for long centuries conceived them to be. They are something different and they live in a disenchanted world that exists for no particular purpose that science can show. Still people continue to try to lead a human life. And this is rather quaint because man is not the comparatively distinguished creature he thinks himself to be. In the new view he is more wretched, animal and common.

In *Ulysses* Joyce gives the novel's fullest account of human life— within this realistic convention. As he sees it the material world is now entirely human. Everything about us—clothing, beds, tableware, streets, privies, newspapers, language, thought—is man-made. All artifacts originate in thought. They are thoughts practically extended into matter. Nature governs us physiologically and the unconscious is still its stronghold, but the external world consists entirely of human inventions and projections. Nature has been beaten out of it. Among these powers—instinct in the depths, language in the middle, artifacts outside—the life of Ulysses-Bloom is comically divided.

Joyce is the complete naturalist, the artist-zoologist, the poet-ethnographer. His account of Bloom's life includes everything. Everything seems to *demand* inclusion. No trivialities or absurdities are omitted. Old bourgeois reticences are overrun zigzag. For what, after all, is the important information? No one knows. Anything at all may be important. Freud taught in *The Psychopathology of Everyday Life* that the unconscious did not distinguish between major and minor matters as conscious judgment did and that the junk of the psyche had the deepest things to tell us. Joyce is the greatest psychic junkman of our age, after Freud. For the last of the facts may be the first. Thus we know the lining of Bloom's hat and the contents of his pockets, we know his genitals and his guts. We are thoroughly familiar with Molly too, how she feels before her period and how she smells.

With so much knowledge we are close to chaos. For what are we to do with such a burden of information? *Ulysses* is a comedy of information. Leopold Bloom lies submerged in an ocean of random facts— textbook tags, items of news, bits of history, slogans, clichés, ditties, operatic arias, saws and jokes, scraps of popular science, a great volume of superstitions, fantasies, technical accounts of the Dublin water supply, observations about hanged men, recollections of copulating dogs. The debris of learning, epic, faith and enlightenment pour over him. In this circumambient ocean he seems at times to dwell like a coelenterate or a sponge. The man-made world begins, like the physical world, to suggest infinity. The mind is endangered by the multitude of accounts that it can give of all matters. It is threatened with inanity or disintegration.

William James believed that not even the toughest of tough minds could bear to know everything that happened in a single city on a given day. No one could endure it. It is probably one of the functions of the nervous system to screen us and to preserve us from disintegrating in the sea of facts. We ourselves, however, seek out this danger, for the Faustian dream of omniscience lives on.

At all events Bloom's mind is assailed and drowned by facts. He appears to acknowledge a sort of responsibility to these facts and he goes about Dublin doing his facts. This suggests that our scientific, industrial, technical, urban world has a life of its own and that it borrows our minds and souls for its own purposes. In this sense civilization lives upon Bloom. His mind is overcome by its data. He is the bearer, the servant, the slave of involuntary or random cognitions. But he is also the poet of distractions. If Bloom were only Everyman, nothing but the sort of person realism describes as "ordinary," he would not be the Bloom we adore.

The truth is that Bloom is a wit, a comedian. In the depths of his passivity Bloom resists. He is said in Dublin to be "something of an artist." To be an artist in the ocean of modern information is certainly no blessing. The artist has less power to resist the facts than other men. He is obliged to note the particulars. One may even say that he is condemned to see them. In the cemetery Bloom can't help seeing the gravedigger's spade and noting that it is "blueglancing." He is receptively, artistically, painfully immersed in his mental ocean. The fact that he is "something of an artist" aggravates the problems of information. He seeks relief in digression, in evasion and in wit.

Why is the diversity of data so dazzling and powerful in *Ulysses*? The data are potent because the story itself is negligible. *Ulysses*, as Gertrude

Stein once said, is not a "what-happens-next" sort of book. A "what-happens-next" story would, like a nervous system, screen out distraction and maintain order.

It is the absence of a story that makes Bloom what he is. By injecting him with purpose a story would put the world in order and concentrate his mind. But perhaps Bloom's mind is better not ordered. Why should he, the son of a suicide, the father who mourns a dead child, a cuckold and a Jew in Catholic Dublin, desire moral and intellectual clarity? If his mind were clear he would be another man entirely. No, the plan of Bloom's life is to be planless. He palpitates among the phenomena and moves vaguely toward resolution. Oh, he gets there, but *there* is a region, not a point. At one of the low hours of his day he thinks, "Nothing is anything." He feels his servitude to the conditions of being. When there is no story, those conditions have it all their own way and one is delivered to despair. The artifact civilization, Joyce seems to tell us, atrophies the will. The stream of consciousness flows full and wide through the will-less. The romantic heroes of powerful will, the Rastignacs and the Raskolnikovs, are gone. The truth of the present day is in the little Blooms whose wills offer no hindrance to the stream of consciousness. And his stream has no stories. It has themes. Bloom does not, however, disintegrate in this thematic flow. Total examination of a single human being discloses a most extraordinary entity, a comic subject, a Bloom.

But the burden of being a Bloom is nevertheless frightful. It is not clear exactly how Joyce would like us to see the Bloom problem. Long passages of *Ulysses* are bound together by slurs (in the musical sense) of ambiguous laughter. It does, however, appear that Joyce expected the individual who has gone beyond the fictions and postures of "individuality" (romantic will, et cetera) to be sustained by suprapersonal powers of myth. Myth, rising from the unconscious, is superior to mere "story," but myth will not come near while ordinary trivial ideas of self remain. The powers of myth can be raised up only when the well-known pretensions of selfhood are surrendered. Therefore consciousness must abase itself and every hidden thing must be exhumed. Hence Bloom's moments in the privy, his corpse fantasies at Paddy's funeral, his ejaculation as he watches crippled Gerty, his masochistic hallucinations in Nighttown. The old dignities must take a terrific beating in this new version of "the last shall be first."

What you feel reading *Ulysses* today is the extent to which a modern society imposes itself upon everyone. The common man who, in the past, knew little about the great world now stands in the middle of it. At least he thinks he does, as reader, hearer, citizen, voter, judge of all public questions. His imagination has been formed to make him think himself in the center. The all-important story appears to belong to society itself. Real interest is monopolized by collective achievements and public events, by the fate of mankind, by a kind of "politics." The voluminous Sunday *Times* is put into our hands together with *Time* and *Newsweek* while images from television flash behind us. This is the week's record of everything of substance relating to the human species. It is about us, our hope for survival, our common destiny. Is it, now? Does this really speak to my condition? Is this mankind, is it me, heart, soul and destiny? No, the nominally central individual studying the record does not feel central. On the contrary he feels peculiarly contentless in his public aspect, lacking in substance and without a proper story. A proper story would express his intuition that his own existence is peculiarly significant. The sense that his existence is significant haunts him. But he can prove nothing. And the business of art is with this sense, precisely.

Though the sun shines sweetly, the modern mind knows that there are devilish processes of nuclear fusion and staggering explosions in the heavens. So as mild Bloom goes down the streets, we are aware of a formidable intellect that follows him as he buys a cake of soap. The modernists are learned intellectuals—Viconians like Joyce, Freudians, Marxians, Bergsonians, et cetera. A technological society produces mental artists and an intensely intellectual literary culture. "Most modern masterpieces are critical masterpieces," writes Harold Rosenberg. "Joyce's writing is a criticism of literature, Pound's poetry is a criticism of poetry, Picasso's painting is a criticism of painting. Modern art also criticizes the existing culture." Rosenberg finds merit in this. "One keeps hoping that the decline in excellence of people and things is an effect of transition. All we have on the positive side is the individual's capacity for resistance. Resistance and criticism." The hope that the decline in the excellence of people and things (the last an effect of technology) is an effect of transition shows Mr. Rosenberg's heart to be in the right place. But the emphasis on criticism shows something else, namely a claim for intellectual priority. Art is something that must satisfy the requirements of intellectuals. It must interest intellectuals by being, in the right sense, critical of the existing culture. The fact is that modern art has tried very hard to please its intellectual judges. Intellectual judgment in the twentieth century resembles aristocratic taste in the eighteenth—in the sense, only, that artists in both centuries acknowledge its importance. Art in the twentieth century is more greatly appreciated if it is directly translatable into intellectual interests, if it stimulates ideas, if it lends itself to discourse. Because intellectuals do not like to suspend themselves in works of the imagination. They prefer to talk. Thus they make theology and philosophy out of literature. They make psychological theory. They make politics. Art is one of the principal supports of this social class.

Gide's *The Counterfeiters* is a cultural product as well as a novel; *The Red and the Black* is no such thing. *The Magic Mountain* belongs to Intellectual History, a category that does not exist for that excellent book *Little Dorrit*. It never occurred to Dickens to run over into cultural criticism or to be Carlyle and Mill as well as Charles Dickens. But in the twentieth century writers are often educated men as well as creators and in some the education prevails over the creation. There are reasons for this. A burden of "understanding" has been laid upon us by this revolutionary century. What I am trying to indicate is that cultural style is not to be confused with genuine understanding. At the moment such understanding has few representatives while cultural style seems to have hundreds of thousands.

One of the problems of literature in this age of technology is the problem of those who preside over literary problems—the specialists, scholars, historians and teachers. Modern writers, themselves more "intellectual" than writers were a century ago, now face a public formed, educated and dominated by professors, "humanists" and "antihumanists," by psychologists and psychotherapists, by the professional custodians of culture and by ideologists and shapers of the future. This critical public has a thousand important (i.e., political and social) questions to answer. It is irritably fastidious. It asks, "To whom should we listen? Who, if anyone, can be read? What is, or can be, really interesting to a modern cultivated intelligence?" Such questions can be answered only with sadness and sighs. To prove that I am not exaggerating, I shall quote briefly from an essay by Lionel Trilling, "Authenticity and the Modern Unconscious." In this essay Professor Trilling argues that in this day and age, things being what they are, novels can no longer be Authentic or appeal to Authentic readers. "It is the exceptional novelist today who would say of himself, as Henry James did, that he 'loved the story as story,' by which James meant the story apart from any overt ideational intention it might have, simply as, like any primitive tale, it brings into play what James called 'the blessed faculty of wonder.' Already in James's day, narration as a means by which the reader was held spellbound, as the old phrase put it, had come under suspicion. And the dubiety grew to the point where Walter Benjamin could say some three decades ago that the art of storytelling was moribund."

Here one cries out, "Wait! Who is this Benjamin? Why does it matter what *he* said?" But intellectuals do refer to one another to strengthen their arguments. It turns out that Walter Benjamin objected to storytellers because they had "an orientation toward practical interests." Stories, Trilling quotes Benjamin as saying, are likely to contain "something useful." Here what I have called "cultural style" begins to show itself. Modern literary culture, which prides itself on being radical, dissenting, free, has its own orthodoxy. Don't we know how it views the Bourgeois, the Child, the Family, Technology, the Artist, the Useful? We do indeed. The idea of usefulness, Baudelaire said, nauseated him—and there in Baudelaire is the foundation of your orthodoxy. Storytellers, Benjamin objects, have "counsel to give," and this giving of counsel has "an old-fashioned ring." Professor Trilling then says that it is "inauthentic for the present time—there is something inauthentic for our time in being held spellbound, momentarily forgetful of oneself, concerned with the fate of a person who is not oneself. . . . By what right, we are now inclined to ask, does the narrator exercise authority over that other person, let alone over the reader: by what right does he arrange the confusion between the two and presume to have counsel to give?"

If there is something old-fashioned and inauthentic for our time in being held spellbound, then Homer and Dostoyevsky, whose works hold us spellbound, are inauthentic. What this professor of literature maintains, therefore, is that literature itself is now inauthentic. Professor Trilling's point seems to be that the modern condition is killing certain human activities (the arts) once highly valued. For an authentic modern man, living in a modern technological society, naïve self-surrender is impossible. Apparently the question is partly one of authority. "By what right does the narrator" presume to invade our minds, deliberately confuse us and give counsel? I don't see what good it does to make a political question of this. By what right do our parents conceive us, or we our children? By what right does society teach us a language or give us a culture? If authentic man had no words, he would be unable to express his longing to be so virginal.

But this I realize is not quite fair. Professor Trilling wishes to leave the surface of life with its stories and descend into the depths of the unconscious in search of truth and maturity, becoming—if he can think hard and face the unconscious fearlessly—one of Aristotle's Great-Souled Men. Thus Professor Trilling seems to agree with Malraux's priest in the Resistance that there is no such thing as a grown-up person. His position is also close to that of Mr. Arthur C. Clarke, who suggests that art is a compensation for the deficiencies of the real world and that "as our knowledge, our power and above all our maturity increase, we will have less and less need for it . . . the ultra-intelligent machine would have no use for it at all."

So Professor Trilling, moving toward "scientific truth," declares that we can no longer be held spellbound, and Mr. Clarke tells us that we can be redeemed by technology from the childish need for art. And art itself is not casting glorious new works upon the world—although if it were the experts might not know it. Perhaps a modest and fair statement of the case is that human beings have always told stories to one another. By what *right* have they done this and on what authority? Well, on none, really. They have simply obeyed the impulse to tell and the desire to hear. Science and technology are not likely to remove this narrating and spellbinding oddity from the soul.

The present age has a certain rationalizing restlessness or cognitive irritability: a participatory delirium that makes the arresting powers of any work of art intolerable. The desire to read is itself spoiled by "cultural interests" and by a frantic desire to associate everything with something else and to convert works of art into subjects of discourse. Technology has weakened certain points of spiritual rest. Wedding guests and ancient mariners both are deafened by the terrific blaring of the technological band.

In a charming and strange book, the prerevolutionary Russian writer V. V. Rozanov argues against repressive puritanism in words that can be applied more widely and are relevant to the subject. He writes: "A million years passed before my soul was let out into the world to enjoy it; and how can I say to her, 'Don't forget yourself, darling, but enjoy yourself in a responsible fashion.' No, I say to her: 'Enjoy yourself, darling, have a good time, my lovely one, enjoy yourself, my precious, enjoy yourself in any way you please. And toward evening you will go to God.' For my life is my day, and it is my day, and not Socrates' or Spinoza's." Thus to the queen or tramp who is his soul Rozanov speaks with an erotic-religious aim of some sort. But we can adapt this to our own purpose, saying, "A million years passed before my soul was let out into the technological world. That world was filled with ultra-intelligent machines but the soul after all was a soul, and it had waited a million years for its turn and did not intend to be cheated of its birthright by a lot of mere gimmicks. It had come from the far reaches of the universe and was interested but not overawed by these inventions."

[1974]

A World Too Much with Us

Wordsworth in 1807 warned that the world was too much with us, that getting and spending we laid waste our powers, that we were giving our hearts away and that we saw less and less in the external world, in nature, that the heart could respond to.

In our modern jargon we call this "alienation." That was the word by which Marx described the condition of the common man under capitalism, alienated in his work. But for Marx, as Harold Rosenberg has pointed out, "It is the factory worker, the businessman, the professional who is alienated in his work through being hurled into the fetish-world of the market. The artist is the only figure in this society who is able not to be alienated, because he works directly with the materials of his own experience and transforms them. Marx therefore conceives the artist as the model man of the future. But when critics influenced by Marxist terminology talk of alienation they mean something directly contrary to Marx's philosophical and revolutionary conception. They mean not the tragic separation of the human individual from himself, but the failure of certain sensitive spirits (themselves) to participate emotionally and intellectually in the fictions and conventions of mass culture. And this removal from popular hallucination and inertia they conceive as a form of pathos." Thus Rosenberg. And why do I associate him with Wordsworth? Simply because we have now a class of people who cannot bear that the world should not be more with them. Incidentally, the amusing title of Mr. Rosenberg's essay is "The Herd of Independent Minds."

I have two more quotations to offer. The first is from a recent statement by Soviet president Nikolai Podgorny. He warns Russian writers that any deviation from the principles of socialist realism is inadmissible and he says, "At a time when ideological struggle between socialism and capitalism is becoming sharper, our art is called upon to constantly raise its ideological arsenal, its irreconcilability to any manifestations of alien views, to combine the assertion of the Soviet way of life with the deflation of apolitical consumer psychology."

Since Mr. Podgorny speaks of "our art" I shall claim the same privilege. In the West *our* art is far from apolitical, if you allow me to give the word *politics* my own definition. When I say *political* I mean that the world is very much with us. The world is more populous, more penetrating, more problematical, more menacing than it was in 1807. We can no longer think of it in contrast to Nature, as Wordsworth did. This is an all-made rather than a naturally created world, a world of artifacts, products of the mind. This world lives so much in us and upon us, so greatly affects our thoughts and our souls, that I can't help thinking of it as having a political character. "Either too much is happening too quickly, or it is simply much more visible and audible than it was in earlier centuries. Society has become more alive," writes Edward Shils. "The populace [Professor Shils is speaking of the West] has become more demanding of services, benefits, attention and a share of authority. This adds to the visibility and audibility. . . . The exhilaration, titillation and agitation have become a continuing feature of our societies." I am inclined to go beyond this. We are in a state of radical distraction; we are often in a frenzy. When Baudelaire spoke of a *frénésie journalière* he was, like Wordsworth and his all-too-present world, describing the condition in its earlier states. The frenzy has accelerated unbearably in our time. We have been, as it were, appropriated mind and soul by our history. We are often cautioned not to exaggerate, not to see our own as the worst or most trying of historical periods. Every generation has assailed itself in this way and cried out against its pains and burdens. But things have happened in the twentieth century for which words like *war, revolution,* even *holocaust* are plainly inadequate. Without exaggeration we can speak of the history of this century of ours as an unbroken series of crises. Not everyone of course responds to crisis with the same intensity, and some of us are more convulsed by events than others. Some take it with existentialist anguish and feel obliged, they say, to suffer through it as nakedly and acutely as possible. Others are more

270 **There Is Simply Too Much to Think About**

tough-minded or better armored or simply disinclined to give up their lives to an interpretation of history—or to surrender their imaginations, since historical interpretations of this sort deprive the imagination of its ability to make independent judgments. But I don't see how we can be blind to the political character of our so-called "consumer" societies. Each of us stands in the middle of things, exposed to the great public noise. This is not the materialism against which Wordsworth warned us. It goes much, much deeper. All minds are preoccupied with terror, crime, the instability of cities, the future of nations, crumbling empires, foundering currencies, the poisoning of nature, the ultimate weapons. To recite the list is itself unsettling. The late John Berryman once told me that T. S. Eliot could no longer read the daily paper. It was too *exciting*, he said. A poet is of course more liable to be unbearably excited, in his tender-mindedness, than a Kansas manufacturer or a Harvard economist. In any case it is business and economics that most people are thinking about. Their minds are turned toward social problems. They are not thinking much of the time about painting or narrative poetry or Platonism or tragedy. They are far too extensively politicized for that. I am not sure that I want to deplore this and complain, Victorian style, of the gross insensitivity, even of intellectuals, to art. I simply note, as one who has lived among serious people and knows something about American intellectuals, that they can't be said to take literature very seriously. It's simply not important to them. It is not a power in life. Power lies in science, technology, government, business, institutions, politics, the mass media, the life of nations. It is not in novels and poems. Few people, very few, will be considering, as Henry James did, that art gives meaning to existence or wondering whether they can afford to neglect the faith of Joseph Conrad, who believed that to understand a human event, to see the color of experience, to grasp it morally, to feel its subtleties, we must have novels—the temperament of a reader must immerse itself in that of a writer. Not even novelists and poets now share this faith. Men like Osip Mandelstam, who believed that there were in Russia only two real powers, the power of Stalin and the power of the truth manifesting itself in poetry, are very rare indeed. The artist must evidently find in his own spirit the strength to resist the principal alienating power of our time, and this alienating power comes

A World Too Much with Us

not from the factory or "the fetish world of the market" but from politics. Marx's "model man of the future" apparently appeared prematurely in Russia.

The man I wish to contrast with Podgorny is Goethe. His view of the writer's social duty is very different. He said in 1830, "I have never bothered to ask in what way I was useful in society as a whole. I contented myself with what I recognized as good or true. That has certainly been useful in a wide circle, but that was not the aim."

Nations and societies torn by conflict, enduring famine, beset by deadly enemies, fighting to survive, may not feel kindly toward Olympian, contemplative Goethe. Russia during the civil war, and again when Hitler invaded it, was such a nation. That, however, was thirty-five years ago. We are all familiar with the tycoon who weeps about his poor childhood and justifies his vices and villainies by telling us how underprivileged he was. Israel is at this moment a country in great peril but it refrains from ordering writers to enter the struggle. It does not deprive them of the right to make the Goethean choice. The creators and rulers of prison-states, dictators and oligarchs, terrorists and their intellectual strategists—the cruelest, most deformed part of our species—force politics upon us and then tell us what "our art" is called upon to do.

In the privileged democracies we find people who force politics upon themselves. I think, for instance, of a Jean-Paul Sartre who expresses his commitment to justice by demanding "action," that is, terror and murder. He tells us in his introduction to Frantz Fanon's *The Wretched of the Earth* that the third world finds manhood by its burning ever-present hatred and its desire to kill us. Us? By us he means guilty and hateful Europe and "that super-European monstrosity, North America." "The native cures himself of colonial neurosis," explains Sartre, "by thrusting out the settler through force of arms. When his rage boils over, he rediscovers his lost innocence and he comes to know himself . . . Once begun, it is a war that gives no quarter. You may fear or be feared; that is to say, abandon yourself to the dissociations of a sham existence or conquer your birthright of unity. When the peasant takes a gun in his hands, the old myths grow dim and the prohibitions are one by one forgotten. The rebel's weapon is the proof of his humanity. For in the

There Is Simply Too Much to Think About

first days of the revolt you must kill: to shoot down a European is to kill two birds with one stone, to destroy an oppressor and the man he oppresses at the same time; there remain a dead man, and a free man; the survivor, for the first time, feels a national soil under his foot."

Sartre reminds us, not altogether unjustly, of our "ideology of lies," the "strip-tease of our humanism," and Europe's "fat, pale . . . narcissism." All that is fair enough. But can we take him seriously when he insists that the oppressed must redeem themselves by violence? I have already suggested that the imagination is being given up by writers. Embracing causes, they have contracted all kinds of political, sexual, ideological diseases; their teeth chatter and their brains are filled with feverish fantasies of purgation and liberation by murder.

Suppose that Sartre had written a novel about the wretched of the earth. He is not a good novelist, but the art itself would have obliged him to deal with real, or approximately real, human beings, not the zombies of a pamphleteer. Suppose the white imperialist killed in a revolt had been a real person. Would Sartre then have been able to show that the slave who had butchered his master was redeemed by violence? Would it be certain that he was at last a free man? I strongly suspect that the banality of this would have sickened the author of *La Nausée*. War certainly filled Tolstoy with fury, but everything in *War and Peace* is humanly tested in full detail, page by page. The novel is for Tolstoy a method of dealing justly. He subjects his own beliefs and passions to the imaginative test and accepts the verdict of an artistic method. His novel shows human beings rooted in reality and it shows that their need for truth is a vital need, like the need to breathe. Swift's Platonist horses in *Gulliver's Travels* spoke of a falsehood as the thing that is not. By truth I mean simply what is. "Truth, Clearness, and Beauty naturally are public matters," writes Wyndham Lewis. "Truth or Beauty are as much public concerns as the water supply." The imagination I take to be indispensable to truth, so defined. *It* is the prior necessity, not the desire or the duty to perform a liberating action. Sartre declares that in the eighteenth century a work of the mind was "doubly an act since it produced ideas which were to lead to social upheavals and since it exposed its author to danger. And this act, whatever the book we may be considering, was always defined in the same way; it was a *liberator*. And, doubtless, in the seventeenth century too, literature had a liberating function."

It is not inconceivable that a man might find freedom and identity by killing his oppressor. But as a Chicagoan I am rather skeptical about this. Murderers are not improved by murdering. Unchecked, they murder more and become more brutish. Perhaps fertilizers and modern methods of agriculture would benefit the peasantry of a famished world more than the melodrama of rebirth through bloodshed. It may do more for manhood to feed one's hungry children than to make corpses.

It is true that the writer no longer holds the important position he held in the eighteenth and nineteenth centuries. He has lost out. He is not at the center of things. The bullying idea that he has a social responsibility, that he must cause upheavals and that in the service of justice he must thrust himself into danger is the result of a certain sense of diminished importance, as well as a boyish nostalgia for eighteenth-century roles. A work of art has many other ways to attain social meaning. The writer whose imagination is passionately moved by political questions and who follows his deepest convictions will write political novels worth reading. But the ideological package, complete with historical interpretations, has no value. I have the greatest admiration for the courage of writers who, having had politics thrust upon them by the ruling brutes of their respective countries, honorably stood their ground. I have great sympathy for them as well. They had no choice but to write as oppositionists. From their side, looking at us in the West, they must be struck by our innocence, our apparent ignorance of the main facts, our self-indulgent playing about with ideological toys, our reckless rocking of the boat. They must often wonder as well at the dull refractory minds, the sleepiness of many of us. For one part of mankind is in prison; another is starving to death; and those of us who are free and fed are not awake. What will it take to rouse us?

I said earlier that we lived in a state of distraction, even of frenzy, and I called this unavoidable immersion in the life of society political. I said also that intellectuals in America did not really take literature seriously but were professionally preoccupied with various scientific, technological or social questions. They were told at their universities that art is very important and are quite willing to believe it; they are

There Is Simply Too Much to Think About

prepared to accept and even to respect those who are described (quite often by themselves alone) as artists. But that is as far as it goes.

Experts know certain things well. What sort of knowledge have writers got? By expert standards they are entirely ignorant. But expertise itself produces ignorance. How scientific can the world picture of an expert be? The deeper his specialization, the more he is obliged to save the appearance. To express his faith in scientific method he supplies what is lacking from a stock of collective fictions about Nature or the history of Nature. As for the rest of us, the so-called educated public, the appropriate collective representations have been pointed out to us and we have stocked our heads with pictures from introductory physics, astronomy and biology courses. We do not, of course, see what is but rather what we have been directed or trained to see. No individual penetration of the phenomena can occur in this way. Two centuries ago the early romantic poets assumed that their minds were free, that they could know the good, that they could independently interpret and judge the entire creation, but those who still believe that the imagination has such powers to penetrate and to know keep their belief to themselves. As we now understand knowledge, does imagination *know* anything? At the moment the educated world does not think so. But things have become dreary and humankind has tired of itself because the collective fictions of alleged knowledge are used up. We now bore ourselves by what we think we know. Either life has already given up its deepest secrets to our rational penetration and become tedious or we have developed a tedious sort of rationality by ruling that certain kinds of knowledge are illegitimate. I am inclined to argue that the tedious rationality of our educated heads is a great breeder of boredom and of other miseries. Our head-culture inordinately respects the collective powers of mind and the technical developments that have produced the most visible achievements of this civilization; it takes little stock in the imagination or in individual talent. It greatly esteems action. It seems to believe that artists should be harnessed to the social system as intellectual workers.

The Western world does not compel the writer to be an intellectual worker or functionary. But feeling no power in the imagination and needing to attach himself to power, under innumerable social pressures and politicized by crisis, the writer begins to think he too must be an activist and exert influence. He must do something, make himself available, be heard in just causes. We are, however, in a position to review the achievements of writers in politics. These are not especially breathtaking. The Tolstoys, the Zolas, yes, those were great. But what of the Célines, the Ezra Pounds, the Louis Aragons, the hundreds who supported Stalinism? And what after all can be said for the view that it is the writer's duty to cause social upheavals? How many of these upheavals have not brought to birth a police state? And if one yearns to live dangerously, is it not as dangerous to persist in the truth as to rush to the barricades? But then it is always more agreeable to play the role of a writer than to be a writer. A writer's life is solitary, often bitter. How pleasant to come out of one's room, fly about the world, make speeches and cut a swath!

For a very long time the world found the wonderful in tales and poems, in painting and in musical performances. Now the wonderful is found in miraculous technology, in modern surgery, in jet propulsion, in computers, in television and in lunar expeditions. Literature cannot compete with wonderful technology. Writers, trying to keep the attention of the public, have turned to methods of shock, to obscenity and super-sensationalism, adding their clamor to the great noise now threatening the sanity of civilized nations.

But isn't there a branch of the wonderful into which wonderful technology cannot lead us? If there is, how shall we know it? Why, we shall recognize it at once by its power to liberate us from the tyranny of noise and distraction. Since 1914, in all spheres of life, crisis has ruled over us, survival anxiety has become permanent with us, and public unrest has been set into our souls. To be free from this would indeed be wonderful. It would mean nothing less than the restoration or re-creation of culture. Indispensable to such a restoration is the recovery of significant space by the individual, the reestablishment of a region about every person through which events must make their approach, a space in which they can be received on decent terms, intelligently, comprehensively and contemplatively. At a time when we are wildly distracted and asking ourselves what will happen, when the end will come, how long we can bear it, why we should bear it, these notions of culture and significant space may seem hopelessly naïve. But for art and literature there is no choice. If there is no significant space there is no judgment, no freedom; we determine nothing for ourselves individually. The destruction of significant space, the destruction of the individual, for that is what it amounts to, leaves us helplessly in the public sphere. Then to say that the world is too much with us is meaningless for there is no longer any us. The world is everything. But it is apparently in the nature of the creature to resist the world's triumph. It is from this resistance that we infer truth to be one of his vital needs. And the creature has many ways of knowing the truth. If not all of these can be certified by our present methods, so much the worse for those present methods of certification.

The German philosopher Josef Pieper speaks in *Leisure, the Basis of Culture* of a purely receptive attitude of mind in which we become aware of immaterial reality. "Is there," asks Pieper, "such a thing as intellectual contemplation? In antiquity the answer was always yes; in modern philosophy, for the most part, the answer is no."

According to Kant, Pieper continues, knowledge is exclusively discursive, the opposite of receptive and contemplative. To Kant knowledge is an activity. Any other claim to know was not genuine because it involved no work. In Pieper's own words, "The Greeks—Aristotle no less than Plato—as well as the great medieval thinkers, held that not only physical, sensuous perception but equally man's spiritual and intellectual knowledge included an element of pure receptive contemplation or, as Heraclitus says, of listening to the 'essence of things.'" Am I proposing, then, that we should take refuge from crisis and noise in a contemplative life? Such a thing is unthinkable. I am saying, rather, that there is a mode of knowledge different from the ruling mode. That this other mode is continually operative—the imagination assumes that things will deliver something of their essence to the mind that has prepared itself and that knows how to listen. I am saying also that full immersion in the Great Noise will kill us. Perpetual crisis will tear our souls from us. Indeed this tearing sensation is experienced daily by many people. What can art and poetry do with this great threat to Life? Has the crisis grown too vast—is it now unmanageable? Only the imagination, by its acts, can answer such questions.

Just now writers are asking themselves how they can be interesting and why they should be taken seriously. Interest follows power and writers do not appear to command the sort of power that is now valued by most of mankind—the power of states or institutions, the power of money or resources, the power of politics, of science and technology, the power that once belonged to religion, the power of ideas, et cetera. What can make a writer truly interesting is an inadmissible resource, something we all hesitate to mention though we all know it intimately— the soul. I don't know what else can possibly obtain and hold the attention of the modern reader who has already become peculiarly difficult to reach. Granted that his tolerance level is low. Bad and boring novels have made him impatient. But he tends to resist all literary influences, especially if he is, or considers himself to be, an intellectual.

Coming from me this may sound a bit odd, for I am thought in America to be something of a highbrow. But it should be noted that the character of the public has changed, that it has become more intellectual, that writers themselves have more intellectual interests and that they have become as concerned to analyze, to investigate problems or to consider ideological questions as to tell stories. The attitude of intellectuals toward literature has become a "serious" one (the quotation marks are heavy). They see in novels, poems or plays a creative contribution often unconsciously made to the study of society or psychology or religion. The plots of Dickens are psychoanalytically investigated; *Moby-Dick* supplies Marxists with material for the study of the factory system. Books are strongly shaken to see what usable things will fall out of them to strengthen a theory or support some system of ideas. The poet becomes a sort of truffle hound who brings marvelous delicacies from the forest. The writer himself begins to accept this truffle-hound role, acknowledging the superior value and greater dignity of ideas and explanations over fancy, play, verve—over imagination. The intellectual makes discourse—a plethora of talk. The novelist and even the painter and musician now imitate him and before long become themselves intellectual workers, discourse makers, serious persons and even functionaries. Obsessive or even monomaniacal professionals do not make wonderful readers. The world is very much with them and their hearts are difficult to reach. One might even call it a political feat to reach their hearts, to penetrate their preoccupied minds and to interest them in a story.

The general view now seems to be that the writer's true province is the unconscious. It is from the unconscious that he brings in his truffles. No one can doubt the existence of the unconscious. It is there all right. The question is what it contains. Is it only the seat of animal nature, of instinct, the libidinal forces, or does it also contain elements of higher life? Does the human need for truth, for instance, also have roots in the unconscious? Why, since the unconscious is by definition what we do not know, should we not expect to find in it traces of the soul as well as of aggression? In any case, the unconscious is today the sole source of impulse and freedom that one branch of science has reserved for art.

What I am saying is that the accounts of human existence given by the modern intelligence are very shallow by comparison with those that the imagination is capable of giving, and that we should by no means agree to limit imagination by committing ourselves to the formulae of modern intelligence but continue as individuals to make free individual judgments.

Wordsworth warned that we laid waste our powers by getting and spending. It is more serious than that now. Worse than getting and spending, modern distraction, worldwide irrationality and madness threaten existence itself. We may not make it. Under the circumstances I have no advice to offer other writers. I can only say, speaking for myself, that the Heraclitean listening to the essence of things becomes more and more important.

[1975]

An Interview with Myself

How do you, a novelist from Chicago, fit yourself into American life? Is there a literary world to which you belong?

When I entered the Restaurant Voltaire in Paris with the novelist Louis Guilloux some years ago, the waiter addressed him as "Maître." I didn't know whether to envy him or to laugh up my sleeve. No one had ever treated me so reverentially. I knew how important literature was to the French. And as a student I had sat (in Chicago) reading of *salons* and *cénacles*, of evenings at Magny's with Flaubert and Turgenev and Sainte-Beuve— reading and sighing. What glorious times! But Guilloux himself, a Breton and a former left-winger, seemed to flinch when he was called "Maître." It may be that, even in Paris, literary culture is now publicly respected only by smarmy headwaiters. Here I am not altogether on firm ground. What is certain is that nothing like this happens here. In America we have no Maîtres except in dining rooms, no literary world, no literary public. Many of us read, many love literature, but the traditions and institutions of literary culture are lacking. I do not say that this is bad, I only state it as a fact that ours is not a society that interests itself in such things. Any modern country that has not inherited these habits of deference simply does not have them.

American writers are not neglected; they mingle occasionally with the great; they may even be asked to the White House, but no one there will talk literature to them. Mr. Nixon disliked writers and refused flatly to have them in, but Mr. Ford is as polite to them as he is to actors, musicians, television newscasters and politicians. At large receptions the East Room fills with celebrities who become ecstatic at the sight of other celebrities. Secretary Kissinger and Danny Kaye fall into each other's arms. Cary Grant is surrounded by senators' wives who find him wonderfully preserved, as handsome in the flesh as on film. They can hardly bear the excitement of personal contact with greatness. People speak of their diets, of their travels, of the vitamins they take and the problems of aging. Questions of language or style, the structure of novels, trends in painting— these are not discussed.

The writer finds Mr. Ford's party a wonderful pop occasion. Senator Fulbright seems almost to recognize his name and says, "You write essays, don't you? I think I can remember one of them." But the senator, as everyone knows, was once a Rhodes scholar. He *would* remember an essay.

It is actually pleasant on such an evening for a writer to pass half disembodied and unmolested by small talk from room to room, looking and listening. He knows that active public men can't combine the duties of government with literature, art and philosophy. Theirs is a world of high-tension wires, not of primroses on the river's brim. Ten years ago Mayor Daley in a little City Hall ceremony gave me a five-hundred-dollar check on behalf of the Midland Authors' Society for my novel *Herzog*. "Mr. Mayor, have you read *Herzog*?" asked one of the reporters, needling him. "I've looked into it," said Daley, thick-skinned and staunch. Art is not the mayor's dish. Indeed, why should it be? I much prefer his neglect to the sort of interest Stalin took in poetry.

Are you saying that a modern industrial society dismisses art?

Not at all. Art is one of those good things that society encourages. It is quite receptive. But what Ruskin said about the English public in 1871 applies perfectly to us: "No reading is possible for a people with its mind in this state. No sentence of any great writer is intelligible to them." For this Ruskin blamed avarice: "so incapable of thought has it [the public] become in its insanity of avarice. Happily, our disease is, as yet, little worse than this incapacity of thought; it is not corruption of the inner nature; we ring true still, when anything strikes home to us . . . though the idea that everything should 'pay' has infected our every purpose so deeply."

You don't see avarice as the problem, do you?

No. "A people with its mind in this state" is where I lay the stress. We are in a peculiarly revolutionary state, a condition of crisis, a nervousness that never ends. Yesterday I came upon a description of a medical technique for bringing patients to themselves. They are exposed for some minutes to high-frequency sounds until they become calm enough to think and to feel out their symptoms. To possess your soul in peace for a few minutes you need the help of medical technology. It is easy to observe in bars, at dinner tables, everywhere, that from flophouse to White House, Americans are preoccupied by the same questions. Our own American life is our passion, the problems of our social and national life with the whole world as background, an immense spectacle presented daily by the papers and the television networks—our cities, our crime, our housing, our automobiles, our sports, our weather, our technology, our politics, our problems of sex and race and diplomacy and international relations. These realities are real enough. But what of the formulae, the jargon adopted by the mass media—the exciting fictions, the heightened and dramatized shadow events presented to the great public and believed by almost everyone to be real? Is reading possible for a people with its mind in this state?

Still, a book of good quality can find a hundred thousand readers. But you say that there is no literary public.

An influential book appears to create its own public. When *Herzog* was published I became aware that there were some fifty thousand people in the United States who had evidently been waiting for something like it. Other writers have certainly had the same experience. But such a public is a temporary one. There is no literary culture that permanently contains all these readers. Remarkably steady and intelligent people emerge somehow, like confident swimmers from the heaving wastes of the American educational system. They survive by strength, luck and cunning.

What do they do while waiting for the next important event?

Yes, what can they read month in, month out? In what journals do they keep up with what matters in contemporary literature?

What about the universities? Haven't they done anything to train judgment and develop taste?

To most professors of English, a novel may be an object of the highest cultural importance. Its ideas, its symbolic structure, its position in the history of romanticism or realism or modernism, its higher relevance, these require devout study. But what has this sort of cultural study to do with novelists and readers? What *they* want is the living moment; they want men and women alive in a circumambient world. The teaching of literature has been a disaster. Between the student and the book he reads lies a gloomy preparatory region, a perfect swamp. He must cross this cultural swamp before he is allowed to open his *Moby-Dick* and read, "Call me Ishmael." He is made to feel ignorant before masterpieces, unworthy; he is frightened and already repelled by the book he is meagerly qualified to begin. And if the method succeeds it produces BAs who can tell you why the *Pequod* leaves port on Christmas morning. What has been substituted for the novel itself is what can be said about the novel by the "educated." Some professors find educated discourse of this kind more interesting by far than novels. They take the attitude toward fiction that one of the church fathers took toward the Bible. Origen of Alexandria asked whether we were really to imagine that God walked in a Garden while Adam and Eve hid under a bush. Scripture could not be taken literally. It must yield to higher meanings.

Are you equating church fathers with professors of literature?

Not exactly. The fathers had sublime conceptions of God and man. If professors of humanities were moved by the sublimity of the poets and philosophers they teach, they would be the most powerful men in the university and the most fervent. But they are at the lower end of the hierarchy, at the bottom of the pile.

Then why are there so many writers at the universities?

A good question. Writers have no independent ground to stand on. They belong to institutions. They can work for news magazines and publishing houses, for cultural foundations, advertising agencies, television networks. Or they can teach. There are only a few literary journals left and those are academic quarterlies. The big national magazines don't want to publish fiction. Their editors want to discuss only the most significant national and international questions and concentrate on "relevant" cultural matters. By "relevant" they mean political. (And *I* mean grossly political.) The "real" questions facing us are questions of business and politics. There *are* questions of life and death at the heart of such important public matters. But these life-and-death questions are not what we discuss. What we hear and read is crisis chatter. The members of our intelligentsia *had* literature in their student days—they *did* it and are now well beyond it. At Harvard or Columbia they read, studied, absorbed the classics, especially the modernist classics. These prepared them for the important, the essential, the incomparable tasks they were destined to perform as functionaries in business, in government, in the professions—above all, in the media. I said before that our common life had become our most passionate concern. Can an individual, the subject of a novel, compete in interest with corporate destinies, with the rise of a new class, a cultural intelligentsia? The rise of a class is *truly* important.

Do you suggest that when we become so extremely politicized we lose interest in the individual?

Yes, if you confuse what is public, or before the attention of the public, with real politics. A liberal society so intensely political—as I have qualified the term—can't remain liberal for very long. I take it for granted that an attack on the novel is also an attack on liberal principles. I view "activist" art theories in the same way. The power of a true work of art is such that it induces a temporary suspension of activities. It leads to contemplative states, to wonderful and to my mind sacred states of the soul. These are not, however, passive.

And what you call crisis chatter creates a contrary condition?

I should like to add that the truth is not loved because it is improving or progressive. We hunger and thirst for it—for its own sake.

To return for a moment to the subject of a literary world . . .

No tea at Gertrude Stein's, no Closerie de Lilas, no Bloomsbury evenings, no charming and wicked encounters between George Moore and W. B. Yeats. Reading of such things is very pleasant indeed. I can't say that I miss them because I never knew anything like them. My knowledge of them is entirely bookish. That Molière put on the plays of Corneille, that Louis XIV himself may have appeared, disguised, in one of Molière's farces—such facts are lovely to read in a history of literature. I'd hardly expect Mayor Daley to take part in any farce of mine. He performs in his own farces only. I have, however, visited writers' clubs in Communist countries and can't say that I'm sorry we have no such institutions here. When I was in Addis Ababa I went to the Emperor's Zoo. As Selassie was the Lion of Judah, he was perhaps bound to keep a collection of lions. These poor animals lay in the filth of dim green cages too small for pacing, mere coops. Their marvelous eyes had turned dull yellow and blank, their heads were on their paws, and they were sighing. Bad as things are with us, they are not so bad as in the Emperor's Zoo or in writers' clubs behind the Iron Curtain.

Not so bad is not the same as good. What of the disadvantages of your condition?

There are moments of sorrow, I admit. George Sand wrote to Flaubert, in a collection of letters I looked into the other day, that she hoped he would bring his copy of her latest book on his next visit. "Put in it all the criticisms which occur to you," she said. "That will be very good for me. People ought to do that for each other, as Balzac and I used to do. That doesn't make one person alter the other; quite the contrary, for in general one gets more determined in one's *moi*, one completes it, explains it better, entirely develops it, and that is why friendship is good, even in literature, where the first condition of any worth is to be one's self." How nice it would be to hear this from a writer. But no such letters arrive. Friendships and a common purpose belong to a nineteenth-century French dream world. The physicist Heisenberg in a recent article in *Encounter* speaks of the kindly and even brotherly collaboration among scientists of the generation of Einstein and Bohr. Their personal letters were quoted in seminars and discussed by the entire scientific community. Heisenberg believes that in the musical world something of the same spirit appeared in the eighteenth century. Haydn's relations with Mozart were of this generous affectionate kind. But when large creative opportunities are

There Is Simply Too Much to Think About

lacking there is no generosity visible. Heisenberg says nothing about the malice and hostility of less lucky times. Writers today seldom wish other writers well.

What about the critics?

Critics use strength gathered from the past to pummel the present. Edmund Wilson wouldn't read his contemporaries at all. He stopped with Eliot and Hemingway. The rest he dismissed. This lack of goodwill, to put it at its mildest, was much admired by his fans. That fact speaks for itself. Curious about Canadians, Indians, Haitians and Russians, and studying Marxism and the Dead Sea Scrolls, he was the Protestant majority's big literary figure. I have sometimes thought that he was challenged by Marxism or modernism in the same way that I have seen the descendants of Orthodox Jews challenged by oysters. Historical progress demands that our revulsions be overcome. A man like Wilson might have done much to strengthen literary culture but he dismissed all that, he would have nothing to do with it. For temperamental reasons. Or Protestant-majority reasons. Or perhaps the Heisenberg principle applies—men are generous when there are creative opportunities and when such opportunities dwindle they are . . . something else. But it would have made little difference. At this moment in human evolution, so miraculous, atrocious, glorious and hellish, the firmly established literary cultures of France and England, Italy and Germany can originate nothing. They look to us, to the "disadvantaged" Americans, and to the Russians. From America have come a number of great irrepressible solitaries like Poe or Melville or Whitman, alcoholics, obscure government employees. In busy America there was no Weimar, there were no cultivated princes. There were only these obstinate geniuses writing—why? For whom? There is the real *acte gratuit* for you. Very different from Gide's gratuitous murder of an utter stranger. Unthanked, these writers augmented life marvelously. They did not emerge from a literary culture nor did they create any such thing. Irrepressible individuals of a similar type have lately begun to show themselves in Russia. There Stalinism utterly destroyed a thriving literary culture and replaced it with a horrible bureaucracy. But in spite of this and in spite of forced labor and murder, the feeling for what is true and just has not been put out. I don't see, in short, why we here should continue to dream of what we have never had. To have had it would not help us. Perhaps if we were to purge ourselves of nostalgia and stop longing for a literary world, we would see a fresh opportunity to extend the imagination and resume imaginative contact with nature and society.

Other people, scholars and scientists, know a great deal about nature and society. More than you know.

True. And I suppose I sound like a fool but I nevertheless object that their knowledge is defective—something is lacking. That something is poetry. Huizinga, the Dutch historian, in his recently published book on America says that the learned Americans he met in the Twenties could speak fluently and stimulatingly, but he adds, "More than once I could not recognize in what he wrote the living man who had held my interest. Frequently repeated experience makes me hold the view that my personal reaction to American scholarly prose must still rest upon the qualities of the prose itself. I read it with the greatest difficulty; I have no sense of contact with it and cannot keep my attention fixed on it. It is for me as if I had to do with a deviant system of expression in which the concepts are not equivalent to mine, or are arranged differently." The system has become more deviant during the last fifty years. I want information and ideas and I know that certain highly trained and intelligent people have it—economists, sociologists, lawyers, historians, natural scientists. But I read them with growing difficulty and exasperation. And I say to myself, "These writers are part of the educated public, your readers." But none of this matters. Philistine intellectuals don't make you stop writing. Writing is your *acte gratuit*. Besides, those you address are there. If you exist, then they exist.

But whether or not a literary culture exists—

Excuse me for interrupting but it occurs to me that Tolstoy would probably have approved of this and seen new opportunities in it. He had no use for literary culture and detested professionalism in the arts.

But should writers make their peace with the academic ivory tower?

In his essay "Bethink Yourselves" Tolstoy advises each man to begin at the point at which he finds himself. Better such towers than the cellar alternatives some writers choose. Besides, the university is no more an ivory tower than *Time* magazine with its strangely artificial approach to the world, its remote-making managerial arrangements. A writer is offered more money, bigger pensions, richer security plans by Luce enterprises than by any university. There too we see an ivory tower of a sort. Even more remote than Flaubert's *tour d'ivoire*. The ivory tower is one of those platitudes that haunt the uneasy minds of writers. Since we have none of the advantages of a literary world we may as well free ourselves from its banalities. Spiritual independence requires that we bethink ourselves. The university is as good a place for such thinking as any other. But while we think hard about the next step we should avoid becoming academics. Teachers, yes. Some are even moved to become scholars. The great danger for writers in the university is the academic danger.

Can you conveniently give a brief definition of an academic?

I limit myself arbitrarily to a professorial type to be found in the humanities. Owen Barfield refers in one of his books to "the everlasting professional device for substituting a plethora of talk" about what matters for—what actually matters. He is sick of it, he says. Many of us are sick of it.

[1975]

The Nobel Lecture

I was a very contrary undergraduate more than forty years ago. One semester I registered for a course in money and banking and then concentrated my reading in the novels of Joseph Conrad. I have never had reason to regret this. Perhaps Conrad appealed to me because he was like an American, speaking French and writing English with extraordinary power and beauty—he was an uprooted Pole sailing exotic seas. Nothing could seem more natural to me, the child of immigrants who grew up in one of Chicago's immigrant neighborhoods, than a Slav who was a British sea captain and knew his way around Marseilles. In England he was wonderfully exotic. H. G. Wells warned Ford Madox Ford, with whom Conrad collaborated in the writing of several novels, not to spoil Conrad's "Oriental Style." He was valued for his oddity. But Conrad's *real* life had little oddity in it. His themes were straightforward—fidelity, the traditions of the sea, hierarchy, command, the fragile rules sailors follow when they are struck by a typhoon. He believed in the strength of these fragile-seeming rules. He also believed in his art. He stated in the preface to *The Nigger of the "Narcissus"* that art was an attempt to render the highest justice to the visible universe: It tried to find in that universe, in matter as well as in the facts of life, what was fundamental, enduring, essential. The writer's method of attaining the essential was different from that of the thinker or the scientist, who knew the world by systematic examination. To begin with, the artist had only himself; he descended within himself, and in the lonely regions to which he descended, he found "the terms of his appeal." He appealed, said Conrad, "to that part of our being . . . which is a gift and not an acquisition . . . to our capacity for delight and wonder . . . to our sense of pity . . . and pain; to the latent feeling of fellowship with all creation—and to the subtle but invincible conviction of solidarity that knits together the loneliness of innumerable hearts . . . which binds together all humanity—the dead to the living and the living to the unborn."

This fervent statement was written some eighty years ago, and we may want to take it with a few grains of contemporary salt. I belong to a generation of readers who knew the long list of noble or noble-sounding words, words such as *invincible conviction* or *humanity,* rejected by writers like Ernest Hemingway. Hemingway spoke for the soldiers who fought in the First World War under the inspiration of Woodrow Wilson and other orotund statesmen whose big words had to be measured against the frozen corpses of young men paving the trenches. Hemingway's youthful readers were convinced that the horrors of the twentieth century with their deadly radiations had sickened and killed humanistic beliefs. I told myself therefore that Conrad's rhetoric must be resisted: resisted, not rejected, for I never thought him mistaken. He spoke directly to me. The feeling individual appeared weak—he felt only his own weakness. But if he accepted his weakness and his separateness and descended into himself, intensifying his loneliness, he discovered his solidarity with other isolated creatures.

I feel no need now to sprinkle Conrad's sentences with skeptical salt. But there are writers for whom the Conradian novel—all novels of that sort—has become invalid. Finished. There is, for instance, M. Alain Robbe-Grillet, one of the leaders of French literature, a spokesman for "thingism"—*chosisme.* In an essay called "On Several Obsolete Notions" he writes that in great contemporary works—Sartre's *Nausea,* Camus's *The Stranger,* Kafka's *The Castle*—there are no characters; you find in such books not individuals, merely entities. "The novel of characters," he says, "belongs entirely in the past. It describes a period: that which marked the apogee of the individual." This is not necessarily an improvement; that Robbe-Grillet admits. But it is the truth. Individuals have been wiped out. "The present period is rather one of administrative numbers. The world's destiny has ceased, for us, to be identified with the rise and fall of certain men of certain families." He goes on to say that in the days of Balzac's bourgeoisie it was important to have a name and a character; character was a weapon in the struggle for survival and success. In that time, "It was something to have a face in a universe where personality represented both the means and the end of all exploration." Our world, he concludes, is more modest. It has renounced the omnipotence of the person. But it is more ambitious as well, "since it looks beyond. The exclusive cult of the 'human' has given way to a larger consciousness, one that is less anthropocentric." However, he offers in comfort a new course and the promise of new discoveries before us.

On an occasion like this I have no appetite for polemics. We all know what it is to be tired of "characters." Human types have become false and boring. D. H. Lawrence put it early in the century that we human beings, our instincts damaged by Puritanism, no longer care for—worse, have become physically repulsive to—one another. "The sympathetic heart is broken," he said. "We stink in each other's nostrils." Besides, in Europe the power of the classics has for centuries been so great that every country has its "identifiable personalities," derived from Molière, Racine, Dickens or Balzac. An awful phenomenon. Perhaps this is connected with the wonderful French saying, *"S'il y a un caractère, il est mauvais."* It makes one think that the unoriginal human race tends to borrow what it needs from sources already at hand, much as new cities have often been made from the rubble of old ones. The viewpoint is perhaps confirmed by the psychoanalytic conception of character—that it is an ugly, rigid formation, something to be resigned to, nothing to be embraced with joy. Totalitarian ideologies, too, have attacked individualism, sometimes identifying character with property. There is a hint of this in M. Robbe-Grillet's argument. Rejection of personality, bad masks, boring forms of being, have had political results.

But this is not my subject; what I am interested in here is the question of the artist's priorities. Is it necessary or even desirable that he begin with historical analysis, with ideas or systems? Proust speaks in *Time Regained* of a growing preference among young and intelligent readers for works of an elevated, analytical, moral or sociological tendency—for writers who seem to them more profound. "But," says Proust, "from the moment that works of art are judged by reasoning, nothing is stable or certain, one can prove anything one likes."

The message of Robbe-Grillet is not new. It tells us that we must purge ourselves of bourgeois anthropocentrism and do the classy things that our advanced culture requires. Character? "Fifty years of disease, the death notice signed many times over by the serious essayists," says Robbe-Grillet, "yet nothing has managed to knock it off the pedestal on which the nineteenth century had placed it. It is a mummy now, but one still enthroned with the same—phony—majesty, among the values revered by traditional criticism."

Like most of us, I share Robbe-Grillet's objection to the mummies of all kinds we carry about with us, but I never tire of reading the master novelists. Can anything as vivid as the characters in their books be dead? Can it be that human beings are at an end? Is individuality really so dependent on historical and cultural conditions? Is the account of those conditions we are so "authoritatively" given by writers and psychologists to be accepted? I suggest that it is not in the intrinsic interest of human beings but in these ideas and accounts that the problem lies. It is the staleness and inadequacy of the ideas that repel us. To find the source of trouble, we must look into our own heads.

The fact that the death notice of character has been signed by the serious essayists means only that another group of mummies—certain respectable leaders of the intellectual community—has laid down the law. It amuses me that these serious essayists should be empowered to sign the death notice of a literary form. Should art follow "culture"? Something has gone wrong.

A novelist should be free to drop "character" if such a strategy stimulates him. But it is nonsense to make such a decision on the theoretical ground that the period that marked the apogee of the individual, et cetera, is ended. We must not permit intellectuals to become our bosses. And we do them no good by letting them run the arts. Should they, when they read novels, find in them only the endorsement of their own opinions? Are we here to play such games?

Characters, Elizabeth Bowen once said, are not created by writers. They preexist, and they have to be *found*. If we do not find them, if we fail to represent them, the fault is ours. It must be admitted, however, that finding them is not easy. The condition of human beings has perhaps never been more difficult to define. Those who tell us that we are in an early stage of universal history must be right. We are being lavishly poured together and seem to be experiencing the anguish of new states of consciousness. In America millions of people have in the last forty years received a "higher education"—often a dubious blessing. In the upheavals of the Sixties we felt for the first time the effects of up-to-date teachings, concepts, sensitivities, the pervasiveness of psychological, pedagogical, political ideas.

Every year we see scores of books and articles by writers who tell Americans what a state they are in. All reflect the current crises; all tell us what we must do about them—these analysts are produced by the very disorder and confusion they prescribe for. It is as a novelist that I am considering the extreme moral sensitivity of our contemporaries, their desire for perfection, their intolerance of the defects of society, the touching, the comical boundlessness of their demands, their anxiety, their irritability, their sensitivity, their tender-mindedness, their goodness, their convulsiveness, the recklessness with which they experiment with drugs and touch-therapies and bombs. The ex-Jesuit Malachi Martin in his book on the Church compares the modern American to Michelangelo's sculpture *The Captive*. He sees "an unfinished struggle to emerge whole" from a block of matter. The American "captive" is beset in his struggle by "interpretations, admonitions, forewarnings and descriptions of himself by the self-appointed prophets, priests, judges and prefabricators of his travail," says Martin.

If we take a little time to look more closely at this travail, what do we see? In private life, disorder or near panic. In families—for husbands, wives, parents, children—confusion; in civic behavior, in personal loyalties, in sexual practices (I will not recite the whole list; we are tired of hearing it)—further confusion. It is with this private disorder and public bewilderment that we try to live. We stand open to all anxieties. The decline and fall of everything is our daily dread; we are agitated in private life and tormented by public questions.

And art and literature—what of them? Well, there is a violent uproar, but we are not absolutely dominated by it. We are still able to think, to discriminate and to feel. The purer, subtler, higher activities have not succumbed to fury or to nonsense. Not yet. Books continue to be written and read. It may be more difficult to cut through the whirling mind of a modern reader, but it is still possible to reach the quiet zone. In the quiet zone we novelists may find that he is devoutly waiting for us. When complications increase, the desire for essentials increases too. The unending cycle of crises that began with the First World War has formed a kind of person, one who has lived through strange and terrible things and in whom there is an observable shrinkage of prejudices, a casting off of disappointing ideologies, an ability to live with many kinds of madness, and an immense desire for certain durable human goods—truth, for instance; freedom; wisdom. I don't think I am exaggerating; there is plenty of evidence for this. Disintegration? Well, yes. Much is disintegrating, but we are experiencing also an odd kind of refining process. And this has been going on for a long time. Looking into Proust's *Time Regained*, I find that he was clearly aware of it. His novel, describing French society during the Great War, tests the strength of his art. Without an art that shirks no personal or collective horrors, he insists, we do not know ourselves or anyone else. Only art penetrates what pride, passion, intelligence and habit erect on all sides—the seeming realities of this world. There is another reality, the genuine one, which we lose sight of. This other reality is always sending us hints, which, without art, we can't receive. Proust calls these hints our "true impressions." The true impressions, our persistent intuitions, will, without art, be hidden from us, and we will be left with nothing but a "terminology for practical ends which we falsely call life."

Proust was still able to keep a balance between art and destruction, insisting that art was a necessity of life, a great independent reality, a magical power. For a long time, art has not been connected, as it was in the past, with the main human enterprise. Hegel long ago observed that art no longer engaged the central energies of man. These energies were now engaged by science—"a relentless spirit of rational inquiry." Art had moved to the margins. There it formed "a wide and splendidly varied horizon." In an age of science, people still painted and wrote poetry, but, said Hegel, however splendid the gods looked in modern works of art and whatever dignity and perfection we might find "in the images of God the Father and the Virgin Mary," it was of no use: We no longer bent our knees. It is a long time since the knees were bent in piety. Ingenuity, daring exploration, freshness of invention replaced the art of "direct relevance." The most significant achievement of this pure art, in Hegel's view, was that, freed from its former responsibilities, it was no longer "serious." Instead it raised the soul through the "serenity of form above painful involvement in the limitations of reality." I don't know who would make such a claim today for an art that raises the soul above painful involvement with reality. Nor am I sure that at this moment it is the spirit of rational inquiry in pure science that engages the central energies of man. The center seems (even though temporarily) to be filled with the crises I have been describing.

There were European writers in the nineteenth century who would not give up the connection of literature with the main human enterprise. The very suggestion would have shocked Tolstoy and Dostoyevsky. But in the West, a separation between great artists and the general public took place. Artists developed a marked contempt for the average reader and the bourgeois mass. The best of them saw clearly enough what sort of civilization Europe had produced, brilliant but unstable, vulnerable, fated to be overtaken by catastrophe.

Despite a show of radicalism and innovation, our contemporaries are really very conservative. They follow their nineteenth-century leaders and hold to the old standards, interpreting history and society much as they were interpreted in the last century. What would writers do today if it occurred to them that literature might once again engage those "central energies," if they were to recognize that an immense desire had arisen for a return from the periphery, for what is simple and true?

Of course, we can't come back to the center simply because we wish to, though the realization that we are wanted might electrify us. The force of the crisis is so great that it might summon us back. But prescriptions are futile. One can't tell writers what to do. The imagination must find its own path. But one can fervently wish that they—that we—would come back from the periphery. We writers do not represent mankind adequately. What account do Americans give of themselves, what accounts of them are given by psychologists, sociologists, historians, journalists and writers? In a kind of contractual daylight, they see themselves in the ways with which we are desperately familiar. These images of contractual daylight, so boring to Robbe-Grillet and to me, originate in the contemporary worldview: We put into our books the consumer, civil servant, football fan, lover, television viewer. And in the contractual daylight version, their life is a kind of death. There is another life, coming from an insistent sense of what we are, that denies these daylight formulations and the false life—the death-in-life—they make for us. For it is false, and we know it, and our secret and incoherent resistance to it cannot stop—that resistance arises from persistent intuitions. Perhaps humankind cannot bear too much reality, but neither can it bear too much unreality, too much abuse of the truth.

We do not think well of ourselves; we do not think amply about what we are. Our collective achievements have so greatly "exceeded" us that we "justify" ourselves by pointing to them. It is the jet plane in which we commonplace human beings have crossed the Atlantic in four hours that embodies such value as we can claim. Then we hear that this is closing time in the gardens of the West, that the end of our capitalist civilization is at hand. This means that we are not yet sufficiently shrunken, we must prepare to be smaller still. I am not sure whether this should be called intellectual analysis or analysis by intellectuals. The disasters are disasters. It is worse than stupid to call them victories, as some statesmen have done. But I am drawing attention to the fact that there is in the intellectual community a sizable inventory of attitudes that have become respectable—notions about society, human nature, class, politics, sex, about mind, about the physical universe, the evolution of life. Few writers, even among the best, have taken the trouble to reexamine these attitudes or orthodoxies. Such attitudes are everywhere, and no one challenges them seriously. They only glow more powerfully in Joyce or D. H. Lawrence than in the books of lesser men. Since the Twenties, how many novelists have taken a second look at Lawrence or argued a different view of sexual potency or the effects of industrial civilization on the instincts? Literature has for nearly a century used the same stock of ideas, myths, strategies. "The serious essayists of the last fifty years," says Robbe-Grillet. Yes, indeed. Essay after essay, book after book, confirms the most serious thoughts—Baudelairean, Nietzschean, Marxian, psychoanalytic, et cetera, et cetera—of these most serious essayists. What Robbe-Grillet says about character can be said also about these ideas, maintaining all the usual things about mass society, dehumanization and the rest. How poorly they represent us. The pictures they offer no more resemble us than we resemble the reconstructed reptiles and other monsters in a museum of paleontology. We are much more limber, versatile, better articulated, there is much more to us—we all feel it.

What is at the center now? At the moment, neither art nor science but mankind determining, in confusion and obscurity, whether it will endure or go under. The whole species—everybody—has gotten into the act. At such a time it is essential to lighten ourselves, to dump encumbrances, including the encumbrances of education and all organized platitudes, to make judgments of our own, to perform acts of our own. Conrad was right to appeal to that part of our being which is a gift. We must look for that gift under the wreckage of many systems. The collapse of those systems may bring a blessed and necessary release from formulations, from misleading conceptions of being and consciousness. With increasing frequency, I dismiss as "merely respectable" opinions I have long held—or thought I held—and try to discern what I have really lived by and what others live by. As for Hegel's art freed from "seriousness" and glowing on the margins, raising the soul above painful involvement in the limitations of reality through the serenity of form, that can exist nowhere now, during this struggle for survival. However, it is not as though the people who engaged in this struggle had only a rudimentary humanity, without culture, and knew nothing of art. Our very vices, our mutilations, show how rich we are in thought and culture. How much we know. How much we can feel. The struggles that convulse us make us want to simplify, to reconsider, to eliminate the tragic weakness that has prevented writers—and readers—from being at once simple and true.

Writers are greatly respected. The intelligent public is wonderfully patient with them, continues to read them, and endures disappointment after disappointment, waiting to hear from art what it does not hear from theology, philosophy, social theory, and what it cannot hear from pure science. Out of the struggle at the center has come an immense, painful longing for a broader, more flexible, fuller, more coherent, more comprehensive account of what we human beings are, who we are, and what this life is for. At the center, humankind struggles with collective powers for its freedom, the individual struggles with

The Nobel Lecture   299

dehumanization for the possession of his soul. If writers do not come again into the center, it will not be because the center is preempted. It is not. They are free to enter. If they so wish.

The essence of our real condition, the complexity, the confusion, the pain of it, is shown to us in glimpses, in what Proust and Tolstoy thought of as "true impressions." This essence reveals and then conceals itself. When it goes away, it leaves us again in doubt. But our connection remains with the depths from which these glimpses come. The sense of our real powers, powers we seem to derive from the universe itself, also comes and goes. We are reluctant to talk about this because there is nothing we can prove, because our language is inadequate and because few people are willing to risk the embarrassment. They would have to say, "There is a spirit," and that is taboo. So almost everyone keeps quiet about it, although almost everyone is aware of it.

The value of literature lies in these intermittent "true impressions." A novel moves back and forth between the world of objects, of actions, of appearance, and that other world, from which these "true impressions" come and which moves us to believe that the good we hang on to so tenaciously—in the face of evil, so obstinately—is no illusion.

No one who has spent years in the writing of novels can be unaware of this. The novel can't be compared to the epic or to the monuments of poetic drama. But it is the best we can do just now. It is a sort of latter-day lean-to, a hovel in which the spirit takes shelter. A novel is balanced between a few true impressions and the multitude of false ones that make up most of what we call life. It tells us that for every human being there is a diversity of existences, that the single existence is itself an illusion in part, that these many existences signify something, tend to something, fulfill something; it promises us meaning, harmony and even justice. What Conrad said was true: Art attempts to find in the universe, in matter as well as in the facts of life, what is fundamental, enduring, essential.

[1976]

Americans Who Are Also Jews:
Upon Receiving the Democratic Legacy
Award of the Anti-Defamation League

How enviable it sometimes seems to have a brief and simple history. Ours is neither simple nor brief. You have honored me with an award and my part, in acknowledging this distinction with gratitude, is to make a short speech about America and its Jews, the Jews and their America. The difficulty of this obligation is considerable for the history we share is full of intricate, cunning and gloomy passages; it is also illuminating and it is noble—it is a large piece of the history of mankind. Many have tried to rid themselves in one way or another of this dreadful historic load by assimilation or other means. I have, myself, never been tempted by the hope of waking from the nightmare of history into a higher state of consciousness and freedom. As much as the next man, I enjoy meditating on such things, but my instincts have attached me to what is actually here, and among the choices that were actually open to me I have always preferred the liberal and democratic ones—not always in the popular sense of these terms.

When I read last summer in the *American Scholar* an article by Professor Sidney Hook on the great teacher and philosopher Morris R. Cohen, I was stirred by Cohen's belief that "the future of liberal civilization" was "bound up with America's survival and its ability to make use of the heritage of human rights formulated by Jefferson and Lincoln." Professor Cohen was no sentimentalist. He was a tough-minded man, not a patriotic rhetorician.

He arrived on the Lower East Side at the age of twelve. He knew the slums and the sweatshops. His knowledge of the evils of American life was extensive and unsparing—the history of the Indians and of the Negroes, cruelty, prejudice, mob violence, hysteria, injustice. *Acidulous* is Hook's word for Cohen's criticism of the U.S.A. Cohen, says Hook, was not a nationalist. He knew that no one chooses the land of his birth. He placed his hopes in the rule of enlightened world law. But Cohen was in some ways piously American. Now *piety* has become one of our very worst words. It used to be one of the best—think of Wordsworth's desire for "natural piety." Maybe we can do something to rehabilitate the term. Cohen accepted Santayana's definition of *piety* as "reverence for the sources of one's being." This emotion, says Hook, was naturally acquired by Cohen without ideological indoctrination or blinding.

I understand this without effort. Most of us do. There *are* people for whom it is entirely natural to despise the life that they were born into. There are others, like myself, who suspect that if we dismiss the life that is waiting for us at birth, we will find ourselves in a void. I was born in eastern Canada and grew up in Chicago. My parents were Jewish immigrants from Russia. They sent me to a *heder*. They didn't want me out in the sandlots or playing pool in the poolroom. All these matters were discussed or disputed by us in Yiddish. But when I went to the public library the books I borrowed were by Poe and Melville, Dreiser and Sherwood Anderson. I did not bring home volumes of the Babylonian Talmud to read. I took myself as I was—a kid from the Chicago streets and the child of Jewish parents. I was powerfully stirred by books from the library; I was moved to write something myself. These are some of the sources of my being. One could have better sources, undoubtedly. I could make a list of those more desirable sources, but they are not mine and I cannot revere them. The only life I can love, or hate, is the life that I—that we—have found here, this American life of the twentieth century, the life of Americans who are also Jews. Which of these sources, the American or the Jewish, should elicit the greater piety? Are the two exclusive? Must a choice be made? The essence of freedom is that one makes the choice, if choices must be made, for the most profound of personal reasons. It is at this very point that one begins to feel how intensively enviable it is to have a brief and simple history. (But is there any such thing?)

In Israel I was often and sometimes impatiently asked what sort of Jew I was and how I defined myself and explained my existence. I said that I was an American, a Jew, a writer by trade. I was not insensitive to the Jewish question, I was painfully conscious of the Holocaust, I longed for peace and security in the Jewish State. I added, however, that I had lived in America all my life, that American English was my language, and that (in an oddly universalist way) I was attached to my country and the civilization of which it was a part. But my Israeli questioners or examiners were not satisfied. They were trying to make me justify myself. It was their conviction that the life of a Jew in what they call the Diaspora must inevitably be "inauthentic." Only as a Jew in Israel, some of them told me, could I enter history again and prove the necessity and authenticity of my existence. I refused to agree with them that my life had been illusion and dust. I do not accept any interpretation of history that declares the deepest experience of any person to be superfluous. To me that smells of totalitarianism. Nor could I accept the suggestion that I repudiate some six decades of life, to dismiss my feelings for some of the sources of my being, *because I am a Jew or nothing*. That would wipe me out totally. It would be not only impiety and irreverence but also self-destruction.

But one need not hold long arguments with views that are so obviously wrong. What underlies the position that I have just rejected is the assumption that America is bound to go the way of other Christian countries and expel or destroy its Jewish population. But *is* it a Christian country like the others? One could write many volumes on what America is *not*. But there is no need, in a brief talk on an occasion such as this, to make grandiose statements about liberal democracy. It is sufficient to say in the most matter-of-fact way what is or should be obvious to everyone: In spite of the vastness and oppressiveness of corporate and governmental powers, the principle of the moral equality of all human beings has not been rejected in the United States. Not yet, at any rate. Sigmund Freud, I remember reading, once observed that America was an interesting experiment but he did not believe that it would succeed. Well, maybe not. But it would be base to abandon it. To do so would destroy our reverence for the sources of our being. We would inflict on ourselves a mutilation from which we might never recover. And if Cohen is right, and the future of liberal civilization is bound up with America's survival, the damage would be universal and irreparable.

[1976]

The Day They Signed the Treaty

The gray skies opened as the historic hour approached, the wind blew the clouds out, the sun shone on the great crowd of guests and journalists who had come to watch the signing of the Egyptian-Israeli peace treaty on the North Lawn of the White House.

Despite the sunshine the wind was stiff; the thermometer stood at forty-five degrees, a nipping and an eager air. On their platforms the TV technicians worked with great-snouted, funnel-eyed cameras and private camera buffs by the hundreds stood on folding chairs to photograph the scene: Prime Minister Begin, Presidents Carter and Sadat, their wives. They were perhaps hoping that their lenses might capture things their own eyes weren't seeing. The Marine band played jazzy, military quickstep music. From Lafayette Park came the amplified screams of demonstrating Palestinians and their sympathizers, kept at a distance by hundreds of riot police. St. John's Church rang its bells to celebrate the occasion and perhaps also to send ecclesiastical blessings over the noise of protest. Secret Service agents checked the papers of invited guests; on the roof of the White House were men with binoculars. From an upper window the White House chef in his tall white hat was looking down.

Beside me, an elderly couple had gotten up on their chairs. The lady said to me with an Eastern European accent, "But I am so small—I can't see." Her husband, in his old-fashioned, voluminous, fur-collared coat, was not much taller. He would, forty years ago, have been well dressed in his conservative pinstripes and homburg. I identified them as Americanized refugees. Greatly stirred, they seemed hardly to hear the indignation of the working press behind the ropes, telling them to step down. Nor did they care much about the eminent persons who went about recognizing one another: Henry Kissinger, Senator Moynihan soaring pleasantly above everyone—the privilege of importance or great height.

Abraham Beame of New York City did not enjoy the same advantage but was unmistakably a "notable"—that is what cops in Chicago call people whose pictures appear in the papers. Hizzoner carries his own sharp little aura. I mistook him for Judge Charles E. Wyzanski of Cambridge, Massachusetts, and had to be corrected by a New Yorker. Arthur Goldberg was present too. About him someone asked, "Why did he let himself be wheedled out of a lifetime job? Some sweet-talker, that Lyndon Johnson." The many celebrities embraced enthusiastically, grappling affectionately, kissing one another. There were wonderful personages to look at: gowned Coptic and Greek Orthodox priests, generals with campaign ribbons, faces familiar to us on the television screen, advancing in the flesh; behind us, masses of cameramen; before us, the alert formations of the Secret Service and flags flapping over the historic table on which the treaty was to be signed.

Until the last moment Sadat and Begin had bickered over wording, Sadat insisting on the Gulf of Aqaba, Begin holding out for the Gulf of Eilat and also, I was informed, for Judea and Samaria. But here they were, differences for the moment composed, ready to sign their names.

Most of those present were moved. Some said they were moved against their better judgment. They hadn't the strength to resist the great moment. "Stupendous," said Arthur Goldberg. I spoke to other observers, however, who could not bring themselves to put aside the habit of a caveat. Well, we'll see, they said. Or, *Pourvu que ça dure*. We are all filled with warm blood; the impulse to hope is very strong in us; those who have seen a great deal of life have learned, however, the wisdom of keeping a quantity of cold blood in reserve.

But even the most reserved and cautious of the Israeli, Egyptian and American diplomats and journalists whose opinions I sought said that this was a most significant advance, a great historic occasion, peace between enemies who have repeatedly spilled each other's blood.

Hardly a man of importance today present has escaped personal suffering. The brother of Sadat fell in the war of 1973. The son of Israeli defense minister Ezer Weizman has never recovered from his wounds.

Israeli foreign minister Moshe Dayan very early suffered the loss of an eye. The families of Begin and of many of his cabinet officers and assistants were destroyed in Hitler's murder camps. One of Begin's staff, Mr. Elissar, was as a boy saved from destruction by the death of another child, whose parents had emigration papers and who took young Elissar in the dead boy's place. Elissar's own family did not survive. Such are the people who this day affix their names to the agreement. The AP reports from Beirut: "Much of the Arab world seethes with outrage today, the day of peace for Egypt and Israel. Palestinian leader Yasser Arafat vowed to 'chop off the hands' of the 'stooge Sadat, the terrorist Begin, and the imperialist Carter.'"

The ceremony of signing is followed by the speeches of the principals. Mr. Carter announces that we must begin to wage peace. Mr. Sadat, a measured, mellowed orator, says, against waves of protest from Lafayette Park, let there be no more bloodshed and suffering. Let there be no denial of rights, he adds, adroitly referring to the Palestinians. He is an accomplished statesman, the most polished of today's speakers.

Begin, taking his turn at the microphones, is aware of his reputation as a chronic objector. "I agree but, as usual, with an amendment," he says. He tells the crowd that this is the third-greatest day of his life, the first being the day in 1948 on which Israel achieved statehood, the second that on which East Jerusalem was taken by Israeli troops.

Thus Sadat tries to assure the Arab world that he continues to represent Arab interests, while Begin still asserts that Jerusalem belongs to the Jews. He speaks of the personal sacrifices exacted by the long treaty negotiations, says that he has been abused by the world, abused by his own people; worst of all, he has been abused by his oldest friends. But he concludes with the 126th Psalm: "They that sow in tears shall reap in joy."

The ceremony ending, my wife and I return to the White House press quarters where we find that crowds of reporters have been watching the event on color television sets. All the vending machines are empty, all the candy has been eaten, everywhere cardboard boxes are stuffed with empty cans and paper plates and cups and sandwich wrappings and cigarette butts.

A weary young woman in slacks and white sneakers is curled up in her paper's cubicle, eating Fritos from a package. The elderly correspondent of *The New Republic* unlocks his confidential file, then with another key unlocks his telephone, pulls out the plug of a lock and dials a number. Egyptian and Israeli newsmen confer in separate groups. One Middle Eastern journalist, a big man, limps by. The look on his face is the look of Androcles's lion before the thorn was removed.

On a day like this, one naturally regrets not being an expert or one of those insiders who thoroughly understand. It's hell to be an amateur. A little reflection calms your sorrow, however. The experts in their own little speedboat, the rest of us floating with the rest of mankind on a great barge—that is the picture. We must do what we can to grasp whatever it is possible to grasp of all these treaties, SALT talks, Iranian revolutions, Russian maneuvers in Yemen, Chinese visits.

President Johnson used to say that he knew what was happening in Vietnam; *he* had information he couldn't share with us and without which we had no opinions worth considering. But he too turned out to be just another amateur. And we nonknowers have our rights. "No annihilation without representation," as Arnold Toynbee once put it. You dare not give up the struggle to form an opinion.

There are moments, certainly, when you feel like Mother Goose's pussycat who goes to London to see the queen. But at other times you refuse to concede that the keenest of professionals and specialists have the right to dismiss any considerable investment of mind, feeling and imagination. When I supported the Israeli Peace Now Movement last summer, I, together with the other signers, was denounced as a meddler and an ignoramus who had no right to a viewpoint. "The notion—how can we criticize when we do not live in Israel?—has been a remarkably powerful slogan," writes the Chicago sociologist Morris Janowitz. From our side we might argue that Israel, for its survival, is obliged to understand certain matters of which we as Americans have some firsthand knowledge. One need not be a professional superstar to understand the fundamentals. Israel's Arab neighbors have until now refused to recognize its legitimacy, its right as a sovereign state, and to this day speak of it as the "Zionist entity." Sadat, for a price, of course, has given Israel this indispensable recognition. Moreover, Israel has until now had to depend for survival entirely on its strength, but it is plain to everyone that the military effectiveness of Israel must eventually reach a limit, perhaps has already reached it.

There are those who question whether Israel won a decisive victory in 1973. They question also whether it can continue to stand the economic and social strains of preparedness, the strain of internal disputes provoked by garrison conditions, the mobilization of reservists, the anxieties and the expenses of siege life, the prospect of further wars and of greater casualties, and the last and most terrible of alternatives—namely, the "nuclear option."

What is fundamental, therefore, and beyond argument, is the need for a political solution—a political-military solution. Israel is in no position to reject this. Begin could not of course publicly state what he assuredly knew about the increasing futility of relying on military strength alone. It would be both demoralizing and dangerous to make such statements.

But since the revolution in Iran, the facts are clear for all the world to see. A complete victory of radical extremism in the Arab world would mean the defeat of all Jewish hopes, the end of Israel. According to President Carter's national security adviser, Zbigniew Brzezinski, with whom I talked briefly after the ceremony, this would present the greatest danger also to Western Europe. What he had in mind, I take it, is what people have begun to call "the Finlandization of Europe." He did not himself use this phrase.

I had met Mr. Brzezinski about a decade ago, at a meeting of some sort. (How many meetings of some sort there have been! You can measure your life out with them, as if they were Mr. Prufrock's coffee spoons.) Mr. Brzezinski has a pleasing face, a narrow aristocratic Polish nose in which I, raised among Poles in Chicago, can identify a characteristic irregularity of line, the Slavic eye frame and a whiteness of the skin more intense than that of Western Europe—not a pallor but a positive whiteness.

Mr. Brzezinski, a fluent and willing talker, necessarily guarded but not dragging his feet, said he was immensely pleased by the treaty—pleased but not exuberant. Brzezinski did not believe the Saudis would discontinue financial support to Egypt although they declared that they would follow the policies laid down at the Baghdad conference last

November, and these include economic sanctions against Egypt. He opined also that the Israelis would prove flexible enough to deal with the Arab problem. He cited in evidence the liberal traditions of Judaism and, more to the point, a recent speech in the Knesset by Shimon Peres, the leader of the opposition.

Mr. Peres, in his desire to come to terms with the Palestinian Arabs, took positions his party would have rejected only a few years ago. Golda Meir refused to acknowledge that there was any such thing as a Palestinian at all. Mr. Brzezinski did not think that Peres was merely sounding off. Peres is a tough politician who expects to return to power and a softening of his views reflects a change in opinion in the country. Mr. Brzezinski evidently believes that responsible Israeli politicians do not intend, cannot afford, to let the treaty unravel and that they understand quite well what the seizure of power by radicals in Egypt would mean for them.

Less guarded officials, off the record, tell you that Sadat was hardly oppressed by the great rage he had generated in the Arab world. Instead Sadat seems fairly lighthearted about it, all things considered. These officials tell you that Sadat has the most violent contempt for his Arab enemies, that his untranslatable purple invectives belong to no minor branch of the art of metaphor. H. L. Mencken once published a dictionary of curses, of all the terrible things his detractors had to say about him. This was purely a local American product. It might be useful to do the same thing on a world scale.

About Jordan's King Hussein the same free-spoken officials say that his recent behavior has been unpleasant, that he complains, beefs and reproaches the Americans. They concede, of course, that he is a man who has been living uncomfortably close to death for many years and that, unable to pursue an independent course in the Middle East, he is intensely frustrated.

In his large hotel suite, Boutros Boutros-Ghali, the Egyptian Foreign Minister, gave us his view of some of the disputed issues. He is a diplomat whose smooth Egyptian-French surface easily deflects unwelcome questions. There are no unmannerly rejections, only an easy, practiced turning aside of things he doesn't intend to discuss. For these things he substitutes certain rhetorical preparations of his own. I have done much the same on some occasions, with less style, and not in a setting of Oriental rugs and cut flowers.

Egypt, he says, has a duty to represent the interests of the Palestinian Arabs since no stability in the region is possible until they receive satisfaction. So peace with Israel requires justice for the Palestinians and is the direct concern of Egypt. I suggest that Egypt might offer more definite plans to mitigate the hardships of Palestinians, especially those in the refugee camps. I am thinking of the camps in Lebanon. Boutros-Ghali counters that the greatest hardship for the Palestinians is that they have no national base, no home to return to. But not that many would want to go back. A large number of Palestinians have prospered abroad. They are among the most advanced, the best educated and skilled, of the Arabs. Some are self-made millionaires and it is unlikely that these would want to live in a Palestinian state, but it is necessary for such a state to exist. It is after all one of the effects of Zionism to sharpen Arab nationalism.

His comment on Dayan, with whom he has had extended discussions in this same hotel suite, is that Dayan is Begin's vizier, that between them there is the Oriental connection of caliph and courtier-statesman. Boutros-Ghali sees Weizman as the crown prince and heir apparent who has the traditional mistrust of the vizier and invariably fires him.

I ask Boutros-Ghali what he thinks of the anti-Westernism of the Iranian Moslems and whether the revolution is evidence that Moslem orthodoxy cannot accept modernism. He answers that Islam is able and willing to accept modern conditions. I suggest that these conditions are not universally attractive and that I can readily understand why the religious are so repelled by them. You foreigners lack the true perspective, says Boutros-Ghali. There are so many factions in Iran that only time will show which will win out. I say nothing of hands lopped off and executions ordered by revolutionary councils. My wife speaks of the woman question in the Moslem world. Mr. Boutros-Ghali does not choose to discuss this.

He is interested, however, in a question about Israeli businessmen and technicians in Egypt. He puts cultural relations in the first place. These, to him, are more important than business connections. The Israelis should learn Arabic, he says. He emphasizes that he does not mean the lower-class Arabic many Jews learned from their neighbors in the old days—the sort of Arabic Dayan speaks. Oriental Jews when they emigrated to Israel should not have discarded their Arabic when they began to speak Hebrew.

Israelis would be wrong to take an attitude of superiority and assume that they would naturally be called upon to improve the backward Egyptians. They must not make the mistake the French made in Algeria of adopting the superior role. I interpret him to mean that a crowd of Israelis will be attracted to Egypt by business opportunities and by the vast sums provided by the United States for the modernization of agriculture and industry. They will not be welcome; they had better proceed with infinite tact.

Boutros-Ghali speaks often of France and the French, of French intellectuals. He recommends an article by Jean-Paul Sartre on Sadat's visit to Jerusalem. His friends call him Pierre, he tells us. Sadat calls him Pierre when he is pleased with him and when he is displeased addresses him as Boutros.

When we leave his suite we see through the open door of an adjoining room the Egyptian musclemen, the hulking guards, coatless, taking it easy, their leather holsters creaking as they move about. They are formidably armed. The American security gentleman sitting quietly in the corridor has a device for messages plugged into his ear like a hearing aid. Under his buttoned jacket he no doubt carries a Magnum: a calm type you might meet at a ticket counter in the airport and exchange the usual inanities about fog on the runway with.

Lastly the party, the Carters' great outdoor bash, to which Joseph Alsop referred as "the President's durbar." A long line of guests waited in the sharp wind to enter the White House and made their way, through a passage walled in fluttering plastic, into the great orange-and-yellow tent.

The Washington Post reported the words of one delighted guest: "It's the first time I've seen so much of Washington's social establishment in the Carter White House." People, the *Post* added, flitted about like mayflies.

Yes, they did flit, and chat, and embrace, and exchange show-business kisses. Well-known people are ecstatic at finding one another on these great occasions. Bands played, the Singing Sergeants sang hard; no one paid much attention to them. The important guests—Vice President Mondale, Mr. Kissinger, Energy Secretary James Schlesinger (a person of monumental presence, a great pillar smoking his pipe)—shook hands, smiled, gave out their views, I presume. I listened to few conversations; there were too many distractions.

I met Mr. Boutros-Ghali again; he bowed with polite charm; in his black-rimmed spectacles he looked extremely Parisian, something like the late actor Sacha Guitry. Senator Moynihan told me how greatly the afternoon ceremony had moved him. Mr. Kissinger told me nothing but coldly endured my handshake. He was very like Queen Victoria, it struck me. ("We are not amused.") Some of my mischievous remarks in print apparently had displeased him.

Our table companions were Congressman Clement Zablocki of Milwaukee, a power in foreign affairs; his young daughter, a student of remedial speech; a Texas businessman, one of Carter's very early supporters, his wife and daughter, all extremely good-looking, silently taking in the celebrity show; Joseph Burg, Israeli Minister of the Interior, a large, amiable, loose-jointed person in an Orthodox beanie, keen to have some good talk but dismayed by the volume of noise.

He did his best. He told me two very good jokes in Yiddish and reminisced about old times at the University of Leipzig, where he had studied symbolic logic. Hearing that my wife was a mathematician, he talked with animation about the great Hilbert and told us what he, Mr. Burg, had had to say in his orals about Immanuel Kant. Later I heard him trying to interest Mr. Zablocki in Tocqueville's *Democracy in America*, suggesting that the congressman read it.

So there were, after all, serious people present who could not easily accept the gala on a day like this and were puzzled and put out by the gaudiness and the noise. But the Americans had apparently tired themselves out making statements about the great event. "Wonderful, the greatest day there's been," Averell Harriman had said. And Arthur Goldberg had told the press, "A stupendous achievement."

Wonderful and *stupendous* bring you to a full stop. For the moment there is nothing to do but eat your salmon mousse, sip your wine, and wait for the powers of mind and feeling to regroup themselves for a fresh start.

You tell yourself that human beings have lived for many thousands of years in the Middle East and in that time have created complex difficulties, beliefs bewilderingly similar and for that reason utterly dissimilar, hatreds and profound needs that cannot be conjured away. What footing rationality can find in these infinitely contorted desires and antipathies, in our revolutionary time, remains to be seen.

[1979]

The Eighties

In the Days of Mr. Roosevelt

I t was in Chicago that Roosevelt was nominated in 1932, when I was seventeen years of age, just getting out of high school. When he defeated Hoover in November of that year he didn't become President, merely. He became *the* President, presiding over us for so long that in a movie of the early Forties, Billie Burke—Silly Billie—said to a fat, flummoxed senator that she had just been to Washington to see the coronation.

Early in the Depression my algebra teacher, an elderly lady whose white hair was piled in a cumulus formation over her square face and her blue-tinted square glasses, allowed herself a show of feeling and sang "Happy Days Are Here Again." Our astonishment was great. As a rule Miss Scherbarth was all business. Teachers seldom sounded off on topics of the day. It's true that when Lindbergh flew to Paris Mrs. Davis told the class, "I do hope, from my heart, that he is as good a young man as he is brave, and will never disappoint us." A revelation to the sixth grade. But that Miss Scherbarth should interrupt her equations to sing out for FDR showed that the country had indeed been shaken to its foundations. It wasn't until later that I understood that City Hall was busted and that Miss Scherbarth wasn't being paid. In the winter of '33, when I was a freshman at Crane College, the whole faculty went to the Loop to demonstrate at City Hall. Shopkeepers were taking their scrip (municipal funny money) at a discount. My English teacher, Miss Ferguson, said to us afterward, "We forced our way into the mayor's office and chased him round his desk."

Miss Ferguson, a splendid, somewhat distorted, but vigorous old thing, believed in giving full particulars. To chant the rules of composition was part of her teaching method. She would dance before the blackboard and sing out, "Be! Specific!" to the tune of Handel's "Hallelujah Chorus." A charming woman, she had overlapping front teeth, like the new First Lady. As she flourished her arms while singing her messages, it was not difficult to imagine her in the crowd that burst through the mayor's doors. They cried, "Pay us!"

In 1931 Chicago had elected its first foreign-born mayor. He was a Bohemian—Anton Cermak—and a formidable politician, one of the builders of the Democratic machine, soon to be taken over by the Irish. Cermak, who had tried to block Roosevelt's nomination, went down to Florida to make peace with the President-elect. According to Len O'Connor, one of the most knowledgeable historians of Chicago, Pushcart Tony was urged by Alderman Paddy Bauler, who bossed the German vote, to come to terms with FDR. "Cermak," Bauler later recalled, "said he didn't like the sonofabitch. I sez, 'Listen, for Cry sakes, you ain't got any money for the Chicago schoolteachers and this Roosevelt is the only one who can get it for you. You better get over there and kiss his ass or whatever you got to do. Only you better get the goddamn money for them teachers or we ain't goin' to have a city that's worth runnin.' So he goes over and, Christ Almighty, next thing I hear on the radio is that Cermak's got shot."

The assassin, Zangara, had supposedly aimed at Roosevelt, although there were those in Chicago who asserted that Cermak was his real target. Lots of people were in a position to benefit from Cermak's death. As he was rushed to the hospital, Cermak supposedly whispered to Roosevelt, "I'm glad it was me instead of you." This legend was the invention of a Hearst reporter, John Dienhart, who was a drinking pal of the mayor, as well as his public relations man. Dienhart's last word on this subject, as quoted in O'Connor's *Clout*, was: "I couldn't very well have put out a story that Tony would have wanted it the other way around."

Years later the *Chicago Tribune* reported that in a letter of thanks to Mrs. W. F. Cross, the Florida woman who had struck away Zangara's arm as he was pulling the trigger, the White House had written: "By your quick thinking, a far greater tragedy was averted." Colonel McCormick's files collected anti-Roosevelt facts as Atlantic beaches gather stones. The Colonel's heart never softened toward the Roosevelts. But the writer of the White House letter, perhaps Roosevelt himself, had it right. Alas for Pushcart Tony Cermak, the tragedy *would* have been far greater.

The Roosevelt era began, therefore, with the unwilling martyrdom of a commonplace Chicago politician who had gone to make a deal—an old deal—with the new guy, an Eastern swell, old money from an estate on the Hudson, snooty people, governor of New York (so what!), a President with a pince-nez and a long cigarette holder. How was Pushcart Tony to know that he had been killed by a bullet aimed at the very greatest of American politicians? Jefferson (himself no mean manipulator) and Madison had had eighteenth-century class. Jackson had had fire. Lincoln was our great-souled man. Wilson was the best America had to show in the way of professorial WASPdom. But FDR was a genius in politics. He was not an intellectual. He browsed in books of naval history, preferring those that were handsomely illustrated, and he pored over his stamp albums like many another patrician. Great politicians are seldom readers or scholars. When he needed brainy men, he sent to Columbia University for them. Following the traditions of monarchy, he created a privy council of brain trusters who had more influence, more money to spend, than the members of his cabinet. Experts now tell us that Roosevelt was an ignoramus in economic matters and the experts are probably right. But it wasn't the brain trusters who saved the U.S.A. from disintegration; it was—oddity of oddities—a country squire from Dutchess County, a man described by a shrewd foreign observer as the Clubman Caesar and by the witty if dangerous Huey Long as Franklin De La *No*. The unemployed masses, working stiffs, mechanics, laid-off streetcar conductors, file clerks, shoe salesmen, pants pressers, egg candlers, truck drivers, the residents of huge, drab neighborhoods of "furriners," the greenhorns today described as ethnics—all these swore by him. They trusted only Roosevelt, a Groton boy, a Social Register nob, a rich gentleman from Harvard and Hyde Park. They did not call for a proletarian president.

There are many for whom it was bliss then to be alive. For older citizens it was a grim time—for the educated and professional classes the Depression was grievously humiliating—but for the young this faltering of order and authority made possible an escape from family and routine. As a friend of mine observed during the complacent Eisenhower period: "The cost of being poor has gone so high. You have to have a couple of hundred bucks a month. Back in the Thirties we were doing it on peanuts." He was dead right. Weekly rent in a rooming house was seldom more than three dollars. Breakfast at a drugstore counter cost fifteen cents. The blue-plate-special dinner of, say, fried liver and onions, shoestring potatoes and coleslaw, with a dessert of Kosto pudding, appeared on the hectographed menu for thirty-five cents. Young hustlers could get by on something like eight or ten dollars a week, with a bit of scrounging. The National Youth Administration paid you a few bucks for nominal assistance to a teacher, you picked up a few more at Goldblatt's department store as a stockroom boy, you wore hand-me-downs, and you nevertheless had plenty of time to read the files of the old *Dial* at the Crerar Library or in the public library among harmless old men who took shelter from the cold in the reading room. At the Newberry you became acquainted also with anarchist-Wobbly theoreticians and other self-made intellectuals who lectured from soapboxes in Bughouse Square, weather permitting.

Between the Twenties and the Thirties a change occurred in the country that was as much imaginative as it was economic. In the Twenties America's stability was guaranteed by big business, by industrialists and by statesmen whose Anglo-Saxon names were as sound as the gold standard. On March 4, 1929, when Herbert Hoover was inaugurated, I was out of school with a sore throat and had the new Majestic radio in its absurd large cabinet all to myself. I turned the switch—and there was the new Chief Executive taking the oath of office before a great crowd. From the papers I knew what he looked like. His hair was parted down the middle, he wore a high collar and a top hat and looked like Mr. Tomato on the College Inn juice bottle. Full and sedate, he was one of those balanced and solid engineering-and-money types who would maintain the secure Republican reign of Silent Cal, the successor of the unhappy Harding. Big Bill Thompson, Chicago's Republican mayor, was a crook—all the local politicians were grafters and boodlers, but nobody actually felt injured by them. Great men like Samuel Insull or General Dawes were very sharp, certainly, but on the whole they were probably okay. The gangsters, who did as they liked, murdered one another, seldom harming ordinary citizens. Chicago, a sprawling network of immigrant villages smelling of sauerkraut and home-brewed beer, of meat processing and soap manufacture, was at peace—a stale and queasy peace, the philistine repose apparently anticipated by the Federalists. The founders had foreseen that all would be well, life would be orderly; no great excesses, no sublimity.

The sun shone as well as it could through a haze of prosperous gases, the river moved slowly under a chemical iridescence, the streetcars rocked across the level and endless miles of the huge Chicago grid. The city greeter, Mr. Gaw, who manufactured envelopes, met all prominent visitors at the railroad stations with old-style pizzazz and comical bombast. Chicago belonged to the Boosters, to the real estate men and the utilities magnates, to William Randolph Hearst and Bertie McCormick, to Al Capone and Big Bill Thompson and to the leafy backstreets where we lived.

A seven-cent streetcar fare took us to the Loop. On Randolph Street, we found free entertainment at Bensinger's billiard salon and at Trafton's gymnasium where boxers sparred. The street was filled with jazz musicians and City Hall types. My boyhood friend Fish, who was allowed to help himself to a quarter from the cash register in his father's poolroom, occasionally treated me to a hot dog and a stein of Hires root beer. When we overspent we came back from the Loop on foot—some five miles of freight yards and factories; joints that manufactured garden statuary like gnomes, trolls and undines; Klee Brothers, where you got a baseball bat with the purchase of a two-pants suit; Polish sausage shops; the Crown Theater at Division and Ashland with its posters of Lon Chaney or Renée Adorée, its popcorn machine crackling; then the United Cigar Store; then Brown and Koppel's restaurant with the non-stop poker game upstairs. It was a good dullness, this Hoover dullness. Higher activities were not prohibited but you had to find them for yourself. If you subscribed to the *Literary Digest* you might get the complete works of Flaubert as a bonus. Not that anybody read those buckram-bound books.

Fish matured before the rest of us. At fourteen he was being shaved by the barber, paying grandly with two bits from his papa's cash register. His virile Oriental face was massaged with witch hazel, his chin was powdered, he came on boldly with the girls. He spent money also on books, pamphlets and magazines. What he wanted from them was no more than a few quick impressions—he was no scholar—and after he had read a few pages he passed the magazines and pamphlets on to me. Through him I became familiar with Karl Marx and V. I. Lenin; also with Marie Stopes, Havelock Ellis, V. F. Calverton, Max Eastman and Edmund Wilson. The beginning of the Great Depression was also the beginning of my mental life. But suddenly the comedy of comfort stopped, the good-natured absurdities of the painted flivver, Pikes Peak or Bust, the Babbitt capers. There were no more quarters in the till.

The tale of America as told in the Twenties by America's leaders was that this country had scored one of the most brilliant successes in history. Hoover boasted in a 1928 campaign speech that the conquest of poverty in the United States was a palpable reality. "The poorhouse is vanishing from among us . . . our industrial output has increased as never before, and our wages have grown steadily in buying power. Our workers, with their average weekly wages, can today buy two and often three times more bread and butter than any wage earner of Europe. At one time we demanded for our workers a full dinner pail. We have now gone far beyond that conception. Today we demand larger comfort and greater participation in life and leisure."

How bitterly Hoover must have regretted the full dinner pail. He had, after all, meant well. To postwar Europe he had been a benefactor. But now the big businessmen who boasted of the bread and butter they were stuffing us with (Silvercup, not European bread) became once more what Eleanor Roosevelt's uncle Teddy had called "malefactors of great wealth." Their factories closed and their banks failed.

Private misery could not be confined: It quickly overflowed into the streets. Foreclosures, evictions, Hooverville shanties, soup lines—old Dr. Townsend of Long Beach, California, was inspired with his plan for the aged when he saw elderly women rooting for food in garbage cans. Maggoty meat for Americans? Were Chicago and Los Angeles to become Oriental cities like Shanghai or Calcutta?

The great engineer had botched his job. What would his successor do? Reputable analysts, taking Roosevelt's measure, were not encouraged by their findings. Walter Lippmann wrote in 1932 that FDR was "an amiable man with many philanthropic impulses," but accused him of "carrying water on both shoulders," of hanging on to both right-wing and left-wing supporters, a politician lavish with "two-faced platitudes." Roosevelt was no crusader, no enemy of entrenched privilege, "no tribune of the people" and Lippmann saw in him no more than "a pleasant man who, without any important qualifications for the office, would like very much to be President."

But Lippmann had examined the wrong musician, studied a different score, for when Roosevelt sat down to play he stormed over the executive keyboard, producing music no one had ever heard before. He was dazzling. And the secret of his political genius was that he knew exactly what the public needed to hear. It amounted to that, a personal declaration by the President that took into account the feelings of the people, and especially their fears. In his first inaugural address he told the great crowd before the Capitol: "This is preeminently the time to speak the truth, the whole truth, frankly and boldly. . . . This great Nation will endure as it has endured, will revive and will prosper." And then: "We do not distrust the future of essential democracy. The people of the United States . . . have asked for discipline and direction under leadership. They have made me the present instrument of their wishes."

With this powerful statement the tale of the Twenties concluded and a new tale began. Against the boastfulness of the Coolidge and Hoover decade were set the humiliations and defeats of the Depression. It was generally agreed that the Depression was to be viewed as what insurance companies term an act of God, a natural disaster. Peter F. Drucker puts the matter correctly in his memoirs: "As after an earthquake, a flood, a hurricane, the community closed ranks and came to each other's rescue . . . the commitment to mutual help and the willingness to take chances on a person were peculiar to Depression America." Professor Drucker adds that there was nothing like this on the other side, in Europe, "where the Depression evoked only suspicion, surliness, fear, and envy." In the opinion of Europeans, the only choice was between communism and fascism. Among world leaders Roosevelt alone spoke with assurance about "essential democracy." It is not too much to say that another America was imaginatively formed under his influence. Recovery programs were introduced with public noise and flourishes during his first hundred days, and although huge sums were spent, it presently became apparent that there would be no recovery. That he was nevertheless elected repeatedly proves that what the voters wanted was to live in a Rooseveltian America that turned the square old U.S.A. of the Hoovers topsy-turvy. I can remember an autumnal Chicago street very early one morning when I heard clinking and ringing noises. The source of these sounds was hidden in a cloud, and when I entered the sphere of fog just beginning to be lighted by the sun I saw a crowd of men with hammers chipping mortar from old paving bricks—fifty or sixty of the unemployed pretending to do a job, "picking 'em up and laying 'em down again," as people then were saying. Every day Colonel McCormick's *Tribune* denounced these boondoggles. In the center of the front page there was always a cartoon of moronic professors with donkey tails hanging from their academic mortarboards. They were killing little pigs, plowing under crops, and centupling the national debt while genial FDR, presiding at the Mad Hatter's tea party, light-heartedly poured out money. The brick chippers, however, were grateful to him. These jobless bookkeepers, civil engineers or tool-and-die makers were glad to work on the streets for some twenty dollars a week. The national debt, which enraged the Colonel, that dotty patriot, meant nothing to them. They desperately needed the small wages the government paid them. The drama of professional dignity sacrificed also appealed to many of them.

Memorable days. In 1934 I took to the road with a pal. With three dollars between us, enough to keep us in cheese and crackers, we bummed the freights. We joined the multitude of men and boys who covered the boxcars like flocks of birds. In South Bend, Indiana, we passed the Studebaker plant and a crowd of sit-in strikers yelling and cheering from the rooftop and the open windows. We shouted and joked with them, rolling at about five miles an hour in summer warmth through fresh June weeds, the Nickel Plate locomotive pulling us toward a horizon of white clouds. It now occurs to me that I didn't know how hard I was grieving for my mother, who had died just before Roosevelt was inaugurated. With her death and the remarriage of my father, the children scattered. I was turned loose—freed, in a sense: free but also stunned like someone who survives an explosion but hasn't yet grasped what has happened. I didn't know anything. At the age of eighteen I didn't even know that I was an adolescent. Words like that came later, in the Forties and Fifties.

Of course I sympathized with the strikers. Thanks to Fish's pamphlets I was able to call myself a socialist, and the socialist line was that FDR's attempted reforms were saving the country for capitalism, only the capitalists were too stupid to understand this. Radical orthodoxy in the Thirties held that parliamentary European reformism had failed and that the real choice, on a world scale, was between the hateful dictatorships of the right and the temporary and therefore enlightened dictatorships of the left. American democracy would not in the long run prove an exception. So said the radicals. One of them, Edmund Wilson, had written in 1931 that if American radicals wished to accomplish something valuable, "they must take communism away from the communists and take it without ambiguities or reservations, asserting emphatically that their ultimate goal is the ownership of the means of production by the government." And in a weird panegyric of Lenin written after his pilgrimage to the tomb on Red Square, Wilson told his readers that in the Soviet Union you felt that you were "at the moral top of the world where the light never really goes out." He spoke of Lenin as one of the very highest products of humanity—"the superior man who has burst out of the classes and claimed all that man has done which is superior for the refinement of mankind as a whole."

I was an early reader of Wilson's *Axel's Castle*. By 1936 I had also read his *Travels in Two Democracies*. Wilson had opened my eyes to the high culture of modern Europe and on that account I was in his debt. Besides, I had met him in Chicago when he was hauling a heavy Gladstone bag on Fifty-seventh Street near the university, hot and almost angry, shining with sweat and bristling at his ears and nostrils with red hairs. A representative of all that was highest and best, on the streets of Hyde Park—imagine that! His voice was hoarse and his manner huffy, but he was kindly and invited me to visit him. He was the greatest literary man I had ever met and I was willing to agree with all his views, whether the subject was Dickens or Lenin. But despite my great admiration for him and my weakness for inspired utterances, I was not carried away by his Lenin worship. Perhaps because my parents were

Russian Jews, I was as distrustful of Lenin and Stalin as Edmund Wilson was of American politicians. I didn't *believe* in Roosevelt as Wilson apparently believed in Lenin. I seem to have sensed, however, that Roosevelt was holding the country together and in my obstinate heart I resisted the Wilsonian program for American radicals. I couldn't believe, anyway, that liberal graduates of Harvard and Princeton were going to abduct Marxism from the Marxists and save the U.S.A. by taking charge of the dictatorship of the American proletariat. I secretly believed that America would in the end prove an exception. America and I, both exceptional, would together elude prediction and defy determinism.

You didn't have to approve Roosevelt's policies to be a Rooseveltian. Myself, I liked his policies less and less as time went by. I can recall the marks I gave him (in my helplessness). For recognizing Hitler as a great evildoer he rated an A. His support of England moved me deeply (high marks). In his judgment of the Russians he fell to a D. With Joe Kennedy in London and Joseph Davies in Moscow, one of the most disgraceful appointments in diplomatic history, he flunked out. For opinions on his dealings with Stalin I refer the reader to the Poles, the Czechs, the Romanians, et cetera. He did nothing to prevent the murder of millions in Hitler's death factories, but of that we were then ignorant.

His most dazzling successes were domestic and psychological. For millions of Americans the crisis of the old order was a release, a godsend. A great gap opened and a fresh impulse of the imagination rushed in. The multitudes were more mobile, diverse, psychologically flexible; they manifested new moods and colors; they were more urbane under FDR's influence. What was most important, for those who had the capacity for it, was the emotional catharsis of making a new start, of falling and rising again. The Thirties were more sociable, more accepting of weakness, less rigid, less idolatrous and less snobbish.

The Roosevelt influence was especially gratifying to the foreign-born. Millions of them passionately hoped to be *included*, to be counted at last as true Americans. Certain of the immigrants were parochial. Poles and Ukrainians, for instance, preferred to keep to their own communities and customs. Others, catching the American fever, changed

There Is Simply Too Much to Think About

their names, made up new personalities and, energized by these distortions, threw themselves into the life of the country. Who knows how many people became somebody else, turned themselves into jazz singers, blackface comedians, sportsmen, tycoons, antebellum Southern ladies, Presbyterian vestrymen, Texas ranchers, Ivy Leaguers, high government officials? It is not too much to say that these self-created people, people with false credentials, actors invisibly consumed by guilt and fear of exposure, were often empire builders. There's nothing like a shameful secret to fire a man up. If Hawthorne had not understood this, *The Scarlet Letter* would never have been written.

For these fertile and productive impostors it was bliss to hear FDR say that in this country we were all of us aliens. An actor himself, he put on the most successful act of all. He even had a secret: He could not walk. Behind this secret much deeper secrets were concealed.

Consider briefly, for the purpose of contrast, the career of Fitzgerald's Jay Gatsby, a pretender who could not forgive himself. Born James Gatz, he was remade (should we say twice born?). Boy Scout motives of self-improvement and naïve love-idealism kept him pure in heart and gullible. What Americans learned from Roosevelt's example was that *amour propre* (vanity, secrecy, ambition, pride) need not give anyone a bad conscience. You could, as Yeats suggested, "measure the lot, forgive myself the lot." Roosevelt, who with his democratic charm, his gaiety, the dramatic nobility of his head, *looked* the great man, sent Americans the message that beyond pretending and theatricality there was a further range in which one's deeper nature could continue to live, its truth undamaged. We may pretend, he seemed to be saying, as long as we are not taken in by our own pretenses. That way schizophrenia lies. From memoirs written by members of his inner circle we have learned that he loved spoofing, he was a gifted comedian who made fun of himself, a practical joker. He was well acquainted with Lear's *Nonsense Rhymes* and with *The Hunting of the Snark*. The irrational has its legitimate place by the side of the rational. Okay, life is real and earnest, but it is also decidedly goofy. With Roosevelt this was always clear. Others were more nebulous and more difficult. Compare, for instance, Roosevelt's Fala with the little dog of Richard Nixon in his "sincere" Checkers speech.

In domestic politics FDR's victorious intuition was that a President must discuss crises with the public in the plainest terms. Democracy cannot thrive if leaders are unable to teach or to console. A certain amount of deception is inevitable, of course. So many of society's institutions stand upon a foundation of fraud that you cannot expect a President to "tell all." Telling all is the function of intellectuals, supposedly. For Roosevelt it was sufficient to attack big business and expose malefactors of great wealth. He was not a philosopher. For his relations with the public he might, however, have taken his text from Isaiah: "Comfort ye." Among his successors in the White House only Truman, in his different "Give 'em hell" style, took a personal line with the voters. Some of our recent Presidents, sophisticated technicians, instinctively resisted the personal line. To Johnson and to Nixon this was an abomination. They were not leaders; they were professional behind-the-scenes operators. The very thought of taking the public into their confidence was horrifying to them. Forced to make a show of candor and an appeal for confidence, they averted their faces, their eyes filmed, their voices flattened. Frightful for a man like LBJ, stuffed with powers and with secrets, to abase himself before the cameras. He was not a Coriolanus but a democratic technician. Under such technicians decay was inevitable.

A civilized man, FDR gave the U.S.A. a civilized government. I suppose that he was what Alexander Hamilton would have called an "elective king," and if he was in some respects a demagogue, he was a demagogue without ideological violence. He was not a *Führer* but a statesman. Hitler and he came to power in the same year. Both made superb use of the radio. Those of us who heard Hitler's broadcasts will never forget the raucous sounds of menace, the great crowds howling as he made his death threats. Roosevelt's chats with his "fellow Americans" are memorable for other reasons. As an undergraduate I was fully armored in skepticism, for Roosevelt was very smooth and one couldn't be careful enough. But under the armor I was nonetheless vulnerable. I can recall walking eastward on the Chicago Midway on a summer evening. The light held long after nine o'clock and the ground was covered with clover, more than a mile of green between Cottage Grove and Stony Island. The blight hadn't yet carried off the elms and under them drivers had pulled over, parking bumper to bumper, and turned on their radios to hear Roosevelt. They had rolled down the windows and opened the car doors. Everywhere the same voice, its odd Eastern accent, which in anyone else would have irritated Midwesterners. You could follow without missing a single word as you strolled by. You felt joined to these unknown drivers, men and women smoking their cigarettes in silence, not so much considering the President's words as affirming the rightness of his tone and taking assurance from it. You had some sense of the weight of troubles that made them so attentive and of the ponderable fact, the one common element (Roosevelt), on which so many unknowns could agree. Just as memorable to me, perhaps, was to learn how long clover flowers could hold their color in the dusk.

[1983]

Reflections on Alexis de Tocqueville:
A Seminar at the University of Chicago

I have for something like forty years written and published stories and novels and I must know *something*. There are, however, happy natures ignorant of their own best insights. I wish I were one of them. Conrad's Captain MacWhirr, who skippered his ship through a typhoon, was too endearingly inarticulate to say how he did it. It is a lucky man indeed who does not need to cope with great complexities. Still, it is part of the fascination of *Typhoon* that Conrad's appreciation of complexity should be so extensive, for without it we should be unable to take the measure of Captain MacWhirr's monumental simplicity. I sometimes wish that I too were a MacWhirr, and the wish itself suggests that I feel I owe my survival to the observance of certain quite elementary rules. These rules, flatly stated, would be of small interest to a lover of complexity but they have seen me over many dark reefs.

What this comes to is that a writer cannot afford to lose his naïveté. It is imperative to add that in the present age he cannot afford to ignore the complexities in which existence is now set. His simplicity will be steeped in complexity. The more tacit the complexity, the better. That goes without saying.

Contemporary American writers (others, too) have been willing, far too willing, to let others perform the essential complex operations for them. One can see why. But it has been a mistake to rely so much upon others. "The good are attracted by men's perceptions, and think not for themselves," said William Blake. "The good" I translate as "the would-be good," the all-too-voluntary innocents who prefer that evil should find them unarmed and unresisting. The opinions of psychologists, critics, sociologists, philosophers cannot however sustain a literature.

Let it be granted then that in the present age it is impossible to escape thinking and that nothing will be accomplished by writers who do not take measures to protect themselves from the tyranny of perceptions—the victorious opinions hanging over us like a smog from which no relief is to be expected. But does that mean that we must devote our evenings to the study of Tocqueville? Lucky writers, born lucid, can get by without reading beautiful books. I myself was not born lucid, unfortunately, and have not been able to manage matters unaided. The anxieties of multiplicity were too much for me. I had to see what it was that had restricted the talents of even the best of modern writers, and I turned therefore to Tocqueville and to others who had what seemed to me a satisfactory, a distinct overview of the modern age. Easily the most important of these was Nietzsche. Less lofty, and for that reason perhaps more congenial, were writers like Wyndham Lewis, himself in his cantankerous way something of a Nietzschean, and two or three modern Russians whom I will presently mention.

I must confess at the outset that in reading Tocqueville I begin with a satisfaction that is presently infected with a growing irritation. He is, to use a word used by sociologists when they review one another's books, so "magisterial." He is all-seeing, in fairness admirably fair, in prescience uncanny. He admits freely, gracefully everything that has to be admitted: Aristocratic Europe, of which he is himself a product, is done for. The new age, which began with Machiavelli, Bacon, Hobbes, Descartes, is upon us. The democratic world with its masses, its miracles, its mediocrities, its splendid opportunities for freedom and development, its monstrous perversions of the same—no need to push this description too hard, to jump up and down on the rhetorical trampoline. These masses are, in a broad sense, our very selves, the families that begat us, the hands that fed us, the school that schooled us, the press that pressed us, even the vulgarities that made snobs of us (such of us as have been seized by impulses of social climbing). Inadequate to say that we are dominated by this—we are a self-saturated population, a collectivity full of itself, viewing, describing, assessing itself. There is one great act and everybody is in it. Allow me to pinpoint these assertions in Tocqueville's own words: "In democratic communities, where men are all insignificant and very much alike, each man instantly sees all his fellows when he surveys himself. . . . I am persuaded," writes Tocqueville—to continue this brief presentation of his views on the sources of poetry in a democracy—"persuaded that in the end democracy diverts the imagination from all that is external to man, and fixes it on man alone. Democratic nations may amuse themselves for a while with considering the productions of nature; but they are only excited in reality by a survey of themselves. Here, and here alone, the true sources of poetry amongst such nations are to be found." He goes further, insisting that democratic nations care little for the past but are haunted by visions of what will be. Here I find one of my cavils in the margin: "Like socialism in one country, or Hitler's thousand-year Reich?" But this is unwarranted, merely a touch of the occasional irritation I have already confessed. My reading continues and soon I come upon the following sentences: Americans, we are told, are "insensible to the wonders of inanimate nature, and they may be said not to perceive the mighty forests which surround them until they fall beneath the hatchet. Their eyes are fixed upon another sight: the American people views its own march across these wilds—drying swamps, turning the course of rivers, peopling solitudes and subduing nature. This magnificent image of themselves does not meet the gaze of the Americans only; it may be said to haunt every one of them in his least as well as in his most important actions, and to be always flitting before his mind. Nothing conceivable is so petty, so insipid, so crowded with paltry interests, in one word so anti-poetic, as the life of a man in the United States. But amongst the thoughts which it suggests there is always one which is full of poetry, and that is the hidden nerve which gives vigor to the frame."

Here Tocqueville anticipates Walt Whitman's celebration of the pioneers. He anticipates also the American skyscraper with its regular masses of cellular units. "Crowded with paltry interests," but forming our celebrated skylines. Tocqueville makes his observations with even-handed poise. He does not, like Nietzsche, burst out against the herds of "voting cattle" and the decadent philistinism of the democratic public; nor does he approach the more sober depths where Nietzsche defines historically the discouragement by which nihilism is identified: "the recognition of the long squandering of strength, the agony of the 'in vain,' the insecurity, the lack of any opportunity to recuperate and to regain tranquility." And yet this would be implicit in the Cartesian view of being ascribed to Americans by Tocqueville. I quote from his chapter on Philosophical Method—Americans follow the maxims of Descartes because their "social condition disposes their understanding to accept them." "Everyone shuts himself up in his own breast, and affects from that point to judge the world." And further, Americans have "little faith for whatever is extraordinary, and an almost insurmountable distaste for whatever is supernatural. As it is on their own testimony that they are accustomed to rely, they like to discern the object which engages their attention with extreme clearness; they therefore strip off as much as possible all that covers it, they rid themselves of whatever separates them from it, they remove whatever conceals it from sight, in order to view it more closely and in the broad light of day. . . . The Americans then have not required to extract their philosophical method from books; they have found it in themselves. The same thing may be re-marked in what has taken place in Europe."

Yes, and this nakedness of the perceptions was noted by Wordsworth as the abstract passion with which a man may "botanize upon his mother's grave" and was denounced by William Blake as "single vision." I will not associate Nietzsche with these romantics, for whom he had little regard. He made his own statement, far more comprehensive, on nihilism and the special meaning of nihilism for world history. Tocqueville, with more modest objectives, seeing in democracy the shape of mankind's future, tried to be nice about the inevitable. He wanted to encourage us, or to put a floor under us. The worst he could foresee would after all be tolerable. Only we have more than once fallen through the floor.

But let me postpone awhile what the collapsing floor may mean and ask you to turn your attention briefly to what art and literature, its theorists and practitioners, have done or might have attempted to do, during the centuries identified by Nietzsche as times in which "the devaluation of the uppermost values" has occurred so swiftly as to leave us standing quite naked. To Nietzsche, as I read him, this nakedness was an exhilarating opportunity, a challenge to find a surer foundation for being. He would have waved away Tocqueville's assurances that democracy would find its floor. Such a floor did not even begin to resemble Nietzsche's far grander quest for a foundation of being. Besides, Tocqueville's project (individuals are negligible and therefore collectivity will be the heroic theme) has the air of being one of those happy French thoughts that sound terribly plausible but won't actually bear much weight.

When he speaks of America's mental life he refers to "a motley multitude whose intellectual wants are to be supplied. These new votaries of the pleasures of the mind have not all received the same education; they do not possess the same degree of culture as their fathers, nor any resemblance to them—nay, they perpetually differ from themselves, for they live in a state of incessant change of place, feelings, and fortunes." Attachments based upon tradition or common habits are hard to find. "It is, however, from the bosom of this heterogeneous and agitated mass that authors spring." In the same paragraph comes the following assertion: "Amongst democratic nations each new generation is a new people." If you join together these two propositions concerning the instability of individuals and the radical alteration of succeeding generations, the time "of the nation itself must be either change or else the elements of permanence resistant to changes." I don't think the "conquest of nature" by the settlers, the theme suggested by Tocqueville, will fill the bill. The "romance of the frontier" was quickly gulped down by the colossus Technology. What then has persisted amid changes, I try to think: for one, using the strength of the Constitution, which was tested by the Civil War, and for another, slavery and the still unresolved problems of race.

There is no need, however, to speculate further upon Tocqueville's forecasts for we live in the future he was so intelligently imagining. My present concern is with various attempts of theorists, historians, artists who in the present democratic ages refuse "absolutely to live without art," cannot even conceive of such an existence. This refusal—or more exactly, this assertion—takes many forms. I will cite several of them, beginning with one familiar to many of you. Henry James, in defending himself from H. G. Wells's charge that his all-too-"aesthetic" novels neglected ordinary human interests, replied that "art *makes* life, makes interest, makes importance." But in this making one must have the strength for what a Russian, Mandelstam, in very different circum-

There Is Simply Too Much to Think About

stances (far from Jamesian amenities) described much later as the "struggle with the barbarism of a new life." And yet those who call it barbarism themselves spring from what Tocqueville called the heterogeneous and agitated mass.

In his essay "Humanism and Modern Life" Mandelstam wrote, "There are certain periods that say they have nothing to do with man; that say he should be used like brick, like cement; that say he should be built from, not for. . . . Assyrian captives swarm like chickens under the feet of the immense King . . . Egyptian builders dispose of the great mass as if it were inert matter." Obviously Mandelstam here is writing of the dictatorship of the proletariat, to which he opposes a personal essence, the true human dwelling utterly different from the constructions of despotism. The "barbarism" of a new life "does not make us deaf to true music"—of which he writes, in an essay on Scriabin, that "it contains the atoms of our being."

But in quoting from Mandelstam I have jumped forward farther than I wished. My first intention was to introduce several statements from those who do not accept the democratic degradation of art and artists as an ineluctable destiny.

"It would be a disaster if we didn't have an art of our own time," said our old friend Harold Rosenberg in what I take to be the last interview he ever gave. And in answer to the next question, "Why is it so important for us to have an art of our own time?" he said, "Art has a lot to do with the level on which the public apprehends events. This is the sense in which art has political significance. Without new relevant art we live in a world in which everything is either of the past or without reference to the deepest developments of the time. Today it's extremely important that we shouldn't be left, as people are in totalitarian countries, with no other public experience than that which the government permits us to have. Yet something close to that takes place with the reign of the mass media, whose managers decide what news you are going to receive, what kind of emotional experience is allowable. What makes a poem acceptable to be printed? How should a picture be organized? If this has been decided in advance by some authority whom one doesn't dare to defy, you are living in a blind world where nobody has any experience to communicate to anybody else. This is called the triumph of communications—which is very much what the state of affairs is now. That's why artists keep struggling to be able to say something new." Two noteworthy suggestions arise from his statement: the first is that the Tocquevillean collective theme (the life of the nation as a whole) is at present in the hands of the media managers; the second is that the capacity to experience is itself threatened by the conditions of our existence.

Now one more quotation, this one taken from Wyndham Lewis's *Men Without Art,* a lengthy study of the subject we are discussing tonight. I give you these sentences with which he concludes: "The valuing of our arts is bound up with the valuing of our life, and vice versa. All I have done here has been, starting from the assumption that a non-material system of values attaches to the exercises of the artist, to denounce the various interferences, by the agency of which, at present, his activities are impaired . . . and at least I may have directed your attention to a question of great moment—namely, whether the society of the immediate future should be composed, for the first time in civilized history, of *Men without art.*"

As to that, it is perfectly possible, as the Russian novelist Andrei Sinyavsky has strikingly testified, to live without art, just as possible as to survive on a salt-free diet, only (I paraphrase him) the trees, the sky, cats, dogs will be obliterated for us and we will inhabit a world that is just as unfurnished as our souls will have become.

I myself perceive something less apocalyptic. The democratic mass itself has begotten a class of persons awakened to thought and art. They temperamentally require it, they refuse privation, they insist on the exercise of their power—they are determined not to be disappointed. This is why a Henry James will maintain that "art *makes* life, makes interest, makes importance" or a Wyndham Lewis will give it as a postulate that the valuing of art is bound up with the valuing of life and vice versa. Lewis goes further in *The Writer and the Absolute* where he declares that "Truth, clearness and Beauty, naturally are public matters. Indeed, Truth (but written truth) . . . is as public and as necessary as the air we breathe. Truth or Beauty are as much public concerns as the water supply." "It is true," he continues, "that the writer in our day— succumbing to the glamour of cryptical techniques and the lure of easy reputation—has allowed himself to be edged into a dark corner of the forum. Progressively he has been pushed away from the center of things. Whatever style he adopts, daily he tends to lose his worldly place. Yet the writer belongs where the public is. . . . In one way or another truth, or what is the same thing, clearness—not the big Victorian abstractions of the classic mind—must be the major object of his search."

I have much more to say on these matters. I might for instance talk about the strangeness and ingenuity, the queer genius, of certain minds and souls developed under the monstrous weight of the modern world or set free, so to speak, by its very momentum, released by centrifugal impulses and liberated above all from the determinist obsession that art depends utterly upon a nourishing or fructifying "culture"—a responsive or properly educated society, the nourishment of traditions, the support of a setting, of manners. To wait upon any of this is to court aggravation and disappointment and perhaps also to betray one's powers, which in this day and age are bound to be the unpredictable powers arising from singularity, from the special perspectives to which history has given us special access. Humankind has today the advantage of an overview—in which ancient epic mingles with modern dehumanization. These are properties of our being in the modern age.

Instead of elaborating these ideas now—and I have already taken far too much time—I will conclude with two statements, very brief, from Osip Mandelstam. The first is: "Do not dare describe anything in which the internal state of your spirit is not reflected in some way or other." The second: "My breath, my warmth have already lain on the panes of eternity."

[1984]

My Paris

Changes in Paris? Like all European capitals, the city has undergone changes. The most unpleasantly conspicuous are the herds of tall buildings beyond the ancient gates. Old districts like Passy, peculiarly gripping in their dinginess, are almost unrecognizable today with the new apartment houses and office buildings, most of which would suit a Mediterranean port better than Paris. It's no easy thing to impose color on the dogged northern gray, the native Parisian *grisaille*—flinty, foggy, dripping and for most of the year devoid of any brightness. The gloom will have its way with these new *immeubles* too; you may be sure of that. When Verlaine wrote that the rain fell into his heart as it did upon the city (referring to almost any city in the region) he wasn't exaggerating a bit. As a onetime resident of Paris (I arrived in 1948) I can testify to that. New urban architecture will find itself ultimately powerless against the *grisaille*. Parisian gloom is not simply climatic; it is a spiritual force that acts not only on building materials, on walls and rooftops, but also on character, opinion and judgment. It is a powerful astringent.

But the changes . . . I wandered about Paris not very long ago to see how thirty-odd years had altered the place. The new skyscraper on the boulevard du Montparnasse seems almost an accident, something that strayed away from Chicago and came to rest on a Parisian street corner. In my old haunts between the boulevard du Montparnasse and the Seine, what is most immediately noticeable is the disappearance of certain cheap conveniences. High rents have driven out the family bistros that once served delicious, inexpensive lunches. A certain decrepit loveliness is giving way to unattractive, overpriced, overdecorated newness. Dense traffic—the small streets make you think of Yeats's "mackerel-crowded seas"—requires an alertness incompatible with absentminded rambling. Dusty old shops in which you might lose yourself for a few hours are scrubbed up now and sell pocket computers and high-fidelity equipment. Stationers who once carried notebooks with excellent paper now offer a flimsy product that lets the ink through. Very disappointing. Cabinetmakers and other small artisans once common are hard to find.

My neighbor the professional packer on the rue de Verneuil disappeared long ago. This cheerful specialist wore a smock and beret, and as he worked in an unheated shop his big face was stung raw. He kept a cold butt-end in the corner of his mouth—one seldom sees a *mégot* in this new era of prosperity. A pet three-legged hare, slender in profile, fat in the hindquarters, stirred lopsidedly among the crates. But there is no more demand for hand-hammered crates. Progress has eliminated all such simple trades. It has replaced them with boutiques that sell costume jewelry, embroidered linens or goose-down bedding. In each block there are three or four *antiquaires*. Who would have thought that Europe contained so much old junk? Or that, the servant class having disappeared, hearts nostalgic for the bourgeois epoch would hunt so eagerly for Empire breakfronts, recamier sofas and curule chairs?

Inspecting the boulevards, I find curious survivors. On the boulevard Saint-Germain the dealer in books of military history and memorabilia who was there thirty-five years ago is still going strong. Evidently there is a permanent market for leather sets that chronicle the ancient wars. (If you haven't seen the crowds at the Invalides and the huge, gleaming tomb of Napoleon, if you underestimate the power of glory, you don't know what France is.) Near the rue des Saints-Pères the pastry shop of Camille Hallu is gone, together with numerous small bookshops, but the dealer in esoteric literature on the next block has kept up with the military history man down the street, as has the umbrella merchant nearby. Her stock is richer than ever, sheaves of umbrellas and canes with parakeet heads and barking dogs in silver. Thanks to tourists, the small hotels thrive—as do the electric Parisian cockroaches who live in them, a swifter and darker breed than their American cousins. There are more *clochards* than in austere postwar days, when you seldom saw them drinking in doorways.

The ancient gray and yellow walls of Paris have the strength needed to ride out the shock waves of the present century. Invisible electronic forces pierce them, but the substantial gloom of courtyards and kitchens is preserved. Boulevard shop windows, however, show that life is different and that Parisians feel needs they never felt before. In 1949 I struck a deal with my landlady on the rue Vaneau: I installed a gas hot-water heater in the kitchen in exchange for two months' rent. It gave her great joy to play with the faucet and set off a burst of gorgeous flames. Neighbors came in to congratulate her. Paris was then in what Lewis Mumford called the Paleotechnic Age. It has caught up now with advancing technology and French shops display the latest in beautiful kitchens—counters and tables of glowing synthetic alabaster, artistic in form, the last word in technics.

Once every week during the nasty winter of 1950, I used to meet my friend the painter Jesse Reichek in a café on the rue du Bac. As we drank cocoa and played casino, regressing shamelessly to childhood, he would lecture me on Siegfried Giedion's *Mechanization Takes Command* and on the Bauhaus. Shuffling the cards, I felt that I was simultaneously going backward and forward. We little thought in 1950 that by 1983 so many modern kitchen shops would be open for business in Paris, that the curmudgeonly French would fall in love so passionately with sinks, refrigerators and microwave ovens. I suppose that the disappearance of the *bonne à tout faire,* the maid of all work, is behind this transformation. The post-bourgeois era began when your housemaid found better work to do. Hence all these *son et lumière* kitchens and the velvety pulsations of invisible ventilators.

I suppose that this is what *modern* means in Paris now. It meant something different at the beginning of the century and it was this other something that so many of us came looking for in 1948. Until 1939 Paris was the center of a great international culture, welcoming Spaniards, Russians, Italians, Romanians, Americans; open to the Picassos, Diaghilevs, Modiglianis, Brancusis and Pounds at the glowing core of the modernist art movement. It remained to be seen whether the fall of Paris in 1940 had only interrupted this creativity. Would it resume

There Is Simply Too Much to Think About

when the defeated Nazis went back to Germany? There were those who suspected that the thriving international center had been declining during the Thirties, and some believed that it was gone for good.

I was among those who came to investigate, part of the first wave. The blasts of war had no sooner ended than thousands of Americans packed their bags to go abroad. Eager Francophile travelers, poets, painters and philosophers were vastly outnumbered by the restless young—students of art history, cathedral lovers, refugees from the South and the Midwest, ex-soldiers on the GI Bill, sentimental pilgrims—as well as by people no less imaginative, with schemes for getting rich. A young man I had known in Minnesota came over to open a caramel-corn factory in Florence. Adventurers, black marketeers, smugglers, would-be *bons vivants*, bargain hunters, bubbleheads—tens of thousands crossed on old troop ships, seeking business opportunities or sexual opportunities or just for the hell of it. Damaged London was severely depressed, full of bomb holes and fireweed, whereas Paris was unhurt and about to resume its glorious artistic and intellectual life.

The Guggenheim Foundation had given me a fellowship and I was prepared to take part in the great revival—when and if it began. Like the rest of the American contingent, I brought my illusions with me, but I like to think that I was also skeptical (perhaps the most tenacious of my illusions). I was not going to sit at the feet of Gertrude Stein. I had no notions about the Ritz Bar. I would not be boxing with Ezra Pound, as Hemingway had done, or writing in bistros while waiters brought oysters and wine. Hemingway the writer I admired without limits; Hemingway the *figure* was to my mind the quintessential tourist, the one who believed that he alone was the American whom Europeans took to their hearts as one of their own. In simple truth, the Jazz Age Paris of American legend had no charms for me, and I had my reservations also about the Paris of Henry James—bear in mind the unnatural squawking of East Side Jews as James described it in *The American Scene.* You wouldn't expect a relative of those barbarous East Siders to be drawn to the world of Madame de Vionnet, which had, in any case, vanished long ago.

Life, said Samuel Butler, is like giving a concert on the violin while learning to play the instrument—that, friends, is real wisdom. I never tire of quoting it. I was concertizing and practicing scales at the same time. I *thought* I understood why I had come to Paris. Writers like Sherwood Anderson and, oddly enough, John Cowper Powys had made clear to me what was lacking in American life. "American men are tragic without knowing why they are tragic," wrote Powys in his *Autobiography*. "They are tragic by reason of the desolate thinness and forlorn narrowness of their sensual mystical contacts. Mysticism and Sensuality are the things that most of all redeem life." Powys, mind you, was an admirer of American democracy. I would have had no use for him otherwise. I believed that only the English-speaking democracies had real politics. In politics continental Europe was infantile— horrifying. But what America lacked, for all its political stability, was the capacity to enjoy intellectual pleasures as though they were sensual pleasures. This was what Europe offered, or was said to offer.

There was, however, a part of me that remained unconvinced by this formulation, denied that Europe—as advertised—still existed and was still capable of gratifying the American longing for the rich and the rare. True, writers from St. Paul, St. Louis and Oak Park, Illinois, had gone to Europe to write their American books, the best work of the Twenties. Corporate, industrial America could not give them what they needed. In Paris they were free to be fully American. It was from abroad that they sent imaginative rays homeward. But was it the European imaginative reason that had released and stirred them? Was it Modern Paris itself or a new universal Modernity working in all countries, an international culture of which Paris was, or *had* been, the center? I knew what Powys meant by his imaginative redemption from the desolate thinness and forlorn narrowness experienced by Americans, whether or not they were conscious of it. At least I thought I did. But I was aware also of a seldom-mentioned force visible in Europe itself to anyone who had eyes—the force of a nihilism that had destroyed most of its cities and millions of lives in a war of six long years. I could not easily accept the plausible sets: America, the thinning of the life impulses; Europe, the cultivation of the subtler senses still valued, still going on. Indeed, a great European prewar literature had told us what nihilism was, had warned us what to expect. Céline had spelled it out quite plainly in *Journey to the End of the Night*. His Paris was still there,

There Is Simply Too Much to Think About

more there than Sainte-Chapelle or the Louvre. Proletarian Paris, middle-class Paris, not to mention intellectual Paris, which was trying to fill nihilistic emptiness with Marxist doctrine—all transmitted the same message.

Still, I had perfectly legitimate reasons for being here. Arthur Koestler ribbed me one day when he met me in the street with my five-year-old son. He said, "Ah? You're married? Is this your *child*? And you've come to *Paris*?" To be Modern, you see, meant to be detached from tradition and traditional sentiments, from national politics and, of course, from the family. But it was not in order to be Modern that I was living on the rue de Verneuil. My aim was to be free from measures devised and applied by others. I could not agree, to begin with, on any definition. I would be ready for definition when I was ready for an obituary. I had already decided not to let American business society make my life for me and it was easy for me to shrug off Mr. Koestler's joke. Besides, Paris was not my dwelling place; it was only a stopover. There was no dwelling place.

One of my American friends, a confirmed Francophile, made speeches to me about the City of Man, the City of Light. I took his rhetoric at a considerable discount. I was not, however, devoid of sentiment. To say it in French, I was *aux anges* in Paris, wandering about, sitting in cafés, walking beside the liniment-green, rot-smelling Seine. I can think of visitors who were not greatly impressed by the City of Man. Horace Walpole complained of the stink of its little streets in the eighteenth century. For Rousseau it was the center of *amour propre*, the most warping of civilized vices. Dostoyevsky loathed it because it was the capital of Western bourgeois vainglory. Americans, however, loved the place. I, too, with characteristic reservations, fell for it. True, I spent lots of time in Paris thinking about Chicago but I discovered—and the discovery was a very odd one—that in Chicago I had for many years been absorbed in thoughts of Paris. I was a longtime reader of Balzac and of Zola and knew the city of *Père Goriot*, the Paris at which Rastignac had shaken his fist, swearing to fight it to the finish, the Paris of Zola's drunkards and prostitutes, of Baudelaire's beggars and the children of the poor whose pets were sewer rats. The Parisian pages of Rilke's *Notebooks of Malte Laurids Brigge* had taken hold of my imagination in the Thirties, as had the Paris of Proust, especially those dense, gorgeous and painful passages of *Time Regained* describing the city as it was in 1915—the German night bombardments, Madame Verdurin reading of battlefields in the morning paper as she sipped her coffee. Curious how the place had moved in on me. I was not at all a Francophile, not at all the unfinished American prepared to submit myself to the great city in the hope that it would round me out or complete me.

In my generation the children of immigrants became Americans. An effort was required. One made oneself, freestyle. To become a Frenchman on top of that would have required a second effort. Was I being invited to turn myself into a Frenchman? Well, no, but it seemed to me that I would not be fully accepted in France unless I had done everything possible to become French. And that was not for me. I was already an American and I was also a Jew. I had an American outlook superadded to a Jewish consciousness. France would have to take me as I was.

From Parisian Jews I learned what life had been like under the Nazis, about the roundups and deportations in which French officials had cooperated. I read Céline's *Les Beaux Draps*, a collection of crazy, murderous harangues seething with Jew-hatred.

A sullen, grumbling, drizzling city still remembered the humiliations of occupation. Dark bread, *pain de seigle*, was rationed. Coal was scarce. None of this inspired American-in-Paris fantasies of gaiety and good times in the Ritz Bar or the Closerie des Lilas. More appropriate now was Baudelaire's Parisian sky weighing the city down like a heavy pot lid or the Paris of the Communard *pétroleurs* who had set the Tuileries afire and blown out the fortress walls. I saw a barricade going up across the Champs-Élysées one morning, but there was no fighting. The violence of the embittered French was for the most part internal.

No, I wasn't devoid of sentiments, but the sentiments were sober. And why did Paris affect me so deeply? Why did this imperial, ceremonious, ornamental mass of structures weaken my American refusal to be impressed, my Jewish skepticism and reticence; why was I such a sucker for its tones of gray, the patchy bark of its sycamores and its bitter-medicine river under the ancient bridges? The place was, naturally, indifferent to me, a peculiar alien from Chicago. Why did it take hold of my emotions?

For the soul of a civilized, or even partly civilized, man, Paris was one of the permanent settings, a theater, if you like, where the greatest problems of existence might be represented. What future, if any, was there for this theater? It could not tell you what to represent. Could anyone in the twentieth century make use of these unusual opportunities? Americans of my generation crossed the Atlantic to size up the challenge, to look upon this human, warm, noble, beautiful, and also proud, morbid, cynical and treacherous setting.

Paris inspires young Americans with no such longings and challenges now. The present generation of students, if it reads Diderot, Stendhal, Balzac, Baudelaire, Rimbaud, Proust, does not bring to its reading the desires born of a conviction that American life-impulses are thin. We do not look beyond America. It absorbs us completely. No one is stirred to the bowels by Europe of the ancient parapets. A huge force has lost its power over the imagination. This force began to weaken in the Fifties and by the Sixties it was entirely gone.

Young MBAs, management school graduates, gene splicers and computerists, their careers well started, will fly to Paris with their wives to shop on the rue de Rivoli and dine at the Tour d'Argent. Not greatly different are the behavioral scientists and members of the learned professions who are well satisfied with what they learned of the Old World while they were getting their BAs. A bit of Marx, of Freud, of Max Weber, an incorrect recollection of André Gide and his gratuitous act, and they had had as much of Europe as any educated American needed.

And I suppose that we *can* do without the drama of Old Europe. Europeans themselves, in considerable numbers, got tired of it some decades ago and turned from art to politics or abstract intellectual games. Foreigners no longer came to Paris to enrich their humanity with modern forms of the marvelous. There was nothing marvelous about the Marxism of Sartre and his followers. Postwar French philosophy, adapted from the German, was less than enchanting. Paris, which had been a center, still *looked* like a center and could not bring itself to concede that it was a center no longer. Stubborn De Gaulle, assisted by Malraux, issued his fiats to a world that badly wanted to agree with him, but when the old man died there was nothing left—nothing but old monuments, old graces. Marxism, Eurocommunism, existentialism, structuralism, deconstructionism, these could not restore the potency of French civilization. Sorry about that. A great change, a great loss of ground. The Giacomettis and the Stravinskys, the Brancusis no longer come. No international art center draws the young to Paris. Arriving instead are terrorists. For them French revolutionary traditions degenerated into confused leftism, and a government that courts the third world made Paris a first-class place to plant bombs and to hold press conferences.

The world's disorders are bound to leave their mark on Paris. Cynosures bruise easily. And why has Paris for centuries now attracted so much notice? Quite simply because it is the heavenly city of secularists. *"Wie Gott in Frankreich"* was the expression used by the Jews of Eastern Europe to describe perfect happiness. I puzzled over this simile for many years and I think I can interpret it now. God would be perfectly happy in France because he would not be troubled by prayers, observances, blessings and demands for the interpretation of difficult dietary questions. Surrounded by unbelievers, He too could relax toward evening just as thousands of Parisians do at their favorite cafés. There are few things more pleasant, more civilized, than a tranquil *terrasse* at dusk.

[1983]

Foreword to The Revolt of the Masses by José Ortega y Gasset

What a mass man is, Ortega amply and indeed elegantly defines for us in Anthony Kerrigan's superb translation of *La rebelión de las masas*, but a rapid sketch of the argument of the book may nevertheless be useful to the reader.

Ortega when he speaks of the mass man does not refer to the proletariat; he does not mean us to think of any social class whatever. To him the mass man is an altogether new human type. Lawyers in the courtroom, judges on the bench, surgeons bending over anesthetized patients, international bankers, men of science, millionaires in their private jets are, despite their education, their wealth or their power, almost invariably mass men, differing in no important respect from TV repairmen, clerks in Army Navy stores, municipal fire inspectors or bartenders. It is Ortega's view that we in the West live under a dictatorship of the commonplace. The triumphs of science and technology have made possible a huge increase in population, and with new multitudes has come a revolutionary change in the character of civilized society, for in Ortega's view revolution is not merely an uprising against the existing institutions but the establishment of a new order that reverses traditional order. The modern revolution has created for the average man, for the great social conglomerate to which he now belongs, a state of mind radically opposite to the old. Public life has been turned inside out. The unqualified individual, "equal in law," belongs to the sovereign mass. Examining the collective assumptions of this sovereign mass, Ortega reaches the conclusion that, although the world remains in certain respects civilized, its inhabitants are barbarians. In Ortega's view barbarism is defined by the absence of norms. "There is no culture where there are no principles of civil legality to which to appeal." In mass society philosophy and art suffer the same fate as the legal traditions.

What are the characteristics of Ortega's mass man? He is unable to distinguish between the natural and the artificial. Technology, which surrounds him with cheap and abundant goods and services, with packaged bread, subways and blue jeans, with running water and electrical fixtures that light up at the touch of a finger, has as it were worked itself into his mind as an extension of the natural world. He expects that there will be air to breathe, sunlight. He also expects elevators to go up, buses to arrive. His ability to distinguish between artifact and organism withers away. Blind to the miraculous character of nature, as well as to the genius of technology, he takes both for granted. So in Ortega's mass society the plebeians have conquered and they do not concern themselves with civilization as such but only with the wealth and conveniences provided by mechanization. The spirit of a mass society bids it to abandon itself freely to itself and to embrace itself; practically nothing is impossible, nothing is dangerous, and in principle no one is superior to anyone else—this, Ortega submits, is the mass man's creed. The "select man," by contrast, insofar as he serves a transcendental purpose, understands that he must accept a kind of servitude. "To live at ease," said Goethe, "is plebeian; the noble mind aspires to ordinance and law." It follows from this that the mass man lacks seriousness. With him nothing is for real, all parts are interchangeable. For him everything is provisional. He may occasionally play at tragedy, but the prevailing mood is one of farce. The mass man loves gags. He is a spoiled child, demanding amusement and given to tantrums, lacking the form, the indispensable tension that only imperatives can give. His only commandment is *Thou shalt expect convenience.* "The only real effort is expended in fleeing from one's own destiny."

And what, according to Ortega, is the destiny of this barbarian? The opening up of life and the world for the mediocre man has led him to shut up his soul. It is the obliteration of the average soul upon which the rebellion of the masses is founded. "Which, in turn, constitutes the gigantic problem facing humanity today." How the soul is going to react to this, or whether it is going to react, Ortega does not tell us in this book. He takes the matter up elsewhere. In *Man and People* he discusses

There Is Simply Too Much to Think About

the psychic struggle of the individual self and the necessity of "being inside oneself" as a prerequisite for the formation of true ideas, for the gestation of those original and creative actions without which societies die.

"The rebellion of the masses is one and the same thing as the fabulous increase in the standard of living in modern times. But the reverse side of this phenomenon is fearsome: the rebellion of the masses represents a radical demoralization of humanity." This is Ortega at his most pessimistic. True, he says, the level attained in the West is superior to any in the past as far as the average man is concerned, but if we look to the future we find grounds to fear that it will neither preserve this level nor reach a higher one. "On the contrary, it may well regress to inferior levels." In the sphere of politics he seems to take it for granted that the masses act through the state and that under the dominion of the masses the state will inevitably crush the independence of the individual.

I think it only fair to point out that the circumstances of the West are vastly different from what they were when this book was first published. Ortega is writing about the West's honeymoon with technology. That honeymoon ended decades ago. Doubts and fears obviously pervade mass society. Although the standard of living has continued to rise, the confidence of modern man has been greatly shaken by the mounting crisis of civilization, by wars and by the speed of change, by the mass man's gradual recognition that the world's resources are after all finite. Besides, the masses do not after all dominate the state. It cannot be said that sophisticated police states express the will of their masses or that Hitler or Stalin led nations of spoiled children in World War II. Nor do the mass media reflect the dominion of the masses; they demonstrate instead the skill of the illusionists who form public opinion and public taste. The average man cannot think that he understands or controls what is happening. He is unable to believe confidently in the explanatory pictures he is shown. Vulgarity in the Eighties is not so sure of itself as it was fifty years ago. Crisis has chastened it considerably. If humanity today is demoralized, the cause is perhaps to be sought not in the rebellion of the masses but in the setbacks suffered by mass society, in the thickening shadow of its all-too-realistic fears, above all in the pain felt by the hounded, mutilated, not wholly obliterated soul.

Foreword to The Revolt of the Masses *by José Ortega y Gasset*   349

Ortega, to be sure, had his ancestors. Earlier writers, Nietzsche among them, had announced with revulsion the advent of a new human type (in *Zarathustra* Nietzsche calls him the "Last Man"), but Ortega is in no sense a derivative thinker. Ortega's mass man is descended from the bourgeois as the nineteenth-century artist saw him— Stendhal's small businessmen and provincial political types, Flaubert's Homais, Dostoyevsky's worshippers of Baal. These writers are among Ortega's predecessors and he sees the twentieth century, in part, from their perspective: A diminished and fatally disfigured human type, a new force in the world numbering hundreds of millions of individuals, has come to dominate modern civilization.

One has only to read a single page of Ortega to see that he is entirely his own man. He has read widely but imitates no one. The French writer David Mata has recently said of him in *Encounter* that he is "a source, a spring. He is so unpedantic, so unbombastic that he is barely a traditional philosopher at all: he seems so transparent that he is nothing, nothing but light. On any theme he ponders . . . he sheds a noonday brightness in which prejudices, idols of the tribe, entelechies, all dissolve." And although he is a civilized European, *un grand Européen*, his light is uniquely Spanish.

[1985]

The Civilized Barbarian Reader

As a Midwesterner, the son of immigrant parents, I recognized at an early age that I was called upon to decide for myself to what extent my Jewish origins, my surroundings (the accidental circumstances of Chicago), my schooling were to be allowed to determine the course of my life. I did not intend to be wholly dependent on history and culture. Full dependency must mean that I was done for. The commonest teaching of the civilized world in our time can be stated simply: "Tell me where you come from and I will tell you what you are." There was not a chance in the world that Chicago, with the agreement of my eagerly Americanizing extended family, would make me in its image. Before I was capable of thinking clearly, my resistance to its material weight took the form of obstinacy. I couldn't say why I would not allow myself to become the product of an environment. But gainfulness, utility, prudence, business had no hold on me.

My mother wanted me to be a fiddler or, failing that, a rabbi. I had my choice between playing dinner music at the Palmer House or presiding over a synagogue. In traditional Orthodox families small boys were taught to translate Genesis and Exodus, so I might easily have gone on to the rabbinate if the great world, the world of the streets, had not been so seductive. Besides, a life of pious observance was not for me. I had begun at an early age to read widely and I was quickly carried away from the ancient religion. Reluctantly, my father allowed me at seventeen to enter the university, where I was an enthusiastic (wildly excited) but erratic and contrary student. If I signed up for Economics 201, I was sure to spend all my time reading Ibsen and Shaw. Registering for a poetry course, I was soon bored by meters and stanzas and shifted my attention to Kropotkin's *Memoirs of a Revolutionist* and

Lenin's *What Is to Be Done?* My tastes and habits were those of a writer. I preferred to read poetry on my own without the benefit of lectures on the caesura. To rest my book-strained eyes I played pool and Ping-Pong at the men's club.

I was soon aware that in the view of advanced European thinkers the cultural expectations of a young man from Chicago, that center of brutal materialism, were bound to be disappointed. Put together the slaughterhouses, the steel mills, the freight yards, the primitive bungalows of the industrial villages that comprised the city, the gloom of the financial district, the ballparks and prizefights, the machine politicians, the Prohibition gang wars, and you had a solid cover of "Social Darwinist" darkness, impenetrable by the rays of culture. Hopeless, in the judgment of highly refined Englishmen, Frenchmen, Germans and Italians, the spokesmen for art in its most advanced modern forms. For some of these foreign observers, America had many advantages over Europe. It was more productive, more energetic, more free and largely immune from pathogenic politics and ruinous wars, but as far as art was concerned it would be better, as Wyndham Lewis put it, to have been born an Eskimo than a Minnesota Presbyterian who wanted to be a painter.

Civilized Europeans, often exceptionally free from the class prejudices of their own countries, were able conveniently to center their not fully mastered biases on the free-for-all U.S.A. What no one was able to foresee was that all civilized countries were destined to descend to a common cosmopolitanism and that the lamentable weakening of the older branches of civilization would open fresh opportunities and free us from our dependence on history and culture—a concealed benefit of decline. To interpret our circumstances as deeply as we can, isn't that what we human beings are here for? When the center does not hold and great structures fall down, one has an opportunity to see some of the truths they obstructed. Long-standing premises then come in for revision and old books are read by a new light.

Many of my own seem now, in retrospect, comedies of wide reading. Henderson, who imagines himself to be an American Caliban, climbs a ladder in the library of the mansion he inherited to look for marked passages in the books of his father, a Prospero who never could forgive his son for being so barbarous. Humboldt the poet, showing off his shack in the barren, chalky backcountry of New Jersey, quotes from *Macbeth*: "This castle hath a pleasant seat." Augie March finds the Harvard Classics in a box under Einhorn's bed. Why was this attachment to high culture so funny? Well, for one thing American society had already set off in a very different direction. In its indiscriminate generosity it had given Humboldt a four-holer Buick to drive over the dirt roads while he was thinking about Yeats, Eliot and Proust, his favorite writers. In the eyes of his fellow Americans he was, God bless him, out of it.

Another, darker cause for laughter is that the best efforts of intellectuals to enlighten us, the books they have written for us, have so often led to deserts of abstraction. After many years of attentive and diligent study we are left with little more than systems of opinion and formulas that hide reality from us. Personal judgment is disabled, crippled by theoretic borrowing. We are bound, in other words, to be skeptical of learning too. Hybrid barbarians that we are, we trusted intellectuals to tell us what was what, we put up with the invented mental language of their "authoritative explanations." But in the end man must master his own experience. He desperately looks for help in books; but it's no good, as Kafka observed, to try to imprison life in a book, "like a songbird in a cage."

Holding such views I find myself, as Americans have taken to saying, between a rock and a hard place. European observers sometimes classify me as a hybrid curiosity, neither fully American nor satisfactorily European, stuffed with references to the philosophers, historians and poets I consumed higgledy-piggledy in my Midwestern lair. I am of course an autodidact, as modern writers always are. That spirited newcomer, the nineteenth-century novelist, guessed, ventured, conjectured daringly. Independent intelligence made its synthesis. "The world," Balzac declared, "belongs to me because I understand it."

From a different standpoint, American readers sometimes object to a kind of foreignness in my books. I mention Old World writers, I have highbrow airs and appear to put on the dog. I readily concede that here and there I am probably hard to read and I am likely to become harder as the illiteracy of the public increases. It is never an easy task to take the mental measure of your readers. There are things that people should know if they are to read books at all and out of respect for them, or to save appearances, one is apt to assume more familiarity on their part with the history of the twentieth century than is objectively justified. Besides, a certain psychic unity is always taken for granted by writers. "Others are in essence like me and I am basically like them, give or take a few minor differences." A piece of writing is an offering. You bring it to the altar and hope it will be accepted. You pray at least that rejection will not throw you into a rage and turn you into a Cain. Perhaps naïvely, you produce your favorite treasures and pile them in an indiscriminate heap. Those who do not recognize their value now may do so later. And you do not always feel that you are writing for any of your contemporaries. It may well be that your true readers are not here as yet and that your books will cause them to materialize.

There are times when I enjoy making fun of the educated American. *Herzog*, for instance, was meant to be a comic novel: A Ph.D. from a good American university falls apart when his wife leaves him for another man. He is taken by an epistolary fit and writes grieving, biting, ironic and rambunctious letters not only to his friends and acquaintances but also to the great men, the giants of thought who formed his mind. What is he to do in this moment of crisis, pull Aristotle or Spinoza from the shelf and storm through the pages looking for consolation and advice? The stricken man, as he tries to put himself together again, interprets his experience, makes sense of life, becomes clearly aware of the preposterousness of such an effort. "What this country needs," he writes at last, surrendering to the absurdity of his state, "is a good five-cent synthesis." Here he echoes Mr. Marshall, Woodrow Wilson's Vice-President, who had said at about the time of the Great War, "What this country needs is a good five-cent cigar."

Certain readers of *Herzog* complained that the book was difficult. Much as they might have sympathized with the unhappy and comical history professor, they were occasionally put off by his long and erudite letters. Some felt that they were being asked to sit for a difficult exam in a survey course in intellectual history and thought it mean of me to mingle sympathy and wit with obscurity and pedantry. But I was making fun of pedantry! The reply: "If that was your purpose, you didn't altogether succeed. Some of your readers thought you were setting up a challenge, something resembling an obstacle course, or an egghead crossword puzzle for members of MENSA." A few may have been flattered, while others resented being tested. People reserve their best thinking for their professional specialties and, next in line, for serious matters confronting the alert citizen—economics, politics, the disposal of nuclear waste, et cetera. The day's work done, they want to be entertained. They can't see why their entertainment should not simply be entertaining and in some ways I agree, for I myself, in reading Montaigne as I sometimes do, am tempted to skip his long citations from the classics, which put my high-school Latin under some strain and it is not amusing to send oneself back to high school.

To finish with *Herzog*: I meant the novel to show how little strength "higher education" had to offer a troubled man. In the end he is aware that he has had no education in the conduct of life. At the university who was there to teach him how to deal with his erotic needs, with women, with family matters? He returns, in the language of games, to square one—or as I put it to myself while writing the book, to some primal point of balance. Herzog's confusion is barbarous. Well, what else can it be? But there is one point at which, assisted by his comic sense, he is able to hold fast. In the greatest confusion there is still an open channel to the soul. It may be difficult to find because by midlife it is overgrown, and some of the wildest thickets that surround it grow out of what we describe as our education. But the channel is always there and it is our business to keep it open, to have access to the deepest part of ourselves—to that part of us which is conscious of a higher consciousness by means of which we make final judgments and put everything together.

The independence of this consciousness, which has the strength to be immune to the noise of history and the distractions of our immediate surroundings, is what the life struggle is all about. The soul has to find and hold its ground against hostile forces, sometimes embodied in ideas that frequently deny its very existence and that indeed often seem to be trying to annul it altogether.

[1987]

A Jewish Writer in America: A Lecture

Afew preliminary words on the title of this talk: It deals with aspects of my personal history and with the substantiality of the person behind this history. The idea of a substantial person has been subjected by modernist, postmodernist and postpostmodernist thinkers to tests that make one think of the rude use of effigies by engineers who simulate car collisions and plane crashes—dummies are dismembered before our eyes or devoured by floods of ignited aviation fuel.

The "identity problem" has vexed and plagued the modern intellect. So what business have I, in view of the "new look" for individuals (in a word, for each and every one of us) sponsored by highly influential existentialist, deconstructionist and nihilist designers, to speak of my personality and my personal history? And the truth is that no such right can be formally defended by a writer—a novelist—who, in any case, would have neither the time nor the metaphysical competency to do the job. All I have to say is that the learned philosophers and critics have raised some questions that perhaps do not have to be raised, sinister questions that I associate with an even more sinister challenge, the challenge, namely, to one's right to exist in any form.

The philosopher Morris R. Cohen was once asked by a student, "Professor, how do I know that I exist?"

"So?" Cohen replied. "And who is esking?"

Thanks to Professor Cohen I feel that I stand on firmer ground and can do what I have done all my life: i.e., fall back instinctively on my first consciousness, which has always seemed to me to be most real and easily accessible. For people who have no access to any such core consciousness, no mysteries exist. Linguistic analysts aim to clear away all mysteries—alleged mysteries, they would say. Facts, however, must be respected and the fact is that, for reasons I can't explain, my own first consciousness has had a long unbroken history. I wouldn't know how to defend my faithful attachment to it. All I can say is that it is a fact and I wonder why anyone should feel it necessary to put its reality in doubt. But our meddling mental world puts all such realities in doubt. This world of truly modern, educated, advanced consciousness suspects the core consciousness, which I take to be a fact, of being inauthentic and probably delusive.

I will ask you for the present to believe that I am right and that what I call the meddling mental world is wrong.

So in my first consciousness I was, among other things, a Jew, the child of Jewish immigrants. At home our parents spoke Russian to each other, we children spoke Yiddish with them and we spoke English with one another. At the age of four we began to read the Old Testament in Hebrew, we observed Jewish customs, some of them superstitions, and we recited prayers and blessings all day long. Because I had to memorize most of Genesis, my first consciousness was that of a cosmos and in that cosmos I was a Jew. I suppose it would be proper to apply the word *archaic* to such a representation of the world as I had—archaic, prehistoric. This was my "given" and it would be idle to quarrel with it, to try to revise or efface it.

A millennial belief in a Holy God may have the effect of deepening the soul, but it is also obviously archaic, and modern influences would presently bring me up to date and reveal how antiquated my origins were. To turn away from those origins, however, has always seemed to me an utter impossibility. It would be a treason to my first consciousness to un-Jew myself. One may be tempted to go behind the given and invent something better, to attempt to reenter life at a more advantageous point. In America this is common, we have all seen it done, and done in many instances with great ingenuity. But the thought of such an attempt never entered my mind. Thus I may have been archaic, but I escaped the horrors of an identity crisis.

There were, however, other crises to face. As a high school boy reading *The Decline of the West*, I learned that in Spengler's view ours was a Faustian civilization and that we, the Jews, were Magians, the survivors and representatives of an earlier type, totally incapable of comprehending the Faustian spirit that had created the great civilization of the West, aliens whose adaptive strategies or mimicries were based on blind survival methods or deceits. Thus Disraeli, often called the greatest of nineteenth-century statesmen, didn't actually know what he was doing. He could not naturally enter into the English spirit and he succeeded only by study and artifice.

Reading this, I was deeply wounded. I envied the Faustians and cursed my luck. I had prepared myself to be part of a civilization, one of whose prominent interpreters (Spengler was an international best seller) told me that I was by heredity disqualified. He did not say that I must be put to death and one might be grateful for that. Yet he did pronounce Jews to be fossils, spiritually archaic, and that was in itself a kind of death. I was, however, an American Jew, not a German or a French Jew, and everything in America was different. My boyish hunch was that America, the enlightened source of a liberal order, might be a new venture in civilization, leaving the Faustians in the rear. So that what Magians were to Faustians, Faustians might very well be to Americans. By such ingenious means I held Spengler at bay.

Later I discerned a kind of Darwinism in his kind of history—mankind advanced by evolutionary stages. In the natural history museum I couldn't reconcile myself to the surrounding pterodactyls and ammonites, to standing on a forgotten evolutionary siding. It did no harm to picture myself in a museum. On the contrary, I realized that I didn't belong there.

Having begun this talk without an adequate perspective, I now begin to see an intent in it. The condition I am looking into is that of a young American who in the late Thirties finds that he is something like a writer and begins to think what to do about it, how to position himself and how to combine being a Jew with being an American and a writer. Not everyone thinks well of such a project. The young man is challenged from all sides. Representatives of the Protestant majority want to see his credentials. Less overtly hostile because they are more snobbish, the English want to know who he is or what he thinks he is. Later his French publishers will invariably turn his books over to Jewish translators.

The Jews, too, try to place him. Is he too Jewish? Is he Jewish enough? Is he good or bad for the Jews? Jews in business or politics ask, "Must we forever be reading about his damn Jews?" Jewish critics examine him with a certain sharpness—they have their own axes to grind. As the sons of Jewish immigrants, descendants of the people whose cackling and shrieking set Henry James's teeth on edge when he visited the Lower East Side, they accuse themselves secretly of presumption when they write of Emerson, Walt Whitman or Matthew Arnold. My own view is that since Henry James and Henry Adams did not hesitate to express their dislike of Jews, there is no reason why Jews, while full of respect for these masters, should not be free to write as they please about them. To let them (the hostile American WASPs) determine once and for all what the American psyche is, not to challenge their views where those views are narrow, or to accept the transmission of European infections and racial poisons, would be disloyal and cowardly.

On the other hand one can't always be heroic, and there were times when shades of Brownsville and Delancey Street surrounded Jewish lovers of American literature and they were unhappily wondering what T. S. Eliot or Edmund Wilson would be thinking of them. Among my Jewish contemporaries more than one poet flirted with Anglicanism, and others came up with different evasions, dodges, ruses and disguises. I had little patience with that kind of thing. If the WASP aristocrats wanted to think of me as a Jewish poacher on their precious cultural estates, then let them.

It was in this defiant spirit that I wrote *The Adventures of Augie March* and *Henderson the Rain King*: "I am an American," et cetera. But of course I was not so simpleminded as to think I had satisfied certain persistent and deadly questions. Those were repeatedly thrust upon me by everyone including Jewish writers and thinkers whom I held in great esteem. Back in the Fifties I visited S. Agnon in Jerusalem and as we sat drinking tea, chatting in Yiddish, he asked whether I had been translated into Hebrew. As yet I had not been. He said with lovable slyness that this was most unfortunate. "The language of the Diaspora will not last," he told me. I then sensed that eternity was looming over me and I was aware of my insignificance. I did not however lose all presence of mind and to feed his wit and keep the conversation going I asked, "What will become of poets like poor Heinrich Heine?" Agnon answered, "He has been beautifully translated into Hebrew and his survival is assured."

Agnon was of course insisting that the proper language for a Jewish writer was Hebrew. I didn't care to argue the matter. I was not in a position to dismantle my entire life and start again from scratch in Hebrew. Agnon did not expect me to. Without a trace of ill will he was simply directing my attention to certain chapters of Jewish history. He was sweetly needling me.

Gershom Scholem, whose books I admire, was less gentle. I am told that a statement that I was said to have made in 1976 when I won the Nobel Prize put him in a rage. I was quoted in the papers as saying that I was an American writer and a Jew. Perhaps I should have said that I was a Jew and an American writer. Because Scholem is one of the greatest scholars of the century, I'm sorry I offended him, but having made this bow in his direction, I allow myself to add that the question reminds me of the one small children used to be asked by clumsy Sunday visitors in olden times: "Whom do you love better, your papa or your momma?" I recognized that I answered the reporters unthinkingly, "Writer first, Jew second."

For easily understandable reasons Scholem immediately placed me among those German Jews who had done everything possible to assimilate themselves and of whom Lionel Abel has written (in *The Intellectual Follies*), "German culture was the culture of the gentile world" that was the most admirable. The tragedy of the German Jews, says Scholem (for Abel too is in this passage referring to Scholem), was "that they were destroyed by the nationalist political movement in the nation they loved best."

This, like so many Jewish questions, is deeper and more tragic than it may appear. I shall examine it from my own standpoint, that of an American Jewish writer, and take the discussion back to Agnon, who needled me so sweetly about the vanishing languages of the Diaspora. One's language is a spiritual location, it houses your soul. If you were born in America all essential communications, your deepest communications with yourself, will be in English—in American English. You will neither lie nor tell the truth in any other language. Without it no basic reckonings can be made. You will not reflect on your own death in Hebrew or in French. Your English is the principal instrument of your humanity. And when the door of the gas chamber was shut, many of the German Jews who called upon God for the last time inevitably used the language of their murderers, for they had no other.

Some such recognition lay behind Agnon's teasing warning. Teasing was his Jewish way of being serious with me. He argued that the soul of the Jew must turn its back on Europe and in the Edenic peace of the Promised Land contemplate *hochma*, wisdom. Yes, but the Jews can neither bear nor afford to confine themselves to the Promised Land. Not even those who make *aliyah* can do without Western science, Western culture, Western financing and technology. How agreeable it would have been to study wisdom at Agnon's feet. He said as much: He told me in Yiddish that if I had had enough Hebrew to understand him, I would have longed to see him again (*ihr volt noch mir gebenkgt*). After the nightmare torments of Nazism we could settle down together at last to await the restoration of God's kingdom.

This seemed to me not only a Jewish but also a European Jewish literary vision. In Europe Jews might be welcomed in almost every field of knowledge, but as artists they would inevitably come up against a national or racial barrier. Wagnerism in one form or another would reject them. Goethe was infinitely more reasonable and balanced than Wagner but even he wrote in *Wilhelm Meister* (third book), "We do not tolerate any Jew among us; for how could we grant him a share in the highest culture, the origin and tradition of which he denies?" And Nietzsche wrote in *Beyond Good and Evil*, "I have not yet met a German who was favorably disposed toward the Jews." He did not mean this to be a compliment to the Germans. And then in 1953 Heidegger, described by many as the greatest philosopher of the twentieth century, was still speaking of "the inner truth and greatness of National Socialism."

A share in the highest culture, the origin of which the Jew himself denies? But it is rather the traditional culture that does the denying.

In twentieth-century Europe the *métèque* writers appear in considerable numbers. *Métèque* is defined in French dictionaries as "outsider" or "resident alien" and the term is pejorative. The word appears in the OED as *metic*, although it is not in general use here. The novelist Anthony Burgess refers to *métèques* and makes a strong defense of the *métèque* writer—the non-native who, being on the fringe of a language and the culture that begot it, is alleged to lack respect (so say the pundits) for the finer rules of English idiom and grammar, for "the genius of the language." For, says Burgess, the genius of the English language, being plastic, is as ready to yield to the *métèque* as to the racially pure and grammatically orthodox: "If we are to regard Poles and Irishmen as *métèques* there are grounds for supposing that the *métèques* have done more for English in the twentieth century (meaning that they have shown what the language is really capable of, or demonstrated what English is really *like*) than any of the pure-blooded men of letters who stick to the finer rules."

Burgess's Irishman is Joyce, his Pole Joseph Conrad, and we can easily add to his list Apollinaire in French, Isaac Babel, Mandelstam and Pasternak in Russian, Kafka in German, Svevo in Italian (or Triestine) and for good measure V. S. Naipaul or Vladimir Nabokov. Indeed it is not easy in this cosmopolitan age to remove the *métèques* from modern literature without leaving it very thin.

I might have asked Agnon how well the Arabic of Maimonides had been translated into Hebrew. I lacked the presence of mind then, and even here my remark is slightly out of place.

In the U.S., a land of foreigners who may or may not be in the process of forming a national type (who can predict how it will all turn out?), a term like *métèque* or *metic* is inapplicable. To renew the purity of the tribe was a French project and a man whose French is acceptable to the French is, at least in the act of speaking, a claimant to aristocratic status. But gentile New York and Brahmin Boston never dominated American speech and the aristocratic pretensions of Easterners were good for a laugh in the rest of the country. Yet when our own metics— the Jewish, Italian and Armenian descendants of immigrants—began after World War I to write novels they caused great discomfort and, in some quarters, alarm and anger.

Irving Howe has noted in a reminiscence of the *Partisan Review* days that "portions of the native intellectual elite . . . found the modest fame of the New York writers insufferable. Soon they were mumbling that American purities of speech and spirit were being contaminated by the streets of New York. . . . Anti-Semitism had become publicly disreputable in the years after the Holocaust, a thin coating of shame having settled on civilized consciousness; but this hardly meant that some native writers . . . would lack a vocabulary for private use about those New York usurpers, those Bronx and Brooklyn wise guys who proposed to reshape American literary life. When Truman Capote later attacked the Jewish writers on television, he had the dissolute courage to say what more careful gentlemen said quietly among themselves."

Capote said that a Jewish mafia was taking over American literature and New York publishing as well. He was to write in a later book that Jews should be stuffed and put in a natural history museum.

I owe too much to writers like R. P. Warren, who was so generous to me when I was starting out, and to John Berryman, John Cheever and other poets, novelists, and critics of American descent to complain of neglect, discrimination or abuse. Most Americans judged you according to your merit and to the majority of readers it couldn't have mattered less where your parents were born.

Nevertheless, a Jewish writer could not afford to be unaware of his detractors. He had to thicken his skin without coarsening himself when he heard from a poet he much admired that America had become the land of the wop and the kike; or, from an even more famous literary figure, that his fellow Jews were the master criminals who had imposed their *usura* on long-suffering gentiles, that they had plunged the world into war, and that the *goyim* were cattle driven to the slaughterhouse by Yids. It was the opinion of the leading poet of my own generation that in a Christian society the number of unbelieving Jews must be restricted.

For a Jew, the proper attitude to adopt was the Nietzschean *spernere se sperni*, to despise being despised.

However disagreeable the phenomenon may seem at moments of sensitivity, it is seldom more than trivial. The dislike of Jews was a ready way for WASP literati to identify themselves with the great tradition. Besides, it is something like a hereditary option for non-Jews to exercise at a certain moment when they discover that they have a born right to decide whether they are for the Jews or against them. (Jews have no such right.) At the beginning of the century it offered an opportunity to stand with distinguished intellectual groups of the right. How nice if you came from Idaho or Missouri to identify yourself with Maurras and the anti-Dreyfusards.

Henry Adams was particularly fond of Drumont, the anti-Dreyfusard journalist. Even the most enlightened minds, if you investigate them closely, have their kinky corners. As an example of kinkiness I offer the remark W. H. Auden made to Karl Shapiro after the Bollingen Prize was awarded to Ezra Pound: "Everybody is anti-Semitic sometimes." True enough. We all know it and we are apt to give our favorites a pass, especially favorites on the whole so free from common prejudices as Auden, the most liberating of the modern English poets. He was in every important respect an exception—just as Capote was in everything trivial, predictably nasty.

"We wanted to shake off the fears and constraints of the world in which we had been born," Irving Howe said, speaking of the Jewish writers published by *Partisan Review* in the Thirties and Forties, "but when up against the impenetrable walls of gentile politeness we would aggressively proclaim our 'difference,' as if to raise Jewishness to a higher cosmopolitan power." As we have seen, the gentiles were not always polite. About the rest Howe is quite right. He errs only in viewing the Jewish contributors to *Partisan Review* as a fully united group, identifying them as the "New York writers." At least two of us thought of ourselves as Chicagoans who had grown up in a mixed district of Poles, Scandinavians, Germans, Irishmen, Italians and Jews. The New York writers came from predominantly Jewish communities. I did not wish to become part of the *Partisan Review* gang. Like many of its members I was, however, "an emancipated Jew who refused to deny his Jewishness," and I suppose I should have considered myself a "cosmopolitan" if I had been capable of thinking clearly in those days.

Delmore Schwartz, whom I looked up to, had written an essay calling T. S. Eliot the "international hero," the poet who had most aptly defined the modern condition: shrinkage, decay, estrangement, disappointment, decline—civilization seen from the vantage point of classicism and aristocracy, all of it framed by a distinguished historical consciousness. I did not fit into any of this. In fact I would have been, in Eliot's judgment, part of the decay and part of the reason for his disappointment. It wasn't that I had any relatives who in the slightest resembled Rachel née Rabinovitch who tore at the grapes with murderous paws, but I did feel that I would be consigned to a very low place in Eliot's historical consciousness. Of course I resisted yielding a monopoly to this prestigious consciousness. I suspected that it was untrustworthy, and despite its attractive and glamorous wrappings I believed it to be more sinister than the simple nihilism of the streets. History? Certainly, but in whose version—whom shall we trust to summarize it for us?

I saw, in T. S. Eliot and in Joyce and the other eminent figures of their generation, history as artists since the end of the eighteenth century had understood it—romantic history. Artists, even the most radical, had orthodoxies of their own and held orthodox views of the history of the West. I saw in art itself, when art was what it could be, a source of new evidence that did not necessarily confirm the judgment on modern civilization as formulated by its most prestigious writers. Art could not be limited by their final judgments. Closed opinions precluding further discoveries resembled, to my mind, a rigged auction.

But I think I may be spending too much time on the culture bosses who dominated writers and ruled over English departments and literary journalism. A genteel dictatorship inspired by T. S. Eliot (with a roughneck faction headed by Ezra Pound) and describing itself as traditionalist was in fact profoundly racist. But such things are ultimately without importance, merely distracting. What is imposed upon us by birth and environment is what we are called upon to overcome. The business of the Jewish writer, as Karl Shapiro rightly says in his indispensable book *In Defense of Ignorance*, is not to complain about society but to go beyond complaint.

These merely social matters (unpleasant, uncomfortable) are reduced to triviality by the crushing weight of the Jewish experience of our own time.

In reading Lionel Abel's memoir, *The Intellectual Follies*, I came upon an arresting passage. During the war he had heard accounts of the Nazi terror, Abel says, and reports of extermination camps in Eastern Europe: "But I had no real revelation of what had occurred until sometime in 1946, more than a year after the German surrender, when I took my mother to a motion picture and we saw in a newsreel some details of the entrance of the American Army into the concentration camp at Buchenwald. We witnessed the discovery of the mounds of dead bodies, the emaciated, wasted but still living prisoners who were now being liberated, and of the various means of extermination in the camp, the various gallows and also the buildings where gas was employed to kill the Nazis' victims en masse.

"It was an unforgettable sight on the screen, but as remarkable was what my mother said to me when we left the theater: She said, 'I don't think the Jews can ever get over the disgrace of this.' She said nothing about the moral disgrace to the German nation . . . only about . . . a more than moral disgrace, and one incurred by the Jews. How did they ever get over it? *By succeeding in emigrating to Palestine and setting up the state of Israel.*"

I too had seen newsreels of the camps. In one of them, American bulldozers pushed naked corpses toward a mass grave ditch. Limbs fell away and heads dropped from disintegrating bodies. My reaction to this was similar to that of Mrs. Abel—a deeply troubling sense of disgrace or human demotion, as if by such afflictions the Jews had lost the respect of the rest of humankind, as if they might now be regarded as hopeless victims, incapable of honorable self-defense, and arising from this, probably the common instinctive revulsion or loathing of the extremities of suffering—a sense of personal contamination and aversion. The world would see these dead with a pity that placed them at the margin of humanity.

"Certainly, the Holocaust was a *tragedy*," Abel says. And with a writer's weakness for literary categories he begins to talk about theories of tragedy: "When we think of tragedy we must remember that the best critics of tragedy considered as an art have told us that at the end of tragedy there must be a moment of reconciliation. The human spirit, offended by the excesses of the pitiable and the terrible, has to be reconciled to the reality of things. Some good must come of so much evil; and for the Jews, this good was found only in the setting-up of the state of Israel. What came out of the Holocaust was the success of Zionism."

My note in the margin was "Do we really need to go into this?" I was far from sure that this was the time to bring down the curtain on the Fifth Act. The struggle still went on. What was certain however was that the founders of Israel restored the lost respect of the Jews by their manliness. They removed the curse of the Holocaust, of the abasement of victimization, and for this the Jews of the Diaspora were grateful and repaid Israel with their loyal support. Perhaps a more appropriate category than tragedy, if a category is what we need, would be epic, for centuries of continuous adherence to Jewish ideas does make one think of a long continuing epic, the dedication of a people to something far higher than itself.

In Germany the revival of the epical theme in Wagnerian and later in Hitlerian form may well have been a bid to supersede the Jewish epic. Even the plan to destroy the Jews was epical in scale. The building up of Israel was a further chapter in the epic of the Jews. It probably matters little which literary label one selects, but then I am speaking of Jews and literature so it is not inappropriate to speculate about tragedy and epic, for what is suggested by the foregoing discussion is that, in the modern world of nihilistic abysses and voids, the Jews through the horror of their suffering and their responses to suffering stand apart from the prevailing nihilism of the West. If they wish to separate themselves from this nihilism, they have such a legitimate option.

At the same time, I have often thought that it would be something of a miracle if they had not been driven mad by their experiences in this century. I look up Yeats's poem "Why Should Not Old Men Be Mad?" and see what the provocations of his old men are: a likely lad who turns into a drunken journalist, a promising girl who bears children to a dunce. Yes, private tragedies—one should not minimize them. But put them up against the project of murdering an ancient people in its entirety, think of what it means that your Jewish birth may condemn you to death, and they seem negligible causes of madness.

And I sometimes glimpse in myself, an elderly Jew, a certain craziness or extremism, as if the vessel can no longer hold what is poured into it, and feel that my mental boundaries are crumbling. I occasionally think that I see evidences in Israeli politics of rationality damaged by memories of the Holocaust. And even if we were to accept Abel's cathartic view of Israel and pronounce its Founding a successful Fifth Act—that play, the play of the Founding, may be over, but Jewish involvement in the history of the West is far from concluded. Our own American chapter of it is certainly opened.

Times have changed (they always do, don't they?) since Karl Shapiro published *In Defense of Ignorance*. I read it during the hopeful Sixties and the chapter on the Jewish writer in America left a permanent impression on me. In it Shapiro argues that Jewish creative intelligence has for centuries been driven into bypaths. "The fantastic intellectual powers of the Jews of our time go into everything under the sun except Jewish consciousness," he wrote. "As far as one can tell these things, there are only two countries in the world where the Jewish writer is free to create his own consciousness: Israel and the United States. . . . The European Jew was always a visitor. . . . But in America everybody is a visitor. In this land of permanent visitors the Jew is in a rare position to 'live the life' of a full Jewish consciousness. The Jews live a fantastic historical paradox: we are the spiritual aborigines of the modern world."

Here, says Shapiro, the American Jew has been able to "emerge from the historical consciousness to a full Jewish consciousness."

Later, when he sees similarities between Judaic mystical humanism and American secular humanism, he loses me. But his prior assertion, namely that in the United States the Jewish writer is free to create his own consciousness, is most appealing.

But in creating his own consciousness, what are the limits our Jewish-American writer must expect to consider? I spoke earlier of the nihilistic abysses of the modern world and suggested that Jews, through the horror of Jewish suffering, the enormity of the Final Solution, might stand apart from the nihilism of the West. If they wished to separate themselves from this modern and European nihilism, they might legitimately exercise the option. What did I mean by this?

These are difficult matters. I shall naturally be asked to define nihilism. What is it? We have our choice of a variety of definitions. For Nietzsche nihilism signifies the abolition of all hitherto accepted measures and fundamental values. But that may be too broad to be useful. More to the point is the assertion that nihilism denies the existence of any distinct substantial self. This lack of self-substance makes all persons nugatory or insignificant. If we are insignificant, what does it matter what becomes of us? Still, those who are killed need not accept their definition from their killers or have their humanity taken from them as well as their lives. The burden of valuation is on the killer whose ground is nihilistic.

Let the country that committed the crimes bear the blame for them. The slain were not invited into Nothingness, they had it thrust upon them. We are free to withdraw (to withdraw our minds where we cannot withdraw our bodies) from situations in which our humanity or lack of it is defined for us. It was the judgment of the slayers that slaughter was permitted, that the slain had at best a trivial claim to existence based on an untenable fiction of inviolate selfhood. Theorists of euthanasia had long ago consented to the destruction of the unfit. Even mild vegetarian Fabians like G. B. Shaw (there were others) agreed that measures should be taken by a progressive society to rid itself of defective types. These socially and historically "progressive" reforms were applied in Central Europe by the Nazis with programmatic rigidity and also a kind of purgatorial irony toward the Jews and other peoples judged superfluous. This is what causes me to speak of nihilism.

It would be a mistake on modern grounds to set aside as unimportant the age-long inclination of connecting the spiritual order in the universe with our own lives. In our pragmatic attitude toward the social order we leave no room for the influence of general beliefs on our own particular views of morality. In his recent short book, *Death of the Soul*, the philosopher William Barrett offers a useful discussion of the consequences of the disappearance (the destruction, in fact) of the self. He examines critically Heidegger's treatment of the human being. How, in Heidegger's view, *are* we in the world? We ask of Heidegger, "*Who* is the being who is undergoing all these various modes of being? (Or, in more traditional language: Who is the subject, the I, that underlies or persists through all these various modes of our being?) And here Heidegger evades us." "We are nothing," he says, "but an aggregate of modes of being, and any organizing or unifying center we profess to find there is something we ourselves have forged or contrived."

Thus there is a gaping hole at the center of our human being—at least as Heidegger describes this being. Consequently, we have in the end to acknowledge a certain desolate and empty quality about his thought, however much we may admire the originality and novelty of its construction.

And Barrett asks, "How could a being without a center be really ethical?" He concludes: "[Heidegger] cannot be dismissed: that desolate and empty picture of being he gives us may be just the sense of being that is at work in our whole culture, and we are in his debt for having brought it to the surface. To get beyond him we shall have to live through that sense of being in order to reach the other side." To this I should like to add that questions which can be closed by philosophical argument often remain open for art. It is therefore a mistake for writers to accept the preeminence of the philosophers, and write poems, novels and plays to illustrate, to confirm, to work out in their art and in human detail the thoughts given to us abstractly by distinguished (and also by undistinguished) thinkers (Cartesians, Kantians, Hegelians, Bergsonians, Marxians, Freudians, existentialists, Heideggerians, et cetera). Neither the philosopher nor the scientist can tell the artist conclusively, definitively, what it is to be human.

But enough of this for the moment. I was saying earlier that the fate of the Jews in the twentieth century was to suffer the cruelties of nihilistic thought and nihilistic politics. I did not say that Jews—the survivors and descendants themselves—escaped the desolate and empty picture of being that Barrett correctly tells us "is at work in our whole culture." All of us living in the West must endure this desolation. The feelings it transmits, the motives it instills in us, the human states our surroundings make us familiar with, the invasive force of these states that we are constrained to submit to, the coloration they give to our personalities, the mutilations they inflict on us, the overwhelming shaping powers of a nihilism now commonplace, do not spare anybody. The argument developing here, using me as its instrument, is that Jews as such are not exempt from these ruling forces of desolation. Jewish Orthodoxy obviously claims immunity from this general condition, but most of us do not share this Orthodox conviction. Closely observed, the Orthodox too are seen to be bruised by these ambiguities and the violence that our age releases impartially against us all.

Israelis are also apt to claim immunity, and to a degree the danger of destruction they have to face justifies this. But they too are part of the civilized West. They have necessarily adopted a Western outlook, Western techniques, Western arms, Western organization, Western

There Is Simply Too Much to Think About

banking, Western diplomacy, Western science. The defense of the Zionist state has led to the creation of a mini-superpower, and thus Israel is to a considerable degree obliged to share the malaise we all suffer—the French, the Italians, the Germans, the British, the Americans and the Russians. Israel is narrowly watched by the West, and the Western press and public try hard to find evidences of Jewish evil, and perhaps their aim is to implicate the Jews in nihilism.

The formation of Israel was a response to the nihilistic rage of the two powerful European states that began the war and the complicity of the rest who could not and perhaps would not protect their Jews, and Israel's founders were aware of this. But the Western world now exhibits a certain unwillingness to sanction the Israeli solution—in other words, to let the Jews get away with it. As for Jews in France, England and the United States claiming a share in the common life of their respective countries, they consent to share also in the desperate sense of non-being-in-being—to experience the gaping hole at the center of the self, that despair arising from the dying heart of every "advanced society."

After these remarks on the actual situation of the Jew and the civilization from which he cannot now be separated, I should like to look again at the statement I made in 1976 by which that admirable scholar Gershom Scholem was so displeased—I am an American writer and a Jew. Or, I am a Jew and an American writer. Evidently it made him angry that I should see myself as a writer primarily. Most Americans, on seeing my name, probably say to themselves, "He is a Jew," and then add, "He writes." Here the priorities hardly matter. I am not an assimilationist. As a Jew, however, I have long been aware of the political significance of America in world history, of the unparalleled hospitality of this country to all the branches of humanity.

Nevertheless I am a Jew and as such I am made to understand by Jewish history that I cannot absolutely count on enlightened laws and institutions to protect me and my descendants. I observe the Jewish present closely and actively remember the Jewish past—not only its often heroic suffering but also the high significance of the meaning of Jewish history. I think about it. I read. I try to understand what it may signify to be a Jew who cannot live by the rules of conduct set down over centuries and millennia. I am not, as the phrase goes, an observant

Jew and I doubt that Scholem was wholly Orthodox. He was, however, immersed in Jewish mysticism of the sixteenth century and studied Kabbalism closely, so it is unlikely that he was devoid of religious feeling.

I, by contrast, am an American Jew whose interests are largely, although not exclusively, secular. There is no way in which my American and modern experience of life could be reconciled with Jewish Orthodoxy. So that my ancestors, if they were able to see and judge for themselves, would find me a very strange creature indeed, no less strange than my Catholic, Protestant or atheistic countrymen. Yet their scandalously weird descendant insists that he is a Jew. And of course he is one. He can't be held responsible for the linked historical transformations of which he became the odd heir.

For writers in the West and particularly in the U.S., it is almost too late to resolve the difficulties described above. Hardly anyone now is conscious of them. Writers seldom give any sign that they are aware of the degree of freedom they enjoy here. Their privilege is to be unrestrained in their destructiveness. They show by this that our giant America does not own them. They are very prickly about not being owned. But then nobody takes them very seriously either. To state the matter more clearly, they are not held to account for their opinions. These opinions are a null dust—weightless.

What does this mean? Can it be said that in our dizziness we are annihilating even nihilism?

Jewish writers, if they wish to exercise their option to reject the nihilistic temper, may do so but it will be all the better for them—for us all—if they do not get themselves up as spokesmen for conscience or try to give the world the business, as it were, by their moralizing.

I never wished to avoid being recognized as a Jew in order to escape discrimination. I never cared enough, never granted anyone much power to discriminate against me—and now it is too late to bother about such matters. My view, a view widely held, is that there is no solution to the Jewish problem. Viciousness against Jews will never end in any foreseeable future; nor will the consciousness of being a Jew vanish, since the self-respect of Jews demands that they be faithful to their history and their culture, which is not so much a culture in the modern sense as it is a millennial loyalty to revelation and redemption.

There Is Simply Too Much to Think About

A philosopher whose views on the subject of Judaism have influenced me, Leo Strauss, says that those modern Jews for whom the old faith has gone will prize it as a noble delusion. Assimilation is an impossible—a repulsive—alternative. What is left to us is the contemplation of Jewish history. "The Jewish people and their fate are the living witness for the absence of redemption," this philosopher writes. And he states further that the meaning of the chosen people is to testify to this: "The Jews are chosen to prove the absence of redemption. It is supposed . . . that the world is not the creation of the just and living God, the Holy God, and that for the absence of righteousness and charity we sinful creatures are responsible. A delusion? A dream? But no nobler dream was ever dreamed."

This is not incompatible with Karl Shapiro's assertion that in the United States the Jewish writer is free to create his own consciousness. In creating it he will find it necessary also to contemplate Jewish history and to attempt to discover its inmost meaning. For a modern man this is perhaps what constitutes a Jewish life.

I said at the beginning of this talk, "My first consciousness was that of a cosmos and in that cosmos I was a Jew." After seventy-odd years, some fifty of which have been spent in writing books, I can do no more than describe what has happened, can only offer myself as an illustration. The record will show what the twentieth century has made of me and what I have made of the twentieth century.

[1988]

Chicago: The City That Was, the City That Is

To be concise about Chicago is harder than you might think. The city stands for something in American life, but what that something is has never been altogether clear. Not everybody likes the place. A Chicagoan since 1924, I have come to understand that you have to develop a taste for it and you can't do that without living here for decades. Even after decades you can't easily formulate the reasons for your attachment because the city is always transforming itself and the scale of the transformations is tremendous.

Chicago builds itself up, knocks itself down again, scrapes away the rubble and starts over. European cities destroyed in war were painstakingly restored. Chicago does not restore; it makes something wildly different. To count on stability here is madness. A Parisian can always see the Paris that was, as it has been for centuries. A Venetian, as long as Venice is not swallowed up in mud, has before him the things his ancestors saw. But a Chicagoan as he wanders about the city feels like a man who has lost many teeth. His tongue explores the gaps. Let's see now: Here the Fifty-fifth Street car turned into Harper Avenue at the end of the trolley line; then the conductor hurried through the car, reversing the cane seats. Then he reset the trolley on the power line. On this corner stood Kootich Castle, a bohemian rooming house and hangout for graduate students, photographers, would-be painters, philosophical radicals and lab technicians (one young woman kept white mice as pets). Harper Avenue wasn't exactly the banks of the Seine; none of the buildings resembled Sainte-Chapelle. They were downright ugly but they were familiar, they were ours, and the survival of what is ours gives life its continuity. It is not our destiny here to get comfort from old familiar places. We can't, we Chicagoans, settle back sentimentally among our souvenirs.

From the west your view of the new skyscrapers is unobstructed. The greatest of them all, the Sears Tower, shimmers among its companions, all of them armored like Eisenstein's Teutonic knights staring over the ice of no-man's-land at Alexander Nevsky. The plan is to advance again westward from the center of the city and fill up the vacant streets, the waste places, with apartment buildings and shopping malls. Nobody at present can say whether this is feasible, whether the great corporations and banks will have sufficient confidence in the future of a city whose old industries are stalled, whose legendary rail yards are empty. Ours is the broadest band of rust in all the Rust Belt.

A fiction writer by trade, I see myself also as something of a historian. More than thirty years ago I published *The Adventures of Augie March*, a novel that is in part a record of Chicago in the Twenties and Thirties. I see by the college catalogs that my book is studied in a considerable number of schools. It is read in Yugoslavia too, and in Turkey and China, so that throughout the world people are forming a picture of Chicago, the setting of Augie's adventures. But that Chicago no longer exists. It is to be found only in memory and in fiction. Like the Cicero of Al Capone, like Jack London's Klondike, like Fenimore Cooper's forests, like Gauguin's Pacific paradise, like Upton Sinclair's Jungle, it is now an imaginary place only. The Thirties have been wiped out: houses in decay, vacant lots, the local characters—grocers, butchers, dentists, neighbors—gone to their reward, the survivors hidden away in nursing homes, doddering in Florida, dying of Alzheimer's disease in Venice, California. A lively new Latin population occupies my old ward, the Twenty-sixth. Its old houses have collapsed or been burned. The school dropout rate is one of the city's highest, the dope pushers do their deals openly. Revisiting Division Street on a winter day, examining the Spanish graffiti, the dark faces, reading strange inscriptions on shop windows, one feels as Rip Van Winkle might have felt if after his long sleep he had found not his native village but a barrio of San Juan. This crude, brazen city of European immigrants is now, in large part, a city of blacks and Hispanics.

The speed of the cycles of prosperity and desolation is an extraordinary challenge to historians and prophets. Chicago was founded in 1833 so it hasn't been here long enough to attract archaeologists, as Rome and Jerusalem do. Still, longtime residents may feel that they have their own monuments and ruins and that accelerated development has compacted the decades, making them comparable to centuries, has put Chicagoans through a crash program in aging. If you've been here long enough, you've seen the movement of history with your own eyes and have had a good taste of history; of eternity, perhaps.

So many risings and fallings, so much death, rebirth, metamorphosis, so many tribal migrations. To young Midwesterners at the beginning of the century this was the electrifying regional capital. Here students from Ohio or Wisconsin studied their trades, becoming doctors, engineers, journalists, architects, singers. Here they made contact with civilization and culture. Here Armour, Insull and Yerkes accumulated huge fortunes in pork, gas, electricity or transit. Their immigrant employees, hundreds of thousands of them, lived in industrial villages— Back of the Yards, out by the steel mills, the Irish on "Archie Road," the Greeks, Italians and Jews on Halsted Street, the Poles and Ukrainians along Milwaukee Avenue.

It wasn't so long ago in calendar years that Carl Sandburg was celebrating Chicago the youthful giant, the hog butcher of the world, the player with railroads. But the farm boys, seduced under streetlamps by prostitutes, have vanished (as have the farms from which they came). The stockyards long ago moved to Kansas and Missouri and the rail yards are filling up with new "Young Executive" housing. And even Sandburg's language is dated. It is the language of the advertising agencies of the Twenties and in part recalls the slogans that came from City Hall when Big Bill Thompson was mayor. "Boost, don't knock," he told us. "Lay down your hammer. Get a horn."

What would we have been boosting? Real power in the city belonged to the Insulls and other magnates, to La Salle Street, to the venal politicians. From his headquarters in Cicero and on Twenty-second Street, the anarch Al Capone and his mob of comical killers sold beer and booze, ran the rackets. They bought cops and officials as one would buy popcorn. Big Bill was one of our fun politicians, like Bathhouse John and Hinky-Dink Kenna, politician-entertainers who kept the public laughing. I was one of hundreds of thousands of kids to whom Big Bill's precinct captains distributed free passes to Riverview Park to ride the Bobs and make faces in fun-house mirrors, to eat cotton candy that tickled you like a beard and disintegrated instantly on your tongue. If you had a nickel to spare you could try to win a Kewpie doll in the shooting gallery. At the age of twelve I was one of Big Bill's fans. Schoolchildren loved him.

The mayor liked to show himself in public and after his retirement, in his declining years, you saw him chauffeured through the Loop in his limousine. He was solitary, glum, silent. One great paw hung through the velvet strap. Part of his youth was spent on the range so he generally wore a cowboy hat. Under it he looked swollen and corrupted. Rouault might have liked to do a portrait of him, one of those mountainous faces he painted—this one against a background of blazing Chicago boredom.

Big Bill is as remote from us today as Sennacherib or Ashurbanipal. Only antiquarians ever think of him. But Chicago still "boosts." Under Mayor Daley (the first) we were "The City That Works." The developers who have remade the north end of Michigan Boulevard announced that they had created a Magnificent Mile. Nothing less. Here Neiman-Marcus, Lord & Taylor, Marshall Field's, Gucci and Hammacher Schlemmer have established themselves in all their pride. A thick icing of comfort and luxury has been spread over the northern end of the business district with its boutiques, bars, health clubs and nouvelle cuisine restaurants. The John Hancock Tower and One Magnificent Mile are the most prestigious addresses in town. From their privileged windows you look over Lake Michigan with its pleasure boats and water-pumping stations. To the south you see the refineries of Hammond and Gary and the steel mills, or what is left of them. Turning westward, you see the notorious Cabrini Green public housing blocks, one of the many projects built for a welfare population. Actually the slums are best seen from the elevation of a ninety-five-story skytop restaurant—a wonderful opportunity for landscape lovers.

You can't be neutral about a place where you have lived so long. You come to recognize at last how much feeling you have invested in it. It's futile to think, like Miniver Cheevy, that you might have done better in another time, in a more civilized city. You were assigned to this one, as were your parents, brothers, cousins, classmates, your friends—most of them in the cemeteries beyond city limits. Where fires, wrecking balls and falling masonry have done so much demolition, human attachments rise in value. So I seek out my cousin the baker, I go to see an old chum try a case in criminal court. I attend city council meetings and public hearings, I talk with Winston Moore about black politics or lunch at the Bismarck with one of the late Mayor Daley's assistants. City politics are comic opera. Circuit judges are convicted of racketeering. One can only guess how many grand juries are hearing testimony and preparing indictments. On my rounds, feeling like an unofficial, unsalaried inspector, I check out the new apartment houses on the banks of the Chicago River, in my time an industrial wasteland. To call these expeditions sad wouldn't be accurate. I am not heavyhearted. I am uneasy but also terribly curious, deeply intrigued. After all I am no mere spectator, for I have invested vital substance in these surroundings; we have exchanged influences—in what proportions I can't say.

In moments of weakness you are tempted to take seriously the opinions of those urbanologists who say that the great American cities of the North are nineteenth-century creations belonging to an earlier stage of capitalism and that they have no future. But then a *Chicago Tribune* article announces that two hundred national retailers, developers and leasing agents have met at the Hilton to plan new stores outside the Loop. Do they see a dying city dominated by youth gangs who do battle in the ruined streets? They do not! Urban shopping strips are "creating vibrant inner-city communities," we are told. Mayor Washington and "city council stalwarts" are "selling Chicago" to dozens of prospective investors.

Like other Chicagoans of my generation, I ask myself how it's all going to come out. In the past we watched events. We had no control over them, of course. But they were lively, they were good entertainment. The Democratic bosses—Tony Cermak, Kelly-Nash and Richard Daley—did not take a terribly high view of human nature, nor were they abstractly concerned with justice. They ran a tight oligarchy. Politicians made profitable arrangements but governed with a fair degree of efficiency. The present administration has little interest in efficiency.

The growing black and Hispanic population has made a successful bid for power. Irish, Greek, Polish and Italian voters are vainly resisting. As conflicts widen and lawsuits multiply, property taxes go up and services diminish. Not many people mourn the disintegration of the machine, but what will replace it? Everything seems up for grabs and everybody asks, "Will we make it?" The city's tax base has moved to the suburbs. For suburbanites the city is a theater. From Schaumburg, Barrington and Winnetka they watch us on their TV screens.

Will Chicago, that dauntless tightrope walker who has never yet fallen, get a charley horse in the middle of the high wire? Those of us like myself who have never abandoned Chicago—the faithful—tell ourselves that he's not going to fall. For we simply can't imagine what America would be without its great cities. What can the boondocks offer us? We too would become mere onlookers and U.S. history would turn into a TV show to be watched like any other program: the death of the tropical rain forests or the history of Egypt's pyramids.

Walking on Le Moyne Street, looking for the house the Bellow family lived in half a century ago, I find only a vacant lot. Stepping over the rubble, I picture the rooms overhead. There is only emptiness around, not a sign of the old life. Nothing. But it's just as well, perhaps, that there should be nothing physical to hang on to. It forces you inward, to look for what endures. Give Chicago half a chance and it will turn you into a philosopher.

[1983]

The Nineties and After

There Is Simply Too Much to Think About

Asked for an opinion on some perplexing question of the day, I sometimes say that I am for all the good things and against all the bad ones. Not everybody is amused by such a dinner-table joke. Many are apt to feel that I consider myself too good for this world, which is, of course, a world of public questions.

Was President Kennedy right to tell us, "Ask not what your country can do for you; ask what you can do for your country"? In the ordinary way of life, what can one do for one's country? One can be preoccupied with it. That is, one can hold enlightened opinions. Most people conclude that there isn't much, practically speaking, they can do. A few become activists and fly around the country demonstrating or remonstrating. They are able to do this in a free and prosperous America. I speculate sometimes about the economics of militancy. There must be a considerable number of people with small private incomes whose life-work is to march in protest, to picket, to be vocal partisans. At this moment the *Roe v. Wade* issue has attracted demonstrators to Washington and to Buffalo. Atomic energy, environmentalism, women's rights, homosexual rights, AIDS, capital punishment, various racial issues—such are the daily grist of newspapers and networks. The public is endlessly polled, the politicians and their advisers are guided in their strategies by poll statistics. And this, let's face it, is "the action." This is where masses of Americans find substance, importance, find definition through a combination of passion and ineffectuality. The level of public discussion is unsatisfactory. As we become aware of this our hearts sink. The absence of articulate political leadership in the country makes us feel that we are floundering.

What are we, today, in a position to do about the crises chronicled daily in *The New York Times*—about the new Russia and the new Germany; about Peru and China and drugs in the South Bronx and racial strife in Los Angeles, the rising volume of crimes and diseases, the disgrace of the so-called educational system; about ignorance, fanaticism, about the clownish tactics of candidates for the Presidency?

Is it possible to take arms against a sea of troubles so boundless?

Wherever it is feasible, arms of course should be taken. But we must also consider what it requires to face the trouble-sea in its planetary vastness—what an amount of daily reading it demands of us, to say nothing of historical knowledge. It was brave of Karl Marx to assert that the time had come for thinkers to be doers. But to consider what his intellectual disciples *did* in the twentieth century will send us back to our seats. It is, after all, no small thing to correct our opinions frequently; and when you come right down to it, the passivity imposed upon us forces us to acknowledge how necessary it is to think hard, to reject what is mentally dishonorable.

We feel heavy when we recognize the limits of our effectiveness in the public sphere, when we acknowledge the weight of the burden laid upon us and the complexities we have to take into account—when we become aware of the impoverished state of public discussion. Reading and hearing what most editorialists and TV commentators tell us about the recent Los Angeles riots, for instance, forces us to recognize that few opinion-makers are able to think at all. To leave matters in their hands is an acute danger.

"The Good are attracted by Men's perceptions, / And think not for themselves." William Blake, who wrote this about two hundred years ago, did not really believe in the goodness of the nonthinking good. He meant that the nonthinking good were inclined to surrender their mental freedom to the cunning—the sharpers and con artists—who would eventually show "their private ends."

It is apparent to experienced observers that well-meaning people emphatically prefer the "good" things. Their desire is to be identified with the "best." The more prosperous and the "better educated" they are, the greater the effort to identify themselves with the most widely accepted and respected opinions. So they are naturally for justice, for caring and compassion, for the abused and oppressed, against racism, sexism, homophobia, against discrimination, against imperialism, colonialism, exploitation, against smoking, against harassment—for all the good things, against all the bad ones. Seeing people virtually covered with credentials, buttons, badges, I am reminded of the layers of medals and campaign ribbons worn by Soviet generals in official photographs.

People who have the best of everything also desire the best opinions. Top of the line. The right sort of right thinking, moreover, makes social intercourse smoother. The wrong sort exposes you to accusations of insensitivity, misogyny and, perhaps worst of all, racism. As the allure of agreement—or conformism—grows, the perils of independence deepen. To differ is dangerous. And yet, as we all must know, to run from the dangers of dissent is cowardly.

So much for the first part of Blake's proposition: "The good are attracted by Men's perceptions." Now for part two: "And think not for themselves."

To illustrate what this may mean, one need go no further than the daily papers. As I write, the *Chicago Tribune* reprints a piece on Michael Jackson, the pop music prodigy, by Charles Burress, a staff writer for the *San Francisco Chronicle*. Michael Jackson's video "Black and White" attracted a worldwide audience of half a billion youngsters. Jackson, Burress says, has achieved "monumental prominence in the cultural landscape." To what is this prominence due? Jackson frolics over the boundaries of race and sex, Burress writes. We've told our children that race shouldn't matter, that boys and girls are equal, and that many sexual roles are arbitrary. Could youngsters be enthralled at seeing these ideas made flesh?

"The refrain in the 'Black and White' video is 'It doesn't matter if you're black or white.' Most riveting is a computer-enhanced segment where a person changes ethnicity and sex in rapid succession. Jackson seems to be saying we are first of all human, and secondarily male or female, one race or another. He urges us toward human unity and away from prejudice."

And finally: "In a world threatened by racial tensions and overpopulation, the survival instinct could summon a new human, one who has no single race and who, by being most asexually androgynous, is less subject to the procreative urge."

Readers may feel that I have gone far out of my way to find such a bizarre example. But no. Those of us who read widely in the popular press and watch the flakier channels of cable TV know that views like Burress's are not at all uncommon. The language he uses identifies him as a college graduate—possibly, though not necessarily, a California product. Besides, his preoccupation is with what appears to have become a national project—namely, the fashioning of a new outlook, a new mind. The mind of this "new human" is synthetic, homogeneous, improved. It transcends the limits of heredity, nature and tradition, goes beyond all limits and all obstacles. "How do we object to [Jackson's] changing his appearance when we tolerate many body alterations, from shaving and bodybuilding to face-lifts and sex-change operations?" Burress asks.

Now, a term widely understood to signify not thinking for oneself is ideology. Ideology for Marx was a class-induced deformation, a corruption of reality by capitalism. Ideology, to make it short, is a system of false thinking and nontruth that can lead to obedience and conformity. In putting Mr. Burress in the high company of Marx, my sole purpose is to throw light on the attempted invention of an altogether new human type. This new and "more desirable" American will be all the good things: a creature of no single race, an androgyne, free from the disturbing influence of Eros. The idea is to clobber everything that used to be accepted as given, fixed, irremediable. Can it be that we are tired of whatever it is that we in fact are—black, white, brown, yellow, male, female, large, small, Greek, German, English, Jew, Yankee, Southerner, Westerner, et cetera—that what we now want is to rise above all tiresome differences? Perhaps gene fixing will eventually realize this utopia for us.

But the rejection of thinking in favor of wishful egalitarian dreaming takes many other forms. There is simply too much to think about. It is hopeless—too many kinds of special preparation are required. In electronics, in economics, in social analysis, in history, in psychology, in international politics most of us are, given the oceanic proliferating complexity of things, paralyzed by the very suggestion that we assume responsibility for so much. This is what makes packaged opinion so attractive.

It is here that the representatives of knowledge come in—the pundits, the anchormen, the specialist guests of talk shows. What used to be called an exchange of views has become "dialogue" and "dialogue" has been invested with a certain sanctity. Actually it bears no resemblance to any form of real communication. It is a hard thing to describe. Two or more chests covered with merit badges are competitively exposed to public view. We sit, we look, we listen, we are attracted by the perceptions of hosts and guests.

When I was young the great pundits were personalities like H. G. Wells or George Bernard Shaw or Havelock Ellis or Romain Rolland. We respectfully read what they had to say about communism, fascism, peace, eugenics, sex. I recall these celebrities unsentimentally. Wells, Shaw and Romain Rolland brought punditry into disrepute. The last of the world-class mental giants was Jean-Paul Sartre, one of whose contributions to world peace was to exhort the oppressed of the third world to slaughter whites indiscriminately. It is hard to regret the passing of this occasionally vivid spirit.

On this side of the Atlantic our present anchormen are the successors of the Arthur Brisbanes, Heywood Brouns and Walter Lippmanns of the Twenties, Thirties and Forties. Clearly, figures like Peter Jennings, Ted Koppel, Dan Rather and Sam Donaldson, with their easy and immediate access to the leaders of the nation, have infinitely more power than their predecessors, those old wordmen. Rather odd-looking, today's tribunes (not magistrates chosen by the people) are—with their massive hairdos—the nearest thing observable to the wigs of Versailles or the Court of St. James's. These crowns of hair contribute charm and dignity but perhaps also oppress the brain with their weight. They make us aware, furthermore, of the study and calculation behind the naturalness of these artists of information. They speak so confidently and so much on such a variety of topics—do they really know enough to be so fluent? On a talk show not long ago, a prominent American declared that the Roosevelt administration had closely supported Hitler until the Pearl Harbor attack. The journalists on his panel made no objection to this. Had none of them heard of Lend-Lease, hadn't they read about FDR, were they unaware of Nazi hostility toward the United States? Can these high-finish, well-tailored and hairstyled interviewers know so little about history?

America is, of course, the land of the present; its orientation is toward the future. That Americans should care so little about the past is fetching, even endearing, but why should we take the judgments of these splendid-looking men and women on public matters seriously? That they have had "backgrounders" or briefings we may take for granted. One is reluctant to conclude that their omniscience is a total put-on. But this too may be beside the point. The principal aim of these opinion makers is to immerse us again in a marinade of "correctness" or respectability.

What is it necessary that we Americans should know? When is ignorance irrelevant? Perhaps Americans grasp intuitively that what really matters to humankind is here—all around us in the capitalist U.S.A. Lincoln Steffens, playing the pundit in Russia after the Revolution, said: "I have been over into the future, and it works." Some secret wisdom! As a horseplayer he would have lost his shirt. Sigmund Freud, visiting the U.S. before World War I, said America was a great experiment that wasn't going to work. Later he called it a *misgeburt*—a miscarriage. This was the judgment of German high culture on us. Perhaps the death camps of World War II would have changed Freud's mind.

That America is an experiment has been said often enough (probably more often said than understood). Consistent with this—in a small way—Charles Burress on Michael Jackson is advocating experimentation. "Suppose Jackson were seen," he writes, "not as a freak, but as a brave pioneer devoting his own body to exploring new frontiers of human identity." The underlying hypothesis seems to be that we human beings, considered as material, are totally plastic and that the material of which we are made will take any (improving) shape we choose to give it. A less kindly word for it is *programming*. The postulate is that it is necessary to reject what we are by nature, that the given, the original, the creature of flesh and blood, is defective, shameful, in need of alteration, correction, conversion, that this entity, as is, can contribute nothing and that it would be better to remake us totally. In my youth the civilized world was taken aback by the Stalin model of Soviet Man as pictured in newspapers and textbooks, in art and literature. Stalinist falsification, we called this. Now we too seem to have come up with a synthetic man, a revised, improved American. What this implies is that the human being has no core—more accurately, that his personal core, if there should be one, would be undesirable, wicked, perverse, a lump of prejudices: no damn good at all.

We are beginning to feel the effects of this project. Perhaps the personal core, or what we are by nature, is becoming aware that what lies behind this drive to revise us is tyranny, that consciousness raising and sensitivity training are meant to force us to be born again without color, without race, sexually neutered, politically purified and with minds shaped and programmed to reject "the bad" and affirm "the good." Will the real human being become *persona non grata*? No wonder so many of us are in a blue funk.

A self-improving lot, Americans have a weakness for this kind of thing: the idealist holding aloft a banner with a strange device. Huck Finn had no use for the nice bright clean New England boy advancing under the motto *Excelsior*. When Aunt Sally threatened to "sivilize" him he decided to "light out for the Territory ahead." There was a time when it was normal for American children to feel that "self-improvement" propaganda would lead us not up the mountain but into the sloughs.

In the matter of opinion, Americans are vulnerable to ideologues, "originators," trendsetters, heralds of better values. Lacking the sustaining traditions of older cultures, we cast about for prescriptions; we seek—in our uncertainty—the next necessary and "correct" step. I can't at the moment remember who it was who said (it sounds like Elbert Hubbard or perhaps R. W. Emerson), "Invent a better mousetrap and the world will beat a path to your door." Revised and updated, this would go: "Invent a new cliché and you will make it big."

Perhaps the worst thing of all is the language used by these "originators," these heralds of the new. Can anything palpably, substantially, recognizably human be described in words like theirs? It was perhaps in reaction to the degradation of this newspeak—the very latest—that I instinctively turned to William Blake:

The Good are attracted by Men's perceptions,
And think not for themselves;
Till Experience teaches them to catch
And to cage the Fairies & Elves.
And then the Knave begins to snarl
And the Hypocrite to howl;
And all his good Friends shew their private ends,
And the Eagle is known from the Owl.

[1992]

Writers, Intellectuals, Politics:
Mainly Reminiscence

When the Bolsheviks took power in 1917 I was two years old. My parents had emigrated from St. Petersburg to Montreal in 1913, so events in Russia were on their minds and at the dinner table the Tsar, the War, the front, Lenin, Trotsky were mentioned as often as parents, sisters and brothers in the old country. Among Jews it was scarcely conceivable that the great monarchy should have fallen. Skeptical older immigrants believed that the Bolshevik upstarts would soon be driven out. Their grown children, however, were keen to join the Revolution and I can remember how my father argued in the street with Lyova, the son of our Hebrew teacher, who said he had already bought his *schiffskarte*, his ticket. My father shouted that the new regime was worthless, but the young were then accustomed to respect their elders so Lyova smiled—deferential but immovable. He went off to build a new order under Lenin and Trotsky. And he disappeared.

Much later, after we had moved to Chicago and I was old enough to read Marx and Lenin, my father would say, "Don't you forget what happened to Lyova—and I haven't heard from my sisters in years. I don't want any part of your Russia and your Lenin."

But in my eyes my parents were Russians, with agreeable Russian traits. They had brought with them a steamer trunk filled with St. Petersburg finery—brocaded vests, a top hat, a tailcoat, linen sleeping suits with pleated fronts, black taffeta petticoats, ostrich feathers and button boots with high heels. Of no use in the dim Ultima Thule of Montreal or in proletarian Chicago, they were the playthings of the younger children. The older ones quickly and eagerly Americanized themselves in the U.S. and the rest soon followed suit. The country took us over. It *was* a country then, not a collection of "cultures." We felt that to be here was a great piece of luck. The children of immigrants in my Chicago high school, however, believed that they were also somehow Russian, and while they studied their *Macbeth* and Milton's *L'Allegro* they read Tolstoy and Dostoyevsky as well, and went on inevitably to Lenin's *State and Revolution* and the pamphlets of Trotsky. The Tuley High School debating club discussed *The Communist Manifesto* and on the main stem of the neighborhood, Division Street, the immigrant intelligentsia lectured from soapboxes while at "the forum," a church hall on California Avenue, debates between socialists, communists and anarchists attracted a fair number of people. This was the beginning of my radical education. For on the recommendation of friends I took up Marx and Engels and I remember, in my father's bleak office near the freight yards, blasting away at *Value, Price, and Profit* while the police raided a brothel across the street—for nonpayment of protection, probably—throwing beds, bedding and chairs through the shattered windows.

The Young Communist League tried to recruit me in the late Thirties. Too late—I had already read Trotsky's pamphlet on the German question and was convinced that Stalin's errors had brought Hitler to power.

Curious how widely information of world politics was disseminated and in what odd corners around the globe positions then were taken. When the poet Mandelstam interviewed a Comintern member in 1923 he asked, "How has Gandhi's movement affected you in Indochina? Have you experienced any vibrations, any echoes?' 'No,' answered my companion"—identified as Nguyen Ai Quoc, known to us as Ho Chi Minh. Mandelstam describes him to us: "At heart he is but a boy, thin and lithe, sporting a knitted wool jacket."

Few boys, I need hardly say, became Comintern members. For millions of them worldwide, however, the October Revolution was a great reverberator whose echoes of freedom and justice you could not choose but hear. That revolution was for many decades the most important, most prestigious event in history. Its partisans held that it had brought to an end the most monstrous of wars and that Russia's revolutionary proletariat had made mankind the gift of a great hope. Now the oppressed everywhere, under communist leadership, would destroy decadent capitalist imperialism. In Depression Chicago, boys at heart—and girls as well—were putting their revolutionary thoughts in order. The program was not very clear but the prospect was immensely thrilling. Full ideological clarity would not arrive for some time.

In college (1933) I was a Trotskyist. Trotsky instilled into his young followers the orthodoxy peculiar to the defeated and ousted. We belonged to the movement, we were faithful to Leninism and could expound its historical lessons and describe Stalin's crimes. My closest friends and I were not, however, activists; we were writers. Owing to the Depression we had no career expectations. We got through the week on five or six bucks, and if our rented rooms were small the libraries were lofty, were beautiful. Through "revolutionary politics" we met the demand of the times for action. But what really mattered was the vital personal nourishment we took from Dostoyevsky or Herman Melville, from Dreiser and John Dos Passos and Faulkner. By filling out a slip of paper at the Crerar Library on Randolph Street you could get all the bound volumes of *The Dial* and fill long afternoons with T. S. Eliot, Rilke and E. E. Cummings. Toward the end of the Thirties *Partisan Review* was our own *Dial*, with politics besides. There we had access to our significant European contemporaries—Silone, Orwell, Koestler, Malraux, André Gide and Auden. *Partisan's* leading American contributors were Marxists—critics and philosophers like Dwight Macdonald, James Burnham, Sidney Hook, Clement Greenberg, Meyer Schapiro and Harold Rosenberg. The *PR* intellectuals had sided with Trotsky quite naturally during the Moscow trials. Hook had persuaded his teacher John Dewey to head a commission of inquiry in Mexico. We followed the proceedings bitterly, passionately, for we were, of course, the Outs; the Stalinists were the Ins. We alone in the U.S.A. knew what a bad lot they were. FDR and his New Dealers didn't have a clue; they understood neither Russia nor communism.

But our own movement, we began to learn, was often foolish, even conspicuously absurd. During the Spanish Civil War the issue of material aid for the Spanish Republic was furiously debated by comrades who didn't have a dime to contribute. A more serious challenge to our loyalty was the invasion of Finland by the Red Army. Trotsky argued

Writers, Intellectuals, Politics: Mainly Reminiscence 393

that a workers' state could not by definition wage an imperialist war. The invasion was progressive since it would nationalize property, an irrevocable step toward socialism. Faithful to the October Revolution, Trotsky fought the dissenters, of whom there were now many. The split this led to did not come to the attention of the American public, which in any case would have preferred Disney's *Fantasia* to our kind.

Although I now drifted away from Marxist politics, I still admired Lenin and Trotsky. After all, I had first heard of them in the high chair while eating my mashed potatoes. How could I forget that Trotsky had created the Red Army, that he had read French novels at the front while defeating Denikin? That great crowds had been swayed by his coruscating speeches? The glamour of the Revolution still cast its spell. Besides, the most respected literary and intellectual figures had themselves yielded to it. Returning from a visit to Russia, Edmund Wilson had spoken about "the moral light at the top of the world," and it was Wilson who had introduced us to Joyce and Proust. His history of revolutionary thought, *To the Finland Station*, was published in 1940. By that time Poland had been invaded and France had fallen to the Nazis.

Nineteen forty was also the year of Trotsky's assassination. I was in Mexico at the time and an acquaintance of the Old Man, a European lady whom I had met in Taxco, had arranged a meeting. Trotsky agreed to receive my friend Herbert Passin and me in Coyoacán. It was on the morning of our appointment that he was struck down. Arriving in Mexico City we were met by the headlines. When we went to his villa we must have been taken for foreign journalists and we were directed to the hospital. The emergency room was in disorder. We had only to ask for Trotsky. A door into a small side room was opened for us and there we saw him. He had just died. A cone of bloody bandages was on his head. His cheeks, his nose, his beard, his throat were streaked with blood and with dried iridescent trickles of iodine.

He is reported to have said once that Stalin could kill him whenever he liked and now we understood what a far-reaching power could do with us; how easy it was for a despot to order a death; how little it took to kill us, how slight a hold we with our historical philosophies, our ideas, programs, purposes, wills, had on the matter we were made of.

The Great Depression was a time of personal humiliation for those who had worked and lived in respectable prosperity. Capitalism seemed to have lost its control over the country. To many, the overthrow of the government looked like a distinct possibility. In the early Depression years the policies dictated by the communist leadership during its rigid and grim third period had had little success in the U.S.A. A new Popular Front policy was announced when Hitler began to demolish the parties of the left. For American communists the Popular Front, temperate and apparently conciliatory, was a bonanza. The Party was freed from its foreign-sounding jargon and began instead to speak the language of Wobblies and working stiffs. Embracing native populism, it sang folk songs and played guitars. Not Lenin and Stalin but Jefferson and Lincoln sat at the center of the new pantheon. The New Deal philosophy of FDR as we heard it in fireside chats generated warmth and confidence. Henry Wallace announced that this was the century of the common man. The Popular Front identified itself with this new populism and the CP learned for the first time how heady it was to be in the mainstream of national life. The country appeared to be having a great cultural revival. Writers and actors were attracted by well-endowed front organizations and fellow-traveling groups. The left had struck it rich.

I was myself a not ungrateful beneficiary of the New Deal. Toward the end of the Thirties I was employed by the WPA Writers' Project. Our stars in the Chicago office were Jack Conroy and Nelson Algren— neither of them out of favor with the Communist Party. Algren was indeed an original, unfortunately susceptible to ideological infection, a radical bohemian in a quickly dated Chicago style. Few of the younger generation of gifted writers were untouched by the Popular Front influence. I refer not only to those who were later victimized in the hysteria generated by McCarthy but also to certain of the more prestigious contributors to *The Nation* and *The New Republic* who had gone along with the CP during the civil war in Spain (e.g., Malcolm Cowley). The Popular Front style was distinctive and its "culture" was easily recognizable in writers like Clifford Odets, Lillian Hellman or Dalton Trumbo, and in critics or radio writers who may as well remain nameless. It survives even now and you need do no more than mention Whittaker Chambers or Alger Hiss or J. Robert Oppenheimer or the Rosenbergs at a dinner table to learn how durable the issues and dogmas of the Thirties and early postwar years have remained.

It is perfectly true, as Charles Fairbanks has suggested, that totalitarianism in our century has shaped the very definition of what an intellectual is. The "vanguard fighters" who acted under Lenin's direction in October were intellectuals and perhaps the glamour of this event had its greatest effect on intellectuals in the West. Among political activists this was sufficiently evident, but the Bolshevik model was immensely influential everywhere. Trotsky and T. E. Lawrence were perhaps the most outstanding of the intellectual activists to emerge from World War I—the former as Lenin's principal executive, Lawrence as the delicate scholar and recluse, a Fortinbras materializing in the Arabian desert. Malraux was inspired by both men, obviously, an aesthete and a theorist eager in his first phase for revolutionary action and manifesting a curious relish for violence in a great cause. It was he who set an example for French writers of the Forties. Sartre was certainly one of his descendants and many in France and elsewhere modeled themselves upon him, up to the time when he abjured revolution. There was a trace of this also in Arthur Koestler, who so often exposed himself to personal danger, but it was especially in France, between the Thirties and the time of Régis Debray, that leftist intellectuals presented themselves in the West as soldiers of the revolution.

The Leninist style had been adopted by Berlin intellectuals in the Twenties. Bertolt Brecht's *The Measures Taken* represents the central precept of Leninism, namely the primacy of the Party, and it dramatizes with great power the tragedy of disobedience—the failure of a Party worker to achieve the utter self-effacement demanded by "History." Martin Esslin tells us most vividly about Brecht himself—the public persona of the literary *enfant terrible,* the truck driver's jacket and dirty visored cap he wore. In proletarian costume he "drove around Berlin at great speed" but wore the steel-rimmed glasses of a "minor civil servant or village schoolmaster." Lenin himself has been characterized as a

There Is Simply Too Much to Think About

gymnasium teacher from Simbirsk: the Great Headmaster is what Edmund Wilson calls him. A powerhouse disguised as a pedant. The Lenin style was also favored by bohemian intellectuals in Greenwich Village. A valuable comment on this has been made by the art critic Clement Greenberg, who was himself preoccupied with the Great Headmaster's personality. He says of Brecht: "Lenin's precepts became for him an eternal standard of conduct, and Bolshevism a way of life and a habit of virtue." And in another place: "the followers of Lenin and Trotsky—like little men aping the externals of those they follow—have cultivated in themselves that narrowness which passes for self-oblivious devotion, that harshness in personal relations and above all that devastating incapacity for experience which have become hallmarks and standard traits of the Communist 'professional revolutionary' . . . it is the cultivated and trained narrowness . . . which frightens away imagination and spontaneity." These animadversions, when I read them years ago, increased my respect for Greenberg; I found in them an unusual gift for self-insight. He had carried himself like a Lenin of the arts. Many of the gifted intellectuals of that time took on a Leninist coloration. They were "hard." To them "lives" and "personalities" were unreal bourgeois conceits, extensions of the idea of property. You eliminated, you cut down to size, you put down frailties and fashions, you welcomed the avant-garde and destroyed kitsch with revolutionary mental rays.

The Russian Revolution was made by a small band of intellectuals under the direction of Lenin, their chief theoretician. Small wonder that intellectuals in the West should have been intoxicated by such an example.

Some of these people were authentic originals and impressively intelligent (Harold Rosenberg, for example). The more clearheaded of the Village intellectuals toward the end of the Thirties were beginning to understand that the Revolution was a disaster. Few of them, however, turned away from Marxism. One way or another they clung to the texts that had made intellectuals of them. The Marxist fundamentals had organized their minds and gave them an enduring advantage over unfocused rivals educated helter-skelter in American universities. What you invest your energy and enthusiasm in when you are young, you can never bring yourself to give up altogether. I came to New York toward the end of the Thirties, muddled in the head but keen to educate myself, and toward the end of the Forties I had become a contributor to *Partisan Review* and a Villager. All around us was commercial America. The Village was halfway between Madison Avenue and Wall Street. Its center lay in Washington Square. From her apartment facing the benches and the elms, Eleanor Roosevelt might have seen, had they been pointed out to her, some of the most eminent intellectuals in the country discussing French politics, American painting, Freud and Marx, André Gide and Jean Cocteau. Everyone was avid for high-minded, often wildly speculative talk.

For Darwin it was the struggle for existence that mattered; for me, in those years, it was the struggle for conversation. There was no existence without it. There were notable talkers in this group of anticommunist leftists: Dwight Macdonald, tall, loosely held together, bearded, goggled, a rapid stammerer; Philip Rahv with his deep, breathy Russian rumble; Harold Rosenberg, extraordinarily fluent, persuasive, domineering, subtle and sharp; Paul Goodman, both canny and visionary, looking beyond you as he laid down the law on psychiatry, poetry, anarchism and sex.

Among these thinkers small distinction was made between an intellectual and a writer. The culture heroes who mattered were those who had ideas. Sidney Hook, in many respects a sensible man, once said to me that Faulkner was an excellent writer whose books would be greatly improved by dynamic ideas. "I'd be glad to give him some," he said. "It would make a tremendous difference. Do you know him?"

There was indeed much for us to understand: history, philosophy, science, the Cold War, mass society, pop art, high art, psychoanalysis, existentialism, the Russian question, the Jewish question. Yet I quickly saw—or rather (since I don't see quickly) I intuited—that writers seldom were intellectuals. "A bit of ideology and being up to date is most *apropos*," Chekhov said—tongue in cheek, I suspect. In a more serious vein he wrote that writers "should engage in politics only enough to protect themselves from politics." "Absence of lengthy verbiage of a political-social-economic nature" was one of his rules, and he recommended also objectivity, brevity, audacity, the avoidance of stereotypes; and compassion. (Ah, for the days before such words had fallen into disrepute.)

I don't intend just now to go farther into the differences between cognition and imagination; I simply note that I avoided anything resembling a choice by following my bent. I can't remember that I ever tried to discuss art versus politics with other writers. At a visiting firemen's dinner, years later, I once asked Günter Grass why he was campaigning so hard for Willy Brandt. Should writers go into politics? He turned a silent glare upon me, as if it outraged him (on this evening, he was the fireman) to be seated beside a village idiot.

Only in America! he may have thought.

For in Europe writers accepted politics as their absolute. This, as I learned during my Paris years (1948–50), was the thing to do. The year 1948 was a peculiarly bleak and bitter one. Coal, gasoline, even bread were still being rationed. That Paris was the capital of world civilization could no longer be taken for granted. French thinkers and writers struggled to maintain its preeminence. Americans, recently cheered as liberators, were not warmly received, the right being nearly as hard on them as the left. Mauriac in his columns expressed a decided preference for the Russians—for Russian rather than American literature. (Up to a point, I could agree with him.) On the left only Americans who had been ideologically vetted were accepted. The rest were thought to be spies. And French speakers were especially tricky—very likely double agents. Lifelong Francophiles like my friend H. J. Kaplan were suspect whereas Richard Wright was immediately welcomed; the existentialists who met in the bar of the Pont-Royal soon had him reading Husserl, whom I ignorantly held in great respect. I might have become an intellectual, but this makes me think of the prostitute in the French cartoon who said, *"J'aurais pu faire la religieuse"*—I might have been a nun. Seeing Wright in Saint-Germain-des-Prés, deep in a thick, difficult book, I asked him why this was necessary and he told me that it was indispensable reading for all writers and that I had better get a copy of my own. I wasn't quite ready for Husserl. As often as possible I went to music halls and the Cirque d'Hiver. Still, I did keep up with French ideas, read Sartre in *Les Temps Modernes* and Camus in *Combat*. I also took in an occasional lecture at the Collège de Philosophie.

The bitterness of defeat, occupation and liberation pervaded postwar Paris. An atmosphere of disgrace and resentment darkened the famous facades and made the Seine (at least to me) look and smell medicinal. This oppressiveness, I was later persuaded, was an early symptom of the Cold War. For the time being the French lay helpless between the USSR and the United States. The communist alternative, so far as I could judge, held an edge in public opinion, so that you couldn't have your hair cut without enduring torrents of Marxism from the barber. I had come to Paris, as Americans generally did, to be educated, and the general ignorance of the history of the Soviet Union in all quarters came as a great surprise. Reading Sartre, I said to myself, Chicago style, "This has got to be a con." A con on my turf was a shade more venial than a lie. I preferred to believe that Sartre's curious behavior was deliberate, Machiavellian. His hatred of the bourgeoisie was so excessive that he was inclined to go easy on the crimes of Stalin. On the intellectual Dow Jones—if there had been such a thing—his credentials, before I began to read him, would have been comparable to preferred stock. But the facts were readily available and that he should know so little about them was a great disappointment. He spoke in Marxist style of an oppressive bourgeois ideology, and while he admitted his bourgeois origins his aim was to create a revolutionary public. Himself an heir of the eighteenth-century *philosophes*, he would speak to the proletariat as his literary ancestors had spoken to the bourgeoisie, bringing political self-awareness to those who were to be the revolutionaries of today. He asserted that the workingman seeking liberation would liberate all of us as well, and for all time. The French CP was an obstacle standing between Sartre and the working class. As for existentialism, he readily conceded that it was a phenomenon produced by the decomposition of the bourgeois carcass. The only public at present available to him came, disgustingly, from the intelligent sector of the rotting bourgeoisie (victims, no doubt, but tyrants also).

"Were the author an Englishman we should here know that our leg was being pulled," wrote Wyndham Lewis in *The Writer and the Absolute*. "But Sartre does not smile . . . he is at his wits' end what to do." Lewis seems wryly sympathetic. And he does here and there agree with Sartre and quotes him approvingly when he declares that we are living in the age of the hoax. "National Socialism, Gaullism, Catholicism, French communism are hoaxes—consciousness is deluded and we can only safeguard literature by disillusioning or enlightening our public. . . . Sartre believes all that the communists believe," Lewis concludes. "But he did not wish to convert this *collage* into a marriage." He says that Sartre was a fellow traveler in the Front Populaire. "He engaged in a path in those days which leads either to communism or to nothing. It was the *néant* that he chose."

My own guess in 1949—when I was immature: not young, only, as I now see; underdeveloped—was that French intellectuals were preparing themselves, perhaps positioning themselves, for a Russian victory. Their Marxism also reflected the repugnance they felt for the other superpower. There were comparable anti-American sentiments in England. Graham Greene, like many writers (and civil servants) of his generation, abominated the U.S.A. and its politics. Successive English governments agreed on the whole with the American line, but Greene found ways to transfer at least part of the odium from London to Washington. On our side of the Atlantic he had a big following. Educated Americans, establishment haters, dearly love to see our society and its official policies loused up. "The main enemy is at home" was Lenin's wartime slogan. Of all his ideas, it may well be the most durable.

When I revert to those times I can take no pleasure in having spotted the errors of Sartre *et al.* I am disheartened rather by the failure of all these aspirations for justice and progress. I can understand that as crisis succeeded crisis no one wanted to surrender to passivity. It is sad to watch so much ingenuity invested in leaky theories. Behind the iron curtain, experiencing totalitarianism directly, people had a clearer orientation.

In the West there was a certain opinion consumerism. One asked oneself, What shall I think, this or that? Sidney Hook in his autobiography scorns the *Partisan Review* intellectuals, the respectable left. His description of them makes them look like small-business types, importers of foreign specialties in a highbrow artistic mall. Mere talkers, Hook thought; no taste for real politics. Moreover, they believed that World War II was an imperialist war exactly like the first. Since they were not the kind of Leninists who aimed to lead a putsch in Washington, their analyses of England and Germany did bring to mind the theologians of Lilliput. The account given by Hook, the stalwart cold warrior, of their confused Marxism was, four decades later, still edged with bitterness. But the fact that we can do nothing does not preclude wanting to be right and everyone was then intent on the one true position. "I had to turn my heavy guns on Dwight Macdonald and the others," Hook would tell me in his last years. But no one has ever examined the connection between helplessness and holding the right views. Following contemporary events is in a way like reading history. To read history is essential but what in actuality can we do about it? The novelist Stanley Elkin, in an essay called "The First Amendment as an Art Form," asks: "Who in old times ever held anything so uncalled for as an opinion? . . . Because history, history *really* was, still is, the agenda of activists. The rest of us, you, me, the rest of us are mere fans of a world view and use the news like theater—episodes, chapters in some Sabbath soul serial." He goes on to say that if we don't have the gift for effecting change, we have the "solace of criticism."

Granted, activists like Hook made a difference. Their contribution to victory in the Cold War can't be measured but must be acknowledged. It was Hook—taking Hook as representative of any number of thinkers and activists—Hook, not Sartre, whose views prevailed and should have prevailed. And what Mr. Elkin does is to report accurately on the state of opinion in a democracy like ours. What we need to consider is the combining of theorizing with effectiveness. I give Hook full marks for the wars he fought and admire him despite his evident lack of sympathy with my way of looking at things. He was the active, not the contemplative, sort, not so much a philosopher as an ex-philosopher. On one of the last evenings I spent with him he told me that philosophy was no more. I asked what the Ph.D.'s he had educated were doing with themselves. They were working in hospitals as ethicists, he said. That didn't make him unhappy either. I don't think that the end of the Cold War signifies that theorizing is bankrupt. To obtain a clear picture of the modern project, to give the best possible account of the crisis of the West, is still a necessity.

Politics as a vocation I take seriously. But it's not my vocation. And on the whole, writers are not much good at it. The positions they take

There Is Simply Too Much to Think About

are generally set for them by intellectuals. Or by themselves, insofar as they are intellectuals (e.g., the case of Sartre). Those anticommunist intellectuals and publicists with whom I have agreed on issues of the Cold War, though they tend to be high-toned and swollen with cultural pride and *suffisance*, are often philistine in their tastes. Their opposite numbers on the left are, in this respect, a mess entirely.

My policy has therefore been to avoid occasions that bring writers together. When President Johnson invited some twenty or thirty "leaders of the arts" to the White House, I foolishly accepted. I thought I would announce my opposition to Vietnam in a letter to the *Times* and I could then attend the jamboree—in order to show my respect for the Presidency. These principles! I have a weakness for stupid loftiness. Robert Lowell, who boycotted the event, had telephoned me more than once to concert a strategy for the afternoon. I gathered that he and his group were giving me a clearance to participate—somebody like me *should* be inside. The White House that day was filled with the cries of Lowell supporters, whom I will call the pros; the cons were in the minority. The journalists covering the event were as noisy and furious as the writers. The climax for me was the appearance of the uninvited Dwight Macdonald, tall, satyr-bearded, walking into the Rose Garden in sneakers, the great bohemian himself going around with a resolution endorsing Lowell's boycott. Many signed. LBJ afterward said the whole thing was nothing but an insult. "They insult me by comin', they insult me by stayin' away."

Philip Rahv set me straight about this. "You got put on the spot by Cal Lowell. He's a crafty schemer. When he gets into maneuvering that way, nobody has a chance with that dreamy poet."

The last literary meeting I can remember to have attended was the International PEN Congress in New York. There I was assigned to a panel on "The State and the Alienation of the Writer"—a superfluous and foolish topic. In a short talk (the shorter the better on this occasion) I said that our government hardly bothered with writers at all. The Founders had put together an enlightened plan for equality, stability, justice, relief from poverty and so forth. Art, philosophy and the higher concerns of mankind are not the business of the state. The emphasis here is on well-being and on a practical sort of humanitarianism. With the help of science we would conquer nature and force her to provide for us. Scarcity was to be abolished. On the whole I believed this program had met with success. In a commercial society nothing prevents one from writing novels or painting watercolors, but culture does not get the same attention as crops or manufacture or banking. I concluded by saying that many of the material objectives of the Founders had been successfully realized.

Before I could step down, Günter Grass had risen to attack me from the floor. He said that he had just visited the South Bronx and that the poor blacks who lived in those monstrous streets could not agree that they were free and equal. The horrors they endured were not at all like the picture of American success that I had described. The hall was crowded with writers and intellectuals. Grass had just lighted the ideological fuse and out came a tremendous boom, a blast of anger from delegates and visitors. Replying as well as I could in the uproar, I said that of course American cities were going to hell in a hurry; they had become monstrous. I tried also to indicate that corrective actions, if there were any, could be taken only by a rich society and this seemed to prove that the material objectives of the Founders had indeed been met. I added, since this was a PEN conference, that writers in politics hadn't done at all well. In this connection I mentioned Brecht and Feuchtwanger in Germany. Grass protested that he was always being put down in America as a communist.

You have to hand it to the social visionaries and liberators: They know how to get the high ground and keep it. They are masters also of the equivalence game: You have spoken well of the American system because you are an apologist for it and a stooge; you are not concerned about the poor and you are a racist, to boot.

He had pressed the agitprop button; up went a familiar semaphore. To his semaphore the agitated crowd responded with a conditioned reflex.

"I am afraid that great German writers do not have to know in order to pronounce," Melvin Lasky has written apropos of Grass.

Grass seems to have believed I was justifying the establishment— that moth-eaten shroud. No, I was simply describing what there is to see.

A brief quotation from an exceptionally clear-minded political theorist, Allan Bloom, will show better than I can the direction I meant to take in my speech before the PEN vipers: "Civil societies dedicated to the end of self-preservation cannot be expected to provide fertile soil for the heroic or the inspired. They do not require or encourage the noble. . . . One who holds the 'economic' view of man cannot consistently believe in the dignity of man or in the special status of art and science."

These are the basics, the first principles of modernity, of the Enlightenment conviction that this is what would be best for most of us. The objectives of Lenin's revolution never materialized in Russia, but they are all about us here in bourgeois America, says the philosopher Alexandre Kojève. In the process, everything worth living for has melted away.

Eastern Europe was "spared" our revolution. Instead Russia had seven decades and more of Stalin, an Oriental despot; and Poland, Hungary and the rest came in for nearly half a century of Soviet rule. The writers who stood their ground against totalitarianism and went to the Lubyanka and the Gulag move us deeply as moralists and artists. I particularly admire Shalamov, the author of *Kolyma Tales*, and Aleksander Wat, who wrote *My Century*, together with many others, Russians, Poles and Jews, who endured Stalin's prisons and Hitler's death camps.

In the West people excused from such torments are, I think it fair to say, inclined to mix self-reproach with their admiration. They wonder how they would have fared under pressure. Terror is the test of tests and I suspect that the Hobbesian or the Darwinian states of nature challenge many of us imaginatively. Intellectuals are particularly susceptible to such challenges and possibly speculate whether living through such ordeals might not have healed their divided souls.

It comes back to me now that Lenin loved Jack London's stories of the Yukon. His favorite, "To Build a Fire," is about a man stopping for the night in a vast snowfield and finding that he has only a single match left. He will freeze to death if it fails to light. I can remember when I was a boy holding my breath as I read the story. Jack London, I later discovered, had a great following in Eastern Europe. This turning back to what precedes civilization is common also among refined people, as is admiration for elemental men, men capable of exceptional violence.

Dostoyevsky, for instance, was greatly impressed by the criminals he came to know in Siberia. One murderer said to him, "'You are very innocent, so innocent that it's pitiful.' . . . Whether it was that he looked on me as somebody immature, not fully grown up, or whether he felt for me that sympathy which every strong creature feels for a weaker, I do not know . . . even in the act of stealing from me he was sorry for me."

Do I seem here to be making a case against the intellectuals, criticizing even the way they read Solzhenitsyn or Shalamov? Well, yes—insofar as they allow tyranny to define the ground rules of existence. The tyrant tells us what true being is and how it should be judged. A scale of suffering is set up for us with the camps at the top and Western societies at the bottom. Those who undergo the most dreadful torments are "serious," the rest of us are not worth bothering about.

My case against the intellectuals can be easily summarized: Science has postulated a nature with no soul in it; commerce does not deal in souls, and higher aspirations—matters like love and beauty—are none of its business; for his part, Marx too assigned art, et cetera, to the "superstructure." So artists are "stuck" with what is left of the soul and its mysteries. Romantic enthusiasm (resistance to bourgeois existence) was largely discredited by the end of the nineteenth century. The twentieth inverted romanticism by substituting hate for love and nihilism for self-realization. Intellectuals seem to me to have turned away from those elements in life unaccounted for in modern science and that in modern experience have come to seem devoid of substance. The powers of soul, which were Shakespeare's subject (to be simple about it) and are heard incessantly in Handel or Mozart, have no footing at present in modern life and are held to be subjective. Writers here and there still stake their lives on the existence of these forces. About this, intellectuals have little or nothing to say.

We yield to these forces when we read a Shalamov or an Aleksander Wat. We recognize them as coming directly from human nature when that nature rejects the imposition of slavery and totalitarian injustice. But among ourselves, in the West, the forces are not acknowledged, they cannot even be recognized.

Here I have no choice but to go overboard. Russia's Oriental despotism comes from the past and the sympathies generated by those who fought for their lives against it have little to do, I suspect, with this present world of ours. Our American world is a prodigy. Here on the material level the perennial dreams of mankind have been realized. We have shown that the final conquest of scarcity may be at hand. Provision is made for human needs of every sort. In the United States—in the West—we live in a society that produces a fairy-tale superabundance of material things. Ancient fantasies have been made real. We can instantaneously see and hear what is far away. Our rockets are able to leave this earth. The flights we make are thoughts as well as real journeys. This is something new and it is of a magnitude too vast to be grasped. To contemplate this can make us tremble for the humanity we miss in everything we see in the incredible upwelling of inventions and commodities that carries us with it. We can't say whether this humanity has been temporarily diminished or has gone for good. Nor can we tell whether we are pioneers or experimental subjects. Russia is perhaps done with tyranny and privation. If it develops a free market and becomes a union of commercial republics it will have to do as we have been doing all along. Kojève hints that we are irreversibly trivialized by our unexampled and bizarre achievements, so that neither life nor death can now be grasped. He seems to accept Nietzsche's appalling vision of the degenerate "Last Man."

I myself believe that everything that can be imagined is bound to be realized at least once—everything that mankind is capable of conceiving, it seems compelled to do. These, for better or for worse, are the thoughts the end of the Cold War suggests to me.

[1993]

Papuans and Zulus

Snowbound in Boston, I watched the blizzard impounding parked cars at midnight. The veering of the snowflakes under the streetlights made me think how nice it would be if we were totally covered by white drifts. Give us a week's moratorium, dear Lord, from the idiocies that burn on every side and let the pure snows cool these overheated minds and dilute the toxins that have infected our judgments. Grant us a breather, merciful God.

Any sensible, feeling person, in the present state of things, might utter such a prayer in the dead of night. In my case the immediate cause was an odd one. I had come under attack in the press and elsewhere for a remark I was alleged to have made about the Zulus and the Papuans. I had been quoted as saying that the Papuans had had no Proust and that the Zulus had not as yet produced a Tolstoy, and this was taken as an insult to Papuans and Zulus and as a proof that I was at best insensitive and at worst an elitist, a chauvinist, a reactionary and a racist—in a word, a monster.

Nowhere in print, under my name, is there a single reference to Papuans or Zulus. The scandal is entirely journalistic in origin, the result of a misunderstanding that occurred (they always do occur) during an interview. I can't remember who the interviewer was. Always foolishly trying to explain and edify all comers, I was speaking of the distinction between literate and preliterate societies. For I was once an anthropology student, you see. Long ago I had been a pupil of the famous Africanist M. J. Herskovits, who had also devoted many decades to the study of the American Negro.

The subject of my senior thesis was "France and the African Slave Trade." Rummaging in the library stacks, I had discovered that two of the French ships involved in the trade were the *Jean-Jacques* and the

Contrat Social. Never a professional anthropologist, I was however a sound enough amateur. I had read widely in the field and immediately after the telephone interview I remembered that there was a Zulu novel after all: *Chaka* by Thomas Mofolo, published in the early Thirties. In my Herskovits days I had read it in translation. It was a profoundly, unbearably tragic book about a tribal Achilles who had with his own hands cut down thousands of people, including his own pregnant wife.

Now why did my remarks, off the cuff obviously and pedantic certainly, throw so many people into fits of righteousness and ecstasies of rage? France gave us one Proust and only one. There is no Bulgarian Proust. Have I offended the Bulgarians too? We, for that matter, have no Proust either. Should the White House issue a *fatwa* and set a price on my head for blaspheming against American high culture?

My critics, many of whom could not locate Papua New Guinea on the map, want to convict me of contempt for multiculturalism and defamation of the third world. I am an elderly white male—a Jew, to boot. Ideal for their purposes.

The literacy of which we are so proud often amounts to very little. You may take the word of a practicing novelist for it that not all novel readers are good readers. The ground rules of the art of fiction are not widely understood. No writer can take it for granted that the views of his characters will not be attributed to him personally. It is generally assumed, moreover, that all the events and ideas of a novel are based on the life experiences and the opinions of the novelist himself.

Our American preference is for the facts—only facts count. A gold miner in Alaska watching an early film and running at the screen to hit the villain with his shovel is my favorite illustration of this low-level bondage to actuality.

Preliterate societies have their own kinds of wisdom, no doubt, and primitive Papuans probably have a better grasp of their myths than most educated Americans have of their own literature. But without years of study we can't begin to understand a culture very different from our own. The fair thing, therefore, is to make allowance for what we outsiders cannot hope to fathom in another society and grant that, as members of the same species, primitive men are as mysterious or as monstrous as any other branch of humankind.

It's no slander to describe a people as preliterate. In any case, preliterate societies are rapidly vanishing. Besides, as we all know, certain forms of literacy are decidedly repulsive. Anyway, the study of culture is our idea. Our civilized demand is for scientific discussions of everything. Papuan fieldworkers do not come here to learn what makes Los Angeles, Las Vegas, Miami or New York tick.

The socialist realism that dominated the literate USSR for many decades forced poets, playwrights and novelists to become part of the official falsehood machine. Those who resisted were sent to die in Kolyma or locked away in psychiatric hospitals. An unpublished poem on Stalin's "cockroach whiskers," brought to the attention of the Kremlin by informers, was the cause of Osip Mandelstam's death.

Despots do not accept the autonomy of the literary imagination. Freedom of the imagination, dangerous to them, is related to the independence of the soul. This independence is not peculiar to artists; it is common to all human beings.

In any reasonably open society, the absurdity of a petty thought-police campaign provoked by the inane magnification of "discriminatory" remarks about the Papuans and the Zulus would be laughed at. To be serious in this fanatical style is a sort of Stalinism—the Stalinist seriousness and fidelity to the party line that senior citizens like me remember all too well. . . .

[1994]

Alone in Mixed Company

Do writers need the company of writers? That, of course, depends. Some writers are better read than met. In every Eastern European capital one finds, or used to find, writers' clubs. In communist Warsaw or in communist Belgrade these clubhouses were nicely furnished and you could sit in leather armchairs, sipping tea and exchanging views. I suppose the Polish or Yugoslav governments found it convenient to corral the writers. The comfortable rooms were bugged. While you chatted with them in Bucharest our novelist or poet colleagues would glance up significantly. In spite of the obviousness of this spying, I think it impressed writers from the West that artists should have clubs of their very own and that these clubs should be maintained at public expense.

Of course, as John Cheever liked to point out when he spoke of his travels in Eastern Europe, "those were odd countries." As proof he cited the fact that in Bulgarian hotels the toilet seats were square. Eastern Europe had not yet discovered the oval, he would say. But toilet seats aside, the writers in Eastern Europe were companionable. They *behaved* like writers; they had an acknowledged position in their respective countries. They lived as writers. At home we had no such distinct identity.

I can't say whether this was a good thing or a bad one. All I can say is that on our side of the Atlantic writers tend to be loners. Before World War II, when I was very young, there were writers who lived independently without the support of universities or other institutions. Those who did well and published widely were called "men of letters"; those who merely got by were freelancers or hacks. Fortunately for all of us, one didn't need much money during the Depression. Greenwich Villagers used to say that on a thousand dollars a year you could be comfortably poor. The Roosevelt-Hopkins WPA programs were a great help. You had to be certified—to prove that you were eligible for welfare. But once hired you found yourself in prosperity. A week's pay was $24.90—a considerable sum in the Thirties when furnished rooms rented at twelve bucks a month. The price of an Automat breakfast was fifteen cents. Now and then you landed a "short notice," an unsigned book review for *The New Republic* or *The New York Times*. Just after the war I was hired to summarize books for Victor Weybright, who was preparing a Penguin list for the U.S. He paid five dollars for a three-page summary, ten for nonfiction. Solid, British, sanguine, smoking pipes, wearing boots not shoes, tweeds not flannels, well satisfied with you, with himself, with the rich fittings of his office, he was a relaxed executive. The job was easy if you didn't mind reading half the night.

So there you were—a man of letters in your late twenties. If you liked that sort of thing, you might even declare yourself an intellectual. Intellectuals were in good supply at *Partisan Review* and *The Hudson Review*, at NYU and uptown at Columbia. Down in the Village there were experimentalists, painters, highly educated young men and women of the *rentier* class—innumerable immigrants from every part of the country who had come to New York to write books, poems, to study painting or to be psychoanalyzed. There were anarchists like Paul Goodman and existentialists like William Barrett; writers of quality like James Agee who worked for Henry Luce; Dwight Macdonald, Nicola Chiaromonte, Meyer Schapiro, Sidney Hook and W. H. Auden were visible and accessible. John Berryman, Delmore Schwartz, Jean Stafford and great theoreticians—tireless talkers like Harold Rosenberg—were among the attractions of the Village in the late Forties. I was not one of the stars in those years. I was part of a considerable crowd of young or youngish writers and painters attracted to New York from every part of the country.

Many of these gifted people were soon drawn back to the interior. The Village population was unstable. Talent proved to be unpredictably, extraordinarily marketable. The GI Bill was then filling and overflowing all American universities. Lucrative teaching jobs were available. Campuses in every part of the country soon had a bohemian population of their own. Greenwich Village, it turned out, was not hard to duplicate. The poets went to Minnesota, to Iowa and to Berkeley as

There Is Simply Too Much to Think About

professors of poetry; men of letters turned into academics. Later generations repudiated literature altogether. Literature and the study of literature went their separate ways.

I do not claim the foregoing to be a definitive analysis of the changes that have obviously occurred. It is only my own, probably erroneous account of what has happened since midcentury.

So—to return to my opening sentence—do writers need the company of other writers? Well, their company can be agreeable; it can be stimulating. It can also generate errors of the deepest sort or foster ideologies that do more harm than good. The modern writer is usually a loner—a prospector, if you like—apt to be a solipsist or crackpot or moral nihilist.

The writer's condition is inevitably problematic. To write, if conditions are favorable, is bliss. To be a writer can be absurd, grotesque. Nowadays I don't seek the company of writers—by now I wouldn't even know how to go about tracking them to their caverns. But from time to time I have found myself—quite suddenly, almost unexpectedly—in a gathering of writers. During the last PEN congress in New York City I was asked to speak on "Alienation and the State" and immediately found myself (perhaps owing to my loathing of the word *alienation*) in a heated dispute. with Günter Grass. . . He convinced himself somehow that I was a conservative who was prepared to accept (even perhaps to endorse) poverty, misery and madness as minor defects in this triumphant superpower of ours, that my sole desire was that America should win the Cold War. Someone must have told him that I was a reactionary. He certainly hadn't formed such a view from reading my books. I don't believe he had read any of them. A political career doesn't leave one much time for reading.

In any case this New York PEN congress was the last one I attended—some twelve years ago. A more pleasant occasion had been President Kennedy's White House banquet for André Malraux in the early Sixties. Scores of writers, composers, painters and performers were present—all in black tie or long skirts. I saw writers there whom I hadn't seen in decades—Edmund Wilson, Thornton Wilder, Allen Tate. Some of these I was never to see again.

I'd never met the godlike Malraux before. It was a very great dinner indeed—every sort of celebrity was invited and more than a few real heroes were present—Charles Lindbergh, for instance. Lindbergh cast a cold eye on us all; everyone was viewed and rejected. And Lindbergh did indeed have the cameo profile with which we were all familiar.

John Kennedy was anything but orthodox. No orthodox President would have invited Lindbergh, an isolationist America-Firster and Nazi sympathizer, to the White House. Edmund Wilson, a lesser offender, had merely failed to pay his income taxes. Irwin Shaw had moved to Switzerland to avoid taxes altogether. The general feeling on that night was that America had taken its first step away from capitalist philistinism and provinciality and that we Americans were—at last!—about to experience national greatness by integrating the arts into the life of this most powerful nation.

To watch Allen Tate, who during the concert kept time with his fingers on the kneecap of the lady in evening dress seated beside him, was proof that writers did indeed benefit from the company of other writers. One more impression—my last: Under Eisenhower, William Faulkner was asked to head the administration's People to People program. I was invited by one of my former Village buddies, Harvey Breit, to a large meeting of novelists and poets. Breit was now a columnist for *The New York Times Book Review* and lived in a large brownstone in the East Sixties. In his grand salon I saw, with awe, writers who seemed to me too eminent to be among the living still. Was it Fanny Hurst I met there or Edna Ferber? I can't now check this with Harvey, because he died decades ago. I saw William Carlos Williams for the first time and, if I'm not mistaken, Conrad Aiken. Every writer on the Eastern Seaboard must have been present. I recognized Steinbeck and, unless I am mistaken, Pearl Buck.

Faulkner, a short but extraordinarily fine-looking man, came in from the cold in a bowler hat (a Baltimore heater, we called it in Chicago), a chesterfield overcoat and a silk polka-dotted scarf. He was curiously self-possessed. The speech he made was mined with ironies: "The President has asked me to head the 'People to People' program for writers," he said. "And I have invited you to assemble here to outline a set of suggestions. My first proposal is that we should take away all U.S. passports and prevent Americans from tourin' foreign countries. That'll restore the good name of the U.S. abroad. Second, we should invite folks from behind the Iron Curtain to come here. Live in a small town, work in a factory, play baseball, have chicken and ice cream on Sunday. Then go back and tell the folks at home about it."

From the assembled writers not a sound was heard. They sat or stood considering these remarks. They were mute. Harvey Breit must have prodded someone to end the embarrassment of this ponderous silence. At last some tentative, respectful, appeasing voice said, "Mr. Faulkner, don't you think that people behind the Iron Curtain already know the difference between their countries and this one?"

"Suh," Faulkner told him, "knowin' is one thing, experiencin' is another!"

[1996]

Ralph Ellison in Tivoli

Some forty years ago I came into a small legacy and with it I bought a house in Tivoli, N.Y. *House* is not the word; it was, or once had been, a Hudson River mansion. It had a Dutch cellar kitchen of flagstones and a kitchen fireplace. There was a dumbwaiter to the vanished dining room above. The first floor had a ballroom, but according to my informants, Tivoli's townspeople, no one had danced in it for eighty years. Tivoli had been the birthplace of Eleanor Roosevelt. The villagers were the descendants of the servants and groundskeepers of the Dutchess County aristocrats.

I shan't be going into the social history of the township or the county. There were great names in the vicinity—the Livingstones, the Chapmans and the Roosevelts—but I didn't know much about them. I had sunk my $16,000 legacy into a decaying mansion. To repair the roof and to put in new plumbing, I drew an advance of $10,000 from the Viking Press to write a novel called *Henderson the Rain King*.

There was a furnace of sorts and a warm-air system that took the moisture out of your nostrils. I was too busy with *Henderson* and with my then-wife to take full notice of my surroundings. The times were revolutionary—I refer to the sexual revolution. Marriages were lamentably unstable and unserious. My wife, tired of life with me in the gloomy house, packed her bags and moved to Brooklyn.

I was naturally wretched about this. I now found the solitude (and the decay of the house) insupportable. Determined to save my $16,000, I threw myself into the work of salvage. I painted the kitchen walls and the bedrooms, as much for therapeutic reasons as to improve the property.

Then Ralph Ellison, who was teaching at Bard College, accepted my invitation to move in. I have always believed that this was an act of charity on his part.

We had known each other in Manhattan. I had reviewed *Invisible Man* for *Commentary*. I was aware that it was an extremely important novel and that, in what he did, Ralph had no rivals. What he did no one else could do—a glorious piece of good fortune for a writer.

Both of us at one time had lived on Riverside Drive. We met often and walked together in the park along the Hudson. There we discussed all kinds of questions and exchanged personal histories. I was greatly taken with Ellison, struck by the strength and independence of his mind. We discussed Richard Wright, Faulkner and Hemingway. Ralph, it was clear, had thought things through for himself and his ideas had little in common with the views of the critics in the quarterlies. Neither he nor I could accept the categories prepared for us by literary journalists. He was an American writer who was black. I was a Jew and an American and a writer and I believed that by being described as a "Jewish writer" I was being shunted to a siding. This taxonomy business I saw as an exclusionary device. Ellison had similar objections to classification. From his side he saw the Negro as one of the creators of America's history and culture.

That was okay with me. We found each other sympathetic. We got along splendidly and went fishing together for striped bass in Long Island Sound.

Ralph drove into Tivoli in his huge old Chrysler. He himself serviced it, coddled it, tuned it, and it ran as smoothly as it had when it came off the assembly line. The trunk, when it was opened, gave me my first hint of Ralph's powers of organization. For hunting there were guns, there were decoy ducks; for fishing, rods, lures and a wickerwork creel; there were tools of every description. Ralph was able to repair radios and hi-fi equipment. I envied him his esoteric technical skills. Where I saw a frightening jumble of tubes, dials, condensers (I can't even name the parts), he saw order. In my trunk I carried the spare wheel, the jack, a few rusty tire irons, rags and brown paper bags from the market. His trunk with its tools and weapons announced that he was prepared for any emergency, could meet every challenge to his autonomy.

Ralph Ellison in Tivoli

He did not come alone. He was accompanied by a young black Labrador retriever who jumped from the Chrysler, eager to play, pawing my chest. Ralph had bought the dog from John Cheever, who was then, briefly, a breeder of black Labs.

The ballroom now became Ralph's studio. It ran the entire length of the house. He set up his typewriter and his desk and we found a bookcase for his manuscripts. You couldn't see the Hudson from the ground floor. Instead you had the Catskills to look at.

In the ballroom Ralph kept African violets that he watered with a turkey baster. It was from him that I learned all that I know about houseplants.

But the important thing was that the gloomy house was no longer empty—no longer gloomy. All day long I heard the humming of his electric typewriter. Its long rhythms made me feel that we were on a cruise ship moving through the woods—the pines and the locust trees, the huge hayfields plowed, planted and harvested by Chanler Chapman, my sometime landlord. Chanler, before I could be aware of it, became Henderson the Rain King. He drove his tractor like a real king, knocking over fences, breaking stone walls and pulling up boundary markers.

Ralph and I brought the house under civilized control.

He came down to get his breakfast in a striped heavy Moroccan garment. He wore slippers with a large Oriental curve at the toe. He was a very handsome man. A noteworthy person, solid, symmetrical and dignified but with a taste for finery, Ralph was never anything but well dressed and he liked clothes of an Ivy League cut. In the days before everybody had elected to go bareheaded, he wore what used to be called a porkpie hat of very fine felt. By comparison, I was a stumblebum. He put on his carefully chosen clothes with aesthetic intent. I often amused him by my (comparative) slovenliness. He studied me silently, deeply amused by my lack of consideration for my appearance. Day in, day out I wore the same blue jeans and chambray shirt.

Our meals were simple. We ate in the kitchen. I learned from Ralph how to brew drip coffee properly. He had been taught by a chemist to do it with ordinary laboratory paper filters and water at room temperature. The coffee then was heated in a *bain-marie*—a pot within a pot. Never allowed to boil.

We saw little of each other during the day. I kept a vegetable garden, and at the kitchen door I planted herbs.

At cocktail time we met again in the kitchen. Ralph mixed very strong martinis but nobody got drunk. We talked a great deal before dinner, before the martinis took hold. Ralph told me the story of his life—told me about his mother, about Oklahoma City; about their years in Gary, Indiana, and later in Cleveland, where he and his brother hunted birds for the table during the Great Depression. He described to me his trip, in freight trains, to Tuskegee; and how he learned to play the trumpet; and how he had come upon certain essays by André Malraux that changed his life. Often we rambled together about Malraux, about Marxism or about painting. Or novel writing.

There were long discussions of American history and of nineteenth-century politics, of slavery and the Civil War and Reconstruction. Ralph was much better at history than I could ever be, but it gradually became apparent that he was not merely talking about history but telling the story of his life and tying it into American history. His motive was in part literary—he was trying to find the perspective for an autobiography. In this respect he much resembled Robert Frost, who had made a routine, an entertainment, of the principal events of his life and polished or revised them again and again when he had the right listeners. But Frost was his own hagiographer. He would tell you how Ezra Pound had received him in his London flat sitting in a hip bath and treated him—Frost—like a plowboy-poet. "I was no Bobby Burns," Frost often said. He was trying to establish his version or picture of a significant chapter of literary history and to spray it with a fixative of his own.

Ralph's purpose was very different from Frost's. He took pleasure in returning again and again to the story of his development not in order to revise or to gild it but to recover old feelings and also to consider and reconsider how he might find a way to write his story.

He and I had our differences. I am not inclined to be sentimental about those arcadian or utopian days. He didn't approve of my way of running the place. I had complained also that his dog relieved himself in my herb garden. I asked, "Can't you arrange to have him do his shitting elsewhere?"

This offended Ralph greatly and he was outraged when in a fit of nastiness I took a swipe at the dog with a broom for fouling the terrace. He complained to John Cheever that, with my upbringing, I was incapable of understanding, that I had no feeling for pedigrees and breeds, and that I knew only mongrels and had treated his *chien de race* like a mongrel.

Cheever was broken up by this. Well, it was very funny. Cheever never spoke of it to me. I learned of Ralph's complaint when Cheever's diary was posthumously published.

When I told Ralph that perhaps it would be a good idea to thin out the locust trees along the driveway, he said, "Well, they're your trees." Immediately I telephoned a woodsman with a power saw. I don't recall that there was such a saw in the trunk of the Chrysler. In my place, Ralph would have cut the trees himself. Nor would he have consulted anyone about it.

But the main cause of trouble between us was the dog. Ralph believed that I had taken against the dog.

I have begun in old age to understand just how oddly we all are put together. We are so proud of our autonomy that we seldom if ever realize how generous we are to ourselves, and just how stingy with others. One of the booby traps of freedom—which is bordered on all sides by isolation—is that we think so well of ourselves. I now see that I have helped myself to the best cuts at life's banquet.

But our boiling paranoias do simmer down, and later on Ralph and I resolved our differences. His dog was after all handsome, intelligent, lively. I didn't hold it against him that he was a thoroughbred, a *chien de race*. We made peace and parted on the best of terms.

Ralph and I afterward agreed that our Tivoli life had been extraordinarily pleasant. The place is no longer a shored-up ruin. Its new proprietor has turned it into a showplace. But Ralph and I, two literary squatters, comically spiky, apart though living together, had been very lucky in the two years we spent in what I called the House of Usher. We did not form a great friendship. What we had was a warm attachment. He respected me. I admired him. He had a great deal to teach me; I did my best to learn.

Since that time I have brewed my morning coffee precisely as he had taught me to brew it.

I often summon him up. He is wearing his Moorish dressing gown and the leather slippers with turned-up toes. Sometimes while pouring water from the measuring cup with one hand, he rubs his nose with the other, rubs it so hard that you can hear the cartilage crack.

[1998]

Literature: The Next Chapter

Wen I was young I had already made plans to write fiction and was not about to undercut myself by discussing the death of the novel. But I am an octogenarian now and see no harm in going public with my views. It is possible that for a majority of readers the question of the survival of the novel is an empty one. It is the scholarly specialist who tells us that every form is born, ripens, ages and finally has to be put down. The scholars and critics identify themselves with the great past of every form and speak with the authority of its best representatives. You can almost hear the voices of the Melvilles and the Henry Jameses laying down the law to a generation of upstarts.

In the earlier decades of the twentieth century writers were less bossy. In putting my thoughts on these matters in order I went back to a straightforward little book by Ford Madox Ford called *The English Novel*. Ford, who fought in the trenches during the Great War (he was described by one of his contemporaries as a "lemony-pink, fleshy man"), tells us at the outset that his remarks will "differ very widely from the conclusions arrived at by my predecessors in this field who have seldom themselves been imaginative writers, let alone novelists." He is prepared to take a more modest line with the novelists he examines as well as with their readers. Those readers represent the common consciousness of their respective countries. The French, German, English, Russian, et cetera readers have a collective familiarity with the facts of life as viewed by their novelist countrymen. They know the going gossip. Like Auden, Ford believed that gossip keeps the minds of a country "aerated," so that even the highly respected "papers of record" find it necessary to report the sex gossip of Prime Ministers and Presidents.

Ford tells us that the novel "supplies that cloud of human instances without which the soul feels unsafe in its adventures, and the normal mind fairly easily discerns what events or characters in its fugitive novels are meretricious in relation to life, however entertaining they may be as fiction." Another way of putting it is that through the reading of novels we come to know others with an intimacy otherwise unfelt. As bookish children we were on familiar terms with a very large number of fictional persons. We knew their hopes, their habits and their thoughts. Readers of my generation were on closer terms with Conrad's Captain MacWhirr, Dreiser's Sister Carrie, Lewis's Babbitt or Lawrence's Lady Chatterley than with their own cousins or classmates. We had a clear view of these characters and were able to observe and know how they felt and what they were thinking. We learned how these people understood life and became familiar with their manners and behavior.

In the early decades of this century of triumphant technics, intellectuals spoke of the mass-man and his inability to distinguish between the natural and the man-made. The mass-man thought that the electricity that lit his rooms was something like a free commodity resembling sunlight or tap water. An educated minority thought of reservoirs or generators. But as technology advanced the educated class was to become as ignorant as the mass-man. In my college days we were taught that metabolism consisted of two processes, anabolism and catabolism. The use of such terms proved you to be an educated person. You needed only to learn the passwords. My heart's rhythm is now regulated by a pacemaker. Once a month it is checked over the phone by a technician several hundreds of miles away—somewhere in New Jersey. Computer chips seem to be running our lives.

On street corners one sometimes sees people apparently staring into space. I am told that the lower lenses of their eyeglasses are programmed to give them up-to-the-minute readings of their Dow Jones holdings. People driving their cars lose control of the wheel as they make assignations on the cellular telephone. The Russian spy recently caught in Washington, who seemed to be idling on a sunny park bench, controlled the switch of a listening device that transmitted classified conversation in a federal building nearby. Minds like our own have broken through into a new technological realm. We haven't made it. This is the work of our cousins, sons and nieces. We trust our lives to the aircraft they design. That we ourselves cannot fly them goes without saying. It goes without saying also that it is possible to manufacture goggles that allow you to follow your investments, but it makes one oddly despondent to think how great our reliance on electronic devices has become. We never did understand the physiology that sustained us, but that was one of the mysteries of nature, an altogether natural ignorance. Now the mystery has become technical. Men, who have created it, should be capable of understanding it as well.

A very long time ago, when I was a teenager, I liked to think of myself as a future historian of culture. I read *The Magic Mountain* and said to myself, "Now that is for you." I pored over John H. Randall's *The Making of the Modern Mind* and said, "This is your cup of tea." I had found the connection between the world of high culture and the slums of Chicago. Just after the end of the war, when I began to contribute stories and articles to *Partisan Review* and learned that I was now thought to be an intellectual, I decided that I was no such thing. To be an intellectual at midcentury meant that you must be capable of arguing points of Marxist doctrine, and since so many people below Fourteenth Street were also in analysis, you could not get by without long days of psychoanalytic study. There was a rift, a gap, a gulf between the intellectuals and their contemporaries, the writers.

A review essay by George Steiner on *The Arcades Project* of Walter Benjamin in *The Times Literary Supplement* for December 3, 1999, now claims my attention because it is involved with the argument I am trying to develop. In Steiner's view the modern has given up its early claim to be systematic. Basic to modernism is that it is incomplete. Adorno has told us that "totality is the lie." Of course truth must come first. Modern literature, writes Steiner, adopts a "poetics of the fragmentary, of fragments shored against the ruins"—every significant modern argument derives its *kashruth*, its rabbinic sanction, from T. S. Eliot. Next—Proust and Schönberg, Ezra Pound and Musil are cited by Mr. Steiner as giants of Art who with their instinct for the genuine have embraced the convention of noncompletion—"a deeper pressure against perfection," Mr. Steiner says. By this he seems to mean that "perfection" should be sabotaged.

He goes on to tell us: "The accelerando and violence of recent history, the large-scale disappearance of the privileges of privacy, of silence, of leisure that underwrote the classic practice of reading and esthetic response, the economics of the ephemeral, of the disposable and recyclable which fuel the mass consumption market, be it in the media or in the factory, militate against enactments of completion and totality."

I know very little about Walter Benjamin. *The Arcades Project* arrived just the other day and I shall try to set aside the first of the many hours it will take to read his 1,073 pages. The man had a bitterly hard life and reading Steiner's review makes you feel even more sympathetic toward him—"his deepening *misère*, what he clearly perceived as the failure of the Front Populaire." As Nazi Germany, Fascist Italy and Soviet Russia poured troops and war matériel into Spain, no one could possibly believe that the Front Populaire would survive. (But what makes *misère* more effective than misery?)

Are we required moreover to think of one vastly extended realm of art-criticism-intellectual-activity-culture, a single sphere where all these things intermingle and touch and are shared somehow by the artists and by the intellectual collaborators of these artists as well? The latter are thought to be indispensable because they focus the light of the mind on every sort of problem. The intellectual appears as a gentle and sapient soul who is fully at home everywhere and indeed is indispensable. He is the artist's kissing cousin. Or perhaps even a brother, as Aaron was to Moses. This is how Mr. Steiner seems to see the existence shared by intellectuals and artists. D. H. Lawrence maintained that "the business of art is to reveal the relation between man and his circumambient universe, at the living moment." A physicist might dismiss this as double-talk or mumbo jumbo, but a novelist would class it as an attempt to express the personal uniqueness of the artist's perspective. A kind of personal natural phenomenology underlies Lawrence's assumption. Because this is universal, a reader will receive and trust the report of the perceiver. This was what Ford Madox Ford meant when he said that "the novel supplies that cloud of human instances without which the soul feels unsafe in its adventures." But this is not the case for an intellectual like Professor Steiner, who misses no opportunity to show his skill with the Baudelairean conjurer's handkerchief: "The resuscitation of the ephemeral, of the unconsidered, of the scorned, makes of the ragpicker a figuration of the Messianic. Of comparable significance is the *flâneur*, again a motif crucial in Baudelaire. The *flâneur* subverts the utilitarian, deterministic program of the city. Perennially the chiffonnier and the *flâneur* will cross paths with the prostitute. She too is essential to the cast. The pavements are her argosy. If the prostitute incarnates archetypal imaginations, of intimacies to be 'picked up,' she is also the emblematic player in the Marxist polemic on capitalist enslavement at its crassest, as well as in the Freudian narrative of middle-class libidinal angst and desire."

Nobody makes my case better than Professor Steiner himself when he cuts loose. He clutches Baudelaire and drags him around in a *pas de deux* over ground that he, Steiner, claims to have mastered in every historical detail. Can this jungle of allusions ever be reduced to order? I really can't say what the future of the novel is, but following Mr. Steiner's lead does not seem promising. A different dance is perhaps still possible.

[2000]

Wit Irony Fun Games

M y topic is fun and games. And invariably the fun goes out of comedy as soon as you lay a theorist's hand on it. The subject for obvious reasons defies definition—it is diabolically resistant to formulation. Something like fifty years ago (possibly sixty) I read some books that analyzed wit, humor, laughter, and found that they had little to tell me. From the philosopher Bergson I learned that we are moved to laugh when the living creature momentarily resembles an artificial one, helplessly subject to the laws of physics. A man slips on a banana peel and when he falls he resembles a bundle of sticks and causes onlookers to laugh. According to Elias Canetti (*Crowds and Power*) we laugh when someone falls because of our dormant cannibalistic tendencies. In showing our teeth to the sprawling accident victim, we notify him that we could eat him if we liked but that civilized persons no longer do that sort of thing. Canetti was a gifted writer but a grim one. Even a comic genius like the Victorian Samuel Butler has written that when a mother says to her infant "I could eat you up" she is prompted by an impulse from her primitive nature to ingest what she loves.

Sigmund Freud also wrote a book about the comic sense. He claimed that wit brought relief from the rigors of repression by means of jokes or slips of the tongue and functioned as a sort of counter-madness, a small garden within the mangrove swamp of the irrational unconscious. Wit is seen as the court fool of the Id, the King.

As you can gather from the samples I have submitted, highly accredited intellectuals have done comedy the honor of taking it seriously. Freud's *Wit and the Unconscious* contains many excellent jokes and even some of the interpretations and commentaries are—for Freud—lighthearted.

With this we abandon the quest for definitions and turn instead to our earliest experiences with comedy. When do we begin to respond to it? To this question the most sensible answer is clearly a personal one. My parents were frequently amused by the antics and outcries of their children or by the unconscious charm, perhaps, of their antics. My eldest brother loved to clown. He was ludicrously overweight, a slovenly eater who dunked bread in his cocoa cup. Frequently scolded, disciplined, slapped by an immigrant father struggling for survival in the New World, the poor greedy brother masked his rage and shot comical looks at the rest of us. He was a huge kid in short pants and a striped jersey pulled over his provoking belly; a misfit, something of a monster. For that very reason, perhaps, he was greatly loved by our mother.

But these kitchen scenes were given a comical spin by the willed idiocy of the stare that went beyond the enraged father to the rest of the kids. This defiant brother, in retrospect, was in his untutored way a humorist and took a sort of angry pleasure in these confrontations over the kitchen table. It was this same brother who brought home books— boys' adventure stories by G. A. Henty, Street & Smith's Nick Carter detective novels. He and I also read the funny papers, of course. There were no comic books in the early Twenties, only funnies from the Sunday papers.

In the children's ward of the Royal Victoria Hospital, where some months of my eighth year were spent, there was not much else to read. Raggedy Ann and Little Lord Fauntleroy could not hope to compete with the violent colors and the sensational burlesques—the huge grins, the fat noses and piercing whiskers, the chases, the punches, the kicks, the *Bams!* and *Ouches!* and *Take Thats!* You may not recognize the names of the cartoon heroes and the girls they loved. They were Slim Jim, Mutt and Jeff, Boob McNutt, Happy Hooligan who carried an empty tin can on his head, Maggie and Jiggs, an Irish couple, he with a top hat, she with a rolling pin. There was Moon Mullins, who wore a derby hat, and his little brother Kayo, who wore a smaller derby and shared Moon's bedroom, sleeping in a dresser drawer. Boob McNutt, overcoming Shrimp Smith his enemy, ties him hand and foot and stows him in the overhead baggage rack on the train, saying, "You're the only man in the world that I can lick."

There Is Simply Too Much to Think About

This meant that even I, a puny child and hospital patient, *could* lick someone.

These funnies took me from the family circle and the narrow neighborhood streets; they carried me into the life of the country—of the entire English-speaking continent. There was no reason why I should not be a part of it. My small mind was added to the millions of other minds that constituted "the public." The greens, the yellows, the boisterous reds of the funnies that overflowed the features, the figures and the frames, also acted as the solvent of many limitations. The fun of all these grotesque absurdities made you feel democracy as a sort of joke in which everybody participated.

"This is a nation of jokes," says a character of Ralph Ellison's. He adds toward the end of his narrative, "some of the things [he] said were amusing but true. And perhaps their truth lay precisely in their being seen humorously."

Wit, this seems to say, is like the forked branch of the water witch or dowser; it will lead us to the truth.

Abraham Lincoln, who prefaced the discussion of very grave questions with lively back-home anecdotes or parables, offended the clergy and the newspaper publishers of the Eastern Seaboard with his unstatesmanlike jokes. The Civil War was no joke, certainly. But it would not be too far-fetched to ponder whether Lincoln's parables and circuit-riding quips might not have been indispensable preludes to his wide and deep mental contrapuntal constructions. It must have been clear to everyone that the casualties his generals reported made him suffer deeply.

But I must check my tendency to ramble.

The Chicago of the Twenties in which I grew up was dominated by machine politicians, lawyers, judges and officials. The bootleggers' gang wars did not affect the man in the street—civilians looked on from a safe distance. The average reader followed the scandals and murders in the papers and enjoyed Chicago's national and international reputation as a gang city, the home base of Al Capone. Mayor Big Bill Thompson was himself a clown and the newspapers made the most of the moonshine wars. They reported them as if they were covering a visiting circus.

It was assumed as a matter of course by the man in the street that public life was corrupt, that the courts were venal, that the police were on the take, that city and county employees had their hands out, that decent simpletons were Johns or marks—that life was a racket. The muckraking writers of the early years of the century—Lincoln Steffens, Ida Tarbell, Upton Sinclair—were followed, after the Great War, by the debunkers. Historians like W. E. Woodward demythologized our great men, lifted up their togas to show us their feet of clay. They told us that George Washington was pompous, that U. S. Grant was a heavy drinker, that Teddy Roosevelt was an exhibitionist and that Woodrow Wilson in Versailles at the peace conference was a long-faced virgin surrounded by whores. This last metaphor came from John Dos Passos's *U.S.A.* trilogy. Dos Passos, a highly gifted novelist, was not primarily a debunker. He was a populist and the currents of populist skepticism eroded the prestige of the founders of great fortunes, the Rockefellers and Harrimans, the master politicians, the famous revivalists, the top brass everywhere, the Jim Crow South, the sex scandals of sugar daddies and the ladies they kept in love nests.

I wish I could transmit the flavor of the *Police Gazette*'s pink pages or of Twenties tabloids—one can occasionally still taste it in the novels of Sinclair Lewis, especially *Babbitt* and *Elmer Gantry*. It occurs, earlier, in the stories of O. Henry: the hicks in their long johns and the grifters and pitchmen who preyed on them. I may be overdoing the skeptical, wise-guy Twenties, but the daily papers in syndicated columns were read by hundreds of thousands, perhaps millions, of schoolchildren. William Randolph Hearst himself seemed to have a taste for them and in Chicago there were two Hearst papers. Everybody followed Odd McIntyre and, in the *Examiner*, a cracked ingenious humorist named Ted Cook. In his Kookoos column I discovered the haikus of a Japanese poet whose name was T. S. Nakano. Cook's parodies led me at the age of thirteen or fourteen to T. S. Eliot, who was himself a humorist, in part, and a satirist.

In the streets, in shops, on the trains, in daily contacts there was an agreeable sociability—banter, an exchange of wisecracks between passengers on the elevated trains of Chicago or with the lady in the change booth beside the turnstile whose name you were never to know. Wit was the nonideological bond, the scarcely conscious ingredient in the

There Is Simply Too Much to Think About

transitory contacts. I see these contacts now as an expression of democratic mutuality—epiphenomena deriving from wit, offerings of well-disposed casual strangers and floating in the streets and shops.

Some of the leading intellectuals of the time were gifted comedians too. That made a substantial difference in the mental life of the country. The chief comedian of the Twenties and Thirties was H. L. Mencken, editor of *The American Mercury*. His gift for invective was remarkably funny. He referred to the average man as *boobus Americanus*. He detested clergymen and college professors, Babbitts; he gave short shrift to men of letters, members of the Congress—the top brass everywhere, Prohibitionists, Southern Bourbons—all the vain idols of the crowd. No vulgarian, Mencken wrote first-rate appreciations of Theodore Dreiser and other American and English novelists. He wrote about Nietzsche; he was familiar with Beethoven and Wagner. In politics he was, generally, a right-winger. German by descent, he sympathized with the Kaiser. He detested Prohibition, he wrote brilliantly about William Jennings Bryan, the representative of the Bible Belt and of creationism at the Scopes Trial. He was a fine literary critic and wrote on the woman question. Mencken's *American Mercury* showed adolescents of my generation how to reject the false teachings of the booboisie (and, I am afraid, many true ones as well). Most of all, we learned from him how to take an independent critical stand against the Press, the Church, the Schools and the Party—against Vulgarity. What we got from Mencken was mainly the idea that dissent was possible and that its sharpest weapons were language and wit. The high school children of the twentieth century were not then aware that Mencken and his *American Mercury* continued the work of Thomas Paine, of Voltaire and Diderot and Rousseau, and that these in turn built on the thought of their seventeenth-century predecessors.

All over the modern industrial world writers are, and have been for the last two centuries, comedians. You will of course be listing the classics—God forbid that we should fail to give *Anna Karenina* or *Moby-Dick* the full measure of respect they deserve. But the odd fact is that by a very wide margin most novels have been written by ironists, satirists and comedians. Even in *The Brothers Karamazov* the murdered father, a great grotesque, overshadows the passionate Dimitri and the holy Alyosha. Only Ivan approaches the old man in stature. So that even in this great tragic work comedy is irrepressible. In *Othello, Macbeth* or *Lear* there are no such comic characters. The modern writer, when he portrays modern man, quickly learns that modern man has chosen to conceive himself as a compound of comical elements. The boldest comedians are the ones who, like Old Karamazov, have revised all social and traditional fictions in the clear light of first principles as *they* see them.

Since the mid-nineteenth century, novelists—and poets too—are deeply concerned about the survival of art and artists in a commercial civilization and their tendency is to charge the language richly and multiply their allusions. There is a lost-cause or last-stand atmosphere about some of them. Flaubert's *Sentimental Education* exhibits a perfection of language and a skill in every detail of the execution that underlines the rift between the wealth of artistic means and the poverty of the human material. The "best" writers of Flaubert's century and of our own (Joyce, Eliot, et cetera) tell us that beauty continues to be made but that the obstacles to its making are very great and that the makers—and their small and shrinking public—are surrounded by a deepening nihilistic darkness. Joyce, in a language that only initiates and connoisseurs can read, describes the kitchen in which L. Bloom fries his pork kidney and the privy where he sits down with his newspaper. He attaches great art to small persons kicking around Dublin on their quotidian errands.

We who follow them out to the cemetery and back again for lunch enjoy the comic contrast between the richness of the art and the Chaplinesque little man, ad-solicitor-father-husband-cuckold-masturbator. And this is what our masterpieces are like. We understand too well for comfort the contrasts between a consciousness swollen with the knowledge accumulated over decades of reading and reflection and the inadequacy of the company we have to keep—knowledge just ain't power. At bottom it is just another form of helplessness. "When I consider the heavens, the work of Thy fingers," asks the Psalmist, "what is man that Thou should'st be mindful of him?"

Some writers tell us that their art, the way they write, gives the only ethical standard we are likely to see. But this too is comedy. Another way to put it is that we are invited to join in the pleasure of seeing the modern world as artists of the greatest power and scope see it. There is something in this. But you can't expect serious persons to refrain from asking for more.

Well, serious people perhaps needn't be as serious as all that. As I see it, their seriousness has been compromised by a vast transformation of the "reality." To be consistent with my view, I have framed the word *reality* in quotation marks. Anyway, these quotes will soon wither away. My aim is to bring to your attention that this "reality" has undergone a series of tremendous transformations. We have been so busy adapting ourselves, bailing out the flood of overwhelming transformations, that there has been little or no opportunity to understand them.

Let me turn to Ortega y Gasset, the Spanish author of *The Revolt of the Masses*, a charming book, who argued that ordinary workaday mankind doesn't distinguish clearly between nature and human invention and that it views electricity (I choose this one item for the purpose of illustration) as something that comes on when you push a button. It doesn't see a difference, really, between the sunlight and the ceiling fixtures. To him these are free or nearly free commodities, like our drinking water. An educated person understands that these are two quite different things.

Ortega gives the educated person far too much credit. Of course, we know that there are generators in which various fuels are transformed into energy and stored and so on. But having said that, how far have we gotten? Not very far at all. Our education is more or less a humbug. We have learned how to conceal the vast extent of our ignorance. . . . Lecturers used to tell undergraduates in my day that anabolism and catabolism were the breaking down and the building up of tissues, and I suppose the satisfaction this gave us was similar to what was felt by children learning the catechism. The children were put at ease about a deep mystery. It was not then as evident as it is now that we were learning what it was to fake knowledge.

Fake knowledge, as I presently understood, was a comical subject. But it was not the biology lecturer who taught me this. I learned it in a French course from Molière's phony, fast-talking "progressive" doctor who listens to his patient's heart on the right side saying, when the invalid sets him straight, *"Nous avons changé tout cela."*

A degree of progress is revealed when we are able to laugh at our ignorance of certain mysteries. This progress is small but it is important. I shall go a step or two further. About twenty-five years ago in Milan I was, so to speak, caught laughing in public. I can no longer recall what caused me to laugh but I remember that I had carried the audience with me—not a very difficult thing to do. As the laughter was dying down a young man stood up and said, "Why do Americans laugh so much— all of them? You never see a U.S. President or even a high-ranking general who is solemn, or even sober-looking. They are always grinning, chuckling, smiling or bursting with laughter."

Today I can't remember just how I answered. It couldn't have been very hard to do. True, you never saw Hitler smiling in public. And the Duce was not one of your smiling men. Stalin as a rule looked severe. De Gaulle wouldn't have dreamed of grinning for the photographers. Churchill for all his burdens did smile occasionally. FDR, undoubtedly, was a fabulous smiler. Truman laughed less often than Roosevelt in his pictures, but he was neither dour nor severe. I believe that in Milan I did speak of these leaders and describe their public faces. I did not fail to add that there was a hint of existentialism about the posture and voice of my questioner; I said that he appeared to be pledged to dreadful freedom or despair and that though the annoying exuberance of the Americans might strike some Europeans as vacuous, it might also be a sign of their belief in the success of their political and economic ideas.

[2003]

Vermont: The Good Place

In 1951, while I was living in a huge brick compound in the borough of Queens, I read a book about rural New England by Odell Shepard and felt that I must go there at once. I packed my knapsack, bought a pair of hiking boots and took the train from Grand Central to Great Barrington. Following a map copied from the book, I made my way by back roads into Connecticut. I met no other walkers. It was early October, bright and warm. The going was good at first but the country was hilly and I began to tire. On steep grades I was overtaken by trucks. The drivers obviously wondered what I was doing there afoot. Some of them stopped to offer me a ride. I thanked them kindly but said that I meant to hike.

"Hike? You could use a lift, couldn't you?"

"I'm here to see the sights."

My refusal puzzled them. A hiker? Here? The sun was still hot, I was obviously bushed. I must have had the look of a determined self-congratulatory crank and the truckers, driving off, had every reason to be glad I hadn't accepted. My map showed a village nearby. When I asked a telephone lineman how far it was, he only shrugged and stepped on the gas. There was no village at the bottom of the next curve, no general store where I could buy a bottle of Nehi to drink on the wooden steps; there were only sleepy hayfields. The landmarks described by Shepard—settlements, farms, taverns, stables—were gone, wiped out.

When a pickup with a horse trailer pulled up for me a few miles down the road, I was grateful to get in and ease my feet. This driver had a foreign accent; he was a Danish horse trainer. The fact that he was a foreigner helped; I might not have been able to tell an American what had brought me here. The horse trainer sympathized with my romantic pilgrimage. He had done the same thing in Denmark. He pointed out, however, that America was too vast for walking. These wide-open spaces were no Arcadia. The weather may have been right for fauns and satyrs but all the other conditions were wanting. The Yankee farmers were gone. Their sons were stockbrokers, their daughters were living in Philadelphia or New York.

I spent the night in a stable among the Dane's horses. The rats were scuffling under my cot.

But my failed expedition did not end my romance with pastures, woods and streams, with what geographers call the Eastern Woodlands, the New England countryside; it only modernized my perspective. I was an Eastern Woodlander by birth, a native of Lachine, Quebec, on the St. Lawrence. True, I had lived most of my life in Chicago but the Middle West had never seemed quite right to me; its soil was different, its very molecules were fatter, grosser. I imagined, apparently, that the East was materially finer.

Millions of farmers were leaving the land; but city dwellers, among them writers, entertained visions of ease and happiness in the fields, under the trees. Edmund Wilson sometimes rusticated himself on the Cape or in upstate New York. Delmore Schwartz settled near French-town, New Jersey; Mr. Salinger withdrew to New Hampshire. Clearly some of these gifted people looked to the country for relief from town-engendered troubles.

I myself, a case of nerves but trembling also with natural piety, moved to the country in the mid-Fifties, investing a small legacy in a house in Dutchess County where I lived for seven or eight years and became countrified. This grand house (fourteen rooms, a Dutch kitchen, a lordly staircase, countless fireplaces, twenty-foot ceilings) turned me into a handyman. I had no money to spend on plumbing and carpentry. I had to paint walls. I mowed and gardened. I had liter-ary neighbors—Richard Rovere, Gore Vidal—but repairs and grounds keeping left me no time for conversation on reading and writing. Be-sides, I couldn't bear to think that I had squandered the money left me by a hardworking father on a collapsing river mansion—"How typical of you," he would have said. I got rid of the place.

For the last ten years (I see that I am old enough now to be prodigal with decades) I have spent much of my time in Vermont.

My guess is that the land between Great Barrington and New Canaan had become too valuable for farming. Perhaps it had been acquired by developers and was temporarily desolate because they had not yet begun to "develop" it. The broader reason for desolation was that America had gone urban after World War II. Land had been sold or abandoned. In the Northeast, a scrubby second growth of new forests had taken over fields and pastures. If you wander in the backlands of Vermont, as I often do, climbing over wavering, dilapidated stone walls and moss-covered ledges, you come upon old foundations, heaps of red brick, overgrown water mills. Along the roads, the sites of vanished farmhouses are marked by pairs of lilac bushes that once grew beside the driveway and by apple trees surviving among the maples and yellow birches. Here you can commune, if you have a taste for that kind of thing, with the premechanized America of horse-drawn harvesters and harrows. Also locks, hinges, doorknobs, old bottles and every sort of treasure trash. The stone walls had made relatively small fields. It takes no great imaginative effort to put in some sheep or cows or crops— Lilliputian in scale to a Middle Western eye.

But in the yard one can sit in peace under a great shagbark hickory, under a maple even greater that began its life in the eighteenth century. The size of these trees seems to give more height to the sky. Few planes pass this way. Except on weekends, the dirt roads are relatively empty. In the town itself there are no shops or taverns, no industries, no gas stations or garages. The occasional sound of a chain saw or the concussions of a hammer can be heard miles away. The nearest farm is half a mile to the east. It is operated by a widow named Verna and her son Hermie, an earnest, solid, silent, simple country laborer. Hermie is known locally as an artist in fence maintenance. He spends no money on barbed wire. His fences, acres and acres of them, are spliced with odd pieces of wire, the greater part of the work well rusted, some of the bits no longer than an inch or two. There is not a whole yard of new wire anywhere. The artist is muscular, uncommunicative, unsmiling, in farm boots, bib overalls and a peaked cap.

I have no near neighbors here. The closest is a biologist from Yale who prefers Vermont to any college town and teaches science in a local high school. His wife designs and makes jewelry. Half a mile to the west is the house of the ingenious, extraordinarily inventive man who built my place. He and his wife, an obstetrical nurse, have become my friends. There are few townspeople out this way; most of us are newcomers or summer people. No township would be complete, I suppose, without its eccentric squatter. Ours collects old heaps—cars and trucks. His huts, plastic fluttering from their windows, are surrounded by ditched machinery of every sort. His livestock browse on weeds or eat broken rice cakes trucked in from a factory somewhere near the Massachusetts line. Enormous long-legged pigs run into the road, looking as if they were wearing high heels. They invade the vegetable gardens of the people along the road and root in them. Some say that the squatter comes of a respectable family and is well educated. In the old days he would have been called a remittance man or a gypsy or a tinker. The property on which he squats adjoins a dam recently abandoned by the beavers.

The Old Vermonters in this neighborhood acquired their land in the reign of George II. Virtually indistinguishable from these are the French settlers who came down from Canada generations ago—people who call themselves La Rock and worship in Protestant churches. There is an immovable, change-resisting population of Vermonters in the backcountry. Some of them claim, with partly defiant pride, that they have never visited a big city. Flossie Riley, who still gets up before daylight to milk her cows (no machines for Flossie), said that she had been to Burlington once and that was bad enough; the noise gave her a headache and the traffic fumes were suffocating; she wouldn't dream of going to New York. She knew perfectly well what Manhattan was like; she had seen it on television and wanted no part of it. Adherents of the ancient ways dig, chop, tend their animals, tap maple trees; their talk is about the roads in mud time, about frostbite or thermal underwear, the price of cordwood or the volunteer fire department. Many of the locals hold jobs in the larger towns—in a surgical-dressing factory, for instance, or in a mill that manufactures old-looking barn board for householders who want a living room that looks rustic. Centers like Brattleboro or

There Is Simply Too Much to Think About

Greenfield, Massachusetts, attract workers who drive in from "bedroom communities" twenty or thirty miles away. Some of the remoter villages resist the real estate developers and the temptation of high land prices. From fear of outsiders and their outside noise and restlessness, they refuse to license new shops. Rural Vermonters install TV dishes in their yards and put up aerials; their children, like children elsewhere, are absorbed in the voodoo beat of a Walkman. No part of this country can be "out of it." What is happening everywhere is, one way or another, known to everyone. Shadowy world tides wash human nerve endings in the remotest corners of the earth. Villages are nevertheless controlled by insiders. Newcomers are accepted on certain conditions. They must pay their taxes, behave decently and follow a few quite minimal rules.

My wife and I arrive in the spring, like Canada geese, sometimes taking off again but intermittently visible until the fall. The postman and the garbage collector have hard information about our comings and goings. There are, however, other mysterious underground channels of information, for when Jack Nicholson, accompanied by William Kennedy, the Albany novelist, and his wife called on me a couple of years ago, advance word got around. Nicholson, then filming Kennedy's *Ironweed* in Albany, had come to chat about a film based on one of my novels. His white stretch limousine could not make the narrow turn between my gateposts. Silent neighbors watched from a distance as the chauffeur maneuvered the long car with its Muslim crescent antenna on the trunk. Then Nicholson came out, observed by many. He said, "Gee, behind the tinted glass I couldn't tell it was so green out here." He lit a mysterious-looking cigarette and brought out a small pocket ashtray, a golden object resembling a pillbox. Perhaps his butt-ends had become relics or collectibles. I should have asked him to explain this; everything he did was noted and I had to answer the questions of my neighborhood friends, for whom Nicholson's appearance here was something like the consecration of a whole stretch of road.

Our roads—the whole township network—were described by another visitor, a motherly old person from Idaho who came here to visit her son, as "one green tunnel after another." From the perspective of a driver, shaded roads would look like that. On warm days a walker is grateful for the shelter, although when the wind dies down the blackflies, deerflies and no-see-ums will be waiting in the hollows. When it rains you are kept almost dry by the packed leaves and you hear the drops falling from level to level. You will have become familiar over the years with each of the beeches, yellow birches and maples, the basswoods, the locusts, the rocks, the drainage ditches, the birds and the wildlife, down to the red newts on the road surface.

People whose leisure time needs to be organized are the profitable concern of professional organizers worldwide. Daily papers and monthly magazines suggest, or advertise, holidays for all seasons, in all zones. East, west, north and south, preparations are made to receive and entertain tourists, swimmers, skiers, diners, loungers, dancers. Whole regions are organized by grant corporations for travelers in quest of new scenes. More important perhaps than palm trees, pyramids, beaches, the temples of Angkor Wat, is the quest for peace. Repose, quiet, peace. But the restless few, longing for singular delights, find themselves once more among the many in facilities the same the world over—room, bed, shower, TV, restaurant, and at 10:00 A.M. your party will be lectured in the Uffizi or on a woodland trail.

But in the Vermont I have been talking about there are no such preparations. In the nearest town, yes, people will be descending from their buses to buy baskets, maple syrup, aged cheddar and knickknacks. But ten miles away, through the woods, you hear no engines. When the birds awaken you, you open your eyes on the massed foliage of huge old trees. Should the stone kitchen be damp, as it may be even in July, you bring wood up from the cellar and build a fire. After breakfast you carry your coffee out to the porch. The dew takes up every particle of light. The hummingbirds chase away hummingbird trespassers from the fuchsias and Maltese crosses. Grass snakes come out of their sheltering rocks to get some sun. The poplar leaves, when you narrow your eyes, are like a shower of small change. And when you walk down to the pond you may feel what the Psalmist felt about still waters and green pastures.

[1990]

Winter in Tuscany

Winter in Tuscany? Well, why not. Millions of Italians do it. The modern tourist takes his winter holidays either in the sun or on the ski slopes. But business brought me to Florence in December and I had put it to my wife, Janis, that with two weeks free when business was done, the Sienese countryside might be just the place to restore the frazzled minds of two urban Americans. The crowds of winter would be madding elsewhere—in the Caribbean or on Alpine slopes—and we should have the whole of this ancient region to ourselves, sharing the cold with the populace.

Anticipating severe weather, we had brought our winter silks, goose downs, rabbit linings, mufflers and Reeboks. Montalcino was cold, all right, but the air was as clear as icicles. Autumn had just ended, the new wine was in the barrels, the last of the olives were in the presses, the sheep were grazing, the pigs fattening, and ancient churches and monasteries were adding yet another winter to their tally. From the heights near Montalcino we could see Siena. In forty kilometers there was nothing to block the view. I have no special weakness for views. It was the beauty of the visibility as such, together with the absence of factories, refineries and dumps, that penetrated the twentieth-century anti-landscape armor of my soul. To admire views, however, you need to stand still, and you had to endure the cold. The *tramontana* was battering the town when we arrived. It forced open windows in the night and scoured our faces by day.

Generations of Americans brought up with central heating can endure the cold on skis, in snowmobiles, on the ice, but they lack the European ability to go about their business in cold kitchens and icy parlors. Europeans take pride in their endurance of winter hardships. It gives them a superiority that to us seems less Spartan than masochistic.

I can remember cursing the management in grim English hotel rooms while going through my pockets for a shilling to drop into the gas meter, and as a guest in a Cambridge college I was driven once to the porter's lodge to ask for a little warmth. The gentleman porter said, "If you will look under the bed, sir, you will discover a heating device."

Under the bedspring when I lifted the coverlet I found a wire fixture holding a naked forty-watt bulb. The heat this bulb threw was supposed to penetrate the mattress and restore you to life. This austerity went with the dusty ragged academic gowns of the dons, held together, literally, with Scotch tape and staples. It pleased these scholars to be dowdy, indifferent to blue fingers and red noses, and heedless of freezing toilet seats. For the mind was its own place and made a heaven of hell. The door to this mental heaven stood open, but I was freezing.

Once freed from dependency on heating, you don't mind the cold. The Tuscan winter didn't affect your appreciation of Tuscan cheeses, soups and wines. On your hummocky mattress you slept well enough, and after breakfast you went to visit a Romanesque church, a papal summer residence; you walked in the fields. You can sit comfortably in sheltered sunny corners and watch the sheep grazing.

The people you meet are happy to have you here; they take your off-season visit as a mark of admiration for the long and splendid history of their duchy and like to reward you with bits of information. In passing, one tells you about the deforestation of hilltops during the Dark Ages; another mentions the ravages of malaria and the Black Death of 1348; a third fills you in about exports to England from medieval Tuscany. The soils of all these fields seem to have passed through millions of human hands generation after generation. Our American surroundings will never be so fully humanized. But the landscape carries the centuries lightly, and ancient buildings and ruins do not produce gloomy feelings. Romanesque interiors in fact are a good cure for heaviness.

The region is as famous for its products—oil, wine and cheeses—as for castles, fortresses and churches. A disastrous freeze killed the olive

There Is Simply Too Much to Think About

groves some winters ago—the ancient trees now furnish farms with winter fuel. The new plantings do not as yet yield much oil but the wine reserves are as full as ever.

In the Fattoria dei Barbi, belonging to the Colombini-Cinelli family, the vats, some of them made of Slovenian oak, resemble the engines of 747 jets in size. On walls and beams there are thermometers and gauges. We are conducted here by Angela, a young woman whose pretty face rivals the wine display in interest. Clean quiet cellars, level after level—the only living creature we meet below is a cat who seems to know the tour by heart. During World War II false partitions were put up to hide old vintages from the Germans. The almost sacred bottles are dimly, somewhat reverentially lighted. You feel called upon to pay your respects to this rare Brunello di Montalcino. With a banner tail the cat is an auxiliary guide and leads the party up and down, in and out, from cellar to cellar. We take to this tomcat, who has all the charm of a veteran of the sex wars.

When we return to ground level the cat leaves the building from between our legs. We enter next an enormous room where white pecorino cheeses, regularly spaced on racks, are biding their time. After the cheeses come the meat-curing rooms. In spiced air the hams hang like the boxing gloves of heavyweights. To see so much meat takes away the desire for food, so that when we go into the excellent Taverna dei Barbi I am more inclined to admire the pasta than to eat it. But you can never lose your desire for the Brunello wine. Your susceptibility returns at the same rate as the glass fills. Once again it makes sense to be a multimillionaire. The Brunello fragrance is an immediate QED of the advantages of the pursuit of riches. (I never joined up.)

"Don't miss Pienza," we were many times advised, so we recruit Angela to drive us there on a sunny but very sharp morning. Pienza was the birthplace, in 1405, of Aeneas Silvius Piccolomini, later Pope Pius II. He was responsible for the handsome group of Renaissance buildings at the center of the town. It is the finest of these buildings, the Palazzo Piccolomini, that we have come to inspect.

From our parking place we ascend to the main street. The first impression is one of stony Renaissance elegance combined with the modern plate glass of shops. The temperature is a bar or two below freezing. A fine group of old gents standing outside the open door of a café acknowledge us with dignity as we move down the all-stone pavement to the palazzo. As cultural duty requires, we look into the church of Pope Pio, where we see long fissures running through the stone nave. (How to keep up with the maintenance of monuments?) Continuing to the palazzo we are overtaken in the courtyard by the custodian. He spots us from the café *en face*, his warm hideout. Thickly dressed in wool and leather, he comes with his ring of silver-glinting keys to lead us up the stairs. We pass through the small living quarters used until not very recently by surviving members of the family. A Piccolomini Count Silvio lived in the three front rooms until 1960. We understand from our guide that a picture of an aviator atop the piano in the music room represented the last of his line. Perhaps he was Count Silvio's son and heir—exact information is hard to come by.

In the living quarters there is a framed genealogical tree weighed down by hundreds of names. We pass through the noble library and the armor room. We circle rugs so ancient, so thin, so pale that a step might shatter them. On bookshelves are huge leather-bound volumes of the classics. I note that fifteenth-century popes were reading Thucydides and even Aristophanes, and as we enter the papal bedroom I think how difficult it would have been to handle these folios in bed. In this freezing chamber the imposing bed is grandly made and formally covered in dark green, a dire seaweed-colored fabric and sinking, sinking, sinking into decay. Perhaps it goes back to the last century. The mattress and bedding may be no more than eighty or ninety years old but the thing carries a threat of eternity; you feel that if you were to lie down and put your head on this seaweed-colored bolster, you would never rise again. There is a fireplace, or rather a Gothic cavity in the wall big enough to accommodate eight-foot logs, but you'd have to stoke it for a week to drive out such an accumulation of cold.

We are happy to escape again into the great-windowed hall. The guide has gone out on a balcony to sun himself. Joining him, we return to Italy itself and latch onto the sun with gratitude.

We order cappuccino in an open-to-the-weather café. The great

There Is Simply Too Much to Think About

espresso machine sizzles and spits and the cups are served on the enormous polished bar. They lose heat so quickly that you'd better down them before ice forms.

Catering to tourists, the boutiques are nicely heated. We go to a stationery shop and buy a minivolume of Petrarch and other Florentine general-issue items—classy clutter for the apartments of the well traveled. The one prize is a Venetian glass pen from Murano, an iridescent spiral.

In Montalcino I am treated for a sprained shoulder by a local herbal specialist. His nickname is "Il Barba" and he is an old man of heroic stature, more stubbly than bearded. He became a local hero by playing the part of the brigand Bruscone (popularly known as "Il Barba") at a party celebrating the new Bruscone dei Barbi wine. Evidently he fell in love with his own portrayal of the legendary bandit. Himself a man of action, he was a resistance fighter and the walls of the narrow front room of his apartment are hung with medals and certificates of valor. There is also a fine display of guns, for he is a hunter. This giant and his small wife conduct us to the long cupboardlike kitchen, where he seats me on a high stool and like any doctor asks me solicitously how I came by this sprain. I tell him I took a header over the handlebars of a bike last summer in Vermont. It doesn't make much sense to him that the likes of me should be an intrepid bike rider. He tells me to strip. I take off my shirt and he examines me. When we have between us located the painful places he pours his mixture into a small saucepan and heats it on the stove. At all times the old wife is close behind him with her arms folded and held tightly to her body. While she gossips hoarsely with our Italian friends he rubs my shoulder with his herbal remedy dissolved in olive oil. He applies the hot mixture using his hand like a housepainter's brush. At a nod from her husband the wife steps out to the porch to fetch a salve to follow the ointment. Enjoying the massage, I begin to feel that this Barba may cure me. I have a weakness anyway for secret herbal remedies and the treatment in the kitchen has its occult side. (Special security measures are taken.) I pull on my shirt again, altogether pleased with the occasion. The exertion of getting into my pullover causes no pain and I tell him he is a wonderful therapist. He bows as though he already knew this. In the parlor he reaches into a cupboard next to the guns and takes down a drawstring sack containing a large number of wild-boar tusks. I should never have guessed that they were so light. Some of these trophies have been tipped with silver and I suppose necklaces or bracelets can be made of them. Thieves would rather have these than the guns, he says.

The great bandit Barba towers over us, smiling, and holds the door open, refusing payment and telling me to come back tomorrow for another treatment. He is so tall that we don't have to duck under his arm. We go down the stairs into the night, very happy.

Further outdoor sightseeing: Habituated to the cold, we no longer shun it. We now prefer outdoor excursions to the inspection of church interiors. There is a charcoal burners' camp nearby, and an elderly gentleman, Ilio Raffaelli, who was himself, until his twenty-fifth year, a *carbonaro*, shows us how the workers lived and how the charcoal was made. The camp, which he has reconstructed himself, is extremely primitive. With soil and grass stuffed into a wooden framework, the little dwelling of the burners reminds me of an American sod hut. The place is windowless. The workmen and their families slept on simple wooden frames that occupied most of the space. One was for man and wife, the other for the children, as many as five or six. All worked in the woods, bringing up water from the spring or, in season, gathering berries and other edibles. There were no metal artifacts except axes and saws. The shovels were wooden, the rakes were skillfully whittled. The burners contracted with the landowners and they camped for half a year or so till they had cut all the usable wood on the property. Then they moved to another estate, where they built a new sod house. The huts, heated by a small fire, were warm enough at night, said our guide.

Raffaelli is a sturdy short man in a cap and an open jacket. (The afternoon was not particularly warm. Our noses and eyes were running; his were dry. He was evidently indurated against natural hardships.) A black thread that had worked loose from the cap hung over his face unnoticed while he gave his explanatory lecture. (With his large

There Is Simply Too Much to Think About

objectives he didn't notice trifles.) In his description of the charcoal-making process, he was exceptionally precise: the cutting of the wood into proper lengths, the stacking of it, the layers of leaves and soil piled on the mound, the space at the center for the fire, which had to be stoked day and night. There were wooden ladders leaning on the cone and screens against the wind, which might drive the blaze too high, endangering the work of months.

So *this* was how people for many centuries lived upon the land, right *on* the packed earth, so to speak, so adept in the management of their pots, spoons, axes and handmade rakes, so resourceful—to see this was a lesson worth a whole shelf of history books. I understood even better what life had been like when our guide said, "Whenever one of our boys in the army sent a letter, we gathered inside the hut and sat on the beds to listen to the reading." He laughed and added that they had all been sent to the priest to learn their letters.

His little Italian car was parked just at the edge of the woods and he would get into it at dusk and drive to Montalcino where he lived. You felt however that his real life was here in this cold clearing. He seemed unwilling to part with the old life and was perhaps not a thorough townsman. A self-taught scholar, he had written a book about the plants and small fauna. Schoolchildren were brought to him for lessons about the woods. He taught them the names of the trees and sang them the charcoal burners' ballads and reminisced about this vanished trade. He was a modest person, without the legendary airs of Signor Barba, the herbal doctor.

Finally we go into the woods near San Giovanni d'Asso with two truffle hunters, Ezio Dinetti and Fosco Lorenzetti, and their dogs, Lola, Fiamma and Iori. On our arrival in San Giovanni we are received by the young dark-haired mayor of the town, Roberto Cappelli, who makes us a little speech of welcome and presents us with a heavy bronze truffle medallion.

The season for truffles is almost over. It has been an unexceptional year—slim pickings. But the dogs are no less keen, rushing from the cars as soon as the doors are opened. There is no breed of truffle hounds.

Lola, Fiamma and Iori appear to be ordinary no-account mutts, but they are in fact highly trained specialists, officially listed, with their own photo-ID license cards and tattooed registration numbers. Turn them over and you can see the numerals under the pink skin. The novice Iori, a skinny dark-brown adolescent, is hobbled with a length of chain to prevent his rushing off by himself in his enthusiasm. The added weight gives him a bowlegged gait. We set out after the dogs on a path through the poplars, tramping over dry leaves. Hurrying after them you find yourself breathing deeper, drawing in the pungent winter smells of vegetation and turned-up soil. The experienced hunters work the dogs earnestly with urgent exclamations and commands: *Lola, dai.* (Come on.) *Qui.* (Here.) *Vieni qui.* (Come here.) *Giù.* (Down.) *Dove?* (Where?) *Piglialo.* (Take it.) They cajole, huff, threaten, praise, caution, restrain, interrogate and reward their dogs. The animals track a distant scent. Though the ground is frozen, they will sniff out a truffle under a foot and a half of earth. Each man has an implement on a leather snap slung over the shoulder, a device about two feet in length with a sharp rectangular blade for digging and sampling the earth. With this *vanghetto* the hunters scoop up a clod of beige-brown mud and nose it with intensity. If the soil is saturated with the truffle odor they halloo the dogs to dig deeper.

Single file we cross a thin bridge, a couple of logs strapped together over a gully. Lola, the gifted matriarch, has found something and the dirt near the streambed sprays behind her. Ezio knows exactly where to intervene and, paying her off with a treat, himself unearths the smallish truffle, a mere nubbin, and slips it into his pocket.

The sun is going down and we stop more often to chat under the chilly poplars. The afternoon has not been a grand success, for the dogs have turned up only three truffles. Ezio and Fosco insist on our taking them. As we head back through the woods we hear a dark story. Sporting honor among the hunters is not all that it used to be, they tell us. Jealous competitors have taken to poisoning the more talented dogs, tossing out bits of sausage containing strychnine when they leave the grounds, Ezio says with anger. A promising pup of his was among six dogs lost to the poisoners last year. Months of training wasted. In the old days it took only a year to break in a dog. Now that there are more

There Is Simply Too Much to Think About

hunters and fewer truffles you need as many as three years of training, so that when a dog dies the loss is considerable.

The ungloved hands of the hunters when we shake them at parting are warmer than ours, for all our leather and wool and Thinsulate. Driving back to Montalcino we consider the mystery of the truffle. Why is it so highly prized? We try to put a name to the musk that fills the car. It is digestive, it is sexual, it is a mortality odor. Having tasted it I am willing to leave it to the connoisseurs. I shall go on sprinkling grated cheese on my pasta.

[1992]

Before I Go Away: A Words and Images Interview with Norman Manea

NM: Could we speak of your mother and father?

SB: My father's name was Abraham, my mother's name was Liza. It was one of these *shadchan* or matchmaker marriages and they were very happy together in Russia before the war. They immigrated in 1913. They had to leave because my father was doing business with fake papers. I don't know what the whole story was. There was a trial. He kept all the newspapers—very mysterious, in the Russian alphabet, printed on green paper—locked away in his desk. And that was the golden time for my mother—that was when she was a young bride and there was plenty of money and they were living in the capital and going to the *cafés chantants* and so forth and so on. She was very happy there. Then she got to Canada and she was washing everything in the tub by herself, by hand. There were no servants, certainly no money to pay for help, and there were no laundries in those days. It was a very difficult time for a fine-looking young woman. And of course my mother would tell her children the story of her fall from grace. We heard all those stories. I know them very well to this day. And of course all their hope was in their children because they were grown adults and there was no way for them to learn the language of the new country. I often wonder how she lived under those circumstances. A few blocks from the house she was lost. In those days every drugstore had an electric mortar and pestle on the sign—you know, the pharmacist's pestle and mortar. Whenever she saw one from the streetcar she would say, "We're here!" "No, Mom, we're not home; it's just another drugstore." And she was continually getting letters from back home of bad news—that people were dying, especially during the Revolution. It was very, very hard. She had a cousin, a famous Menshevik who used to go around lecturing for socialist societies, but he didn't want to have anything to do with her. She was a green cousin. So that was how it was. We all lived in her hope, which was that her children would restore the wonderful position that she'd had as a young woman in St. Petersburg.

I have a sister. As the Jews would say, she was the princess of the family. There was very little money for clothing and what there was she got first chance at, so we wore each other's hand-me-downs. You know, you'd wear your brother's jacket of three years ago as soon as you could shorten the sleeves a bit. New clothes were very seldom bought for us. Before Rosh Hashanah your father would take you down and buy you a pair of pants or something—clean pants to wear to *shul*. That's the way things were. My father, at that time, was working in a bakery, a job for which he had no experience. But he had a cousin who owned a bakery in the Polish neighborhood in Chicago. So my father worked nights and slept during the day and we had to be very quiet around the house. That's an outline of the situation.

NM: How were the alliances? In a family you establish alliances and complicities, don't you? There were three boys and one girl; a mother and a father. Where were your alliances?

SB: There was a great deal of affection flowing around very freely, and my Americanized brothers saw this affection as a bad influence. They wanted to get rid of it immediately because it enslaved them to my father's will, but the rest of us enjoyed this affection and kindness. There was also a kind of campaign against it inside the family. This was part of the American process for me. It lasted quite a long time. I was already in my forties when my father died. When I wept at the funeral my eldest brother said to me, "Don't carry on like an immigrant." He had business friends there and was ashamed of all this open emotionalism. This should give you a little bit of a handle.

NM: You kept a good grip on that sort of thing, and it became your material.

SB: That's right.

NM: So you found another solution. You said your father was a kind of Abraham, a man who was tough.

SB: He was tough.

NM: Did your mother protect you, defend you?

SB: Yes, but it wasn't as though my father had no affection for the children. He was the disciplinarian. She didn't discipline us. She would threaten us, say, "I'm gonna tell Pa about this." That was bad because you'd get a motorized slap back and forth. Such was the discipline in the family. It was muscle.

NM: What about books and literature?

SB: My father was a reader. He read a great deal and in those days there was a lot of reading. I have an idea that the Yiddish papers were very good and very helpful to the immigrant Jews—to explain things and to acquaint them with the history of the U.S. And my father would surprise me from time to time because he would ask me questions about the founding of the colonies, and then it turned out that he was reading about this in the Yiddish papers. *Forwerts* was a powerful influence, a beneficial one. The Yiddish press did try to educate these European Jews and connect them with the Constitution, the framework of the country, all the rest of that. The papers were always filled with interesting historical data and the immigrants were always learning a great deal—that is, if they were willing to read, and my father was a devoted reader. I started to read in the hospitals where I spent a lot of time. They would come around with a cart and with books and you would pick some books; mostly foolish fairy tales but occasionally there was some real book among them.

NM: For the better part of a year in Montreal you were hospitalized for pleurisy and pneumonia. Do you think that isolation was important in shaping your sensitivity, your reading?

SB: I suppose so. One of the things you learned about was anti-Semitism. You were a little Jewish kid and they kept reminding you of it. The nurses would keep reminding you of it, which would make me very angry. I was mad enough to kill but I was also very puny. I was eight years old and I weighed forty pounds or something like that. I felt very receptive to what I was reading in these books about life in America, pioneers, farmers, immigrants, hunters, Indians. The Indians had a most terrific effect everywhere, especially in Europe, I understand. They were also very popular in the U.S. and Canada.

NM: Do you remember how the family first responded when they learned that you were not only a reader but maybe also a writer? Jewish families tended to fear that such boys would grow up to be *Luftmenschen*, dreamy and impractical.

SB: My mother got sick early on, when we came from Canada. She had cancer. She had a breast removed and then she died of cancer and that was the main drama of family life. And my father was frantic and didn't have time to bring up the children himself, and he wouldn't have known how to do it anyway. So what happened was we had a dying mother, as we discovered after a few years in Chicago. We had to lean toward her emotionally.

Of course they were very suspicious of my outside contacts,

which they considered wild, as indeed they were. Wild high school intellectuals—there used to be such a thing in the old days when kids had developed an interest not only in literature but also in politics, and not just politics but left-wing politics. My people worried about that, and they thought my school friends were *messhugoyim*, crazy people. Indeed some of them were; but some went on to become fairly important in the community—newspapermen, for instance. My family was afraid these were all alienating influences.

My mother was very Orthodox, my father was not. My father had been disaffected from Orthodoxy as a *yeshiva bocher*, a young student of Talmud, and then later in Petersburg, where it was just an impediment to have all these religious practices. He didn't turn his back on them; but neither did he recommend them to his children.

There was also the economic struggle, which was very severe for them, and they felt that the children should be earning and bringing in money as soon as possible to help the family. My sister, I think, was taken advantage of because she went through high school and then she stopped. They couldn't afford her going on to school when she should be bringing money in. So she, at an early age, became a stenographer. She worked in offices. My brothers were what we used to call hustlers. They sold papers in the streets, peddled chocolate bars on the commuter trains. They sold magazines until they could get jobs, though they were low-paying jobs. I know my brother Sam wanted to go to medical school, but there wasn't a chance we could afford it. My eldest brother went to some cheap law school in downtown Chicago and eventually he became a lawyer, but it didn't do him any good. He was also a businessman and blowhard. He was a very picturesque character altogether. He introduced me to the idea of chasing women, drinking, being at wild parties. I didn't have much taste for all that—my friends were mainly the high school intellectuals—but it was fascinating to see how life was shaping up. I clung to the family—I have an instinct for clinging to affection and the family—but my brothers didn't, and insofar as I respected them and was guided by them I was taken away from family influence at an early age. Especially by my eldest brother, who was a great Americanizer: We hadn't been here two or three years and he was wearing fancy clothes, loud clothes. Loud shirts. And he was full of contempt for *kashruth*, the Jewish dietary laws, and all Jewish observances. He was the hostile element in the family, the antireligious element.

NM: We see that a bit in *Augie March*. The older brother, the tough one; the younger, sensitive. What happened when they saw you were this special beast?

SB: They gave up on me and they decided that I was fair game, that I could be taken. They could use me advantageously. Of course when I was a schoolboy there wasn't much they could get out of me. But it's a long and complicated story. I don't think it's necessary to go into it.

NM: At some point you ran away with a friend of yours to conquer the world, and it seems you didn't succeed on that first try.

SB: No! We succeeded! He was quite a politician, Sydney J. Harris, if not much of a writer. A gifted journalist, actually, and at an early age. He didn't go to college. His family wouldn't send him to college. It was probably the making of him because he created a position for himself, quite a good position—he became a reporter on the *Chicago Newspaper* and the *Daily News*. And while I was still in college he was getting a byline on the papers. But he was a wild one too. They were all fairly wild. Of course people seemed a lot wilder to me than they may have been in reality because I came from a family where parental control was so strong. They did things that I envied but didn't dare to do.

NM: And how did your father respond to all this?

SB: My father, who didn't know English well, needed his English-speaking sons in the business. With Maurice and Sam he had lots of quarrels because he was *ungeklapteh,* as they say in Yiddish—hot-blooded, full of passion, fighting with everyone. He was a very feisty man, enviably I think, because he wasn't big and strong. He was just willing to fight. My second brother was a mild person, clever and thoughtful. It was the oldest brother who was the agitator, the Americanizer. He had almost consciously fought the Orthodox influence and, as much as he could, dragged us along with him. Not my brother Sam who then backed away, but me. I was very happy to be Americanized; being Americanized in those days meant the way you dressed, the way you spoke, the way you viewed yourself, the things you read and how you imagined your future, your career. Of course, as far as they were concerned there was only one future and one career and that was business and nothing else mattered and you were made of disagreeably soft stuff if you went in for art and ideas. You were not a *mensch*, you'd never amount to anything. They were all convinced that I had no center to me and that I didn't know where I was going or what I was doing and up to a point they were right.

NM: Did you give business a try?

SB: Yes, because my father owned various businesses, always very strange businesses. For instance, he sold wood to the Jewish bakeries of Chicago as fuel. He had this bakery experience so he knew all the Jewish bakers in Chicago. Of course they wanted to buy from him. But this involved going to the lumber mills in Michigan and Wisconsin and buying up the scrap wood, the reject wood, and bringing it to Chicago in freight cars and then selling it to his bakeries. This meant there were truck deliveries, so before I knew it I was in the railroad district of the city, which very few kids of my background ever got close to. And we knew all the Jewish bakeries in Chicago. That was a great privilege for me. We would come into the shop from the back where the baking was done. When they brought gas ovens into baking my father got into the coal business. That was another non-Jewish business— there were very few Jews who ran coal yards and it meant that my weekends were taken up with being on the scale. The truck came in empty. You weighed it. Then it was loaded. You took the weight a second time and then you billed for the coal they had bought. During those days, during the Depression, they would drive their trucks up and down the street and sell their coal by the bag for people to cook with and to heat their houses. And this brought me into the slums in a way I never had been. Those are tough people and fighting and guns were common; the unions were present, and there was a lot of tough life, and by himself my father couldn't have made it. His sons became indispensable to him. We ordered, bought, paid bills, sold and so forth; they trucked the coal, found the customers. Suddenly my father was in a business he'd never in his wildest imagination dreamed about, and it was through his sons that he was able to do this. My two brothers became very wealthy. But of course I had my own engagements and departed very soon.

NM: What does it mean, very soon?

SB: By the time I was in college I was already taking my distance. Of course coal was paying my way through college and so I had to work behind the scales in a semi-industrial neighborhood where there was light industry, poultry markets, wholesale markets all around and railroad people coming in. It was actually a better education for me than the university.

NM: But in college you already felt that your path was different?

SB: Yes. In college I behaved as though my career was to be a writer and that guided me. Not a career as a teacher or any other professional activity. As a writer. Of course my family paid very little attention to the writing and attributed it to adolescent foolishness. Maybe it was.

NM: I assume you were still obsessed with Americanization. It's evident in *Augie March* and in other places where you're obviously searching for your vocation, experimenting with Marxism, Trotskyism, Freud and other excitements.

SB: That's perfectly true. In high school I was a socialist. We had a socialist club, and we read and debated and disputed and some of the people we went to school with became communist leaders and well-known Trotskyites. For some reason Trotsky took a very powerful hold in certain American cities and Chicago was one of them. To read Trotsky's *History of the Russian Revolution* was an eye-opener even though most of it was party line. We didn't know that at the time, and this caused conflict at home because my father didn't want me reading Trotsky. He was very shrewd about such things and he knew a lot about what was going on in the Soviet Union in the Twenties, much more than I did. I would have done well and saved myself a lot of trouble if I had listened to him because he had it straight from the very beginning; that was a very important matter because so many Russian Jews in the United States, either for sentimental reasons or opportunistically, even if they were not given to radicalism themselves, took advantage of this fascination with Russian revolutionary Marxism. Because it brought Russia into the news, and they had a Russian past, it gave them a kind of authority they wouldn't otherwise have had.

But my father drew the line against any of that and when I brought people home, especially people who had been to the

Soviet Union, young Americans who had done some kind of work there, he gave them a hard time. "You don't really know Russia. You don't really know what's happening there." And he was right. But I felt ashamed that he should be such a reactionary.

Then when I was still quite young, I went to Mexico. That's a separate matter. One of my reasons for going was to have some conversation with Trotsky. My mother had died and she left me a five-hundred-dollar insurance policy and my father wanted the money and I refused to give it to him. I said, I'm going to Mexico. I don't know why I said that. So I went with a friend of mine, Herbert Passin, who later became a professor of Japanese literature and culture at Columbia University. He was there too. We had an appointment with Trotsky, and we came to the door of the house. An unusual amount of excitement. We asked for Trotsky, and they said who are you and we said we're newspapermen. They said Trotsky's in the hospital. So we went to the hospital and we asked to see Trotsky, and they opened the door and said he's in there, so we went in and there was Trotsky. He had just died. He had been assassinated that morning. He was covered in blood and bloody bandages and his white beard was full of blood. Well, I remained a Trotskyite for a time after that but I soon turned away from all of that stuff. During the war a great many of us gave up on the whole revolutionary ideology because it was so crazy, so false, and we had watched the Popular Front going to pieces in Spain and we knew what was behind it. The whole thing was very disillusioning, and as a matter of fact we were drifting away from Trotskyism because of the line Trotsky had taken on the Russian invasion in Finland.

You know, you never realize how crazy your life has been until you tell the story and then it's you, a *meshugener*. It doesn't make sense. At least I could have divided the money, my mother's legacy, with my father. He needed it very badly. In those days two hundred fifty dollars was a lot of money.

NM: Interesting that you were there with Trotsky at the wrong moment, not only because Trotsky was dead, but also the wrong moment for you because you were already ceasing to believe in him.

SB: I thought, how could I go see the great man and take up his time by discussing theoretical questions that he understood a thousand times better than I, especially since he invented the theory himself? It's an elaborate position he held. I couldn't possibly have argued with him; I saw it would be pointless; it would be the cat visiting the queen. I thought, I have an introduction and I am in Mexico and I will take the bus and make an appointment.

NM: Did you want to discuss the Finland War with him?

SB: Yes, that was the issue at the time and it broke the American Trotskyite movement into two parts, one headed by James P. Cannon, who was an old party-liner Stalinist type really, and the other by Max Shachtman, who was a very clever and engaging personality. I suppose I felt that as a writer I had some latitude to go in on my own and talk to him about the way things were. Anyhow I was always a little reticent to push myself on people, especially in those circumstances; Trotsky was continually under attack and they had already tried several times to kill him. The villa was an armed camp and yet this young assassin, Rámon Mercader, got in with his Alpine ax.

NM: Had the American Trotskyites made an effort to convince Trotsky that he was wrong about the Finland War? Was his position that it was still a just war for the Soviets, no matter what others thought?

SB: Well, it was very strange because people were still arguing esoteric questions in Marxism. That's what was strange about it. It was not a question of stopping the war in Finland. We couldn't

There Is Simply Too Much to Think About

stop it. There was nothing you could do about it. But there remained a theoretical question to be decided: Could a workers' state, even a corrupt workers' state, wage an imperialist war? And the answer for Trotsky was no, and for the others the answer was yes. That split the movement in the United States.

NM: How many days did you stay in Mexico?

SB: Oh, I was there a few months.

NM: So you were at the funeral?

SB: Yes.

NM: How was it?

SB: It was the usual Trotskyite oratory about the career of the great man who had been our leader and had been a mastermind, and he and Lenin had made the Revolution but Stalin had taken all the credit and gotten rid of everyone; and this was another of the great crimes of Stalin—to have had Trotsky murdered. So you heard all these Marxist sermons with a review of the entire revolutionary picture and so on and so forth. It was more an occasion for piety than for education, let's put it that way.

NM: So you had Marxism, you had Trotskyism. You also had a bit of Freudianism, probably.

SB: Yes.

NM: Were you also involved in existentialism? I mean, did it have an influence on you?

SB: No, it didn't have an influence on me. By the time that had become the big new thing I was a little bit alienated. I'd already belonged to one or two crazy movements. I didn't need another.

NM: You said at some point that in the that first period in Paris, after the war, you tended to speak about Céline and Sartre in the same way—that you could happily have killed them both.

SB: Céline is a terrible puzzle, as you know, to all novelists. He is a superb writer but he's also humanly so impossible. You say, this is nihilism. Yes, but it's nihilism plus. People said that for Céline to have taken the line on the Jews that he took during the Holocaust and after—he was just being a playboy, it was nonsense, nonsense, he couldn't have meant it, because where did he get all his refinement of spirit to write those extraordinary novels? He was an unpleasant puzzle for us and I couldn't understand why so many Jews in good faith and in good conscience joined the army of his supporters. I used to argue about this but no, no, no, they said—he was a great artist and therefore everything must be forgiven. Well, I'd heard this argument used on behalf of Wagner till it was coming out of my ears and I wasn't going to have it again. With Sartre, of course, I felt another kind of exasperation.

NM: There are some Americans who think the Holy Land is here in the U.S. A kind of reverse Zionism. They think you don't necessarily have to go to Israel and start a new state because you can find here opportunities and a sense of freedom, of identity. Some American Jews, Philip Roth for example, are quite furious when they are told that they are in Diaspora. He used to say, "What kind of diaspora? I'm not in any diaspora. I am in my country and I'm here and I'm free and I can be whatever I want to be." Are you still in Diaspora or not?

SB: I'm older than Philip and my parents were older than Philip's parents and they were Europeans through and through. They came here in 1913 as grown, mature people and for them the problem could not be disposed of so easily. I grew up under this influence myself. Philip, I think, did not. So he did have that alternative of being an American. I had it too, but in my case it would need to have been announced with a certain bravado because the alternatives are altogether too clear for me. They're not so clear for Philip and the simple reason is that he grew up as a different Jew in a different America.

NM: Is it all right if we go back a bit to the hospital? There you encountered death—and also Jesus. A Christian lady had come through the ward and given you a New Testament.

SB: I was in the small boys' ward in the Royal Victoria Hospital in Montreal, and occasionally one of the kids would die and there was a lot of fuss in the darkness with a few lights on and then the stretcher would be brought in and in the morning there was the empty bed. Of course all the kids understood, although nobody talked about it. The beds were a little too far apart for us to have discussions and there was nobody to talk to about any of these things. You had to make your own record of them. You knew what an empty bed in the morning meant and by noon there was another kid in the bed and that was how it went. I knew myself that my life was in danger. I had multiple abdominal surgeries while I was there and each time, as I realized later, my life was in danger. I had serious infections caused by surgery and I was on the edge myself. Also, you're without your mother, without your father, for the first time in your life and you can't call out in the night for anybody because nobody is going to come. My parents took turns visiting me. They were not allowed to come at the same time and meanwhile I was eating diced pork on a tin plate.

NM: An additional guilt.

SB: Yes, but I knew enough about Jewish tradition to know that this was permitted if it kept you alive. This horrible diced pork was keeping me alive—all the food was terrible but this was especially awful—and there was nobody to talk to except the ladies from the Bible Society, the Christian ladies we used to call them, with copies of the New Testament, which I finally read because I read everything I could lay my hands on. I was eight years old and I read the Gospels and they were tremendously moving.

NM: Was it like a fairy tale, reading it?

SB: I suppose you could say that, except it was a fairy tale in which the hero was killed. It was unlike other fairy tales.

NM: What about the Jewish Bible, the Old Testament—was it a fairy tale too? Did it have another kind of substance?

SB: No, it was not a fairy tale. It was a holy book, in Hebrew, and you knew that it had to be true because it said God created the world—and here was the world, here was the proof! Right outside the window was proof. And Abraham was our first Jew, so designated by God himself, and my father was Abraham, so there we were: It was a continuing thing. It was impossible for a child of eight to make all the necessary distinctions and I didn't even try to make any distinctions because I was so enchanted with the whole thing: It was a straight line from the top, where God was, to the bottom, where I was.

NM: But the story with Jesus seemed to you *treif,* forbidden?

SB: No. I knew that my parents would think it *treif* so I decided not to talk to them about it. They would have been horrified. Especially my mother.

NM: So to you it was okay?

SB: There were moments when I had some trouble with it, for instance when the Jews are asked by Pontius Pilate what to do

There Is Simply Too Much to Think About

and they cry out, "Crucify him!" I thought the Jews should really not have done that. Anyhow, I made a fairy tale of it for myself and it didn't have much immediate human meaning, it was something that had happened a very long time ago and to Jesus, who was a Jew, and that counted heavily. But I would never have joined the enemies of the Jews as supporters of Jesus. That would have been impossible. Of course nobody was recruiting me, but I couldn't have been recruited.

NM: It is different if you see him as the Son of God, the Messiah.

SB: Well, I didn't have it all quite straight at age eight, but I knew enough.

My guilt as a young boy was the guilt of one of those Jews who cried out, Crucify him! Because I wasn't about to abandon the Jews over this matter. It was something in need of explanation but I knew that my family would never provide the explanation; and besides, they would be horrified. So this became one more secret that estranged me from my family. Mind you, it didn't estrange me from the affections. It was just that I felt I understood things they didn't understand, or they understood things I didn't understand. I was not ready to give up the Jewish religion; but all of the important things I knew or thought or felt I'd found in books written in a language that was not my parents'—English—including the children's books I'd been reading about another world, another life, about children visiting their grandparents who were farmers who lived in the country, who had cattle and poultry and so forth. These were the books that you read. I put religion in the closet and didn't take it out for many years.

NM: Not only religion but ideology?

SB: I suspect every ideology at that age presented itself to me as orthodoxy. There was something about radical ideology that resembled orthodoxy in that it was enforced by people who insisted rigidly on the legitimacy of their political position. After all, being a Trotskyite was in a way like being a Jew. Although Trotsky denied that he was a Jew.

NM: You say somewhere, "I have perhaps a slavelike constitution which is too easily restrained by bonds. It then becomes rebellious and bursts out in comic revolution."

SB: Did I say that?

NM: Yes. You, yourself.

SB: Well, it's probably the truth.

NM: Does it happen also in your books?

SB: I think it does. In the books I can really put all sorts of strange things in an amusing light, which is the way I choose to do it. Not deliberately choose, but that's the way it comes out.

[1999]

"I Got a Scheme!": With Philip Roth

On a summer afternoon in 1998, while I was visiting Saul Bellow and his wife, Janis, in their rural Vermont home, I proposed to Saul that he and I do an extensive written interview about his life's work. We had been talking for hours on the deck at the rear of the house, along with other friends who'd driven to Vermont to see the Bellows—the Romanian writer Norman Manea and his wife, Cella, who is an art restorer, and the writer and teacher Ross Miller. The four of us tried to get up to Vermont for three or four days every summer because Saul demonstrably enjoyed our visits, and we had a good time together staying at a nearby inn. The conversation was sharp and excited, lots of lucid talk directed mostly at Saul—whose curiosity was all-embracing and for whom listening was a serious matter—and much hilarity about the wonders of human mischief, particularly as we evoked them around the dinner table at the Bellows' favorite local restaurant, where Saul would throw back his head and laugh like a man blissfully delighted with everything. The older Saul got—and in '98 he was eighty-three and growing frail—the more our annual pilgrimage resembled an act of religious devotion.

Once I was home, I phoned Saul to suggest how we might proceed with the interview, if he was still interested in my idea. I would reread the books (some, like *The Adventures of Augie March* and *Herzog*, for the third or fourth time), then send him my thoughts on each, structured as questions, for him to respond to at length however he liked. As it turned out, we never got much beyond a beginning, despite Saul's willingness and my prodding. Every few months, in response to a letter or a phone call from me, some pages would arrive in the mail or through the fax machine, but then months would pass without a word from him, and, despite a weeklong visit I made to his Boston home one December, when he and I sat together for several hours every day talking about the books in the hope of stimulating his memory and his interest, the project petered out, and, reluctantly, I let him be. In time, I enlarged my "thoughts" into an essay on his work, and filed away the pages that Saul had sent sporadically in the course of the two and a half years that I'd tried to keep the interview alive.

Only recently have I taken the pages out to reread. They appear here as he wrote them, without any editorial correction or alteration—his sentences like his memories left to stand as they are—and with bracketed material added by me only for the sake of clarity. They focus on the early books *Augie March, Seize the Day* and *Henderson the Rain King,* published between 1953 and 1959. We got no further than that. Most of the pieces are about *Augie* or are recollections—of Saul's Chicago childhood or of Paris in 1948, where the book was begun—prompted by his thinking about *Augie;* sometimes it appears that he has forgotten having already answered my questions about *Augie* and, zestfully, with great precision, begins to develop a new line of thought that repeats details and incorporates motifs from a previous response. The pages about *Seize the Day* arrived in May of 2000 and those on *Henderson the Rain King* several months later, and that was the end of it.

It's too bad that I couldn't get him to go on to *Herzog, Mr. Sammler's Planet, Humboldt's Gift* and *The Dean's December,* as I planned to do, but he just wasn't interested enough in contemplating his own achievement anymore. Also, he was writing *Ravelstein* at the time, and the energy and concentration weren't there for this sort of retrospective pursuit. It's too bad, because what he wrote about the Fifties books constitutes a singularly Bellowesque mix of mind and memory, the opening of an aged writer's autobiography, unplanned, extemporized, and yet comparable in its vividness and evocative charm to Hemingway's farewell to the world, the posthumously published memoir *A Moveable Feast.*

—Philip Roth

I certainly was transformed [by writing *Augie March*] and I'll probably be the last to understand how this happened, but I am very willing to look for the cause. I had written two very correct books [*Dangling Man* and *The Victim*] and I shall try to explain what I mean by correct: I seem to have felt that I, as the child of Russian Jews, must establish my authority, my credentials, my fitness to write books in English. Somewhere in my Jewish and immigrant blood there were conspicuous traces of a doubt as to whether I had the right to practice the writer's trade. Perhaps I felt that I was a pretender or an outlaw successor. After all, it wasn't Fielding, it wasn't Herman Melville who forbade me to write, it was our own Wasp establishment, represented mainly by Harvard-trained professors. I must say that these guys infuriated more than they intimidated me.

Well, I got a Guggenheim, thanks to Jim Farrell [James T. Farrell, the author of *Studs Lonigan*] and Edmund Wilson, and with wife and child I crossed the Atlantic on a ship named *De Grasse* carrying about a hundred Southern college girls practicing their French on stewards and deckhands with no intention of getting rid of their Southern drawl. The voyage lasted nearly two weeks. The men slept in the hold while the women and children had tiny cabins.

We got off the train in the Gare Saint-Lazare and went to the apartment Kaplan had rented for us (H. J. Kaplan, of Newark, N.J.). The Guggenheim grant amounted to five or six thousand dollars but the rate of exchange was five hundred and fifty to one. We were rather well-to-do.

I had brought several hundred pages of manuscript with me. This third book of mine was even more depressing than the first two. Two men in a hospital room, one dying, the other trying to keep him from surrendering to death.

Okay, the Americans had liberated Paris, now it was time for Paris to do something for me. The city lay under a black depression. The year, if I haven't said so before, was 1948. The gloom everywhere was heavy and vile. The Seine looked and smelled like some medical mixture. Bread and coal were still being rationed. The French hated us. I had a Jewish explanation for this: bad conscience. Not only had they been overrun by the Germans in three weeks, but they had collaborated. Vichy had made them cynical. They pretended that there was a vast underground throughout the war, but the fact seemed to be that they had spent the war years scouring for food in the countryside. And these fuckers were also patriots. La France had been humiliated and it was all the fault of their liberators, the Brits and the GIs.

Depressed like everybody else, I went around looking for traces of the old Paris of Balzac, et cetera. But Balzac had been pre-nihilistic. Of course, there was something in me perhaps of Jewish origin that had nothing at all to do with nihilism. But if I wasn't nihilistic, I was terribly downcast and writing about a hospital room, and coaxing a dying man to assert himself and claim his share of life, and thinking my gloomy thoughts beside the medicinal Seine and getting no relief from the great monuments of Paris. I sometimes wondered whether I shouldn't be thinking about a very different course of life. Maybe I should apprentice myself to an undertaker.

Apart from Kaplan, I had no friends here. Kaplan, a French-speaking Francophile, was a writer with a job at UNESCO. We were never able to say anything that mattered to each other. I used to see Jimmy Baldwin quite often, mostly at mealtimes, and I had other acquaintances as well, Herb Gold [Herbert Gold, the American writer], a bohemian comedian named Lionel Abel, and the Italian philosopher Chiaromonte, whom I had known in New York. My general impression was that Europe was defying me to do something about it, and I was deeply depressed. I seem to have been a good solid sufferer in my youth.

We arrived in the fall, and when spring came I was deep in the dumps. I worked in a small studio, and as I was walking toward it one morning to wrestle yet again with death in a Chicago hospital room, I made the odd discovery that the streets of Paris were offering me some sort of relief. Parisian gutters are flushed every morning by municipal employees who open the hydrants a bit and let water run along the

There Is Simply Too Much to Think About

curbs. I seem to remember there were also rolls of burlap that were meant to keep the flow from the middle of the street. Well, there was a touch of sun in the water that strangely cheered me. I suppose a psychiatrist would say that this was some kind of hydrotherapy—the flowing water, freeing me from the caked burden of depression that had formed on my soul. But it wasn't so much the water flow as the sunny iridescence. Just the sort of thing that makes us loonies cheerful. I remember saying to myself, "Well, why not take a short break and have at least as much freedom of movement as this running water?" My first thought was that I must get rid of the hospital novel—it was poisoning my life. And next I recognized that this was not what being a novelist was supposed to have meant. This bitterness of mine was intolerable, it was disgraceful, a symptom of slavery. I think I've always been inclined to accept the depressions that overtook me and I felt just now that I had allowed myself to be dominated by the atmosphere of misery or surliness, that I had agreed somehow to be shut in or bottled up. I seem then to have gone back to childhood in my thoughts and remembered a pal of mine whose surname was August—a handsome, breezy, freewheeling kid who used to yell out when we were playing checkers, "I got a scheme!" He lived in the adjoining building and we used to try to have telephone conversations with tin cans connected by waxed grocery string. His father had deserted the family, his mother was, even to a nine-year-old kid, visibly abnormal, he had a strong and handsome older brother. There was a younger child who was retarded—a case of Down syndrome, perhaps—and they had a granny who ran the show. (She was not really the granny; she'd perhaps been placed there by a social agency that had some program for getting old people to take charge of broken families.) Now, just what had happened to handsome, cheerful Chuckie and to his brothers, his mother and the stranger whom they called Granny? I hadn't seen anything of these people for three decades and hadn't a clue. So I decided to describe their lives. This came on me in a tremendous jump. Subject and language appeared at the same moment. The language was immediately present—I can't say how it happened, but I was suddenly enriched with words and phrases. The gloom went out of me and I found myself with magical suddenness writing a first paragraph.

I was too busy and happy to make any diagnoses or to look for causes and effects. I had the triumphant feeling that this is what I had been born for. I pushed the hospital manuscript aside and began immediately to write in a spirit of reunion with the kid who had shouted, "I got a scheme!" It poured out of me. I was writing many hours every day. In the next two years I seldom looked into Fowler's *Modern English Usage.*

Perhaps I should also add that it has been a lifelong pattern with me to come back to strength from a position of extreme weakness: I had been almost suffocated and then found that I was breathing more deeply than ever.

It was enormously exhilarating to take liberties with the language. I said what I pleased and I didn't hesitate to generalize wildly and to invoke and dismiss epochs and worlds. For the first time I felt that the language was mine to do with as I wished.

In writing *Augie March,* I was trying to do justice to my imagination of things. I can't actually remember my motives clearly, but I seem to have been reacting against confinement in a sardine can and evidently felt I had failed to cope with some inner demands. Reading passages from *Augie,* I seem to recognize some impulse to cover more ground, to deal with hundreds if not thousands of combined impressions. To my cold octogenarian eye, it seems overblown now, but I recognize nevertheless that I was out to satisfy an irrepressible hunger for detail. The restraint of the first two books had driven me mad—I hadn't become a writer to tread the straight and narrow. I had been storing up stuff for years and this was my dream opportunity for getting it all out. I was also up to my eyes in mental debt. By this I mean that in becoming a writer I hoped to bring out somehow my singular reactions to existence. Why else write? I had prepared and overprepared myself by reading, study, and fact-storage or idea-storage and I was now trying to discharge all this freight. Paris (Europe) may have set me off. I didn't actually understand what had happened during the Second World War until I had left the U.S.A. I now seem to have been struck by the shame of having written my first book under Marxist influence. In 1939 I had seen the Second World War as a capitalist imperialist war, like the First World War. My *Partisan Review* Leninist friends (especially Clem

There Is Simply Too Much to Think About

Greenberg [Clement Greenberg, the art critic]) had sold me on this. Even in writing *The Victim* I had not yet begun to understand what had happened to the Jews in the Second World War. Much of *Augie* was for me the natural history of the Jews in America. The Jews in Germany, Poland, Hungary, French Jews, Italian Jews had been deported, shot, gassed. I must have had them in mind in the late Forties, when I wrote *Augie*.

We the children of immigrants had lots of languages to speak and we spoke them with relish. We were prepared, braced, to answer questions in half a dozen tongues. The older children had not yet forgotten their Russian, and everybody spoke Yiddish. At the age of three, I was sent to Mr. Stein across the way to learn Hebrew. I was not aware as yet that languages existed. But I soon learned that in the beginning God created heaven and earth out of *Tohu v'vohu*. In Genesis 11, He decided that He did not want all of mankind to speak a single language, it was too dangerous. "Nothing will be restrained from them, which they have imagined to do." Rabbi Stein was our neighbor on St. Dominique Street, Montreal. When the lesson was over, I went down and sat on the curbstone to think it over.

The French Canadian kids as they marched by twos to their classes shouted obscenities and insults at us, and I soon understood that I was a *zhwiff*—a *muzhi* (*maudit*) *zhwiff* at that. At six, I was enrolled in the first grade at the Devonshire School. There we sang "God Save the King" and recited the Lord's Prayer. On the way home we stopped on Roy Street to look at the Chinese in their laundry. They wore black pajamas and skullcaps as they painted their crimson labels with India ink. There was not a chance in the world that we would ever understand what they were writing or saying.

In 1924, we moved to Chicago, and there we lived among Poles and Ukrainians. Everybody spoke a sort of English, and we learned certain key words, like *piva*—Polish for beer. Or *dupa*, backsides, or *kapusta*, pickled cabbage. On Division Street, the main drag, men carried office typewriters—we called them uprights—in their arms and for twenty-five cents the scribe would mount this machine on a ledge and write letters to parents or sisters in the Old Country.

The larger community was of course American and at school you were told in textbooks and by teachers that George Washington and Abraham Lincoln were *your* Presidents. You could not be excluded when the common language became your language—when you knew the National League standings, when you had learned about the Chicago gang wars. In the papers, you followed the events leading to the killing of Dion O'Banion, of the North Side bootlegging gang, and of the indictment of Al Capone for tax evasion. You knew all the facts about the death of Lingle, the *Tribune*'s gang reporter who was shot down in the Illinois Central Randolph Street tunnel. The papers informed you that Big Bill Thompson, the mayor, was in the pocket of Capone. All this was available in the dailies, when you had become familiar with the language of the historians, chroniclers, and the lingo of the insiders. You didn't know the full story from sober, reliable, dependable sources. You had come to know it by mastering the language in which it was gussied up by newspapers and by magazines like *Ballyhoo*, *College Humor* and Henry Luce's *Time*.

Chicago was big on gab in the Twenties and Thirties, and under the influence of gab you came to feel yourself an insider. Verbal swagger was a limited art cultivated in the Hearst papers by contributors like O. O. McIntyre and Ted Cook. On a higher level was H. L. Mencken of *The American Mercury*. Mencken comically expressed the dissatisfaction of intellectuals with the philistinism and comical bourgeois provinciality of the "booboisie" American in the years of prosperity that followed the First World War. He found his largest public among schoolboys like me or village atheists and campus radicals. It seemed to me that he didn't expect his prejudices to be taken very seriously.

At school, we, the sons and daughters of European immigrants, were taught to write grammatically. Knowing the rules filled you with pride. I deeply felt the constraints of "correct" English. It wasn't always easy, but we kept at it conscientiously, and in my twenties I published two decently written books. In 1948 I went to Paris to write a third novel. But by the winter of 1949 it became miserably—hatefully—apparent that I was once again on the wrong track. I fell into a depression thicker than the palpable soddenness of Paris. In those early postwar days, the city defeated and recently occupied by the Germans was experiencing a second and even more disgraceful occupation by the dollar-proud

There Is Simply Too Much to Think About

Americans, moronically happy, stupid and *mal élevés*. But the French were no more unhappy than I was when I began to recognize the extent of my latest failure. I had come to great humanistic Paris to reach what was deepest in my nature and the best I was able to do was to begin to realize the scope of my failure. Proud of my freedom, I turned out to be the least free of all the people I met. Every morning when I walked to my rented workroom I stopped to watch the municipal workers who turned on the water for the daily street wash. In the streets there was just slope enough to sluice the gutters, and watching the flow of water between the curb and the barrier of wet burlap gave me the only ease I was getting on those gray days, and the release that came with this was inexplicably verbal in form. I was not much interested in explaining this transfer from fluidity and low sparkle to . . . well, to polyglot versatility. I discovered that I could write whatever I wished, and that what I wished was to get into words the appearance of a gallery of personalities—characters like Grandma Lausch or Einhorn the fertile cripple, or Augie March himself. Years of notation ended in the discovery of a language that made everything available. A language might be restrictive or it might be expansive. An excess of corrections caused shrinking. Philip Roth puts it well when he speaks of the teeming, dazzling "specifics" in the opening pages of *Augie March*. These specifics were not deliberately accumulated for some future release. They were revealed by the language. They represent the success of the unconscious strategy. You might put it that Mr. Einhorn had been in hock for years, for decades. He and I together had been waiting for an appropriate language. By that language and only that language could he be redeemed. I couldn't have been aware of this development. It was not an invention; it was a discovery.

The novel I now began to write wrote itself: "I am an American, Chicago-born." The narrator was a boyhood friend whom I had lost track of thirty years ago, when my family had moved from Augusta Street. I often wondered what had become of this handsome impulsive kid. The book I found myself writing was therefore a speculative biography.

There was something deeply unsatisfactory about the language used by contemporary writers—it was stingy and arid, it was not connected with anything characteristic, permanent, durable, habitual in the writer's outlook. For as long as I could remember I identified body and limbs, faces and their features, with words, phrases, and tones of voice. Language, thought, belief were connected somehow with noses, eyes, brows, mouths, hair—legs, hands, feet had their counterparts in language. The voice—the voices were not invented. And whether they knew it or not all human creatures had voices and ears and vocabularies—sometimes parsimonious, sometimes limitless and overflowing. In this way the words and the phenomena were interrelated. And this was what it meant to be a writer.

Before I forget the name of the man who trained the eagle: He was an American called Mannix who had materialized in Taxco. [Chapter XVI of *Augie March* is about the attempt by Thea Fenchel, Augie's lover, to train an eagle to attack and capture the large lizards inhabiting the mountains of central Mexico.] My memory works by fits and starts and I didn't want to have to grope through my head in vain. The late Mannix, no longer among us, was one of those American eccentrics who do great and also grotesque things and arrange somehow a wonderful press for themselves.

As so often, I begin with a footnote.

Day in, day out, I watched Mannix and his eagle on a sharp slope outside the town. But I think I should go back a bit and explain what I was doing in Mexico in the summer of 1940. My late mother had paid twenty-five cents a week to an insurance agent, a stout man who used to come by regularly to collect his money. He carried a very thick black portfolio secured with many rubber bands. He was a bookish type himself, and was forever trying to engage me in conversation about the books he saw in my mother's kitchen. He was extremely keen to discuss *The Decline of the West*. Smart Jewish schoolboys in Chicago were poring over Spengler at night. But to keep to the point, I was the beneficiary of an insurance policy on which my mother paid two bits weekly. She died when I was seventeen and the policy matured eight years later. My father wanted me to turn the money over to him, all five hundred bucks of it. He needed it badly, but I refused to part with it. Now, my father was a tyrant, with a perfectly good claim to his place in the all-time gallery of great tyrants. Three years earlier I had defied him by

There Is Simply Too Much to Think About

getting married. Now I declared that Anita and I would go to Mexico. It was essential that we should go. Europe was out of the question since the Germans had just overrun Paris. Deprived of Paris, I simply had to go to Mexico. Looking back, I see more agony than boldness in this decision. I was, as kids were to say later, making a statement. I had spent most of my life in weary, stale, flat and unprofitable Chicago, and I needed barbarism, color, glamour and risk. So Anita and I took the Greyhound bus to New York. I can't remember why we didn't go directly to Texas, but there was some compelling reason to go to New York. Perhaps I needed to see my uncle, Willie Bellow, a brush maker, unemployed and brooding his life away in Brownsville, Brooklyn. I didn't clearly understand at the time, but it is easy today for me to see that he had been punished by my grandfather for joining the Bund at an early age. The Bellows did not work with their hands, they were not tradespeople, and to apprentice Willie to a brush maker was meant to be especially humiliating and punitive because he would be working with hog bristles. It seems that in my rebellion I turned to him for support. He was an affectionate uncle, but he was an unemployed worker with a family to feed. I ought to have shared the five hundred bucks with him. I was however headed for Mexico. We went on the Greyhound by way of Augusta, Georgia, where my uncle Max was selling *schmattes* on the installment plan to black field hands. Our next stop was New Orleans. After hanging around the Latin Quarter pointlessly for a few days, we went on to Mexico City.

Now, Mexico in those years was everything that D. H. Lawrence said it was, and a good deal more besides. Here there were no uncles, no family bonds. I was somewhat frightened, I must admit, but certainly not intimidated. It seems to me now that I was determined not to be made by my father in Chicago, nor by my older brothers. Uncle Willie in Brownsville illustrated what might happen to a Bellow who rebelled. He would be humiliatingly shot down. Uncle Max in Georgia was a cheerful, engaging hand-to-mouth *ganef.* And now here I was in Mexico to stay as long as my four hundred and fifty dollars lasted. After drifting around for several weeks in places like Michoacán, we were drawn to Taxco, which had a sizable foreign colony, mostly American, but also Japanese, Dutch and British.

I had been brought up to worry, but the lesson seems somehow not to have taken. None of the people I met in Taxco had a very firm grip on anything at all. I never gave a thought to what would happen after my money had run out. We rented a very nice house with two servants for about ten bucks a week and the Indian women shopped, cooked and washed our clothes. I have to say also that I very rarely gave my father a thought. I was very *happy* to submit to the influence of my betters. I was intrigued with what I took to be the imaginative powers of the people I met. I see all too clearly now how limited they were, but everybody has his own pattern for liberation and my own liberation took the form of an escape from anxiety. My mood was investigative. I wanted to see firsthand what the characters I was spending my time with were up to. I sent my wife away to Acapulco—then a beach with a few huts. My strong desire was to go it alone. It never occurred to me that it might be a danger to Anita to be shipped off. Evidently I discovered a talent for doing things in a headlong style. Perhaps I was fascinated by Mannix's eagle because he was such a plunger.

The challenge was to emerge intact from the grip of these would-be dominators. To extract the secret of their powers from them while eluding their control became my singular interest. If I had any game, it was this independence game. Perhaps it was not so much an interest as it was a spiritual exercise. I recognized that I did not have to do the will of others.

In Paris, where the book was being written, it was Charlie (Augie) who resisted influence and control. Childish and fresh, he sat at the checkerboard and shouted "I got a scheme!" I, the writer, might be hampered, depressed. Charlie, however, was immune, defying Grandma Lausch. She took a dim view of his schemes. He, however, was prepared to light out for the territory ahead.

In mountainous Mexico, where the sun shone so dramatically, so explicitly, you were never allowed to forget death. Women bought tiny coffins in the marketplace for their dead infants and carried them on their heads to the cemetery. After ten years, graves were dug up and bones thrown into a charnel house. The Day of Death was a national holiday. Although I was most keenly aware of this, I was too roughly excited for any sense of fear to take a grip on me. And then the eagle was a death-dealing life force. Seven mornings a week I was out with Mannix. I also drank far more than was good for me with American buddies in the *zócalo* (the town square). I took riding lessons and I hung out with the hard-drinking professionals who wrote for *Black Mask* and other pulps. Mannix and his eagle were my antidotes to the low company of the pulp writers. It was hard for me to grasp the fact that the free could be taught to hawk. It surprised me to learn that such a predator would obey his trainer like any lesser creature. I felt a boundless respect for the eagle nevertheless. Mannix I saw as just another showman. Later, when *Augie* was published, Mannix demanded billing in his own name and Viking Press advised me to give him a footnote. I can't recall whether this was mentioned in the text, but the eagle perched atop the water tank in Mannix's toilet, just under the ceiling. Just another domestic fowl. On the mountainside a creature of boundless freedom and power, he caught lizards and brought them to his showman master.

Robert Penn Warren once said that he liked to write in a foreign country "where the language is not your own and you are forced into yourself in a special way." I suppose it is essential that one should be forced into oneself and perhaps the foreign language is important—perhaps not. Plausible speculation after the fact can be pleasant. When I began to write *The Adventures of Augie March*, I was living in Paris and I now ask myself whether I was at that time forced into myself in a special way and find that I am able to answer in the affirmative. It seems to me that I felt very much as I had felt in 1923, when we, the family, were reunited with my father and his cousins in Chicago. My father, who had preceded us a year earlier, and Cousin Louie were waiting for us at the Harrison Street Station when the Montreal train arrived. The date was July 4th, Independence Day. The brick streets were hot. In the Midwest everything was alien—nature itself was different—the air, the leaves and bushes, the soil, the water, the very molecules were unfamiliar. Breathing would not be here what it had been in Canada. My father, whom I had longed to see, was now clean shaven. I had never seen him without his mustache, and the bareness of his upper lip was a shock to me.

In the street near the platform, Cousin Louie's Dodge touring car was parked. Its celluloid panels were kept unbuttoned so that the air could circulate. Sitting at the wheel, Louie wore his hair in a long crest, like an Iroquois warrior. He belonged, physically, to a different branch of the species. He had a big thriving nose and a ruddy color. Louie had saved us, and brought us to the promised land.

We followed the trolley lines up Milwaukee Avenue to the northwest side of the city, and since this was July 4th, the streetcars set off the powder caps the children had taped to the rails, and in this ripping noise and smoke we drove to Cousin Flora's house. Flora, Louie's sister, welcomed us into her bungalow and fed us on smoked Great Lakes whitefish. We had come by coach, sitting up all night, and were very tired. So the living-room furniture was pushed aside and we slept on the floor. The Chicago neighborhood was raw and new. The streets had just been paved and along the Sanitary District canals the newly planted trees were coming into meager leaf. Orange striped awnings shaded the windows. Old Montreal lay one sleepless night behind us. Chicago with its stars and stripes was utterly new. Rummaging in Cousin Flora's closets, I found a coverless prose translation of the *Iliad* (Andrew Lang, Leaf and Myers). Achilles and Agamemnon therefore stood between me and the Chicago of Al Capone and Big Bill Thompson. It was up to me to find ways to reconcile the Trojan War with Prohibition, major-league baseball, and the Old Country as my mother remembered it. After school, in the cellar of the synagogue on Rockwell, I studied Old Testament Hebrew. At home I followed the Leopold and Loeb case in the papers. In 1926 there was the Dempsey-Tunney fight and Charlie Chaplin's *Gold Rush*. By 1930 I was an American entirely. I read *The American Mercury*, the novels of Edith Wharton, Sinclair Lewis and Sherwood Anderson.

I shall never understand how *The Adventures of Augie March* came to be written. I had arrived in Paris with wife and child to complete another novel—something about two men who shared a hospital room in Chicago and came to be close friends. The story was told by the survivor. I said to myself that I ought not to be writing such dreary stuff. What I needed was something more open and generous—a freewheeling, hang-loose book. But I was unable to shake off the hospital room and the dying man who had become my close friend. I was desperately depressed.

I had rented a room near the Place Saint-Sulpice, where the shops sold ecclesiastical goods, and I was walking heavyhearted toward my workplace one morning when I caught up with the cleaning crew who opened the taps at the street corners and let the water run along the curbs, flushing away the cigarette butts, dogs' caca, shredded letters, orange skins, candy wrappers into the large-mouthed sewers. The sanitation sweepers dragged the soaking burlap downhill to keep the water from dispersing. Watching the flow, I felt less lame, and I was grateful for this hydrotherapy and the points of sunlight in it—nothing simpler. I did not have to kill myself in the service of art.

That *Augie March* happened in dismal postwar Europe (knowledge of the Holocaust was slowly coming to us back then) is evidence of an independent move of the mind, a decision not to surrender to horror. I discovered that I no longer wanted to be put upon by art seriousness.

My oldest brother was a lesson to me in this respect. He was determined to become a world-beater. He did, as a matter of fact, very well for himself. He became very rich. From the first he would say to me, when we moved from Canada, enough of this old crap about being Jewish. Also, my old man was oddly enough a great American patriot. He had no picture of himself as a man beating America, but my brother did. My middle brother, Sam, was also a successful businessman, and he was certainly American in hatching deals and multiplying bank accounts. But he was of the Old World with his wife and children, and granddaughters who had to be married off. There were no such compromises for Morris, the entirely American brother. We were united in our disapproval of brother Sam and his formal Orthodoxy.

Paris was turning out to be a mistake. "Living up to it" consumed too much energy. Madame Lemelle, my landlady, told me that André Gide lived just down the way, and if I had answered, I would have said that competition was actually good for business. In any case, Mme. Lemelle was more interested in the automatic water heater I had bought and installed in her kitchen. This might have been the right kind of American gesture to make. But my real interests just then were not in the technological transformation (improvement) of Europe by America.

I had walked away from the streetwashing crew saying under my breath, "I am an American—Chicago-born." The *I* in this case was not autobiographical. I had in mind a boyhood friend from Augusta Street in Chicago of the mid-Twenties. I hadn't seen Augie since the late Twenties; the Forties were now ending. What had become of my friend, I couldn't say. It struck me that a fictional biography of this impulsive, handsome, intelligent, spirited boy would certainly be worth writing. Augie had introduced me to the American language and the charm of that language was one of the charms of his personality. From him I had unwittingly learned to go at things freestyle, making the record in my own way—first to knock, first admitted.

Of course, I improvised freely from the events of my own life. Immigrants differed considerably in their attitudes toward America. Some continued to live mentally and emotionally in the Old Country. Others "Americanized" themselves. To Jews from other parts of the country, the Eastern Seaboard Jews seemed less confidently American, more cowed by old money and old names. My father understood the U.S.A. rather well. I discovered that Abraham Cahan of the Yiddish *Forward* made a serious effort to educate his immigrant readers. Though he was a socialist, he understood that the older Europeans had little use for Marxism. My father knew quite a lot about the Constitution, the Congress and the Presidency. I remember being lectured by him on Roger Williams's banishment from Massachusetts Bay Colony and his hospitality to the Jews and Quakers. My old man would say that in the Old Country Jews had to carry masses of identification papers—*cartes de séjour*. Here you were never stopped and asked for your papers.

I had an eighth-grade teacher—Mrs. Jenkins was her name, a wonderful old woman. Her father had been a prisoner in Andersonville, and in the mid-Twenties she would tell the kids his Civil War stories. Mrs. Jenkins herself was white-haired. The Grand Army of the Republic was still a lively topic in Chicago. On Memorial Day, the old men lined up on Randolph and Michigan in front of the public library. The public library was built on land given by the Civil War veterans. On the second floor of the north end there was a war museum. People were not familiar with it. They were at the south end, where the books were. But upstairs at the north end was an enormous display of regimental flags, guns, photographs, and on Veterans Day old soldiers lined up for the annual march. The Grand Army of the

Republic was still represented. I read a lot about the Civil War—Grant's memoirs and Sherman's as well.

I took a tiny hotel room on Rue des Saints-Pères. Across the way pneumatic drills were at work on the construction of a hospital or medical school. The room below mine was occupied by an old Italian scholar named Caffi. He was tall but frail and had an immense head of hair and a small nervous laugh, but he was a serious man. In 1917, as an Italian journalist in Petersburg, he had spent the funds his paper sent him to feed starving children. Now he lived on the money raised by his devoted followers. His supporters kept him alive and would occasionally come from Italy to visit him. Apparently he was an accomplished Greek scholar. Most of the day he passed in bed drinking coffee and writing learned notes to himself.

I tried occasionally to be helpful. As he was washing his feet in the sink one day, the bowl of the washstand broke and a chunk of it fell on the instep of the supporting right foot. The wound was painful. He wrapped a large towel around it and did not leave his bed for an entire week. Among his acquaintances and followers there were some who said he had wounded himself on purpose, from resentment toward a friend who had tried to get him a job. A strange theory. When one of his visitors remarked that I did not seem to be getting what an American should get out of Paris, Sr. Caffi wisely replied that it was only natural that I should be thinking of America most of the time. It was Chicago before the Depression that I went to in my room in the morning, not misty Paris with its cold statues and admirable bridges. The book had taken off, writing itself very rapidly; I was coming to be strangely independent of place. Chicago itself had grown exotic to me. A descendant of Russian-Jewish immigrants, I was writing about Chicago in odd corners of Paris and, afterward, in Austria, Italy, Long Island and New Jersey. To speak of rootless or rooted persons is all very well, but I felt that the cultural vocabulary of the university crowd should be avoided. I listened to Mr. Caffi when he described America as the new Rome. I was deferential and respectful, aware that he was trying to do good, to raise my mental level. He did as much for his young Italian disciples—his helpers. They brewed his coffee and mothproofed his winter clothes. Half-blind and often bedridden, Caffi directed his activities. He evidently saw that I was an American doing something characteristically American—a latter-day Roman. What I learned in Europe was how deeply involved I was with the U.S.A.

A major figure in Europe was an intellectual—poverty was one of his badges and he was supported by his followers. A young Italian had attached himself to Caffi as his delegate, representative and helper. I was fascinated by this very different un-American version of a higher life, but I pursued very different aims. Sr. Caffi probably saw this more clearly. I think also that I was very lucky. For me the overpowering brother was the totally American brother. He overpowered me and in a sense he led me to write *The Adventures of Augie March*. He didn't like the book when he read it, but he granted that I had in my cockeyed way done something significant and it was necessary that he should figure in the book. He was aggressive and I recognized in him the day-to-day genius of the U.S.A.

In the opening sentence of my work in progress I don't say that l am an American Jew. I simply declare that I am an American. My eldest brother was the first to point out the advantages of this. America offered to free us from the control of the family and of the Jewish community. After school he was a "baggage smasher," loading trucks with suitcases and trunks for home delivery. He wore football jerseys with broad bands of orange and purple. In a few years, he had City Hall connections. He wore a derby and a velvet collar to his topcoat, a silk scarf with polka dots and pointed shoes of patent leather. He was slick, savvy and combative. He was preparing for the bar exam, and he described himself as bagman for a member of the House of Representatives. He opened his Gladstone bag for me once and showed me paper money it was crammed with.

He brought home copies of *The Saturday Evening Post, Collier's, Liberty Magazine* and *The Literary Digest*. These influential papers gave you an idealized orientation to the mental life of the country—its farmers, its laborers, its wives and mothers, its mechanics and athletes, its heroes—its promoters and opportunists, its social climbers, its White Pants Willies and marketers of drowned Florida real estate, New England boy prodigies like Mark Tidd—Marcus Aurelius Fortunatus Tidd: images of what Americans were, or might become. There was a great demand for images or models of rough-and-ready frontier types such as Walt Whitman had offered to the country in *Leaves of Grass* and *Democratic Vistas*. In a country of immigrants, there was a singular need for prototypes, especially among the young.

In my father's generation, there was a great sense of release from tsarist officialdom, not merely oppressive but downright crazy. My father believed that the U.S.A. offered the Jews unheard-of opportunities for development—the first rational government in history. And the law of the land, guaranteed in the founding documents. My father took an exceptional interest in the U.S. Constitution and the privileges of citizenship, for which Leviticus, Numbers and Deuteronomy had prepared him. He said, "That's what I call a deal. I'm glad to pay taxes in a country where the Constitution says I'm a citizen, not a Jew." This put the work of the founders under some strain, he thought, but there was no danger in this since justice as the world acknowledges was taught to Israel by Moses under the direct supervision of God. But from the beginning the life of the Jews in America was not what it had always been in Europe, with the ghettos—the Jews in each country belonging to a separate community of Jews. They were taxed not as Jews but as citizens; nor were they subject to special levies. As a Jew, you have a connection of your own to the life of the country, and in many respects you could be as American as you pleased. Naturally, there were private organizations that excluded you from membership, but such conduct would force you to remember the mass murder, gassing camps, the contrast of seriousness with sophomoric provocation.

My old man was odd that way; he was a great patriot, seeing the safety of the Jews as dependent on the stability and balance of the rational founders.

My brother's Americanism was altogether different. He was made for Chicago. He adopted the style of a racketeer and put himself over as a wheeler-dealer. An underworld coloration made legitimate business seem or sound crooked.

And, strangely enough, my father became a patriotic American. He knew quite a lot of U.S. history, though he read only the Yiddish papers. He often took me aback. He'd say, "Tell me about this man Roger Williams." "Where did you find that name?" I said. "I read about him in *The Forward*," my father said. "There was a series of articles on Rhode Island." Cahan, editor of the Yiddish paper, saw to it that his readers received instruction in the rights and duties of citizenship.

I remember that we arrived at the Dearborn Street Station in Chicago on July 4th. We were met by my father and his cousin and employer, Louie, who owned a bakery on Marshfield Avenue. A tall, vigorous man, with a red Indian strip of hair down the middle of his head. But I was truly astonished by my father—he had shaved his mustache and the nudity of his face shocked me. Among the alien phenomena of Chicago, this was, on that first day, probably the hardest to absorb. We climbed into Cousin Louie's touring car with its flapping celluloid curtains and we followed the car tracks, on which the kids had laid small explosive devices that were set off by the trolley cars. The air smelled of gunpowder. War veterans were firing the guns they had brought home from France. I was too big a boy, at nine, to be dandled on my father's knee and, besides, the disappearance of his cigarette-saturated mustache had made another man of him, temporarily. Montreal was nice, it was old-fashioned, European, its parts were interconnected. The crude Chicago of those days was described by an English visitor as a string of industrial villages from factory to factory. The streets of the Polish neighborhood where we settled smelled of sauerkraut and home-brewed Prohibition beer. Mechanical player pianos everywhere played polkas and waltzes. In proletarian immigrant Chicago of the Twenties there was little culture, but schoolchildren didn't know what culture was, and I was in any case at a level of development below books, music, painting and conversation. I found myself in a place where everything was strange—even the trees and their leaves. Colors, spaces, the air itself was different, clumsier, coarser—as if made of heavier molecules. I was now, as my parents had been earlier in Canada, an immigrant in an altogether different physical reality. Here everything demanded revision, and I was aware that my senses were being adapted to the chemical or tactile demands of the new place—its atmospheres, its hidden variations had to be absorbed. The rest—classrooms, playgrounds, marching in the corridors—came easily. Baseball gave me a certain amount of trouble at first, because I had spent my eighth year in the hospital. [The eight-year-old Bellow was hospitalized with acute

There Is Simply Too Much to Think About

appendicitis and peritonitis that led to life-threatening complications.] I worked hard at physical fitness, but when a grounder passed, one of the boys said, "You looked at that ball as if it was an object of idle curiosity."

Pittsburgh was famous for steel, Detroit for automobiles, Akron for rubber tires; Swift and Armour exported beef and bacon from their South Side Chicago plants. Donnelly the printer published telephone directories of many cities, and in Chicago the educated classes thought of the city as a literary center. Dreiser, Sherwood Anderson, Willa Cather, Edgar Lee Masters, Sandburg, Vachel Lindsay came here to study, to write for the newspapers or the ad agencies. The *Chicago Journal,* a paper that did not survive the Depression, published a weekly literary supplement. The two Hearst papers were hospitable to writers. High school children also read Mencken's *American Mercury.* One of the most notorious crimes of the mid-Twenties was committed by Leopold and Loeb, university students whose heads were turned by the Nietzschean ideas they wildly misunderstood. They were defended by Clarence Darrow, whose courtroom speeches ran in the papers together with the gang killings and the urban sketches of Ben Hecht. In high school, at the age of fourteen, we were doing *The Merchant of Venice* and *Julius Caesar* and, on our own, Dos Passos's *Manhattan Transfer* and Dostoyevsky's *Crime and Punishment.* We read the "Chicago authors," of course, Dreiser's *Sister Carrie* and, a little later, Farrell's *Studs Lonigan.* My closest friend, in early adolescence, was Syd Harris, who lived on Iowa Street, just east of Robey. An only child and a difficult one, he tyrannized his London-born mother and his Russian papa. Skinny Sydney, with his wild ways, his tics and his rages, ran the show—he lied, he threatened and he stormed, he played the genius and the dictator. A large dinner table occupied the little parlor and there we read our esoteric books. We wrote at opposite ends of the big table, on yellow second-sheets from the Woolworth ten-cent store. At this square borax table, its surface protected by a carpet-like cover, we wrote stories, poems, essays, dialogues, political fantasies, essays on Marxism—on subjects we didn't really know too much about.

When the well-meaning Mrs. Harris looked in on us to ask some harmless, encouraging question, Sydney would shout, "Get back to the kitchen, you old Cockney bitch! How dare you interrupt!" And, losing her temper, one eye jumping out of focus when she bristled, his mama would answer, "Yer no child of mine! They switched yer on me in the hospital!"

It was theater, of course.

Mrs. Harris thought of me as a well-behaved boy of good family from whom he, Sydney, could learn to be civil and show proper respect. I was brought up to defer to my elders. Millennia of correct conduct, I thought, and much good they did us, I think today. But I am still shocked by Sydney's false rages, as when he shouted at his ma, get out you old "whore." This was pushing outrage and bohemian swagger too far. I thought, my mother wouldn't have let me get away with it, and my father would have knocked me down.

At fifteen, we wrote a book together, and one winter day on Division Street we flipped a coin to see which of us would take the manuscript to New York City to be published. Sydney, when he won the toss, stuffed the pages under his sweater. We pooled our money—some sixty cents—and immediately he was in the street, with his thumb up. In a matter of days, he was in New York. He wrote that he was staying on Riverside with John Dos Passos, who was dazzled by Sydney's gifts. Dos Passos had six white spitz dogs who were walked on triple leashes, twice a day.

Meantime, Mrs. Harris had reported the disappearance of her only child to the Missing Persons Bureau. She came to the house and questioned me in my mother's sickroom. [Bellow's mother was dying of breast cancer.] I said I knew nothing. Adolescents in those days were bound by gangland rules. You didn't rat on a buddy. My eldest brother said that I should be questioned at police headquarters. We went to Eleventh and State Streets, Sydney's mother weeping, my bossy brother determined to tag me hard and teach me a lesson. I repeated my lies to the Missing Persons Bureau and felt that I could tough it out with the best of them.

But my brother now broke into my locked drawer and found Sydney's letters. After dinner that night he read them to the family. In the opinion of the New York experts who had read our manuscript, Sydney was an obvious winner. Covici the publisher [Pascal Covici, destined many years later to become Bellow's editor at Viking] had commissioned a book on Chicago's revolutionary youth and paid Sydney an advance of two hundred dollars. In the judgment of the publishing illuminati, I would do well to enter my father's business. Only my mother grieved for me. Everybody else was delighted to see me go down in flames.

Famous and rich, Sydney came home on the train. He was far too busy now to write a book for Covici. He soon became the legman for Milton Mayer, who covered Chicago for *PM*, the New York paper founded by Marshall Field. Eventually, Sydney became a *Chicago Daily News* columnist who specialized in the education of adolescents. Sydney's early schooling in avant-garde literature was singularly advantageous. Beneath his ivory tower there was a gold mine.

I don't like that book, *Seize the Day*. I never think about it, I never take it up, I don't touch it. But I have to admit that you ask the question of questions, and that I don't know how I can possibly answer. [I'd asked him if he knew why, in writing *Seize the Day*, he'd moved from the euphoric openness of *Augie March* back into the dour ethos of the pre-*Augie* world of *The Victim* and *Dangling Man*.] Augie is the freest of the free, while Wilhelm is a full catalog of repressions and civilized mantraps. I sympathize with Wilhelm, but I don't like him. Seated at the checkerboard, he has no scheme. The reader, however, is attracted to him because of his "sensibilities." His is, of course, a common type—he calls on others to "give" or "encourage." It is the commonest of stories. But my task was to represent him, not to recommend him. In him we see the failures of "feeling"—the characteristic American slackness of virtues and the inanity of good counsel.

Many readers assumed that as an enlightened person I would naturally be on Tommy Wilhelm's side. On the contrary, I saw him as a misfit wooing his hard-nosed father with the corrupt platitudes of affection, or job-lot, bargain-sale psychological correctness. I thought he was one of these people who make themselves pitiable in order to extract your support. The clue to my true opinion about this may be found in the zany mental-health lectures of Dr. Tamkin. The absurd, phony Dr. Tamkin was a great help to me—the advice-giving phony we turn to for guidance, the false man of science who has all the answers.

I've thought quite a lot about the New York setting of *Seize the Day* and I'm inclined to agree that the loneliness, shabbiness and depression of the book find a singular match in the uptown Broadway surroundings. I think that for old-time Chicagoans the New Yorkers of *Seize the Day* are emotionally thinner, or one-dimensional. We had fuller or, if you prefer, richer emotions in the Middle West. I think I congratulated myself on having been able to deal with New York, but I never won any of my struggles there, and I never responded with full human warmth to anything that happened there.

I lived on the Upper West Side for some time. Adam's mother, Sondra, lived in the Ansonia before we were married, and I used to spend my nights there. That was in the early Fifties, and that hotel lent itself to *Seize the Day*—the Insomnia, I liked to call it.

I found a nice apartment on Riverside Drive. But somehow it just didn't work. I never knew any real comfort in New York. I always felt challenge and injury around the corner. I had always considered it a very risky place, where one was easily lost. And I think I saw New York through the being of Isaac Rosenfeld. [Rosenfeld, a fiction writer and essayist, was a Chicago native and had been a friend of Bellow's since childhood.] He came to take the town and he got took. From his standpoint it proved to be a very dangerous place. He came with this pretty wife to qualify for his Ph.D. He came from Chicago and he got himself deeper and deeper into the pit.

Isaac would almost certainly have agreed that New York might save him. Chicago had no hope to extend to him. The just-married pair, Isaac and his Greek-American bride, found a flat in Greenwich Village. His "carefree" circus on Barrow Street attracted the bohemian intellectual crowd. Isaac became one of the wits of this group, a serious person who allowed himself to play the clown following the example of the Dostoyevskian underground man. During the war, he was in command of a barge in New York Harbor. An ingenious, playful father, he filled the apartment with cats, dogs, guinea pigs, parakeets with whom the two kids were on excellent terms. The son, like Isaac himself, died of a heart attack in his mid-thirties. The daughter is now a Buddhist nun and resides in a French convent. Isaac's wife remarried when she was widowed and in her late eighties lives on in Honolulu. She's partially paralyzed. His considerable gifts as a writer never matured in New York. He became a follower of the onetime Freudian Wilhelm Reich. This would not have been possible in any other American city. It took Isaac years to cast off the Reichian influence.

Also, New York was the place where *I* did the Reichian therapy. That was really a horror. I didn't realize how terrible it was, and that it happened under Isaac's influence. Because he insisted that I had to have this done, since he was doing it. About three years. Once or twice a week. There was a box in the doctor's office, and you had to take off every stitch and lie on the couch. I think I probably was doing this during that *Seize the Day* period. Not anything I'm terribly proud of, but you could not keep your respect for yourself if you had not faced the ultimate rigors. And it was a link between Isaac and me. I felt that I could not let him go through this without going through it myself so that I would know what was happening to him.

I suppose I felt utterly isolated in New York. It was the sort of place that generated such feelings, and there was nothing you could turn to. I mean, if you turn to somebody for help, you'd make the biggest mistake in your life if you choose Dr. Tamkin. I knew the original of Dr. Tamkin. He was a friend of two friends. The second friends were a European couple whom I liked very much, and their only child had been killed in an accident, and "Dr. Tamkin" came and took charge, emotional charge, of the family, as he would. And I hated him for it. I saw what he was doing; he had no feeling for these people. He was just a scatterbrain, a poseur. Self-anointed helper of mankind, full of generosity to everybody. That was the real background of this foolish grotesque.

She was a Jewish Frenchwoman. He was a German Jew. Their child, about fifteen years old, was knocked down in the street by a truck on his way home from school. She went to the hospital, where she was told that he was okay. Then he had an embolism, as a result of this accident. And when she got home from the hospital, the phone was ringing to tell them that he was dead. They had just lost their son whom they loved with all their hearts and he put himself forward as their protector and their guide, with all this psychological garbage of his.

It was a very bad time. Maybe what I was thinking is if you bring your hopes to New York, this inevitably happens to you. There's a connection between Tommy Wilhelm and Isaac. Because he does come to New York again, to reestablish his connection with his father and his mother, his grave, and so on.

Still, having said all this, I can't really see that I am so utterly place-dependent. I've never taken much stock in the notion that London, Paris, St. Petersburg and other great capitals have *made* the literature of their respective countries. The cities are wonderful, but one must be wary of historicism. Historicism is an academic product whose premise is that urban multitudes make the culture of their countries. Together we share the high significance or glamour of Paris and London. During the Depression, I bought a set of Balzac and was taken over by the glamour of the great joint enterprise of the city of Paris and its triumphant capitalism, its erotic oddities and vices, the mixed legacy of its Revolution, its Napoleonic days of triumph, its *jeunes ambitieux,* its inventive restless criminals, its bankers, its lovers. This wonderful mixture or compound had a glamour of its own. We wanted to know all that could be known about it.

Its attractions are boundless, but is it everything it claims to be? We are fascinated by it, but we are also wary of its claims to be the setting of settings and the formative power behind the phenomena. We had learned in our Chicagos and New Yorks that the great treasures of culture were not indispensable—that one can live without them.

It may be that the swing from *Augie* to *Seize the Day* was part of a lifelong pattern. It seems to have started when I was a kid in Montreal, dying in the hospital; when I was released from the Royal Victoria Hospital, we went immediately to Chicago. There I grew up, worshipped health, became muscular and chinned myself and so forth. I was making it, emotionally, in Chicago. After that, when I got out of college and went to New York, it was more of the same. But I had an Uncle Willie Bellow, in Brownsville, who was a very gentle, depressed man. He was a brush maker. He disappointed his father, my grandfather. My grandfather apprenticed him to a brush maker. This apprenticeship contained a hidden disgrace, because as a brush maker he would have to deal with hog bristles. This was actually my grandfather's point. So there was poor Willie, an illegal immigrant in New York. I don't know how he ever got there—he took a train with his family from Montreal to New York, but there was no record of his entry into the country, so he couldn't apply for citizenship papers. I loved him dearly. He was a very very feeling, cheerful, generous humorist, without much power of self-expression. And he died in the early Fifties in his place of work, at the brush factory, in Brooklyn. It's true, many dark things were happening as I came to write *Seize the Day.*

"As much a disease as he is a man" perfectly sums up *Henderson the Rain King.* [Bellow is alluding to a description of Henderson I'd used in my question.] Henderson *is* of course looking for a cure. But the bourgeois is defined by his dread of death. All we need to know about sickness as it relates to bourgeois *amour propre* and death we can learn from Thomas Mann's *The Magic Mountain.* The difficulty in approaching Henderson following this outlook is that Henderson is so unlike a bourgeois. In his case, the categories wither away.

It seems to me that I didn't know what I was doing when I wrote *The Rain King.* I was looking for my idea to reveal itself as I investigated the phenomena—the primary phenomenon being Henderson himself, and it presently became clear to me that America has no idea—not the remotest—of what America is. Europeans would agree, enthusiastically, with this finding. They will tell you that America is *inculte* or *nyekulturny.* But how far does that get us? It is true that culture is not one of Henderson's direct concerns. He could not compete with his father's gentlemanly generation—his immediate ancestors who knew Homer and read Dante in Italian. He had a very different take on American life. You refer to this, rightly, as his wacky anthropology. To a young Chicagoan it seemed the science of sciences. I learned that what was right among the African Masai was wrong with the Eskimos. Later I saw that this was a treacherous doctrine—morality should be made of sterner stuff. But in my youth my head was turned by the study of erratic—or goofy—customs. In my early twenties I was a cultural relativist. I had given all of that up before I began to write *Henderson.*

Roth likes *Henderson,* and I am grateful to him for that. He sees it as a screwball stunt, but he sees, too, that the stunt is sincere and the book has great screwball authority. I was much criticized by reviewers for yielding to anarchic or mad impulses and abandoning urban settings and Jewish themes. But I continue to insist that my subject ultimately was America. Its oddities were not accidental but substantial. Again, Roth puts it better than I could have done. Henderson is that "undirected human force whose raging insistence miraculously does get through." The wacky Henderson led me through my last and wackiest course in anthropology. My diploma, if I had been given one, would have told the world that I was a graduate of the college of dionysiacs. Did I know what I was doing? Not very clearly. My objective was to "burst the spirit's sleep." Readers would share this—or they would not. Alfred Kazin asked what Jews could possibly know about American millionaires. For my purposes, I felt that I knew enough. Chanler Chapman, the son of the famous John Jay Chapman, was the original of Eugene Henderson—the tragic or near-tragic comedian and the buffoon heir of a great name. I can't imagine what I saw in him or why it was that I was so goofily drawn to him. Those years were the grimmest years of my life. My father had died, a nephew in the Army had committed suicide. My wife had left me, depriving me also of my infant son. I had sunk my small legacy into a collapsing Hudson River mansion. For the tenth time I went back to page 1, beginning yet another version of *Henderson*.

[1998–2000]

Coda: Why Not?

I want to consider some of the difficulties faced by young Americans who are determined to write poems or novels or paint pictures. I emphasize the difficulties not because beginners are unhappy—they are, for a time at least, happier than most people, and we have it on good authority that they begin in gladness—but because the problems that await them are peculiarly troublesome.

Why are the beginners glad? Well, they've read masterpieces or looked at them, they've studied the lives of writers and painters and have said to themselves, greatly stirred, "I must do something like this myself. Why not?" A staggering declaration. Highly magnanimous too, for as Matthew Arnold once wrote, the world "is forwarded by having its attention fixed on the best things." He said also, about poetry, that it was "nothing less than the most perfect speech of man, that in which he comes nearest to being able to utter the truth." Why then should a beginning writer not be happy? He intends to fix the attention of the world on the best things, to make his own individual approach to the truth, and he intends to do this with words, familiar words available to everyone. For this he needs no elaborate professional training; schools can't help him much. He must form himself, learn his trade, and he must take up a position in the middle of the world. But what a world it is!

Now there are specialists who are obliged to set the world aside as alien to their professional interests. Astrophysicists or neurophysiologists, for instance, have to turn their attention away from the world. And of course these are very superior persons. W. H. Auden has written somewhere that a poet among physicists feels like a shabby curate among the bishops.

The "hard scientists" know extraordinary things to which the rest of us have no access, and many of them are obviously men and women of genius. But when they discuss matters the rest of us understand somewhat, they can be very disappointing. Then we can see for ourselves the effects of these long absences from the world. They don't always sound like men of genius when they discuss China or Washington, D.C., or the Middle East. And they often appear to take a patrician view of themselves. I am quite willing to agree that this is justified. But what accounts for their political opinions is perhaps *noblesse oblige.* Revisiting the earth after their intergalactic or infra-atomic journeys, these aristocrats of the mind prefer, in an abstract way, to advocate the best, the most advanced and the most beneficial positions. It is from them, therefore, that you hear the most progressive clichés going. They know one thing well, they know it superbly. The interests of a writer must be wider, perhaps impossibly wide. He takes a common central human ground open to everyone who will come and consider and see and hear and feel.

But to return to the beginner, the young man or woman who has said, "Well, why not?" He begins, as Wordsworth said, "in gladness"; he often ends in despondency and madness. It isn't as though he hadn't been warned by many intelligent and experienced people. Samuel Butler says in his *Notebooks* that you must be careful in youth to wish for the right things because you are all too likely to get exactly what you wished for. You storm the walls and are rewarded for heroic achievement. There you stand weighed down with medals and itching under the honorific brocades, but when the ceremonies end you learn that you have taken not a famous city but a dump with insoluble urban problems.

And what, according to Butler, did the right thing look like? In advance of his times, exceedingly modern, Butler believed such things as that parents were harmful and families a hindrance to the free development of children; and that your really lucky person was born alone, among the cabbages, with a ten-thousand-pound note pinned to his diapers. Butler was a cheerful, sadistic, shrewd, no-nonsense sort of man and a keen gadfly who had a dependable Victorian horse to sting. Our post-industrial, post-Christian, post-everything period of flux and crisis does not breed stingable horses, only millions of gadflies.

There are a good many beginners—too many of them. Not all of them are gifted, some of them are deluded, many are impure. There are opportunists, exhibitionists and future racketeers among them. It is, I suppose, the responsibility of the critics to sort them out, to maintain standards, to protect the arts, to keep the game honest. But the critics do not do this. Oh, those critics!

Reading, some days ago, a collection of essays by Hilton Kramer, a most intelligent and conscientious critic, one who is trying to keep the game honest, I came upon the following remarks. Of Jackson Pollock, Mr. Kramer says: "The display of ambition in Pollock's art, the naked attempt of an artist to invest his entire being in a style that might compete with the greatest achievements in Europe—and to do so in a quintessentially American manner—answers to something deep in the American intellectual community. We have seen the same thing happen more recently in the case of Allen Ginsberg, who has become an international legend while remaining a poet of small, fragmentary accomplishment. And, indeed, Pollock stands to Picasso as Ginsberg stands to Whitman and Pound: provincials aspiring to a status which their intrinsic gifts deny them. But the exact quality of their gifts does not matter: the whole momentum of our culture shares in this unearned aspiration and rewards its exemplars with the trappings of authenticity."

I often think that critics are harder on artists than economists are on businessmen or journalists on politicians. What was Pollock's sin? A lively young man from the sticks (he came from Cody, Wyoming) decided that he was born to be a painter. Coming to New York, he studied at the Art Students' League under Thomas Hart Benton, soon rejected regionalism and realism and turned to abstraction, to Action Painting. Before he knew it or was able to grasp the consequences of his new ideas (one of which seems to be that traditional control is death to the contemporary artist) he had uttered the fatal "Why not?" Was Pollock working at the painter's trade or was he more interested in defining himself? Was his principal effort to define? Was he primarily an intellectual—or a gambler? Kramer is in part right when he says that Pollock nakedly attempted "to invest his entire being in a style," but I don't see how the investment of a man's entire being can be based on the ordinary calculations or motives of ambition. It can be argued that Pollock was trying to do what Walt Whitman wanted American artists to do. Whitman thought it a mistake to compete with the great achievements of Europe. Those magnificent achievements, he told us in *Democratic Vistas*, could not serve us as models; in America they are "exiles and exotics." The American should, he said, wisely gather, cull, absorb, but he should not overlay his "precious idiocrasy and special nativity and intention." If he did this the man himself, however wide his cultivation, was a failure. Whitman attacked the "refinement and delicatesse" that threaten "to eat us up, like a cancer. Already, the democratic genius watches, ill-pleased, these tendencies," said Whitman. "Provision for a little healthy rudeness, savage virtue, justification of what one has in oneself, whatever it is, is demanded. Negative qualities, even deficiencies, would be a relief."

What threatens to eat us up now is certainly not refinement. And how much is "a little healthy rudeness"? What would Whitman have thought of the "savage virtue" of Allen Ginsberg? Mr. Kramer is rather hard on Ginsberg, for wasn't Ginsberg too trying to satisfy Whitman's requirements? Of course an artist should know when he is going too far, but it isn't so easy to be very ambitious and very objective at the same time. And why scold? To pay for the errors of ambition when the years of full objectivity arrive is painful enough. That is the point of Butler's warning. And then why does Kramer speak of aspiring provincials? Were Ezra Pound of Idaho, T. S. Eliot of Missouri, Walt Whitman of Long Island less provincial than Jackson Pollock of Cody, Wyoming? But critics often enjoy bringing down the glittering ax of European high culture on the heads of Americans. It is as if they were saying to them, "Look, we *know* you, you come from Cincinnati, and you grew up like the rest of us among shopping centers, garages and factories. You can't pull the wizard bit on us." What they imply is, "If it were as easy as you make it look we'd have done it ourselves." And who is not, in the new order of things, with the world opening before him (or gaping for his destruction), a "provincial"? We are all, in one way or another, from Cincinnati. Even Romans and Parisians are, as they face the post-everything world, newborn babes and uncultivated rubes. Was the Picasso who drew the Peace Dove not a hick?

But I am not quite ready to drop the question I asked a moment ago: How might Whitman have felt about the "healthy rudeness" and "savage virtue" of Allen Ginsberg? He might have liked his candor, his naturalness, his passion; he might have approved of his turning the weapons of philistinism against the philistine. But what would he have made of dope, jazz, the Beat routine? Whitman's priorities are quite clear. By "idiocrasy" he did not mean boundless, ungoverned self-expression. "Idiocrasy" had for him a natural root and a moral meaning. He believed that when we read, we must first satisfy ourselves that a poem, the work before us, is indeed the work of a poet, and that its art qualities are genuine. The next question, however, is moral. Has this work "helped any human soul"? Does it "free, arouse, dilate"? Whitman asks.

Although I esteem him, I shall continue for a while to nag at Mr. Kramer, for he has raised some remarkably interesting questions. And he has, moreover, tried seriously to protect us from fakers and from our own gullibility. We are easily taken in by phonies, reputations are too easy to make, and we know perfectly well what Kramer means when he speaks of "unearned aspirations." The American is a great backer of dark horses and dreams of coming from behind and stunning the handicappers. When he says "Why not?" he enters the race as an unknown favorite, the darkest phantom of them all, the unpredictable winner. The exaggerated ambitions of American artists, or would-be artists, are directly related to the leveling tendency of their society. Leveling inevitably breeds megalomania, but one should not strengthen the hand of the leveler by speaking of "unearned aspirations." And on the whole my sympathies are with the young man from Cody, Wyoming, or Paducah, Kentucky, and I defend his right to make the naked attempt as an artist to invest his entire being et cetera. I do not say that I will like his gaudiness, his self-promotion, his effrontery, but if I am forced to a choice, I will accept exaggeration, callowness, vanity. Even megalomania is better than a lobotomy performed by high-culture surgeons. For there are always some beginners who write for the reasons William Carlos Williams gave once in an interview. He said quite simply that he was trying to get said what was most important to him. "Like those desert plants that are all closed and brown until you put them in water . . . resurrection plants. They unfold and put out green leaves. We are like that in wanting to expand." It is the penetration of experience by the imagination that Williams is talking about, the illumination of the surrounding world by art. It will not do to be snooty with those who from such motives utter the words "Why not?"

Mr. Kramer is not a critic of narrow sympathies; quite the contrary. I have caught him in a moment of punditry and while he was yielding to a weakness common to critics, that of using artists to make points about American society and American culture. Many critics seem far more interested in sociology than in literature or painting. But then the arts are dependent on the help of the social body and sociological interests are, up to a point, legitimate. It is only when critics clearly prefer sociology and cultural analysis to the arts that I turn away from them. I should be unfair to Kramer if I failed to mention that he expresses great sympathy with Pollock. He says that the facts of Pollock's life might have offered a subject to a major novelist like John Dos Passos. For Pollock the painter he has small use; Pollock the American phenomenon fascinates him. For how does a young American become, or imagine he has become, an artist? What impels him to utter the fatal "Why not?"

The country is sold on "creativity." Do what comes natural, express yourself; it may turn out that you too are an artist. Everyone has a right to take a shot at the title. Besides, the figure of the artist generates a quantity of social excitement, pleasant and desirable in itself. It adds perhaps to our sense that America's resources are inexhaustible. The artist is a significant part of that vast unending daily show, the common life of the American people. Art often seems to borrow significance from what Americans obviously feel to be an infinitely greater phenomenon, namely, their national life, their public existence. Artists themselves often concede this. A writer like Norman Mailer (consciously or unconsciously following the example of Lord Byron) develops his talents in the Town. But the Town has become enormous, a national and even an international entity. We have no convenient way of referring to it; its realities are ungraspable. The Town now comprises New York, London, Paris, Jerusalem, Calcutta, Beijing. How are we to speak of the mixture of technological changes, economic transformations, wars and revolutions of this extraordinary century?

How? I said at the outset that I would consider certain peculiarly

There Is Simply Too Much to Think About

troublesome and puzzling problems faced by young Americans who were determined to write or paint. Here is one of them, inherited from an earlier generation, or imposed upon us by that generation. There was a time, so Wyndham Lewis tells us in his autobiography, *Blasting and Bombardeering*, when civilization was still in equilibrium, still possessed the will to play, the will to create art. But, says Lewis, "the war to end war" did not end war, it merely ended art. He continues: "Great social changes which with such uncouth and wasteful violence started to get themselves born, in that tragical atmosphere, extinguished the arts which were supposed to be their expression, and which had been their heralds." No one, he says, "ever supposed that some bigoted theorist of the mass-life, or some Brass hat, either—much less the 'Financial Wizard' who controlled the Brass hat and subsidized the bigot—would ever feel drawn toward an art." But without the artist "the world ceases to see itself and to reflect. It forgets all its finer manners. For art is only manner, it is only style," says Lewis. Without art, "life instantly becomes so brutalized as to be mechanical and devoid of interest."

This was what my generation heard from the old boys. Or from those who made old boys of themselves, the epigones. On our side of the Atlantic, some of these associated the golden lull preceding the Great War with the golden day of the American Protestant Majority. But then came the effects of capitalism, of technology, of immigration, hybridization, degradation. The Twenties—so goes their account of literary history—produced a few twilight masterpieces. The Jazz Age was pleasant but by the Thirties the Ice Age had begun. Lewis in *Blasting and Bombardeering* concedes that it is still possible to write a good book or paint a good picture; but, he says, "the mass stupidity and helplessness of men, with all the power of machines to back it," is against us. "An artist starting his career today does so under the most enormous handicap. And today we are only half way to full collectivism, to the consummation of the capitalist materialism."

We had better not avoid such facts. We had better have nothing to do with stratagems of disingenuousness or false optimism. We do, however, have the right to ask how true these "historical truths" are. The beginner who said "Why not?" only to hear, in immediate reply, that his wish to illuminate the surrounding world and penetrate experience with imagination is absurdly out of date—he will want to know what there is to these devastating descriptions or charges; whether it is a fact that the war to end war ended art; whether he, the beginner, is condemned to lead a life irremediably brutalized, mechanical and devoid of interest. Some of his most respected seniors have said so. Lewis was at least generous enough to keep an eye out for the occasional good book. Others of his generation or outlook could not be bothered, among them several of our most famous critics.

But there is the beginner still persistent, wanting to know what he is to do with his intuitions, his impulses, his occasional states of exaltation. Are these, in the circumstances, only afflictions? Had he better try to cure himself, to rid himself of the art-instinct that, no less than the sexual, refuses to let him be? What, in a word, is he to do about a cultural situation that so many respected people have told him is beyond redemption?

The consummation of the capitalist materialism, Wyndham Lewis calls it. After reading an interview with Mr. W. Michael Blumenthal in *The New York Times* on the occasion of President Carter's appointment of him as Secretary of the Treasury, I went back to Lewis's *Blasting and Bombardeering* to look for the passage from which I have just quoted. Mr. Blumenthal, an authentic Financial Wizard, does not subsidize bigots or control the Brass. An educated man, he told the interviewer that he was not the sort of intellectual who worried about the differences between Rilke and Hofmannsthal. He is, if I interpret correctly, too concerned with the growth rate and the balance of payments, the stock market, the Fed, to "feel drawn to an art." It must be a substantial satisfaction to him to be where the action is and not on some waterless moon where the Rilkes are thinking about Orpheus or trying to speak to the angels. Of course it is better to be big in Washington than to be an afflicted poet or, even more profoundly afflicted, a pedant digging blindly in the stacks, mole-wise, under the roots of masterpieces. The busy powerful executive, by contrast with poet or pedant, is something of an aristocrat and resembles the type designated by Matthew Arnold as the "barbarian." Arnold distinguished the barbarian from the dismal, stiff-necked, illiberal middle-class philistine devoid of sweetness and light. Aristocrats, said Arnold, did have a certain external sweetness and

There Is Simply Too Much to Think About

light about them, but were lured off from following the light by the "mighty and eternal seducers of our race . . . by worldly splendour, security, power and pleasure. These seducers are exterior goods, but in a way they are goods; and he who is hindered by them from caring for light and ideas, is not so much doing what is perverse as what is too natural."

So we are doing what is natural. And the bosses of modern democracy or of "revolutionary" socialist republics or police states, established in power and surrounded by splendor, adopt an aristocratic attitude. The Bolsheviks, too, as Andrei Sinyavsky argues in his essay "On Socialist Realism," appropriated the severest aristocratic and classical traditions of eighteenth-century literature. For the revolutionary masses nothing but the best was good enough and the only best the Bolshevik bosses knew was the antecedent best. Which was aristocratic.

Someone should bring these facts to the attention of those who are fated to utter the irrepressible "Why not?" I promised to discuss the difficulties that face them. I have not done so. And there are more.

"It seems," wrote Whitman, "as if the Almighty had spread before this nation charts of imperial destinies, dazzling as the sun . . . making history a dwarf." He foresaw that new history would swell into a leviathan. But these charts of imperial destinies that Whitman foresaw obsess rather than dazzle us. We Americans are enchanted with the American phenomenon itself. And this phenomenon is not there only to be looked at; it demands to be experienced, and it is intimately and overwhelmingly experienced by us with an intensity that leaves little room for anything else. We have got to think about oil and the Middle East and the Chinese and the SALT talks. In Mr. Blumenthal's view this is no time for spirited and intelligent men to be fooling about with Rilke or Proust. It is the lessons of the Bendix Corporation and not those of *Malte Laurids Brigge* or *Swann's Way* that matter now. Consider what OPEC has done to prices and to employment, the instability it has produced in our economy and in the weaker economics of Europe, the responsibilities it has laid on our government, the burdens it is preparing for us. The technocrat statesman, our guardian, keenly aware of the fragility, the immensity and the complexity of the structure in his care, keeps himself light and mobile, ready to dart from one point of crisis to

Coda: Why Not?

the next. He deals with conditions the majority of mankind most readily understand. He is at the center of the political life that is, in many respects, identical with mental life as a whole.

Our world has been made—or ruined—by politics. "You deny the existence and the power of the political sciences?" Tocqueville asked in 1852. "Look around you and see these monuments and these ruins. What raised the former and brought the latter down? . . . It was political science, and often that science at its most abstract, which put into our fathers' heads the germs of those new ideas which have since suddenly blossomed into political institutions.

"Among all civilized people the political sciences create, or at least give shape to, general ideas; and from these general ideas are formed the problems in the midst of which politicians must struggle, and also the laws which they imagine they create. The political sciences form a sort of intellectual atmosphere breathed by both governors and governed in society, and both unwittingly derive from it the principles of their action."

To return now from Tocqueville to Mr. Blumenthal. Mr. Blumenthal is not considering political science in the abstract. He feels that mankind must make mental decisions (only mental ones?) about its continued existence. And I understand him to mean that our intellectual talents must concentrate on the survival of our elaborate civilization. It may not, therefore, be the most admirable minds that will be drawn toward literature and painting.

Allow me to contrast with this the position taken by Proust in *Time Regained*. He is discussing his vocation and he speaks of the act of creation with which no one can help him and he says, "No one can do our work for us or even collaborate with us." This is the essence of unpolitical activity—a man doing what only he himself can do. He continues, "How many for this reason turn aside from writing! What tasks do men not take upon themselves in order to evade this task! Every public event, be it the Dreyfus affair, be it the war, furnishes the writer with a fresh excuse." The writer, says Proust, wants "to ensure the triumph of justice, he wants to restore the moral unity of the nation, he has no time to think of literature. But these are mere excuses, the truth being that he has not or no longer has genius, that is to say instinct. For instinct dictates our duty and the intellect supplies us with pretexts for evading it. But excuses have no place in art and intentions count for nothing: at every moment the artist has to listen to his instinct, and it is this that makes art the most real of all things, the most austere school of life, the true Last Judgment."

So, beginners, we have Matthew Arnold on the seductions of exterior goods, only too natural; we have Tocqueville on the power and prevalence of political ideas; and we have Proust on the obligation of the artist to follow his instincts. Proust was writing during the Great War, when so many artists and intellectuals were drawn irresistibly into the world, into public affairs. And of course the real interests of most people do lie at this moment in great events. Their thoughts are framed and their vocabularies are produced by public discussion of this astonishing phenomenon, the advanced industrial society with its idols of production, idols of consumption and its political necessities. And how will these thoughts, these vocabularies, these necessities affect the finer manners, the style that Wyndham Lewis identifies with art? For art, he says, "is only manner, it is only style." Perhaps it will help us to listen to the testimony of a contemporary Russian writer. The Russians, after all, are on the other, the collectivist, side of Wyndham Lewis's equation. It will be better for us not to compare the two superpowers on Mr. Lewis's scale. Andrei Sinyavsky, released not long ago from a forced labor camp, made the following remarks in an interview given to *The Times Literary Supplement*. He lives in Paris now, in exile after a long sentence for circulating his writing abroad. What he says is this: "You see, the whole meaning of my life is in art. I do not set myself any great tasks of a didactic or moralizing nature. I am in no way a preacher or a moralist; it is something which is lacking in me. Different people specialize in different things; someone may have a gift for preaching, teaching, for leading people in some particular direction. I don't have that gift. My specialty is creating images by a process of transformation, and that is all. . . . All my life I have wondered what art is and why it exists. We can all manage perfectly well without art. The Soviet regime, for instance, does without it almost entirely. We cannot get by without food, without drink, without other essentials—but we can survive without art. It's like a kind of bonus, a luxury. Yet as soon as we consciously remove art from life, then life ceases. It is thanks to this unnecessary, inessential thing that life exists at all . . . the whole world is God's art. At the level of mere existence we can survive without art, but if we consciously do away with art, then being—in the sense of a universe full of mysteries, wonders, individuality, personality, cats, weeds, flowers—will disappear. All that will remain is flatness. And then art to me is salt: in principle you can eat unsalted food and not die, but it is salt which gives life."

This, you see, argues that the great, uncouth, wasteful social changes of which Mr. Lewis spoke, however negative their effect on the arts as a whole, cannot extinguish the art impulse. We can agree that the process of dehumanization has intensified in the twentieth century. (Can we agree to anything else?) But need we also say that all resistance of the imagination (of the intellect too; these should not be separated) is now useless? We cannot allow critics and historians to turn the leaves of the album for us, to tell us, "Those were the palmy times. The days of style. Now we are in an Ice Age." Albums? Baedekers? Is it some sort of conducted tour we have signed up for?

I have just outlined what I consider to be the central question confronting the contemporary artist. That is, I have arranged to have Arnold and Tocqueville and Proust and Blumenthal and Sinyavsky outline it for me. Now I should like to say a few words about several peculiar dangers that lie in wait for American writers. Some of us have watched soldiers prodding their way gingerly through a minefield, marking the safe path with a wire to which they tie strips of rag. I shall try to add a few rags to the literary wire.

A young American writer is not likely to be aware that his countrymen (those who read books) expect him to provide them with attitudes or to confirm their favorite opinions, to give them practical ideas, behavioral models. It often appears that what Americans want is "a way to be"—if possible, "a beautiful way to be," a way to define oneself, to achieve the power to experience by so defining oneself. The famous Lost Generation originated gestures and attitudes that hundreds of thousands of Americans found wonderful and valuable. What Lionel Trilling characterized as the "adversary culture" deals with certain aspects of this quest for usable forms. Trilling spoke of "the actually subversive

There Is Simply Too Much to Think About

intention that characterizes modern writing." It was one of the objectives of this adversary subversion "to liberate the individual from the tyranny of his culture in the environmental sense and to stand beyond it in an autonomy of perception and judgment." This was not its general effect. Instead the modern adversary culture "developed characteristic habitual responses to the stimuli of its environment." Certain of these habitual responses, the political ones, for instance, are clearly visible and identifiable while others are more elusive, ectoplasmic, and require subtler methods of detection.

"A beautiful way to be," I said. What this implies is that the condition of middle-class America is deplorably vulgar, graceless, benighted, lacking in style or manner. Hemingway offered attractive alternatives to the children of this middle class. Hemingway, whose genius as a storyteller becomes more apparent with every decade, seemed aware that these children needed another, truer father to develop their virtues and to lead them toward manhood. He offered them "a beautiful way to be"—dignity in hardship, colorful independence, the rejection of comforting illusions, stoicism in suffering, grace under pressure. Some of this goes back, I suppose, to chivalry, to Castiglione's courtier, to nineteenth-century ideas of honor, to the schoolboy's and soldier's code in Rudyard Kipling. Americans will quickly recognize the phenomenon as soon as I have mentioned some of the forms it has taken on this side of the Atlantic—the rough, free man of the wilderness, the Huck Finn who lights out for the territory ahead and, later, the beautiful and damned of the Jazz Age, the Loner, the Hippie, the Child, the representative of the Counter Culture and a multitude of special cases whose neuroses or addictions require special understanding. Patience is the tribute offered by the capitulating adult middle class and becomes a distinction widely claimed and greatly valued by the defeated. They appear to take pride in their ability to endure the abuses visited upon them whether on the streets of their own cities or in international relations. Week after week *The New York Times* raises monuments of patience in its editorial columns. The adult middle class is pleased when those who have achieved the "beautiful way to be" accept them, recognize them for one of themselves—almost. There is a strangely touristic element in it—that is, the natives prefer you to the rest. In the early

Fifties I met in Florence a young GI I had known in Minnesota. Just out of the Army, he had opened a caramel-corn shop near the Uffizi. Through caramel corn, which the Florentines loved, he was connected with all the best people. He was their closest American friend, the only one they fully accepted, trusted and spoke frankly with. He showed me his address book. It contained the names of the Florentine Four Hundred. At this I remembered how Jake, in Hemingway's *The Sun Also Rises*, is questioned by the innkeeper about the American friends he has brought with him to the bullfights at Pamplona. The interrogation (I am quoting from memory, but I can't be far off) goes like this, "Are these visitors *aficionados* like you?" "Yes, they are *aficionados* like me." "No, they are not *aficionados* like you." In the same book Lady Brett, introducing her friend the Greek merchant who is at first face too gross to be accepted, says that he has been wounded in Ethiopia by Stone Age arrows and has scars to show. Again, the "beautiful way to be."

An interesting contemporary case is that of an elderly professor whom I have known for nearly forty years and who introduced me long ago to the novels of Fitzgerald. Recently divorced, he tells me in a long letter that he has little to do with anyone of his generation. He prefers youthful company. Almost all his friendships are with young lesbians. He is having a love affair with one of them. She tells him that he is the only man she can make it with. And this young woman is, for my friend, *dans le vrai*. She is free, she is far out. She is pure in heart, she is beyond success or failure, she is a stranger to philistinism and all its wearisome prejudices, she is beautifully true to herself. And he, the older man who has not done too well in life, is qualified precisely by his misfortunes and by his sensibility to enjoy a privileged relationship with her. The beautiful way to be. He believes that the verdict on a ruined civilization given by such a pair (two castaways who have found the only real center that can be found) is the only just verdict.

There is, in short, a culture more inclusive than the adversary culture and more pervasive; its clichés are more sophisticated, more tolerant and, I believe, more dangerous to the beginner who has learned to identify the subversive modernist adversary culture in its broadest outlines.

I don't know which is the more difficult to break away from, one's

There Is Simply Too Much to Think About

own stupidity or those collective stupidities stealing into us subtly because they have the prestige of literary tradition behind them. To put the matter as simply as possible, "a beautiful way to be" is simply a stylish strategy for ignoring ignorance and getting through despair.

It will not be necessary to tell the beginners that they must make a particular effort to be truthful. They wish to begin because they already sense that every human being needs truth as he needs air to breathe and water to drink. As I am no metaphysician I will not try to be precise about truth. When a writer has it, his readers will be sure to know it. He must not look to prestigious intellectuals to lead him to it. Attitudes will not help him, nor "positions" on the modern, the new, the revolutionary. Writers toward the close of the nineteenth century became part of the intellectual world, were themselves in many instances intellectuals, wrote increasingly for an intellectual public. This was inevitable. Artists could not hold themselves apart from the high culture of their time. There occurred, however, a loss of confidence, an absorption of ideas with which their intuitions could not live. As John Lukacs puts it in *The Passing of the Modern Age*, "The world of artists and the world of the intelligentsia overlapped more and more. They came to depend on each other, especially in countries such as the United States where both felt they were a small, indeed a misunderstood, minority among the large mass of their countrymen. Soon this mutual dependence became more and more lopsided, as the artists turned to depend on the intellectuals for their sustenance. Eventually the intelligentsia would devour and absorb them, the world of art having become but one portion of the world of intellectual reputation."

There cannot be much argument about the accuracy of this account. We see now why the interests of art critics do not lie in the arts themselves but in the intellectual activities suggested by the arts. The next question, although rhetorical, cannot be shirked: Do the intellectuals represent the intellect? The answer to this is a heavy sigh. Intellect must not be surrendered to the intelligentsia. The beginner must achieve independence of thought. He must not—like "the good" of Blake's statement "The good are attracted by men's perceptions and think not for themselves"—give his mind into the hands of those who "know better." He must not, in the "weakness" of his difference and isolation, concede all strength and all knowledge to the victorious communities of scientific or scholarly specialization. It is for the victorious culture (with which the beginner comes into contact if he has any higher education) to come to the phenomenon. Why should the phenomenon run after it, asking to be interpreted and forcing its own imagination or intellect to move over and make room? The young writer is surrounded by its formulations and attitudes, by its authority, its prejudices. He has usually begun by accepting its outlook, its theory of knowledge, its description of the external world that puts him, as an object, into a universe of objects; by accepting its account of his evolution and nature, the structure of his society, its history of civilization. Those who in recent generations bathed that civilization in negatives, the "adversaries," became its most influential shapers, their radicalism our ruling prejudice.

No, without independence and individuality the phenomenon has no reason to exist. The victorious culture (containing most of what "enlightened" people now think) will only take up the surrendered phenomenon and move on—toward quicker breakup and dissolution. I am not, by the way, recommending a return to the culture of "the good old days," rejected by the modernist adversaries. For us there are no "good old days."

There is a growing point in human beings that cannot be enclosed by the hard forms we construct.

I have quoted from many writers. I hope I may be forgiven one last quotation, singularly appropriate. It comes from a writer I greatly admire, Ignazio Silone. He relates in his last book, *The Story of a Humble Christian*, that in a provincial Italian library he met a literary friend who asked him why he was doing research on Celestine V, a pope of the Middle Ages. The friend said, "In these visits of yours to convent libraries, I imagine you are obliged to meet some of the monks. Aren't you repelled by that?"

Silone answered, "Don't you consider them the same as other human beings?"

The friend insisted, "Don't you feel an instinctive sense of repulsion when you're with them?"

"Does something of that sort happen to you?" Silone asked.

"Frankly, yes," the other writer answered. "I don't believe it's an entirely personal reaction. I think every writer with a liberal or radical training . . ."

At that, Silone understood what he meant and interrupted him. "Although you and I are about the same age," Silone said, ". . . I consider myself post-Risorgimento and even post-Marxist. Both in ideology and sensibility."

Note that Silone's colleague first said that he felt an instinctive repulsion when he was with monks. He then added that this was not entirely a personal reaction. Silone answers that to him the monks are the same as other human beings, and that he considers himself post-Risorgimento, post-Marxist—post other things obviously—and in this answer we may observe the growing point of the spirit finding its way out of the "liberal" or "radical" rubbish. For to live, to breathe, to be, we must get clear of the rubbish, the clichés.

Luckily, what we live by is not what we say we live by. We have a secret intelligence that helps us. We have a certain ability to detect the falseness of the most widely accepted postulates. There are metaphysical and moral intuitions that turn us away from what we have been taught, from the "knowledge" we have hoarded up. Say what we may in the way of tomfoolery—or obediently, for the wildest of us often prove to be extraordinarily obedient—we work in our inner lives to reunite imaginatively what has been put asunder by history. Our instinct is to release ourselves from the bottles into which we have been processed and to recover our universal affinities. For we have been stuffed into our own isolated heads, locked up, corked in. There are gaps in comprehension and gaps in feeling that we publicly agree, under the ruling conventions, we can never hope to bridge. But in our souls we never stop trying to bridge them. The ruling conventions were created by some of the most prestigious thinkers of the modern period. And I am suggesting that one need not be bound by them, that the phenomena should not tamely and without resistance take their places in the assigned categories. I am taking a position taken by a German savant who, when his students told him that his theories did not square with the facts, said, "So much the worse for the facts."

Beginning writers often ask me practical questions about agents and publishers and special courses, and whether they should take sanctuary in universities (among the clichés?) or try to hold their own in the media world. All these are serious questions, but they are not the important ones, and since the latter are so seldom raised, I thought this a good occasion to raise them. But I shall go no further now, my real business being, as Defoe says somewhere, "not to preach but to relate."

[1978]

Acknowledgments and Editor's Note

"Starting Out in Chicago" appeared first in *The American Scholar*. "The University as Villain" appeared first in *The Nation*. "The Sharp Edge of Life," the text of a talk left among Bellow's papers, appears here for the first time; it has been titled by the editor of this volume. "Laughter in the Ghetto: On Sholom Aleichem" appeared first as "Laughter in the Ghetto" in *The Saturday Review of Literature*. "Dreiser and the Triumph of Art" appeared first in *Commentary*. "Hemingway and the Image of Man" appeared first in *Partisan Review*. "Man Underground: On Ralph Ellison" appeared first as "Man Underground" in *Commentary*. "The 1,001 Afternoons of Ben Hecht" appeared first in *The New York Times Book Review*. "The Swamp of Prosperity: On Philip Roth" appeared first as "The Swamp of Prosperity" in *Commentary*. "The Writer and the Audience" appeared first in *Perspectives U.S.A.* "Distractions of a Fiction Writer" appeared first in *New World Writing*. "Deep Readers of the World, Beware!" appeared first in *The New York Times Book Review*. "On Jewish Storytelling" appeared first in *The American Jewish Historical Quarterly*. "Up from the Pushcart: On Abraham Cahan" appeared first as "Up from the Pushcart" in *The New York Times*. "Where Do We Go from Here? The Future of Fiction" appeared first in *The Michigan Quarterly Review* and is adapted from the Hopwood Lecture. The four sections of "At the Movies"—"The Art of Going It Alone," "Buñuel's Unsparing Vision," "The Mass-Produced Insight" and "Adrift on a Sea of Gore"—all appeared first in *Horizon*. "On Shakespeare's Sonnets" appeared first in *The Griffin*. "The Writer as Moralist" appeared first in *The Atlantic Monthly*. "Beatrice Webb's America" appeared first in *The Nation*. "Recent Fiction: A Tour of Inspection" combines the contents of "Literature," which appeared first in *The Great Ideas Today* (Encyclopaedia Britannica, 1963), and "Some Notes on Recent American Fiction," which appeared first in *Encounter*. "Barefoot Boy: On Yevgeny Yevtushenko" appeared first as "Barefoot Boy" in *The New York Review of Books*. "My Man Bummidge" appeared first in *The New York Times*. "The Thinking Man's Waste Land" appeared first in *The Saturday Review of Literature*. "Cloister Culture" appeared first in *The New York Times*. "Skepticism and the Depth of Life" appeared first in *The Arts and the Public*. "On America: Remarks at the U.S. Cultural Center in Tel Aviv" appeared first as "Postscript: Some Answers to Questions after the Address in Tel Aviv" in *Congress Bi-Weekly*. "Machines and Storybooks: Literature in the Age of Technology" appeared first in *Harper's*. "A World Too Much with Us" appeared first in *Critical Inquiry*. "Americans Who Are Also Jews: Upon Receiving the Democratic Legacy Award of the Anti-Defamation League" appeared first as "Americans Who Are Also Jews" in *Jewish Digest*. "Reflections on Alexis de Tocqueville: A Seminar at the University of Chicago" appears in print for the first time here. "Foreword to *The Revolt of the Masses* by José Ortega y Gasset" appeared first as "Foreword" in the 1985 Notre Dame University Press edition of Ortega's treatise. "The Civilized Barbarian Reader," adapted from the introduction to Allan Bloom's *The Closing of the American Mind* (Simon and Schuster, 1987), appeared first in *The New York Times Book Review*. "A Jewish Writer in America" is excerpted from a lecture delivered at the Jewish Publication Society in Philadelphia and appeared first in two parts in *The New York Review of Books*. "Papuans and Zulus" appeared first in *The New York Times*. "Alone in Mixed Company" appeared first in *The Boston Globe*. "Ralph Ellison in Tivoli" appeared first in *Partisan Review*. "Wit Irony Fun Games," adapted from a lecture, appeared first in *The Public Intellectual: Between Philosophy and Politics*, an anthology of essays published by Rowman & Littlefield in 2003. "Literature: The Next Chapter" appeared first in *National Review*. "Before I Go Away: A Words and Images Interview with Norman Manea" is taken from an interview originally published in *Salmagundi,* and originally conducted in December 1999 on behalf of Words & Images, The Jerusalem Literary Project, in conjunction with Ben Gurion University of the Negev, Israel; it is licensed by Words & Images. "I Got a Scheme!" With Philip Roth" appeared first in *The New Yorker*; Mr. Roth's words appear by his kind permission. "Why Not?"

appeared first in *The Bulletin of the American Academy of Arts and Sciences* and is adapted from an address to that organization.

"In the Days of Mr. Roosevelt," "A Talk with the Yellow Kid," "The Sealed Treasure," "An Interview with Myself," "The Nobel Lecture," "Writers, Intellectuals, Politics: Mainly Reminiscence," "There Is Simply Too Much to Think About," "Spanish Letter," "Illinois Journey," "Israel: The Six-Day War," "New York: World-Famous Impossibility," "The Day They Signed the Treaty," "My Paris," "Chicago: The City That Was, the City That Is," "Vermont: The Good Place" and "Winter in Tuscany" all appeared in *It All Adds Up* (Viking Penguin, 1994). Each of these has been edited anew for this volume. ("An Interview with Myself," as it appears here, reincorporates several sentences from its original published version, "Some Questions and Answers," in *New Review* and, subsequently, *The Ontario Review*.)

I wish to express my gratitude, in each instance, for permission to reprint. This book's contents have been culled from a very wide variety of periodicals, with differing house styles. In the interest of consistency, adjustments and adaptations have been necessary here, particularly with respect to punctuation. All his writing life Saul Bellow broke certain of the rules that Chicago's public school system had drilled into him. Throughout, I have asked myself what sounds most Bellovian rather than adhering mechanically to the printed record. Spellings and transliterations have been made uniform. In a few instances, I have adjusted paragraphing to clarify meaning. Certain of the very long pieces are modified here for reasons of space. Sentences unconnected to the main argument have occasionally been elided. Very lengthy quotations from other writers have sometimes been abbreviated.

While the book's table of contents is organized according to decade, within those subheadings—Sixties, Seventies, etc.—I have let other considerations than chronology determine the order of the pieces.

Bellow's references are typically to well-known persons and phenomena and I have preferred not to impose on the reader with unnecessary footnotes. If certain of his allusions are less familiar, details about Viscount Bryce, Elbert Hubbard, Freud's Rat Man, Boob McNutt, Colonel Bertie McCormick, Billie Sol Estes and *Oh! Calcutta!* are nowadays at one's fingertips.

There is simply too much gratitude to express, but I will briefly try. I thank those at the Wylie Agency who have served Saul Bellow so long and well: Andrew Wylie, Jeffrey Posternak and Jennifer Henderson. Viking's copy editors treated the manuscript with unstinting attention and exemplary judgment. My dear friend Joel Conarroe read the manuscript first and made numerous editorial suggestions. More than I can say is owed to my assistant, Patrick Callihan, without whose hardihood, meticulousness and good cheer the collection could not have been assembled. My profoundest thanks I reserve for last: to Janis Freedman Bellow, who gave me the privilege of editing this all-purpose education and book of wonders.

—*Benjamin Taylor*

Index

Liebknecht, Karl, 66
Lincoln, Abraham, 35, 36, 57, 319, 429
Lincoln, Robert, 167
Lindbergh, Charles, 414
Lindsay, Vachel, 3, 83, 105
Lingle, Jake, 474
Lippmann, Walter, 322–23, 387
Literary Digest, The (periodical), 321, 484
literary intellectuals, 207–10, 230–34
literary quarterlies, 231
literary tendencies, of twentieth century,
    237–38
literary world or culture, lack of in
    America, 280–81, 282–83, 285–89
"Literature: The Next Chapter" (Bellow),
    422–26
literature professors, 230–31
Little Dorrit (Dickens), 265
Little Fugitive, The (film), 132, 134
Little Review, The, 65
Loeb, Richard Albert, 487
Lolita (Nabokov), 193
London, Jack, 405
Long, Huey, 319
Longfellow, Henry Wadsworth, 155
Lorenzetti, Fosco, 447, 448
Lovers and Lollipops (film), 132–34
Lowell, Robert, 403
Luce, Henry, 412
Lucian of Samosata, 114
Lukacs, John, 509

Macbeth (Shakespeare), 392, 432
MacDonald, Dwight, 393, 398, 403, 412
Machen, Arthur, 65
"Machines and Storybooks: Literature in
    the Age of Technology" (Bellow),
    253–68
McCarthy, Eugene, 2
McCarthy, Joseph, 395
McCormick, Robert "Colonel" (known
    also as "Bertie"), 318, 321, 324
McIntyre, Odd, 430, 474
Madame Bovary (Flaubert), 108, 172
Madison, James, 319
Madrid, Spain, 15–19
Magic Mountain, The (Mann), 123, 265,
    424, 493
Mailer, Norman, 158, 247–48, 500
Making of Americans, The (Stein), 123
Making of the Modern Mind, The
    (Randall), 424
Malamud, Bernard, 2

Malraux, André, 126, 145, 255, 256, 267,
    345, 393, 396, 413–14, 419
Man and People (Ortega y Gasset), 348–49
Mandelstam, Nadezhda, 7
Mandelstam, Osip, 271, 334–35, 337, 362,
    392, 410
Manea, Cella, 467
Manea, Norman, 450–66
Mangano, Silvana, 148
Manhattan Transfer (Dos Passos), 487
manhood, 58–59
Mann, Thomas, 74, 112, 121, 150, 164, 193,
    493
Mannix, 476, 478–79
"Man Underground: On Ralph Ellison"
    (Bellow), 60–64
Marcel, Gabriel, 180
Marjorie Morningstar (Wouk), 70
Mark the Match Boy (Alger), 156
Marquand, John P., 157
Marshall, Thomas R., 354
Martin, Malachi, 295
Marx, Karl, 90, 259, 269, 272, 384, 386,
    392, 406
Marxism, 269, 393, 394, 397–98, 400–401,
    458–61
mass man/mass society, 347–50, 423
Masters, Edgar Lee, 3
Mata, David, 350
Matthiessen, F. O., 50
Mauriac, François, 399
Maury, Lucien, 147
Mayer, Milton, 489
meaning, 92–95
Measure Taken, The (Brecht), 172, 396
Mechanization Takes Command (Giedion),
    340
Meir, Golda, 310
Melville, Herman, 93, 127, 173, 287, 393
Memoirs of a Revolutionist (Kropotkin),
    351
Mencken, H. L., 65, 310, 431, 474
Men Without Art (Lewis), 336
Mercador, Rámon, 460
Merchant of Venice, The (Shakespeare), 487
Mérimée, Prosper, 75
messages, 155
Metatheatre (Abel), 173, 176
métèque writers, 361–62
Michelangelo, 295
middle class, in America, 244–45
Mill, J. S., 173, 183
Mill, James, 244

Index   525

Miller, Henry, 157, 190
Mimesis (Auerbach), 172
"Miniver Cheevy" (Robinson), 377
Misfits, The (film), 143
Moby-Dick (Melville), 93, 124, 431
modern industrial societies
   art and, 281–82
   noise of modern life, as enemy of
     poetry, 7
   separation of writers from, 203–4
   writer's approaches to life in, 107–12
modernism, 206–7, 311, 424–26
Mofolo, Thomas, 409
Molière, 191, 208, 433
Mondale, Walter, 313
Monroe, Marilyn, 143
Monsier Verdoux (film), 245
Montaigne, Michel de, 169, 188, 355
Moore, Winston, 378
"Moral Equivalent of War, The" (James),
   82–83
moralist, writer as
   affirmation and, 160–61
   Alger and, 156
   art-for-art's-sake novelists' rejection of,
     163
   Cleans *versus* Dirties, 157–58, 160
   commitment and, 163–64
   Emerson and, 155, 156
   experiencing self, reevaluation of, 161
   nihilism and, 161–62
   Thoreau and, 156
   Tolstoy on, 162–63
   truth and, 159–60
   Whitman and, 156
Moravia, Alberto, 51
Mormons, 31
Mortre D'Urban (Powers), 177–80
Moveable Feast, A (Hemingway), 469
movie critiques, 131–49
   of Buñuel's movies, 136–41
   of Engel's films, 131–35
   gore and violence in service of spiritual
     themes, 145–49
   psychological insight in American film,
     141–45
"Movies Aren't Movies Any More"
   (Farber), 142
Moynihan, Daniel Patrick, 306, 313
Mozart, Wolfgang Amadeus, 286, 406
Mumford, Lewis, 340
Musil, Robert, 424
Mussolini, Benito, 434

My Apprenticeship (Webb), 166
My Century (Wat), 405
"My Paris" (Bellow), 338–46

Nabokov, Vladimir, 193, 362
Naipaul, V. S., 362
Nakano, T. S., 430
Naked Lunch (Burroughs), 160
Nash, Patrick, 378
Nasser, Gamal Abdel, 212–13, 220, 221
Nation, The (periodical), 89, 395
naturalists, 109, 156–57
nature mysticism, 124, 127
Nausea (Sartre), 292
Nauvoo, Illinois, 31
Nazarin (film), 136, 140
Nazis/Nazism, 67, 344, 361, 365, 366, 369
Nerval, Gérard de, 162
Never on Sunday (film), 132
New Deal, The, 1, 395
New Orleans, Louisiana, 225–26
New Republic, The (periodical), 395
New Salem, Illinois, 36
New Testament, The, 463, 464–65
New York City, 226, 227–28, 249–52,
   490–91
"New York: World Famous Impossibility"
   (Bellow), 249–52
New Yorker, The (periodical), 52, 190
New York Journal (newspaper),96
New York Review of Books, The
   (periodical), 251
New York Times, The (newspaper), 2, 68,
   221, 222, 251, 384, 403, 502, 507
Nicholson, Jack, 439
Nietzsche, Friedrich, 43, 73, 98, 259, 331,
   332–34, 350, 361, 368, 407
Nigger of the "Narcissus," The (Conrad),
   291
nihilism, 161–62, 332–33, 342–43, 368–71,
   462
1984 (Orwell), 260
Nixon, Richard, 280, 327, 328
"Nobel Lecture, The" (Bellow), 291–300
Noble Savage, The (periodical), 114
No Exit (Sartre), 139
noise of modern life, as enemy of poetry, 7
Nonsense Rhymes (Lear), 327
Notebooks (Butler), 496
Notebooks of Malte Laurids Brigge (Rilke),
   343
Notes from Underground (Dostoyevsky),
   43, 86–87

Index   527

Index

Index

Index

Index